The Instant Enlightenment of Ordinary People

Nichiren Buddhism 2.0 for the 21st Century

Yukio Matsudo

COPYRIGHT

© 2018 Yukio Matsudo

This English edition was published in June 2018 by DPI Publishing, Heidelberg, Germany.

https://www.facebook.com/DPIpublishing

ISBN: 978-1724519849

Contents

Foreword — 11
On my personal background in innovative Nichiren study — 11
Involvement in a new forum to complete my thesis — 12
SG's final separation from NS — 13
A One Volume Trilogy — 14
A Nichiren Teaching for the 21st Century — 15
I propose to update to version 2.0 — 15

Preliminary Remarks — 17
An additional note on the English version — 18

Introduction to the English version — 19
A comprehensive reassessment of SG's own ideologies — 19
Toda's idea of returning to the cosmic original life — 20
Ikeda's idea of returning to human life — 22
In line with SG's tradition of Buddhist humanism — 24

Part One
The Doctrine of Nichiren as the Eternal Original Buddha and the Renunciation of Faith in the Dai-Gohonzon

Chapter 1
The Turn to a More Universal Understanding of the Three Great Secret Laws — 26

Chapter 2
Criticism of the Doctrine of Nichiren as Eternal Original Buddha — 30

Chapter 3
An alternative to the "Doctrine of Nichiren as the Eternal Original Buddha" — 38

Chapter 4
An Interview "Thought of Change, A Thesis on the Ordinary Person as True Buddha" — 42
Humanism against authoritarianism — 45
"The Person" becomes an object of worship — 46

Consequently, always abide in the principle of "Rely on the Dharma and not on the Person" – The "ideology of high priest endowed with absolute authority" leads only to the worship of persons   47
The Bodhisattvas of the Earth as embodiments of the "Principle of the Ordinary Person as True Buddha"   48
Both the "theoretical stage" and the "verbal stage" of identity are found within the ordinary person   49
Self-perfection from the bottom up – The Daishōnin's view with respect to self-realization and the attainment of enlightenment   51
The Eternal Original Buddha is wholly imaginary   52
The Buddha of the Latter Day of the Law is a Bodhisattva of the Earth   52
Not a person but the Dharma alone should be the object of worship – Practicing to gain "immediate enlightenment" in order to "attain Buddhahood in this lifetime"   53
Striving for spiritual independence – Everyone will grow spiritually like "Nichiren"   55

Chapter 5
Unfounded and Contentious Criticism from NS   58

Chapter 6
The Dai-gohonzon is a Past Forgery   60
The legend of the Persecution at Atsuhara   60
The fabricated myth about the Dai-gohonzon   62

Chapter 7
An objective assessment of the "Theory of the Ordinary Person as True Buddha"   64
Nishiyama's book review   64
Sueki's book review   66
    How will the doctrinal controversy develop now that SG has separated from NS?   66
    Doctrinally Placing the Theory of the Ordinary Person as True Buddha   67
    An Evaluation of Original Enlightenment Thought   68
    Gosho considered to be Apocrypha   68

Part Two
Whither SG's Doctrine of Nichiren as the True Buddha?

Chapter 1
On Organization, Doctrine and the Unity of Master and Disciple   72
1. Organizational transformation by way of doctrinal change   72

2. Ambiguity in the master/disciple relationship ... 73

Chapter 2
The Gohonzon considered in »The Wisdom of the Lotus Sutra« ... 77

1. Time and Eternity, after the abandonment of faith in the Dai-gohonzon ... 77
2. The Multilayered structure of the discourse ... 79
3. The Gohonzon Understood as a Unity of Buddha and Dharma ... 82
4. The meaning of "Revealing the true identity by casting aside the shadow" ... 83
5. Summary of the multilayered structure ... 86
6. A Nichiren Buddhist Humanism ... 88
7. The Chapter on Emerging from the Earth ... 90
8. The Chapter on the Tathāgata's Supernatural Powers ... 92
9. The Dharma Body of Essential Entrustment ... 93
10. The Eternal Bodhisattva as Buddha ... 99
11. The Theory that Every Ordinary Person is a True Buddha ... 102
12. Transcending the Philosophy of Original Enlightenment ... 103

Summary ... 107

Chapter 3
Comments on the Miyata/Suda Controversy ... 109

1. Can the Believers of all other Nichiren sects also obtain merit by faith in any "honzon of the essential teaching"? ... 109
2. Is it a failure to make claims with respect to "merits and punishment"? ... 113
3. Matters Relating to Modern Buddhist Studies ... 116
   ① *The Mahayana Sutras do not represent the actual spoken teachings of Shakyamuni Buddha* ... *117*
   ② *"The Five Periods"* ... *117*
   ③ *"The Latter Day of the Law"* ... *117*
   The matter of authenticity: significant or not? ... *119*
4. The Doctrine of Nichiren as the True Buddha ... 120
   ① *Does such a doctrine lead to the cult of an image?* ... *120*
   ② *Nichiren's own Theory of the True Buddha* ... *123*
   ③ *The reason why Nichiren should be considered the teaching lord in the Latter Day of the Law (or the True Buddha)* ... *124*
   ④ *The reason why Nichiren revered Shakyamuni Buddha* ... *125*
   ⑤ *Nichiren's intention as represented by the figurative design of the Mandala-honzon* ... *126*
   ⑥ *T'ien-t'ai's understanding of the role of the teaching lord for each age* ... *128*

⑦ Buddhism spreads to the East and then returns to the West: the principle of change in Buddhist teachings   129
⑧ Significance of the entrustment to Jōgyō – The idea of the change of teaching master   129
⑨ Gosho of undetermined authenticity   131
⑩ The Heritage of the Doctrine of Nichiren as the Original Buddha within the Nikkō lineage   132
5. Is worship of a Buddha statue to be accepted?   133
6. Can an academic theory alone be a sufficient foundation for doctrinal understanding?   135
7. Can one's own judgment be the standard for everything?   135
Summary   138
Additional remarks on the present revised version   139

Chapter 4
Comments on the SG Study Document   142

1. Some terms and definitions found in the SGDB   142
Hosshaku-kenpon: Revealing the true identity by casting aside its shadow, or according to SGDB: Casting off the transient and revealing the true   142
Kuonganjo jijuyūhōshin nyorai: The Tathāgata of the wisdom body of limitless joy at the original beginning of eternity   143
Nichiren Daishōnin   144
Honmon no Honzon: The object of devotion of the essential teaching   145
Gohonzon: The object of Devotion   146
Nam-myō-hō-ren-ge-kyō   146
2. The basic doctrinal concepts used in SG Silent Prayer   148
Summary   150

Part Three
The Theory of the Ordinary Person as Buddha based on the Principle of the Mutual Containment of the Ten Worlds

Introduction   153
Discarding the dogma of authenticity   154
Philosophical evaluation of the non-authenticated writings   158

Chapter 1
The Process of Formation of the Three Principles for Realizing Buddhahood   159

1. Elucidating the Multilayered Character of Nichiren's Teachings   159

2. The Difference in Nichiren's Teaching before and after the Sado Exile 160
   The Dual Identity of the Tendai Monk and the Bodhisattva Jōgyō   *160*
   The Dual Practice of Chanting Daimoku and Meditation on Ichinen Sanzen   *161*
3. The essential consistent focus on the multiple significance of the Daimoku   163
4. The three fundamental principles for realizing Buddhahood in our time   165
   Chanting Daimoku remains the essential practice   *165*
   The three principles for establishing the practice of Daimoku   *166*
5. The starting point of Nichiren's teaching   169
6. The early form of the theory of the ordinary person as Buddha   172
   The principle of the dual structure of life as a universal condition for attaining enlightenment   *172*
   The Complementarity of self-power and other-power   *173*
   Realizing the enlightenment of ordinary people based on the tenfold life structure   *175*
7. The early theory of Instant Enlightenment based on the principle of Eternal Realization   176
   Manifesting the Buddhahood inherent within the ordinary person   *176*
   A pitfall of the autographed-centered view   *177*
   This World of Suffering where the Eternal Buddha resides   *178*
   The dual Structure of Original Enlightenment   *179*
8. The case of the dragon girl   182
   The immediate enlightenment of the dragon girl as prototype   *182*

Chapter 2
The Multiple Structure of Nichiren's Comparative System   189

1. The multifaceted and multilayered character of Nichiren's comparative system   189
2. Classification in terms of shallow / deep, superior / inferior, offering / receiving, and primary / secondary   190
3. The Practice of Nenbutsu leads to the hell of incessant suffering   194
   Nichiren's Reaction to the new exclusive teaching of Hōnen   *194*
   The Mystic Law itself led Amida Buddha to enlightenment   *195*
   The Slander of the Law leads to falling into hell   *196*
4. Witnessing to the pervasion of hell throughout the whole of society   197
5. The age of miscellaneous forms of faith and practice   198
6. The Daimoku and Honzon of the Essential Section for our current time   200
7. A doctrinal heritage which transcends the Eight Teachings   202

Chapter 3
Nichiren's own system of critical evaluation   204

1. The Five Principles of Propagation	204
2. The National Master of the Latter Day	207
3. The Fivefold Comparison	210
The superiority of the Lotus Sutra in comparison to the pre-Lotus Sutra teachings	*211*
The superiority of the essential section in comparison to the theoretical section	*213*
From the perspective of a contemplative reading of the essential section for the Latter Day	*214*
The superiority of Sowing in comparison to Harvesting	*218*
4. The doctrine of Ichinen Sanzen and the object of devotion	220

Chapter 4
From the perspective of a Contemplative Reading of the Essential Section for the Latter Day — 225

1. Nichiren's own system of critical evaluation of the Essential Section	225
2. The Five Guides to Propagation based on a Contemplative Reading of the Essential Section for the Latter Day	228
3. Some characteristic features of Nichiren's system of comparative evaluation	229
4. The seed which brings forth all Buddhas is the Mystic Law	235
5. The Fourfold interpretation level of the Buddhism of Sowing	236
6 The four-layered dimensional structure of the Gohonzon	240

Chapter 5
The Honzon of the Essential Section — 243

1. The Three Great Secret Laws of the Essential Teaching	243
Two references to the concept while on Minobu	*243*
A definition of the One Great Secret Law	*245*
2. The multilayered structure of the Three Great Secret Laws	246
3. The Multifaceted Significance of *Honmon no Honzon*	251
4. The Ambiguity of the *Honmon no Kaidan*	257
The place for observing the indestructible diamond-like precepts	*257*
5. The Three Great Secret Laws as inherited by Jōgyō	260
6. The bloodline of the faith which flows to the votaries of the Lotus Sutra	266

Chapter 6
The Principle of Attaining to Buddhahood — 268

1. The Bodhisattvas of the Earth embody the principle for activating Buddhahood	268
2. The duality of the primordial Buddha without beginning	270
3. Instant Enlightenment is exclusively for ordinary people	273
4. The inter-relationship between Daimoku and chanting Daimoku	275

Chapter 7
A systematic interpretation of the Gohonzon — 279

1. Ambiguities in any theory of the Honzon with respect to the Person and the Law — 279
2. Three different types of Gohonzon — 281
3. The significance of the "essential version of the Gohonzon" — 283
   Chanting Daimoku is the primary practice for our times — 283
   How to deal with the statue of Shakyamuni Buddha — 285
   Shakyamuni as the Buddha of Ichinen Sanzen — 286
   Daimoku as the power of transformation — 287
4. The Law-centered Honzon attended by the eternal Buddha — 288
   The One Buddha and the Four Bodhisattvas — 288
   Jōgyō appears at the dawn of the Latter Day — 290
   Who is Attending whom? — 292
5. Concerns about the use of statues of "the one Buddha and the four bodhisattvas" — 293
6. Is the Eternal Buddha identical to Shakyamuni Buddha in the Treasure Tower? — 294
7. The relationship between the Daimoku and the Eternal Buddha — 300
8. An Appropriate Limit to any worship of the sect's founder — 303
9. Toward a theory of Nichiren as true Buddha in the sense of "ordinary person as Buddha" — 305
   The significant unity between the central Daimoku and Nichiren's Signature — 305
   Making a single individual a prototype for all without distinction — 307
   Some examples of substituting another's name for Nichiren's signature — 310

Chapter 8
The Ten-Worlds-Mandala of Ichinen Sanzen — 313

1. The Fusion of Wisdom and Actuality — 313
   The fusion of wisdom and actuality represents Instant Enlightenment — 313
   The fusion of wisdom and actuality represents the essence of the eternal Buddha — 315
2. The theoretical and practical consequences for the theory of the ordinary person as true Buddha — 317
   Keeping the Treasure Tower in one's own heart — 318
   The two Buddhas represent the function of the Mystic Law — 319
   The practitioner of the daimoku will manifest as the true Buddha who exists in actuality — 320
3. The Ten World Mandala as the Realization of Ichinen Sanzen in Actuality — 322

> *This world of suffering itself is the enlightened world of eternal*
> *realization*   *323*
> *Ichinen Sanzen in Actuality for the Latter Day*   *325*
> *Eternal Realization manifests in one's own heart*   *326*
> 4. The Mystic Law is itself the original master of the eternal Buddha   328
> 5. Fusion with the Mandala-Honzon   333
> 6. Buddhahood omnipresent throughout the whole cosmos   336
> 7. The four-fold level of interpretation of the Buddhism of Sowing
>   and the four-layered structure of the Gohonzon   338
> Concluding Remarks   340

Reference   **342**

Glossary   **346**

About the Author   **351**

Foreword

On my personal background in innovative Nichiren study

I first encountered *Nichiren Buddhism* (NB) in Germany in 1976, and since then I have consistently practiced it against a Western cultural background. Consequently, my basic understanding of the doctrine and practice of NB has been cultivated within the framework of "Soka Gakkai International" (SGI), a globally active lay Buddhist organization. This basic understanding remains the same. Yet, much more than that, I hope to encourage Nichiren Buddhists all over the world to ever deeper realization at the doctrinal level, as I feel a special affinity and responsibility to them both within Japan and overseas who take the practice of Nichiren Buddhism seriously. In this respect, I hope to update the traditional understanding of NB, in order that it may better meet the aspirations and needs of our contemporary global society.

I got the idea to reconstruct SGI teaching for the future at the time that Soka Gakkai (SG) was "excommunicated" by Nichiren Shōshū (NS) on November 28, 1991. Shortly before, in 1990, I had gained a doctorate in Philosophy (PhD) at Heidelberg University. Consequently, SGI President Ikeda arranged for me to succeed to the newly founded position of Director of Research at the European Center of the "Institute of Oriental Philosophy" (IOP) in Taplow Court, UK. This appointment gave me the opportunity to deepen my studies during a fruitful intellectual exchange with Japanese researchers in Tokyo. As a result of this exchange and my own reflections, I became convinced of the necessity to modify, renew and transcend the traditional rigidity of NS doctrine and I published a series of books in order to promote such renewal. They were:

- »In search of a Humanistic Doctrine of "Nichiren as Original Buddha" – for the Foundation of the Soka Renaissance Movement« (1992),
- »An Innovation of Nichiren Thought – About the Thesis on "Ordinary Person as True Buddha"« (1994), and
- »The Doctrine Controversy of the *Heisei period*[1] – Laughing at the "Refutation" of Nichiren Shōshū« (1995).

In short, the intention of all these publications was to highlight the much more contemporarily relevant doctrine on "The Ordinary person as a Buddha" against the pre-modern doctrine of "Nichiren as the eternal Original Buddha", the latter itself emblematic of NS doctrine. I continued this effort until 2000 when I finished my appointment as research director.

---

[1] "Heisei" is the current era in Japan that started in 8 January 1989 after the death of the Emperor Hirohito and when his son, Akihito, acceded to the throne.

As to this doctrinal problem, as is briefly summarized in »Human Revolution«, Vol. 11, "Trial", there was a particular context behind that new wave oriented toward that Renaissance and toward a new humanism.

Soka Gakkai gave it the name "The year of Soka Renaissance" to mark 1992 and so took the first step into a new era. "Soka renaissance" was considered to be a movement of spiritual reinvigoration, seeking to build a new era based on a true humanism and democratic values, by encouraging all people with the compassionate light of the Buddhism of Nichiren Daishōnin, while struggling against all authority and power which threatened human rights. It was a step toward a human revival, which the modern Renaissance did not achieve, for human beings generally were unable to actualize those high ideals for society at that time. (From »Human Revolution« Volume 11 "Postscript")

By publishing all of the above-mentioned books, I intended to establish a "foundation for the Soka Renaissance movement," and I continued with this doctrinal reconstruction until 2000, by when I had completed my appointment as the Director of Research at the European Center of the Institute of Oriental Philosophy (IOP).

Subsequently, I spent all my time and energy in completing my post-doctoral thesis, in order to obtain accreditation to teach in the capacity of professor at a German University. This weighty German thesis was finally published in two works:
- »Nichiren, der Ausübende des Lotos-Sutra (Nichiren, the votary of the Lotus Sutra)« (2004) and
- »Hairetischer Protest – Reformatorische Bewegungen im Buddhismus und Christentum (Hairetical Protest – Reformatory Movements in Buddhism and Christianity)« (2009).

Involvement in a new forum to complete my thesis

Although my direct connection with Nichiren research in Japan had been broken for 15 years, *Fumihiko Sueki*, a well-known Professor of Buddhist Studies, had written an article with the title »Secularization and Nichiren Buddhism – Around Yukio Matsudo's "Ordinary Person as True Buddha"« in »Contemporary World and Nichiren, Series Nichiren, Vol. 5« (2015). Since Sueki also offered me an opportunity to criticize his review on my thesis, I immediately published an article with the title "For a Contemporary Reconstruction of Nichiren Buddhism" in »Lotus Buddhist Studies (*Hokke bukkyō kenkyū*) No. 21« (2015). As a result, I became involved in the "Lotus Study Group (*Hokke bukkyō kenkyūkai*)", presided over by Jūdō Hanano, an expert of NB and an ex-NS priest. I also then got the chance to read its periodically-published research magazine.

The researchers in this group are from various Nichiren-related organizations such as Nichiren Shū, NS and SG (IOP) as well as independent researchers. They regularly exchange their own views and opinions on sectarian doctrines, as well as disseminate the results of their own research. It is a valuable academically oriented forum in which to inform, learn and reflect together on the multifaceted aspects and perspectives of NB. Historically, Nichiren Buddhist organizations have been very contentious, and they have frequently abused and slandered each other. Given this historical reality, the research group gains a revolutionary significance. For contemporary Nichiren Buddhists or those interested in NB, it is an opportunity and a challenge to transcend both dogmatism and exclusivism in order to successfully propagate NB as *itai dōshin*, i.e., working together in essential unity while accepting and valuing difference of opinion or difference of doctrinal understanding.

After reading issues Nos. 21 and 22 of the Magazine »Lotus Buddhist Studies«, I felt a sense of discomfort not only about NS doctrines but also about the traditional sectarian interpretation of Nichiren Shū. Consequently, in order to take a clear position against the traditional doctrines of Nichiren Shū, I expanded my draft on "The Ordinary Person as True Buddha." Subsequently, this article became too long for it to be published in the magazine. On the other hand, it was not suitable for publication as an academic research paper, because I had myself aimed to construct a "practical teaching." Thus, I decided to publish this thesis in a monograph independently.

SG's final separation from NS

There was another circumstance which led me to publish this book. On November 7, 2014, SG pronounced a revision to the Doctrinal Clause of the Constitution and expressly rejected the teaching on the "Dai-gohonzon of the High Sanctuary of the Essential Section," held by the NS Head Temple Taisekiji. In fact, this indicated that SG now rejected the very core of the fundamental doctrines of NS and especially the particular interpretation of NB propagated by *Nichikan* (1665-1726), the 26th High Priest of NS. For the traditional NS doctrines that the SG had adopted from its beginning in the 1930's had been characterized by Nichikan's particular exegetics built upon belief in the Dai-Gohonzon. The subsequent renunciation of this particular belief meant an official declaration of doctrinal separation from NS, followed by SG's organizational separation from NS with SG's "excommunication" on November 28, 1991. As a result, SG has determined to follow a path completely independently of NS. Nevertheless, the doctrinal direction of SG remains ambiguous.

Under these circumstances, the 74th Academic Conference, organized by the Society of Japanese Religious Studies, took place at Soka University on September 5, 2015. *Kōichi Miyata*, professor of philosophy at Soka University, gave an oral presentation with the title "Academic Research and the Doctrine of Denominations – The case of Soka Gakkai". A supplementary revised paper of this speech has been published on Miyata's own website. To this paper, *Haruo Suda*, a former vice chief of the SG study department, responded in his blog on September 14, 2016, in an article entitled: "Doubting Miyata's Thesis - One Consideration on the Thesis of Nichiren as True Buddha." I am eager to participate in this ongoing debate, so I will summarize the essential points of each of them.

A One Volume Trilogy

Consequently, in this book I consider the doctrinal controversy against three different contexts., Thus it consists of three parts.

➤ The first part is meant as a summary of the issues raised by several of my critics with respect to my criticism of NS doctrines published in the 1990s. In short: more than twenty years ago, I proposed the rejection of the NS core doctrines, especially *the thesis of Nichiren as the eternal Original Buddha* and *faith in the Dai-Gohonzon*.

> This doctrinal position of mine has now, 20 years later, become officially recognized by SG.

My own awareness of this fundamental problem remains unchanged to this day. As all the books from that time are now out of print, I would like to now outline the essential points which remain relevant and important, given the theoretical development delineated in this book. Consequently, I consider it to be an essential introductory background to this book.

➤ Part two deals with the ongoing debate relating to the future direction of SG teachings after the rejection of belief in the Dai-Gohonzon. I would like to explore the controversies of Miyata and Suda, especially to take a closer look at the debate on the "theory of Nichiren as True Buddha." With respect to this, I will also consider the doctrinal implications found in the dialogue of Ikeda published as »The Wisdom of the Lotus Sutra« (1995-1999), as well as the most recent doctrinal position propagated by the SG Study Department.

➤ In Part three, I will consider some representative interpretations of fundamental Nichiren doctrines, such as *Daimoku* and *Gohonzon*, as well as the *Teaching Master* presented in the recent »Lotus Buddhist Studies". As well as considering them as focal points in a critical review, I would like also to systematically present my own thesis of "the Ordinary Person as True Buddha based on the principle of the Mutual Containment of the Ten Worlds" under the new heading "the theory of the Instant Enlightenment of ordinary people".

> The three parts of this book correspond accordingly
> to SGI study in the past, present and future.

A Nichiren Teaching for the 21st Century

In particular, although I consider various doctrinal interpretations of NB in the second part and the third part, the intention of this book is to reconstruct SGI teaching by way of proposing an innovative interpretation and understanding of NB for lay people chanting Daimoku in the global society of the 21st Century. Consequently, I will avoid any heavy debate at the philological, historical or ideological level. To stress once again, this book does NOT consider purely academic questions such as:

- What should be considered to be original and authentic Nichiren doctrine?
- Against what kind of ideological and historical context was Nichiren doctrine formed?
- What kind of interpretative theories have developed among scholars and in the various Nichiren sects up to today?
- Which writings of Nichiren can be regarded as authentic and which as apocryphal?

As for myself, I will only make use of the valuable fruits of academic research, by way of reference or in support of my own doctrinal conclusions.

> For the future rather than the past,
> for the whole world rather than only for Japan,
> for lay Buddhists rather than for Temple Buddhism, and
> for the unfolding of Buddha nature in one's own life
> rather than faithful devotion to the Buddha.

The purpose of reconstructing the innovative teachings of Nichiren is so that they can be reasonably understood and practiced by lay Buddhists living and working in a global contemporary society. For this purpose, I am attempting to establish a solid foundation for NB in the 21st Century.

I propose to update to version 2.0

This book continues the project of my previous publications from the 1990s, in seeking to transcend traditional NS doctrines, but it is also meant as the conclusion to this series. To my mind, the former SG/SGI teaching based on the traditional NS doctrines should be designated as version 1.0, while the present book, as an example of a new innovative approach, should be designated version 2.0.

In fact, other than some articles and other publications in Japanese relating to NB, version 3.0 had been published already in June 2016: in English as »Transform your energy - Change your life! Nichiren Buddhism 3.0". This was the first book of the series outside the framework of Buddhist studies, traditionally more concerned with philological, historical and doctrinal aspects. Further, this series focuses on an explanation of the principles and practices of NB from the perspective of the New Science of quantum physics, energy, consciousness, brain, heart, cells, genes and the like. I obtained significant scientific data on changes to the body's energy and brain waves during chanting, and intriguing conclusions can be drawn. The second book in this series was published in August 2017 under the title »Change Your Brainwaves - Change Your Karma! Nichiren Buddhism 3.1«.

To avoid misunderstandings here, these version numbers like 2.0 and 3.0 refer to the different fields and perspectives on NB, so a later version does not imply a later edition. Of course, there is a fundamental difference between the traditional closed system of NS doctrine (NB 1.0) and this more open universal system of NB2.0, that can be extended to 3.0 and more.

> I propose to upgrade NB 1.0 founded on traditional NS doctrine to a contemporary understanding of NB 2.0.

In March 2017 in Heidelberg
Yukio Matsudo

Preliminary Remarks

- In the Japanese original, I used the SG version »*Nichiren Daishōnin Gosho Zenshū*« for the citation of Nichiren writings (Gosho) with the respective page number. For the Gosho that are not included in the SG version the »*Shōwateihon Nichiren Shōnin Ibun*« (**SS**) is used.
- For the present English book, the English translation of the SG version, »The Writings of Nichiren Daishōnin« (**WND**), is used, that is available in: http://www.nichirenlibrary.org/en/. In this internet site, »The Lotus Sutra« (**LS**) and »The record of Orally Transmitted Teachings« (**OTT**) are also available and used.
- I may have partly modified each quotation taken from these works to aid understanding, where necessary. The bold character and the sign of [...] for omission in the quotation are the author's addition.
- Every quotation is marked like (»On Establishing the Correct Teaching for the Peace of the Land«, p. 17 / I. 6), referring to the title, the page of Japanese Gosho, followed by WND consisting of two volumes.
- The following terms that will be often used in the text are abbreviated to spare the paper:

Nichiren Buddhism	NB
Nichiren Daishōnin	ND
Nichiren Shōshū	NS
the »*Shōwateihon Nichiren Shōnin Ibun*«	SS
Sōka Gakkai	SG
Sōka Gakkai International	SGI
The Writings of Nichiren Daishōnin	WND
The Lotus Sutra	LS

- This book aims to develop a particular understanding of Nichiren's thought based on my own interpretation and should not be considered a purely academic contribution to Nichiren research. Consequently, I avoid referencing or referring to previous research. I will only use the most recent discussion as "reference" for critical examination and demonstration of my own theory.
- I will not touch on the authenticity of Gosho. I basically use the writings of Nichiren, whose authenticity has been established due to the discovery of original writings or authenticated copies by his disciples. However, with respect to those writings whose authenticity has not been established, I will make use of them not as a means not to establish my thesis but as further validation of parts of my thesis established by the authentic writings.

An additional note on the English version

➤ The Japanese original of this book was conceived to provide Japanese readers with necessary information for understanding SGI study in the past, present and future. However, for a better understanding, I added some more explanations regarding historical, conceptual and terminological issues that are self- evident for Japanese readers but not for others. Thus, this English version will be expanded in detail. The outline remains the same, but some parts will not correspond exactly to the Japanese original.

➤ Prefixing of the person's name is, where as possible, omitted according to the academic convention so far as I refer to the person.

Introduction to the English version

A comprehensive reassessment of SG's own ideologies

After the Japanese version of this book was published in May 2017, the "Lotus Buddhist Studies No. 24" appeared in July 2017, and included a paper with the title "The Basis Thinking of Soka Gakkai" by *Shigeru Nishiyama*, professor of sociology of religions, who has specialized in research on the religious movements based on NB and the historical development of SG. In this paper he pointed out that the separation of SG from NS was historically inevitable as SG had developed its own religious thought parallel to but originally distinct from traditional NS doctrines.

According to his analysis, this original thought can be characterized as Makiguchi's "theory of value," Toda's "theory of life," as well as Ikeda's "humanistic view of NB" and his new understanding of Kōsenrufu. This understanding is consistent with Miyata's opinion, and I also analyze in this book the multilayered structure of Ikeda's thinking as implicitly expressed in his dialogue on »the Wisdom of the Lotus Sutra«, e.g. with reference to NS doctrines, the theory of life, the thought of Original Enlightenment, and the doctrine on Ordinary People as True Buddha.

Interestingly, Nishiyama notes in Toda's thinking not only his theory of life, but also the concept of Ordinary People as the True Buddha founded on the »Orally Transmitted Teachings.« Moreover, he emphasizes that by Kōsenrufu Ikeda didn't intend to simply mean the dissemination of the Gohonzon of NS, but rather to inspire and carry forward a "great cultural movement that expands throughout the earth based on the Mystic Law", i.e. based on a humanistic interpretation of NB (ibid., p. 116).

This was the main reason for the recognized fact that why the NS head temple repeatedly made claims that SG was preaching doctrine "at variance with traditional NS doctrine". In other words, the fundamental doctrinal stance and orientation of SG was not to promote traditional Temple Buddhism based on the teachings of NS but rather to propagate a form of NB more relevant to lay Buddhists active in contemporary global society. From now on, this humanistic approach to NB will be pushed forward. And this at my own suggestion!

Additionally, I would like to quote some remarks made by Nishiyama which refer to myself.

> Toda's theory of life was handed over to Soka Gakkai, and Ikeda was frequently mentioning that "You are all a Buddha." Yukio Matsudo, former director of Research in the European Center of the Institute of orien-

tal Philosophy, stated in his books »In search of a humanistic understanding of Nichiren as True Buddha« (1992) and in »An innovation of Nichiren Thought« (1994), that the Honzon represent a *"mirror reflecting one's own enlightened life"* while the ordinary person is identical with a Buddha body. Thus, it becomes clear that both Ikeda and Matsudo were faithful disciples of Toda who wrote the theory of life... (ibid.)

I have been flattered by the great honor of being mentioned along with Ikeda in relation to Toda. Yet, this complimentary evaluation by an impartial researcher with a well-established reputation made me think anew about my own humanistic interpretation of NB throughout the course of the history of SG studies.

It cannot be denied that SG had consistently applied the NS Nichikan doctrine, but it is also a fact that at the same time, it had developed a contemporary doctrinal standpoint focused on the needs of a lay Buddhist movement concerned to promote peace, culture and education throughout global society. Especially, I would like to refer to the discourse which both Toda and Ikeda employed, as examples of a particular universal and humanistic understanding of NB. For this purpose, I will refer to two of their speeches, which have been helpfully provided to me by a SG member.

Toda's idea of returning to the cosmic original life

First, let us refer to a lecture entitled "Causality in the past, present and future" which Toda gave at the 2nd Soka Gakkai general meeting on October 19, 1947 (enclosed in »Lecture Collection of Toda Josei Sensei«).

That life is subject to the constant cycle of birth and death as well as to the sufferings of the present is the characteristic teaching of karmic retribution, which says: you will reap what you have sown. This view of karma as expounded in the context of Shakyamuni Buddhism is called by Nichiren *"the usual law of cause and effect"* (»A Letter from Sado« p. 960 / 305). However, in order to break through the causal chain of karmic retribution, Toda emphasizes the Law of Causality which Nichiren taught. That is to say, a "law according to which we ordinary people break through the usual law of cause and effect and unfold the natural Buddha's body", i.e. the "law that brings us back to the eternal past". In other words, because we can transcend all causalities of the past and manifest as "ordinary people of the eternal past", we are able to change our destiny.

Toda explained the meaning of this law by quoting the passage about the "remote past (*kuon*)" which says: *"Kuon means something that was not worked for, that was not improved upon, but which exists just as it always has"* (From "the 23rd important point in Chapter Sixteen of the Lotus Sutra": "The Life Span of the Tathāgata" in the »Orally Transmitted Teachings« (p. 759 / 141).

The "Buddha of the remote past" may sound like a very difficult word. However, the "remote past" simply means that "it is as it is originally, nothing more nor some wondrous effect" and the Buddha is nothing but life itself. Thus, when we realize that the Buddha of the remote past means "original life as it is", all causal chains on the way will disappear and the Lotus Buddha endowed with the principle of simultaneity of cause and effect will be born.

Since Toda has assumed a certain knowledge regarding the doctrine, some basic points need to be summarized for ease of understanding:
- The historical Buddha Shakyamuni explained in the 16th chapter of the Lotus Sutra that he had already attained enlightenment in the unaccountably remote past and that he had been preaching the Right Dharma (Sad-Dharma; the Mystic Law) to lead all people to enlightenment. This Eternal Buddha Shakyamuni is the Original Buddha of all Buddhas in the entire universe and through all time.
- Nichiren picked up the Right Dharma from this story around the Eternal Buddha and formulated it as Nam-myō-hō-ren-ge-kyō. This is the law that enabled himself to attain enlightenment in the remote past and is, therefore, able to lead all people to enlightenment.
- This Mystic Law represents the logical structure of the "simultaneity of cause and effect" in the sense that an ordinary person can activate the potential of enlightenment inherent in his own life.
- In activating this eternal potential which is available from time without beginning and end, you will enter the realm of the Eternal Buddha beyond time and space[2].
- In this spiritual dimension you are free of karmic influences from the past. At this moment you are the "Lotus Buddha", as Toda expresses it. In this capacity you can set a completely new course, as you wish, and it evokes immediately the effect that will sooner or later appear in the realm of our everyday reality.
- Thus, the Mystic Law that we are practicing represents the "principle of the Simultaneity of Cause and Effect," which breaks through the usual law of karmic retribution and creates new value in our lives.
- To put it another way, in chanting Daimoku before the Gohonzon we transcend the consciousness level of our everyday life which is subject to the usual law of karmic retribution and activate the cosmic enlightened state inherent in our lives. This eternal Buddha potential works, when activated, beyond the consciousness level of our everyday ego. In this state of Instant Enlightenment during chanting Daimoku we can set a new

---

[2] In our book "Transform Your Energy, Change Your Life. Nichiren Buddhism 3.0" this state is described as *the cosmic, non-local consciousness*.

course with an intention that will be realized independent of the law of karmic retribution.

Now, based on this understanding of the significance of chanting Daimoku, Toda continues to talk about another practical consequence, i.e. *"eliminating negative karma caused by slander of the Dharma"*. We may be doomed to repay and erase them one by one for the entire future, but due to the working principle of the Mystic Law we can endure a heavy karmic destiny lightly and purify our lives. This is, so Toda emphasizes, "faith in the Gohonzon".

Ikeda's idea of returning to human life

Ikeda has inherited Toda's idea of "the ordinary person of the remote past", but it designates nothing other than the fact that Buddhahood, the enlightened state of life, will appear while chanting Daimoku. This concept provides the very basis for a humanistic understanding of NB.

In support of Ikeda's innovative idea, I would like to refer to a speech that he made on the occasion of the 3rd German Supreme Conference, which was held near Frankfurt on May 24, 1994 (included in »Renaissance of Soka 72«). I was lucky enough to attend this meeting and to listen to his guidance directly at that time. Having attended a number of these occasions abroad, I must have become aware of this new direction in SG philosophy, i.e. its innovative humanistic understanding of NB. Unlike in Japan, where the SG members had been burdened by the heavy weight of traditional NS doctrine and practice, outside Japan we faced a different situation that made us much more susceptible to easily accept the new SG orientation.

Among other things, Ikeda introduced an episode in which Jawaharlal Nehru (1889-1964), the prime minister of India at that time, told Andre Malraux (1901-1976), that *"Buddhism had been destroyed and disappeared from India when the Buddha came to be regarded as a deity and ceased to be a human being"*. In pointing out the problem of the "deification of the historical Buddha", Ikeda highlighted the general tendency of institutionalized temples with priesthoods towards "authoritarianism".

Against this authoritarian tendency within any religious institution, he insisted that Buddhism had originally taught the way of "how to live as a human being" and that the Buddhism of *Nichiren Daishōnin* was a battle for the *"humanization of Buddhism"*.

> In considering the reason why ND engaged in such virulent criticism of the religion and politics of the Shogunate and the other Buddhist schools, we may arrive at the conclusion that he struggled to "humanize Buddhism". He wanted to bring a Buddhism astray from reality back to a more humane focus and to teach a way of how to live in accordance with the reality of life.

At that time in Japan, many Buddhist teachings were prevalent which preached devotion to "Buddhas" such as *Amida Butsu* (Buddha Amitabha) and *Dainichi Nyorai* (Tathāgata Vairochana), who were seen as distant and transcendent. Even the Buddha in the Lotus Sutra was generally regarded as transcendent of humanity. However, the Daishōnin radically reversed this perceived relationship between the Buddha and human beings. In this sense, the philosophical significance of the "Doctrine of Nichiren as Original Buddha" might be considered to be a doctrinal attempt to radically "humanize Buddhism".

In »The True Aspect of All Phenomena« it states: *"A common mortal is an entity of the three bodies, and a true Buddha. A Buddha is a function of the three bodies, and a provisional Buddha"* (p. 1358 / p. 384). Yes, it is this Buddha. This means that those human beings who believe in and practice the Mystic Law are exactly Buddhas. The "Buddha world" exists in "faith" in the Mystic Law.

Ikeda stresses that it is in this respect that the origin or starting point of SG must be found.

Soka Gakkai has practiced Buddhism "in the midst of daily life" and in the "way of how to live as a human being" in accordance with the spirit of the Daishōnin. As the Daishōnin returned to the origin of Buddhism, Soka Gakkai likewise went back to the origin of faith in the Buddhism of the Daishōnin, i.e. in a return to "human being". Toda Sensei said on one occasion: our religion is a "school for human beings". A thorough form of "humanism" is the essence of the Buddhism of the Daishōnin. Likewise, he stressed one should worship neither a god nor a Buddha if considered completely distinct from common humanity, for the object of worship should be the "unchangeable law".

That which links Gandhi and Einstein or that which connects religion and science, should be considered a "law". Similarly, Dr. Arnold Toynbee frequently spoke of *"the ultimate spiritual reality behind the universe"* and told me personally in our dialogue that the "ultimate reality" should ultimately be viewed not as a personal God but as a "law". And in the time of that "ultimate law" we are now living. I want you to realize that you are at the cutting edge of human civilization. "God" is transcendentally separated from humans, but "law" is universal to all things including human beings. If you live according to the correct "law", you can all equally become "Buddha" and realize "happiness". A person living in accordance with the Mystic Law will without fail become "Buddha". He or she can build "absolute happiness" without fail.

In line with SG's tradition of Buddhist humanism

In the above speeches, both Toda and Ikeda emphasized and outlined the humanistic direction in which NB should travel in the future. This can be summarized in the following points:
- Buddhism is not a religion worshipping Gods and Buddhas, rather its objective is for everyone to practice a universal law to realize the Buddha state and become happy.
- The reason why we can change our karmic destiny by chanting Daimoku is, metaphorically speaking, because chanting enables us to return to the remote past beyond karmic causality, but more practically because in the body of every ordinary person there exists a potentiality for Buddhahood, so that the eternal Buddha nature will appear quite naturally.
- The purpose of NB is to practice it "in the midst of daily life" and "in the way of how to live as a human being". SG has made this standpoint as its own.

Following this line of thought, I have developed my "Theory on Ordinary People as True Buddha" (based on the principle of Mutual Containment of the Ten Worlds), yet now in an innovative new form as "The Instant Enlightenment of All Ordinary People". In conclusion, I am aware that in developing my own standpoint, I am very much within that humanistic strand of Nichiren thought, first initiated by the SG presidents.

Consequently, I passionately urge you to radically revise the traditional sectarian-oriented teachings and practices and to update to the NB 2.0, for lay people practicing in the global society of the 21st Century.

Last, but not least, I would like to thank Nigel Wray from the UK for his extraordinary help in proofreading and editing the English version of this book in a very elegant and clear manner. We both share a deep love for Nichiren as a great Buddhist master and a passion for Nichiren Buddhism. While working together on this English version we also discussed how best to translate Japanese Buddhist terms. For a better understanding of these terms a concise glossary is provided as an appendix.

I also express my gratitude to Robert Mann who helped me with materials from SGI-USA.

In June 2018 in Heidelberg, Germany
Yukio Matsudo

Part One

The Doctrine of Nichiren as the Eternal Original Buddha and the Renunciation of Faith in the Dai-Gohonzon

Chapter 1
The Turn to a More Universal Understanding of the Three Great Secret Laws

On Nov. 7, 2014, SG President *Minoru Harada* announced a revision to Chapter 1, Article 2, of the Rules and Regulations of Soka Gakkai. This amendment reflected the decision of SG, no longer to hold belief in the Dai-Gohonzon, which had previously been considered as having been personally inscribed by Nichiren on Oct. 10, 1279 in order to be placed in "the High Sanctuality of the Essential Section" (*Honmon no kaidan*) and which is still maintained at the NS Head Temple, Taisekiji. This announcement was published in the SG daily newspaper "Seikyo Shinbun" the next day and the doctrinal change was formulated as follows.

> This Association shall honor Nichiren Daishōnin as the *True Buddha of the Latter Day of the Law*. It shall believe in the *Three Great Secret Laws* embodying the fundamental Law of Nam-myō-hō-ren-ge-kyō, chant Daimoku encompassing *practice for oneself and others* to the Gohonzon and base itself on Nichiren Daishōnin's writings. It shall strive, by way of each individual achieving their *Human Revolution*, to realize as its ultimate goal [*Kōsenrufu*], the worldwide propagation of Nichiren Daishōnin's Buddhism, thus fulfilling the Daishōnin's mandate[3].

In order to further clarify its meaning, the SG Study Department subsequently published in Seikyo Shinbun a "Commentary on the revision to the doctrinal clause of the constitution", published on January 29 and 30, 2015.

It is natural to review doctrinal interpretation, in order that an association globally promoting world propagation [Kōsenrufu] can face the new challenges consequent upon successful expansion. By taking into account contemporary thought and culture, as well as by adopting empirical research methods, the dissemination of the means to human salvation in the modern world should be regarded as the primary mission of that association which is moving forward to ultimately realize world peace [Kōsenrufu]. We want to strive to build a more universal SG teaching.

The importance of the doctrinal change is related specifically to a revised understanding of the "Three Great Secret Laws" which form the foundation

---

[3] The Enligsh translation is quoted from:
https://www.worldtribune.org/2016/07/nichiren-buddhism-people/
Marking the fixed terms with italics and complement with bracket are added by the author.

of Nichiren's teachings. According to the "NS-Nichikan doctrine"[4] the "Dai-gohonzon of 1279 of the High Sanctuality" is taught as the "Principal Great Secret Law representing all three aspects of the Great Secret Laws", that are then unfolded into six aspects. These are as follows:

One Great Secret Law	Dai-gohonzon The Unity of the Eternal Original Buddha and the Mystic Universal Law		
Three Great Secret Laws	*Honmon no Honzon*	*Honmon no Daimoku*	*Honmon no Kaidan*
Six Great Secret Laws	Person & Law	Faith & Practice	Fact & Meaning

Each of the Three Great Secret Laws is distinctively identified by the term "*Honmon*" which is a reference to the "*Essential Section of the LS*". This is emblematic of Nichiren's particular view that the latter half of LS from 15th until 28th chapter, called the "Essential Section", should be considered to be of far greater value than the preceding half, i.e. from the beginning until 14th chapter. We shall discuss this in more detail later. For the moment, it is enough to remember that the Three Great Secret Laws were established by Nichiren on the foundation of the Essential Section of the LS.

Chapter	Lotus Sutra
1. – 14.	The Theoretical Section *(Shakumon)*
15. – 28.	The Essential Section *(Honmon)*

In fact, SG decided not to maintain these NS-Nichikan teachings, as explained further by SG's study department:

> In NS "the One Great Secret Law" means "the Gohonzon of the second year of Kōan period (1279)". Based on this the "Three Great Secret Laws" are to be unfolded and they are explained as follows: The "Honzon of the Essential Section" is the "Gohonzon of 1279", the "Daimoku of the Essential Section" is the "Daimoku" that we recite toward this object of worship and the place where this Honzon resides is the " High Sanctuary of the Essential Section". [....]

---

[4] The wording "NS-Nichikan doctrine" refers to the traditional NS doctrine brought to completion by Nichikan. This distictive teaching and practice even today still plays a dominant role in NS, although there have been some different doctrinal emphases introduced by other high priests since *Nikkō* (1246-1333), one of the six senior disciples and successors of Nichiren as well as the founder of the *Fuji* line.

According to this amendment, the meaning of "the Three Great Secret Laws" is defined as follows: "The mandalas equipped with the Ten Worlds that ND inscribed personally by hand for all people of the Latter Day of the Law and the Honzons in the transcribed form, are all the manifestations of the fundamental Law of Nam-myō-hō-ren-ge-kyō and they should be regarded equally as being the "Honzon of the Essential Section"; Nam-myō-hō-ren-ge-kyō that we chant toward the "Honzon of the Essential Section" is the "Daimoku of the Essential Section"; The place where we chant Daimoku is as such considered to be the "High Sanctuary or Altar of the Essential Section".

This difference in understanding of the three Great Secret Laws can be summarized as follows.

Three Great Secret Laws	Doctrine of NS	Revised edition of SG
Honmon no Honzon	The Dai-gohonzon only	Each kind of Ten World Mandala
Honmon no Daimoku	Daimoku to chant toward the Dai-gohonzon	Daimoku chanted toward each Gohonzon
Honmon no Kaidan	The place where the Dai-gohonzon resides	The place where we chant Daimoku toward the Honzon of the Essential Section

It is only natural that SG, as an independent organization, should "make a revision to clarify its religious uniqueness". Furthermore, as a consequence of this new understanding of the Three Great Secret Laws, SG announced a change in the content of Gongyo on November 18, 2015. This issue will be treated at the end of Part II to give a summarized overview on the new SG teaching.

Such a series of doctrinal changes has had a significant effect, determining the direction of SG / SGI subsequently and in the future. The Dai-gohonzon for the High Sanctuary of the Essential Section is the very foundation of a rigid exclusive dogmatism, which considers all other schools, religions and beliefs as slander of the Law. As is well known, SG was one of NS lay Buddhist organizations and previously propagated the NS doctrine based on this fundamental belief in the Dai-gohonzon. Despite this fanatical fundamentalist conviction that the Dai-gohonzon alone should be considered to be the sole and absolute truth, while all other schools and religions should be considered false and decadent, SG achieved a remarkable growth in the decades following the war. This exclusive and self-righteous dogmatism was the driving force behind its development, yet at the same time its fierce attacks against slander of the Law provoked antipathy, conflict and harsh criticism from families, temples and society more widely. Consequently, abandoning the foundation of this absolutist claim, as well as casting off a rigid exclusivism and dogmatism, has had the effect of shifting SG to a more positive position from now on, a position characterized by greater tolerance and cooperation with others. This type of philosophical orientation can best be characterized as a "shift from exclusivism to universalism".

Chapter 2
Criticism of the Doctrine of Nichiren as Eternal Original Buddha

I had critically dealt with the problems of faith in the Dai-gohonzon in a previous book »In search of a humanistic theory of "Nichiren as True Buddha" – for the foundation of the Soka Renaissance Movement« (hereafter »Humanism« of 1992). NS teaching is constructed on the basis of the "Doctrine of Nichiren as Eternal Original Buddha" which Nichikan expressly defined. He asserted the true identity of Nichiren as the "Tathāgata of the wisdom body at the primordial origin of the beginning of eternity in the remotest past" (*kuonganjo jijuyū hōshi nyorai*), who was characterized as being more fundamental than the "Buddha Shakyamuni who attained enlightenment in the remotest past" (*kuonjitsujō no Shakuson*). To explain this particular doctrine of Nichikan, we need to bear in mind Nichikan's understanding of a significant difference in person and function between Shakyamuni and Nichiren:

- Shakyamuni Buddha reveals in the 16th chapter of the LS that he attained enlightenment not for the first time under the bodhi tree at Bodhgaya but much earlier in an unimaginably remote past.
- This revelation meant for Nichiren that the eternal Buddha Shakyamuni must have practiced the Dharma as preached in the LS, which Nichiren calls Nam-myō-hō-ren-ge-kyō.
- However, Nichikan interpreted this relationship in a manner which asserted that the eternal Buddha Shakyamuni had previously practiced the Dharma to attain enlightenment under a primordial Buddha, known as the "Buddha body of wisdom of the Primordial Original at the Beginning of the remotest past".
- Further, this Primordial Original Buddha was asserted to be non-other than the true identity of Nichiren himself, who then appeared in the Ceremony in the Air as the leader of the Bodhisattvas of the Earth. This Bodhisattva *Jōgyō* was especially entrusted to preach and propagate the Lotus Dharma in the Latter Day of the Law, i.e. 2,000 years after the death of Shakyamuni Buddha, the age in which Nichiren himself appeared.
- Consequently, the Dharma that Nichiren embodied and preached is characterized as the Mystic Principle of Original Cause, while the enlightenment of the eternal Buddha Shakyamuni who practiced this Dharma is characterized as the Mystic Principle of Original Effect.

I considered this NS doctrine of "Nichiren as the Eternal Original Buddha" problematic as Nichiren's true identity was conceived to be "more primordial" than the eternal Buddha Shakyamuni of the 16th chapter of LS. To my mind, this NS view amounted to nothing but a particular form of "founder worship", i.e. a hagiographic deification of Nichiren himself.

Lotus Sutra	
Chapter 1. – 14.	Theoretical teaching
Chapter 15. – 28.	Essential teaching
Chapter 11. – 22.	Ceremony in the Air
11.	The Emergence of the Treasure Tower
12.	Devadatta
15.	Emerging of the Bodhisattvas from the Earth
16.	The Life Span of the Tathāgata (Revelation of the Eternal Buddha)
21.	Supernatural Powers of the Tathāgata
22.	Transmission of the Dharma to the Bodhisattvas

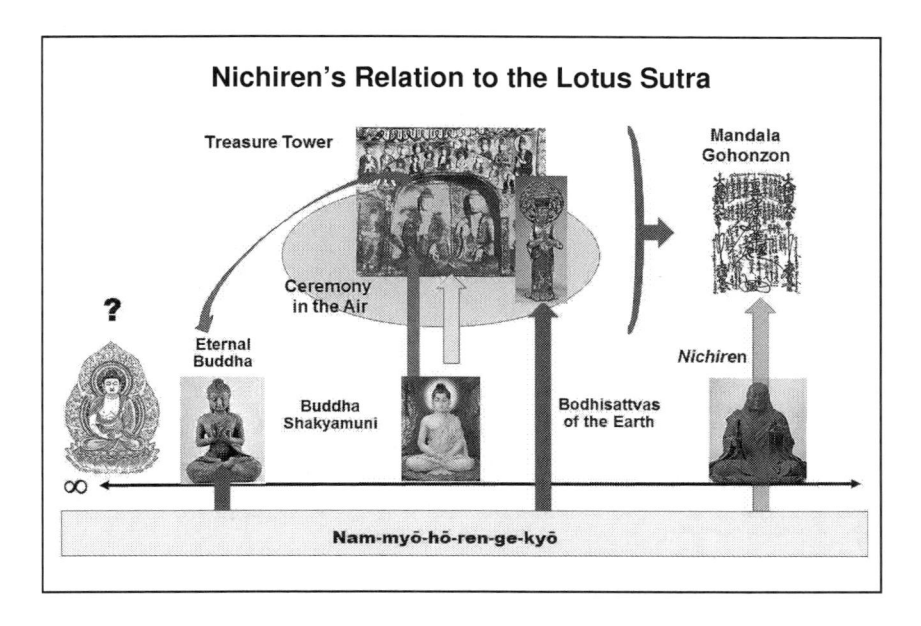

Nichiren's Relation to the Lotus Sutra

Treasure Tower — Mandala Gohonzon — Ceremony in the Air — Eternal Buddha — Nichiren — Buddha Shakyamuni — Bodhisattvas of the Earth

Nam-myō-hō-ren-ge-kyō

Consequently, already at that time, I proposed a radical dismantling of this NS-traditional doctrine. I will provide some quotations from my previous books in order for the reader to better understand the context at that time and the reason for my making such a radical proposal.

At the end of last year [1990], NS suddenly made much harsher its internal regulations and unilaterally dismissed SG honorary president Ikeda, who had served as the general chairman representing all affiliated lay believers. After that, NS head temple introduced new measures, such as a restriction on pilgrimage to the head temple, a suspension on presenting Gohonzons, and a drive to convert SG members to membership of NS's own lay group, both domestically and outside Japan. Furthermore, NS published a "Recommendation for the Dissolution of SG", followed by a "Letter on the Excommunication of SG", dated November 28, 1991. This situation remains the same today (»Humanism« of 1992, p. 5).

This conflict with NS is now known as "SG's second conflict with NS" as it followed the "SG' first conflict with NS", which had only been resolved by the bold action of Ikeda, who, after having served for 19 years as the third president of SG, resigned in April 1979. At that time *Nittatsu* (1902-1979, tenure: 1959-1979), the 66th high priest of the NS head temple Taisekiji, was deeply involved in the conflict with SG which had grown to be a gigantic lay Buddhist organization.

In this development process the SG president Ikeda took an initiative to build *Shōhondō* in the temple terrain of Taisekiji by donation of SG members. This special temple building was completed in October 1972 to fulfill the supposedly proclaimed wish of Nichiren for establishing the "High Sanctuary of the Essential Section in Actuality" for enshrining the Daigohonzon. Later in 1998 this construction was completely destroyed by the order of *Nikken* (1922-, tenure: 1979-2005), the 67th high priest of the NS head temple Taisekiji, who enacted the excommunication of SG from NS in November 1991.

Shōhondō completed in October 1972

Destroyed in 1998

The renewed confrontation with NS led SG to officially to declare the time as the "religious reformation of the Heisei period". This reformation movement was pushed forward by such means as: the demand for the equal treatment of priests and lay believers as well as a radical democratization of all administrative structures and activities, the admonishing of priestly behavior generally and the abandonment of traditional Buddhist practices, mostly relating to the funeral ceremony. However, apart from these organizational and management problems, there still remained a doctrinal problem that SG would need to resolve in the future. This was essentially due to the fact that there remained a fundamental contradiction within SG itself: while promoting "Soka renaissance" which criticized the authoritarian culture and structure of NS, it was not possible to continue to adhere to traditional NS doctrine, which formed the ideological basis for the very same authoritarian structure.

During the period when I was reflecting on this problem, it was really the "letter on the excommunication of SG" which allowed me insight into an important dimension with respect to SG's fundamental doctrinal problem. Among other matters, the "§2 The doctrinal violation of SG" asserted that "SG is committing a serious and obvious violation of the traditional doctrine of the NS sect" and stated as follows.

> (1) Regarding the Dai-gohonzon as a Oneness of Buddha and Dharma which comprises one of the Three Great Secret Laws, Daisaku Ikeda has often stated that "the Dai-gohonzon is the mandala in which the fundamental law of the universe is manifested". He continues to assert such a false teaching which places more significance on the Law [Dharma] than the Person [Buddha] and thus, he is deviating from the teaching of the secret enlightenment of the True Buddha Nichiren Daishōnin. This kind of assertion made by Ikeda exactly amounts to a great slander of the Dharma which destroys the doctrine of the Nichiren Shōshū sect. (ibid., p. 8)

From the perspective of NS, the Dai-gohonzon has been interpreted in the sense of the "Oneness of Buddha and Dharma" (*ninpō ikka*), with Nichiren as identical to the Mystic Law since the Primordial Origin of Eternity in the Remotest Past. In contrast, already by that time, Ikeda had detached the relationship between the Dai-gohonzon and the doctrine of Nichiren as Eternal Original Buddha and interpreted its meaning in a more universal sense that *"the Dai-gohonzon is the mandala in which the fundamental law of the universe is manifested"*. This innovative view was then condemned by NS as a false teaching deviating from the secret enlightenment of the True Buddha ND because it places greater significance on one aspect: i.e. on that of the Law [Dharma] rather than that of the Person [Buddha].

I responded to this evaluation of NS as follows:

> However, the (present) NS head temple has further developed a far more pernicious ideology about *"the infallibility of the Dharma transmission of the High Priest"* according to which *"the priests and lay believers of this sect must faithfully obey the guidance of the High Priest (who ob-*

tained the Dharma transmission solely from the former Hight Priest) regarding both practice for oneself and for others as well as for the development of Kōsenrufu". For the very reason that this anachronistic ideology represents the undercurrent of NS doctrine, the traditional NS dogmatism itself must be critically reviewed, especially all assertions about the "secret enlightenment of the True Buddha Daishōnin" and "the Dharma body of the secret enlightenment of the Daishōnin". The doctrine of the Daishōnin as True Buddha as traditionally taught in NS implies, at least theoretically, an ideology which asserts the High Priest to be True Buddha. (ibid.)

That is to say, in the situation at that time, *the ideology concerning the infallibility of the Dharma transmission by each successive High Priest* has been widely propagated. This dogmatic ideology can be summarized as follows:
- The Dai-gohonzon is the essence of the Eternal Original Buddha Nichiren.
- The high priest Nikken obtained the Dharma transmission in his capacity as the sole entitled person and, thus, he is endowed with the absolute authority & infallibility with respect to both faith and administrative operations.
- Therefore, all believers must faithfully obey and accept his guidance.

Against this background it is clear that the doctrine of Nichiren as Eternal Original Buddha provided not only the foundation of faith in the Dai-gohonzon as a manifestation of the Oneness of Buddha and Dharma, but it had contributed to establish an institutional system of absolute infallibility focused on the high priest. Consequently, it was inevitable that I would seek to overcome the doctrine of Nichiren as Eternal Original Buddha and faith in the Dai-gohonzon as the sole authentic mandala. In this context, the significance of the "High Sanctuary of the Essential Section" would change.

The "letter on the excommunication of SG" refers to this point as follows:

(2) The High Sanctuary of the Essential Section establishes the most important of the Three Great Secret Laws found in the teachings of the founder Daishōnin. Regarding the significance of this High Sanctuary Ikeda asserted, based on a shallow view, the following, disregarding the true intention of the Daishōnin: *"Constructing the High Sanctuary means only a form to be fulfilled. Its real essence lies in the intention that all people in the world should become happy. As a result of this accomplishment, the construction of an Sanctuary can be carried out in order to set a symbolic mark like a stone monument. Therefore, it can be regarded as a subordinate minor issue, just one of formality"*. (ibid., p. 9)

Given these critical remarks made by NS, we can conclude that Ikeda had perhaps already been oriented toward a more universalist signification of the

"High Sanctuary of the Essential Section" by seeking to overcome the spatially limited significance given to it by NS. In order to successfully further develop Ikeda's new orientation, I proposed a radical humanist understanding of NB as follows:

> For what purpose was the Gohonzon inscribed by Nichiren? For what purpose arqe we chanting Daimoku in a faithful manner? As the "notice on SG excommunication" asserted that Ikeda's guidance violated NS doctrine, the statements of SGI president Ikeda with respect to the "Daigohonzon" and the "Construction of the High Sanctuary" clearly expressed the "humanist" position that NB should serve to promote the happiness of all people and the establishment of world peace. And this position is the final goal of the „Reformation movement of the Heisei period" and the philosophical basis of the "Soka renaissance".
>
> In this respect, it would be valuable to doctrinally elucidate the humanistic Buddhism which Nichiren intended, in order that NB can truly expand as a world religion after the collapse of the "Nikken Cult". This book is an attempt at a radical deconstruction of the traditional doctrine of "Nichiren as True Buddha". To summarize its conclusion, it asserts only one fundamental philosophical basis: the foundation of the thought of the Daishōnin on the doctrine of the "Mutual Containment of all Ten Worlds based on the Original Enlightenment of the Buddha" and, consequently, the Dharma of Nam-myō-hō-ren-ge-kyō that Nichiren manifested in his own life is nothing other than the "mystic principle that is originally inherent in all living beings"[5]. This view represents a humanistic position that paves the way to attaining Buddhahood equally by all people. (ibid., p. 10)

Against this background, my first book published dealing with the problem of NS bears the title »In search of a humanistic theory of "Nichiren as True Buddha"«. The NS doctrine asserts "Nichiren as Eternal Original Buddha" based on the particular view of Nichiren as the "Tathāgata of the wisdom body at the primordial origin of the beginning of eternity in the remotest past". This presumes a very specific mythology with regard to Nichiren as an

---

[5] In the "Foreword" of »Humanism«, written in December 1991, this "mystic principle" was taken from the gosho »On Attaining the Buddhahood in This Life time« of 1255 (WND, p.3). And this inherent principle was regarded as the universal essence of enlightenment. This is why the five characters of Myō-hō-ren-ge-kyō actually mean the principle of mutual inclusion of all ten worlds based on original enlightenment". This Dharma for enlightenment will in Part 3 of this present work be argued for in more concrete detail, i.e. that it is the "three great principles of the mutual inclusion of all ten worlds, Ichinen sanzen and instant enlightenment". To practice this Mystic Law, designated as the five characters of Myō-hō-ren-ge-kyō, is nothing other than the chanting of daimoku, the practice of the seven characters of Na-m(u)-myō-hō-ren-ge-kyō.

exceptional holy and enlightened person by way of "transferring him back into the remotest past". If the eternal original Buddha Nichiren is upheld, he would indeed be a person who is radically distinct from our own ordinary selves. This is a dogmatic, exclusivistic and fundamentalist understanding of Nichiren. However, if we adopt a more humanistic viewpoint, i.e. by "Transferring the remotest past to the present time", a new horizon is opened up which manifests the universal and eternal Buddhahood (the Buddha World) inherent in all ordinary people (the Nine Worlds), both in Nichiren and in our ordinary selves. The "humanistic thesis on Nichiren as True Buddha" [which I suggested in the book] necessarily implies a principle that is universally applicable to every ordinary person who chants Daimoku. That means quite simply that "the ordinary body manifests the Buddha body as a matter of fact" (ibid., p. 150), or to put it in relation to our practice, "the very emergence of our chanting Daimoku means nothing other than that Nam-myō-hō-ren-ge-kyō designates originally existing enlightenment and the principle of the mutual inclusion of all Ten Worlds" (ibid.).

I summarized this new way of thinking in the "postscript" as follows.

> If ND is regarded as the Eternal Buddha without beginning and end, he would cease to exist as an ordinary person and become an object of worship in the form of the "Dai-gohonzon as the Oneness of Buddha and Dharma". The theoretical problem with this particular view is that the Daishōnin would then be relocated into the remotest past and function in the capacity as the single original Buddha. In this case the Eternal Buddha and we, ordinary people, would remain radically distinct eternally. The conclusion should be that the Buddhism of the Daishōnin teaches us thoroughly, that in order to reveal our ordinary body as the Buddha body, i.e. by "revealing true identity by casting away its shadow", which the Daishōnin demonstrated at Tatsunokuchi, merely by manifesting his "wisdom body at the Primordial Origin of the Beginning of the remotest past", which is inherent in all sentient beings. Consequently, it is not about transforming the Daishōnin himself into an extraordinary being who existed in the remotest past but rather the exact opposite, i.e. the means by which the remotest past is transformed into the present. It implies that the same path that initially awakened the Daishōnin to his own "entity endowed with the three bodies of Original Enlightenment without intention" has opened up the way to the realization of enlightenment in the sense of "immediate enlightenment as original enlightenment", a way open to all living beings. An eternal Buddha is radically distinct from all ordinary people, but the "ordinary body as Buddha body" in terms of original existence without intention reveals a pioneer who opens up the Buddha way to all ordinary people, i.e. the way of true humanism. Let's be adamant that there lies the greatness of Nichiren in his capacity as the

Buddhist master of the "mystic principle of the original cause". (ibid., p. 167)

In this initial discussion in the 1990s, I was still trying to dismantle the traditional NS doctrine within its own framework. For example, even in this quotation, I used the particular NS terms, such as the *"wisdom body at the Primordial Origin of the Beginning of the remotest past* which is inherent in all sentient beings". For I was attempting to give a new meaning to these traditional terms. In response to my first book, there were some sharp criticisms from NS priests and lay believers. These diatribes against my new interpretations led me myself to sharpen my own position by way of reaction. Sueki who understood my reasons made the following comment.

In his »Humanism« of 1992, Matsudo was struggling to rearrange the existing teachings based on the NS doctrines. Therefore, his arguments partly remained difficult to follow for he didn't yet use the word "Ordinary Person as True Buddha" that might make clearer his own doctrinal position. However, his endeavor must be much admired, as he is seeking a new theory which can be the foundation for the secular social activity of lay people, yet which is still nourished by traditional teachings. Hence, there is an unavoidable tension between the desire to be radically novel and yet true to the spirit of the traditional teachings.

In his »Innovation« of 1994 Matsudo described his own position as the "Theory of the Ordinary Person as True Buddha", following his reflections published in his first book. Subsequently, after further revision and refinement, his second book appeared, which can be regarded as an attempt to advance a far more developed theory. [Though the third book about his debates with several NS priests followed...], this »Innovation« should perhaps be regarded only as a matrix for the time being. (»Sueki's Comments« of 2015, p. 95)

Chapter 3

An alternative to the "Doctrine of Nichiren as the Eternal Original Buddha"

In my next book »Innovation« of 1994 I drew attention to the problematic "claim of the high priest to be the representative of the Original Buddha". Given the assumption that the secret dharma body of the Daishōnin is the Dai-gohonzon, it is asserted that the high priest who succeeds in the lineage of the Dai-gohonzon holds his appointment within NS as the representative of the Eternal Original Buddha Nichiren. This assertion can be summarized as follows.

Nichiren Daishōnin

= the *Tathāgata of the Wisdom Body present at the Primordial Origin of the Beginning of the remotest past*, therefore he is more fundamental than *the Buddha Shakyamuni who attained enlightenment in the remotest past*
= the supreme master of the mystic principle of the original cause,
= the rebirth of Jōgyō bodhisattva in the Ceremony in the Air
= the True Buddha in the Latter Day of the Law
= the Dai-gohonzon which is the Oneness of Buddha and Dharma

The High Priests in succession

= the transmission of the dharma body within the lineage from each high priest successively to another alone
= the deputy to Nichiren for today
= the authoritarian hierarchical system in which all priests, novices and lay believers are obliged unquestionably to obey the high priest who alone can guide the faithful to salvation

The particular kind of authoritarian system and doctrinal understanding established by NS, is based fundamentally on the "doctrine of Nichiren as the Eternal Original Buddha" and "faith in the Dai-gohonzon". Against this dogmatic belief system, I myself proposed a radically contrasting "Theory of the Ordinary Person as True Buddha". My intention of innovating the doctrinal understanding has not changed until today. The 1994 "Preface" of »Innovation« concluded with the following words.

> For myself, I consider the traditional doctrine of Nichiren as eternal original Buddha is deeply problematic and that it should be dismantled if the study of Nichikan is to be radically transformed. In other words, as already pointed out in my previous book, I consider that the traditional

doctrine of Nichiren as eternal original Buddha is unpersuasive and it is a doctrinal disaster, as it bears no relevance for our practice today. Discarding the framework of the established doctrines and viewpoints found within NS, is not simply negative: it is an attempt to review those doctrines once again from the perspective of our own lived experience based on faith. It is essential, that we seek a contemporary philosophical theory that reflects our current life experience. That is, a contemporary and innovative form for NB. I consider that this is the task facing the Soka Renaissance movement.

The fundamental stance of humanistic Buddhism is its radical anti-authoritarianism based on the "Theory of the Ordinary Person as True Buddha" according to which we, as ordinary people who are practicing Daimoku, are the Buddha of Nam-myō-hō-ren-ge-kyō. This "humanistic Theory of the Ordinary Person as True Buddha" should not be considered as identical with medieval "Original Enlightenment Thought", which uncritically affirms the status quo of existing society and all other things existing in the world. On the contrary, because it is based on a particular theory which stresses the unique value of each person individually, it represents a theory of radical change aiming at the "human revolution" of each individual who struggles against the misery and misfortune of this world and at breaking down the institutional status quo, the unjust structures which form our contemporary social reality. An elucidation of these humanistic ideals, in strict relation to NB, is the theme of this book.

Thus, in order to argue effectively against the "doctrine of Nichiren as Eternal Original Buddha", given that this doctrine was the foundation upon which a fundamentalist, exclusivist and authoritarian sectarian mind set had arisen, I actively promoted a radical alternative, i.e. a universalistic, humanistic and egalitarian "Theory of the Ordinary Person as True Buddha", in which Buddhahood was now properly conceivable as attainable by all ordinary people just as they are. Of course, when I talk about the "thesis on the ordinary person as true Buddha", this runs the risk of being immediately confused with the "medieval Tendai idea of original enlightenment", which had affirmed the status quo, whether personal, natural or social. Additionally, all works of ND sympathetic to such a thesis have generally been treated as apocryphal or falsifications, simply because they are rich in allusions to the idea of original enlightenment. The roots of this prejudice run deep.

I had been aware of the above problems in 1994, when I summarized as below:

> In this book I actively sought to extract both the Essential Section of the LS and the idea of Original Enlightenment found in the teachings of the Daishōnin and then to expand upon this into the Theory of the Ordinary Person as True Buddha. However, mainstream scholars engaged in

Nichiren Buddhist studies were at that time generally suspicious of (& sought to exclude as discourse) any "idea of original enlightenment", especially radical presentations, such as that found in the "Theory of Ordinary Person as True Buddha". Even in philological debate around the "authenticity" of many of Nichiren's Gosho, the mainstream became dominated by the view that elements of some Gosho apparently inspired by "ideas of original enlightenment" must necessarily be fabrications and interpolations from a later age.

Based on the above considerations, to my mind, any understanding which regards an ordinary person as the original enlightened subject is not satisfactory, for it implies a particular idea of Original Enlightenment which merely affirms the status quo, thus making Buddhist practice unnecessary and futile. Nevertheless, it would be wrong to discard all ideas of original enlightenment. The Theory of the Ordinary Person as True Buddha developed by the Daishōnin is succinctly characterized below:

- The Daishōnin viewed the Dharma body of Original Enlightenment as indicating the Buddha Shakyamuni, who attained enlightenment in the remotest past, as revealed in the LS. This Dharma body is nothing other than Nam-myō-hō-ren-ge-kyō. Initially, the starting point is the preaching of the LS, at the literal textual level. He contrasts and compares Original Enlightenment with Initial Enlightenment, and similarly with causality, i.e. where "original cause = original effect" at the very moment of attaining enlightenment in the remotest past.
- This immediate enlightenment consists in the faith and practice of the Dharma of Nam-myō-hō-ren-ge-kyō. It is not an idea about Original Enlightenment that is in any way detached from practice. It means to manifest Original Enlightenment at the moment of Initial Enlightenment and thus, "practice (cause) = attaining Buddhahood (effect)".
- Practice enables the ordinary person dwelling in concrete reality to open up to the enlightened life of Nam-myō-hō-ren-ge-kyō. Any Buddha who dwells beyond the realm of the ordinary person is thereby revealed to be only a fiction, a provisional Buddha. Only ordinary people can reveal their capacity as truly existing Buddhas.
- Therefore, Nam-myō-hō-ren-ge-kyō which leads all people to enlightenment is the true master of eternity. Until this revelation, even Shakyamuni Buddha and the Daishōnin himself, as well as any other person or divine being, are unable to lead people to salvation. Not the Buddha, but the Dharma is the foundation of Buddhism.
- Nevertheless, as it was Nichiren Daishōnin who embodied and preached the Dharma of Nam-myō-hō-ren-ge-kyō, he alone should be considered to be the "true Buddha in the latter day of the law", endowed with the three virtues of sovereign, teacher and parent or "the

supreme master of the mystic principle of the original cause". (ibid., p. 202)

At that time, as noted above, I considered the "Dharma body of Nam-myō-hō-ren-ge-kyō" to be identical to the "Dharma body of Original Enlightenment". This in fact means the *"mystic truth that is originally inherent in all living beings"* (»On Attaining Buddhahood in This Lifetime«, p. 383 / 3). Consequently, this Wonderful Dharma should be understood in terms of the "simultaneity of cause and effect", found deep within the lives of ordinary people, i.e. Nam-myō-hō-ren-ge-kyō as Dharma body cannot be understood as "something" that a high priest may transfer from one generation to another. In contrast to this material and utterly limited view of Dharma, I stressed the *"mystic truth that is originally inherent in all living beings in the sense of the Buddhahood of all people"*.

However, when I now reflect once again upon it, this understanding has remained rather idealistic. Consequently, even though at that time I had already developed a "Theory of the Ordinary Person as True Buddha" based on the "Principle of the Mutual inclusion of the Ten Worlds", the task remained to me to elaborate on this further, especially in relation to the actual practice of chanting Daimoku.

Chapter 4
An Interview "Thought of Change, A Thesis on the Ordinary Person as True Buddha"

After the publication of my »Innovation« (1994) an "interview with the author" was posted in a daily newspaper specializing in religious issues in Japan »Chūgai Nippō« on April 14, 1994. This interview was included in chapter one of the third book »The Doctrinal Controversy of the Heisei period – Laughing at the "Refutation" of Nichiren Shōshū« (1995). Since the explanation concerning my intention in publishing my works summarizes the basic orientation of my argument concisely, I will quote the complete article here, as an introduction for non-Japanese readers:

The religious thought and the practice of faith established by Nichiren Daishōnin is completely different from the traditional doctrine of "Temple Buddhism" which is characterized by a particular form of Buddhism focused on funeral and merit transference ceremonies for the dead. The Daishōnin himself was a religious revolutionary condemned and exiled by the Shogunate for propagating false religious beliefs and sedition. An important dimension of his efforts to propagate exclusive belief in the LS was that he virulently denied any form of "salvation from above" and "disengagement from the present world". Instead, as the doctrine of Immediate Enlightenment and the metaphor of the "lotus flower in muddy water" suggest, Nichiren propagated a way of practice and faith, which would open up the Buddhahood within our own lives. (Quoted from the foreword of »Innovation«)

Since the severe conflict between SG and NS broke out, a series of scandalous incidents, such as some priests' corrupt and violent behavior, sloppy or inadequate administrative treatment of the bones of the dead, as well as a truly premodern segregation of lay believers from priests and the hierarchical and authoritarian power structure centered around the NS head temple. In the middle of this process a strange new idea emerged within NS, i.e. the idea of the "High Priest *Nikken*, the 67th high priest, as true Buddha". It was perhaps but a "nodal flower" which bloomed out of the defective doctrine of "Nichiren as Eternal Original Buddha", the traditional doctrine unique to NS.

Yukio Matsudo, Director of Research in the European Center of the "Institute of Oriental Philosophy" (IOP), recently wrote »An Innovation of Nichiren Thought – About the thesis on "Ordinary Person as True Buddha" « for "the foundation of the Soka Renaissance Movement". In his book he developed a radical critical buddhological theory to assault and undermine the traditional key NS doctrines, which had long upheld a temple- and funeral-centered form of Buddhism, in an attempt to return NB back into the hands of ordinary people. The interviewer asked the author about his motivation in writing "The Theory of the Ordinary Person as True Buddha".

A document which raises questions from European SGI

– Please tell us about the intention behind or the background to this book.
Matsudo: I went to Germany in 1971 and later began to study Western philosophy at the University of Heidelberg. In 1976 I joined the German SGI (it was called at that time "Deutsche Nichiren Shōshū" DNS). Since then I have been studying and practicing Nichiren Buddhism in the German SGI and I have been in constant Buddhist dialogue with Germans and other nationalities. Consequently, I have naturally gained a particular understanding of NB through their eyes, as a result of this dialogue and through participation in organizational activities with German people.

In other words, it was impossible to propagate a particular Japanese form of temple- and funeral-oriented Buddhism, which was quite alien to Germans and other Westerners. Given that, we did practice NB as a wholly lay Buddhist movement, much more than SG in Japan, which has been mired in Japanese tradition.

– What does that mean exactly?

Matsudo: Firstly, we do not have either a NS temple or priest in Europe. Consequently, the SGI movement has had an exclusively lay Buddhist orientation. Secondly, it has been natural for us to conduct ceremonial events, such as marriages and funerals, as well as propagation of the teachings. For example: the particular form of "funeral service with friends", i. e. without the leadership and guidance of priests, has been quite normal, indeed it represents a great success for the "reformation of the Heisei period" in Japan. Thirdly, in Europe where individualism and democracy form the cultural basis of social life, many people looking for a faith outside of Christianity will only accept and practice a faith that is theoretically reasonable. They will not accept any form of authoritarian belief or any hierarchical structure which places limitations on thinking and acting. Fourthly, traditional Japanese beliefs and assumptions emphasize the accumulation of merits and worldly benefits, although this aspect is likewise important in Europe, much greater emphasis is placed on the inner nature of faith and the ethics of spiritual independence and responsibility. In other words, aspects such as the transformation of individual and collective karma and an individual's self-realization are far more significant.

Thus, in Japan and Europe, it would seem that the needs and the ritual forms demanded of religion are quite different.

Against this background, from the beginning of the SGI movement in Europe, Japanese temple- and funerary-oriented Buddhism was never practiced. Instead inspired by the guidance of SGI President Ikeda, a much more modern understanding and practice of NB was initiated. **In fact, his speeches and guidance touched the hearts of** SGI members much more directly than in Japan. **Being oblivious of Japanese "double-standards", such as "outer and inner face"** or "diplomatic manner and real intention", European members, including myself, have understood NB as a contemporary humanistic and pacifist Buddhist teaching.

To my critical understanding, I considered the current conflict between SG and NS essentially as indeed a confrontation between Japanese temple- and funeral-oriented Buddhism and an internationally engaged lay Buddhist movement. Such an antagonism appeared to be a historical necessity and was evidenced on the doctrinal level as a confrontation between the "doctrine of Nichiren as the eternal original Buddha" and the "doctrine of the ordinary person as Buddha", which is founded on the eternal Mystic Law.

Consequently, the argument I have developed in both the above books is nothing other than the idea that SGI president Ikeda has been espousing. I simply represented at the doctrinal level an implicit understanding which SGI had been promoting within Germany or Europe.

− Do you mean in short that the conflict with NS was not caused simply by the financial corruption and other moral failings of the NS priesthood, but also to doctrinal defects which had permitted such decadence?

Matsudo: Yes. Historically the decadent and corrupt priesthood may have been a harmful consequence of the temple patronage system established during the Edo period (17th Century)[6]. Thus, it became inevitable that the traditional doctrines which had sanctioned and thereby deformed Temple Buddhism should be challenged. This challenge poses the question as to how best to advance into the future. I consider that it is necessary to carry out a kind of ideological struggle to challenge and push for fundamental and radical reform of the status quo. **Otherwise, even if the present high priest Nikken abdicated, nothing would be essentially altered.** For behind the dogmatic assertions on "the absolute power of the high priest" and "the high priest as

---

[6] The Tokugawa Shogunate compelled all Japanese households to belong to a Buddhist temple in their local area. The initial intention had been to prevent the Christianization of Japan; however, later the temple partronage system was used to enforce resident registration. Further, lay believers belonging to a particular Buddhist temple were permitted to administer family tombs and to preside over funeral and memorial ceremonies for the dead.

true Buddha", lies the traditional "doctrine of Nichiren as the eternal original Buddha".

Since Soka Gakkai, which criticizes Funeral Buddhism, has been consistently promoting slogans such as "The Daishōnin First" and "Gosho First", I revisited the existing teachings of SG, which had been strong influenced by NS, in order to seek to rediscover and present anew the original and authentic teachings and practice of Nichiren Daishōnin. The first book that I wrote has the title »In search of a humanistic theory of "Nichiren as True Buddha"« (1992), published two years ago.

– Followed by a sequel: »The Innovation of Nichiren Thought – About the thesis on "The Ordinary Person as True Buddha"«.

Matsudo: Yes. In the first book I critically referred to the "doctrine on the unity of Shakyamuni and Jōgyō" elaborated by *Nichijun* (1898-1959, the 65th high priest of NS) and the doctrine of his disciple *Jijō Ōhashai* (priest and professor at the NS college). In reply to my critical article, someone describing himself as "an independent NS believer" published an article with the title "A discussion forum: Pointing to problematic views in Yukio Matsudo's »In search of a humanistic theory of "Nichiren as True Buddha"« in the magazine »Kōfu« of the NS temple *Shōkōji*. In a further reply, I once again summarized my arguments which had formed the basis of my criticism. Indeed, I was grateful for the further opportunity to refine my critical argument. As an author, as a general rule, one welcomes criticisms raised against one's work, which is highly preferable to others' neglect of one's work. Only in this way, can one deepen one's intellectual insight!

Humanism against authoritarianism

– What is the main theme of this book expressed concisely?

Matsudo: It is that which concerns the "theory of the ordinary person as a Buddha" and about "humanism" resisting "authoritarianism". The fundamental position of ND is, as I understand it, that we, ordinary people who chant the Daimoku for our own realization of Buddhahood and spiritual liberation, in order that we may help all other beings, just as we are, embody the dharma of **Nam-myō-hō-ren-ge-kyō**, i.e. we are Bodhisattvas of the Earth.

This theory of "the ordinary person as Buddha" is fundamentally humanistic. I sought to elucidate a theory of radical change aiming at Human Revolution, in order to undermine the global status quo to more effectively struggle against the misery and injustice of this world.

The contents are divided into two parts, one part seeks to undermine the "doctrine of Nichiren as the eternal original Buddha", which has traditionally supported the dogma that the "high priest has infallible authority". The other part seeks to present the "theory of the ordinary person as Buddha", in radical contrast to the "doctrine of Nichiren as the eternal original Buddha". As some may raise the question that this theory might be nothing other than a novel representation of the medieval Tendai Philosophy of Original Enlightenment, the fifth chapter serves as "An objection to concerns raised that my theory is nothing other than a novel representation of the doctrine of original enlightenment".

— If one speaks of the essential Buddhahood of ordinary people, this can easily be mistaken as nothing other than a representation of the Tendai Philosophy of Original Enlightenment, i.e. that "even deluded people are manifestations of Buddhahood itself", a doctrine which has traditionally been complicit in upholding and justifying political and social inequalities, "just as they are". Is this what you mean?

Matsudo: Yes. This Original Enlightenment Thought has become an ideology of affirmation, justifying status quo. On the other hand, the question of whether or not my theory is distinct from the traditional doctrine of Original Enlightenment poses a serious problem. As such questions directly relate to a fundamental problem: which Gosho are apocryphal among the received writings of ND. With respect to this question I feel uneasy, as many of ND's important writings which contain elements of the Doctrine of Original Enlightenment have been systematically redacted by some scholars. I consider that it is preferable to accept that quite understandably there are some elements of the traditional Doctrine of Original Enlightenment which have emerged in the thought of the Daishōnin, as he had received a traditional medieval Tendai education. Nevertheless, Nichiren's thought is radically distinct from the traditional Tendai doctrine, as the potential for enlightenment can only be activated by practice.

The late Professor *Yoshiro Tamura* of Risshō University noted in this regard that: *"Although the thought of Kamakura New Buddhism[7] stood on a foundation akin to the Doctrine of Original Enlightenment, the traditional doctrine was radically reinterpreted with reference to new exclusive forms of Buddhist practice and fundamentally new much more practical theories with respect to human realization and spiritual development."*

"The Person" becomes an object of worship

— So, from an European religious perspective, you are criticizing traditional Japanese Funeral Buddhism.

---

[7] The term "Kamakura New Buddhism" refers to the new Buddhist movements, established and promoted during the Kamakura period: e.g. Jōdoshū of *Hōnen* (1133-1212), Jōdo-shinshū of *Shinran* (1173-1262), Rinzaishū of *Eisai* (1141-1215), Sōtōshū of *Dōgen* (1200-1253), Hokkeshū of *Nichiren* (1222-1282), and Jishū of *Ippen* (1239-1289).

Chapter 4

Matsudo: Among all the existing Buddhist schools, I can only talk about the so-called Funeral Buddhism in the lineage of the Nichiren school. There has been a doctrinal culmination within the Nichiren lineages generally, which is independent of any particular doctrinal and/or institutional differences. For example, within Nichiren Shū the person of Shakyamuni Buddha, while within Nichiren Shōshū the person of Nichiren Daishōnin, have been transformed into "objects of worship", as each is considered to be a transcendent or deified being who brings salvation to the faithful devotee. This transformation has meant that the priesthood has assumed a crucial role in "mediating salvation brought by the Buddha" to the faithful believer. Consequently, the priesthood has assumed (or rather presumed) itself to have a crucial role with respect to the "salvation" of the individual lay believer. Contrary to this type of faith in the person of the Buddha, the authentic teaching of ND makes the Dharma of Nam-myō-hō-ren-ge-kyō itself the origin and foundation of the enlightenment of all Buddhas, past, present and future.

Consequently, always abide in the principle of "Rely on the Dharma and not on the Person" – The "ideology of high priest endowed with absolute authority" leads only to the worship of persons

— So, you mean that faith should be based only on the Dharma, although speaking of the "Oneness of Buddha and Dharma", do you?

Matsudo: By single-mindedly practicing the Dharma of Nam-myō-hō-ren-ge-kyō, every one of us, ordinary people living in the Latter Day of the Law, are able to manifest Buddhahood.

— Buddha Shakyamuni taught also that "he leads us to the same level of realization as himself", i.e., we can attain in the same way the same level of realization as the Buddha himself.

Matsudo: Yes. The Buddhist teaching with respect to this is the principle of *"Relying on the Dharma and not any person"*.

— Again, the foundation of Buddhism is the Dharma.

Matsudo: So, if you set up any person or Buddha as an object of worship, another person will be needed to "mediate" him. And this leads inevitably to a hierarchical structure which can then coalesce into an authoritarian system, such as the ideology of the high priest endowed with infallibility.

— You are also referring to the "theory of the high priest as the representative of ND," aren't you?

Matsudo: Based on the doctrine which considers ND to be the eternal original Buddha, a privileged caste will surely emerge, which will claim to inherit the "blood line" of the Buddhist Dharma. Indeed, the person at the apex of the hierarchy will come to be considered as a Buddha. In such a way, an authoritarian structure will be erected around this privileged especially empowered person. In stark opposition to this mystification of ND and the high priest as his alleged successor, my "theory of the ordinary person as Buddha" intends to return to and clarify the original authentic view of ND, who had constantly stressed that any Buddha, whether Amida or Shakyamuni, only attained enlightenment by practicing the Dharma of Nam-myō-hō-ren-ge-kyō as an ordinary person. It is only in this way that the Daishōnin explained how the "Buddha Shakyamuni had attained enlightenment in the remotest past". For this Buddha represents the Mystic Principle of Original Effect, while the Mystic Dharma he practiced is called the Mystic Principle of Original Cause. He actually became awakened to the truth that an ordinary person only becomes a true Buddha by activating the potential for Buddhahood found within this very body. This cause of all Buddhas is nothing other than Nam-myō-hō-ren-ge-kyō.

The Bodhisattvas of the Earth as embodiments of the "Principle of the Ordinary Person as True Buddha"

ND considers the Bodhisattvas of the Earth as embodying the "Principle of the Ordinary Person as True Buddha". In fact, he identified himself as the rebirth of Bodhisattva Jōgyō, he embodied the principle that an ordinary person is in essence a Buddha. ND considered the chanting of Daimoku based on this principle is the only means to activate the Buddha potential in the body of an ordinary person. Hence the "Theory of the Ordinary Person as True Buddha".

In this respect, there is another dimension which was important to ND: i.e. any Buddha who is no longer also an ordinary person is false. Thus, Amida Buddha (Tathāgata Amitabha), Dainichi Nyorai (Tathāgata Vairochana) or even Shakyamuni in a deified form as a majestic or brilliant golden Buddha, have simply ceased to be ordinary human beings. In these forms, the Buddha is worshipped as a transcendent being or deity. This should be regarded as false, as only a person with an ordinary human body can exist in this actual world, and so too only a Buddha with an ordinary human body can be considered real and true.

— You deal with the "Theory of the Ordinary Person as True Buddha" in the second chapter, don't you?

Matsudo: According to the "doctrine of Nichiren as the Eternal Original Buddha", it is claimed that, "There was a Buddha at the Primordial Origin of the Beginning of the remotest past". However, with a "Theory of the Ordinary Person as True Buddha", from first to last, there exist only ordinary people.

— I see.

CHAPTER 4

Matsudo: It is taught that Amida Buddha residing in the Pure Land to the West had at first also been an ordinary man, but who subsequently, as *Hōzō* Bodhisattva, vowed to become a Buddha. However, if he didn't exist in this actual world with an ordinary human body, then his story is nothing but a myth. Thus, if anyone should become a Buddha, that would mean that he attained enlightenment in this world in an ordinary human body. This is what the term the "Three Bodies of Dharma, Wisdom and Manifestation" actually implies. An actually existing Buddha in the form of an ordinary person is endowed with these "three aspects of the Buddha body (trikaya)".

For the Daishōnin, an ordinary person awakening to Buddhahood means quite simply to realize the Mystic Law of Nam-myō-hō-ren-ge-kyō. Similarly, the Eternal Original Buddha Shakyamuni necessarily can only have realized Buddhahood as an ordinary person at the moment of his enlightenment. This significant moment is best expressed as "Initial Enlightenment is identical to Original Enlightenment". This means that at the very moment you become enlightened for the first time, you will also immediately realize that you are "originally" a Buddha. Then you will experience, as ND describes it, "the greatest joy of all joys" in the Latter Day of the Law.

Both the "theoretical stage" and the "verbal stage" of identity are found within the ordinary person

— By the way, you also mention that the theoretical and the verbal stages of identity are particularly related to the practice of the ordinary person[8].

---

[8] There are "six progressive stages of identical enlightenment (roku-soku)" which T'ien-t'ai formulated regarding the practice of the Lotus Sutra. These stages differ with respect to a difference in the progression of practice, yet they are always related to Buddhahood, which forms *the identity* of practitioners. Applying this classification to daimoku, ND explains in »The Record of the Orally Transmitted Teachings« as follows:

Speaking in terms of the six stages of practice, the Tathagata in this [16th Life Span] chapter is an ordinary mortal who is in the first stage, that of being a Buddha in theory [(1) "*theoretical stage of identity*"]. When one reverently accepts Nam-myōhō-renge-kyō, one is in the next stage, that of hearing the name and words of the truth [(2) "*nominal stage of identity*"]. That is, one has for the first time heard the daimoku. When, having heard the daimoku, one proceeds to put it into practice, this is the third stage, that of perception and action [(3) "*active stage of identity*"]. In this stage, one perceives the "object of devotion that embodies the three thousand realms in a single moment of life". When one succeeds in overcoming various illusions and obstacles, this is the fourth stage, that of resemblance to enlightenment [(4) "*resembling stage of identity*"]. When one sets out to convert others, this is the fifth stage, that of progressive awakening [(5) "*participating stage of identity*"]. And when one comes at last to the realization that one is a Buddha eternally endowed with the three bodies, then one is

Matsudo: In *Hokkekō*, the lay organization of NS, they use these terms as a teaching which justifies the logic of discrimination. For example, the strident declarations of Mrs. Uchida that *"His Holiness is the Honorable Daishōnin in our modern times"*: *"In speaking of the fundamental relationship between priests and lay believers, the Honorable Daishōnin has made it clear that the 'verbal stage of identity' can only be applied to him. Therefore, His Holiness is the only person who has inherited from the Honorable Daishōnin the 'Dharma body comprising the Oneness of Buddha and Dharma' in a pure form. Consequently, the relationship between priests and lay people should be understood in the form of master and slave, or as upper and lower."* Of course, she has uttered illogical and incoherent nonsense. She sought to give expression to the bizarre notion that ND might himself be uniquely a person at the "verbal stage of identity", who would then without contradiction, propagate a teaching established on a master-slave relationship between priests and lay believers.

Nevertheless, in reality, this "verbal stage of identity" still belongs to a status which is that of the ordinary person. From this stage the ordinary person enters into each subsequent stage of practice, including hearing and accepting the Dharma. Mrs. Uchida may have based her argument on the passage: *"Nichiren is in the 'verbal stage of identity' while his disciples and lay followers are in the 'theoretical stage of identity'"* (»On the Mystic Principle of Original Cause«, p. 873). But, the main question here is why the Daishōnin should distinguish himself in this way from his disciples and lay followers.

With reference to the conclusion, what is most decisive is not this distinction itself, but the fact that these two stages belong to that of the ordinary person. So long as you are not practicing the Dharma you are an ordinary person at the "theoretical stage of identity". Yet as soon as you accept and begin to practice the Dharma of Nam-myō-hō-ren-ge-kyō, you enter the "verbal stage of identity".

The above quotation is in accordance with the following statement: *"Both from the literal and the meditative viewpoint which I apply in order to understand the meaning of the Lotus Sutra indicate that foolish and evil people with false views remain at the theoretical and verbal stage of identity"* (ibid.). The Daishōnin stresses that his teachings are for people with limited capacity in the evil world of the latter Day of the Law. So, everyone is initially at the "theoretical stage of identity" and only comes into the "verbal stage of identity" once the practice of chanting Daimoku begins. The Daishōnin himself has already attained this stage as he is already practicing Daimoku. That's all.

---

a Buddha of the sixth and highest stage, that of ultimate enlightenment [(6) *"ultimate stage of identity"*]. (p. 752 / OTT p. 124;

*The terms inserted with [...] are my supplementary expressions that I use in the text here.)

After all, it is simply indicating that the Daishōnin, his disciples and lay people are all equally ordinary people.

Nevertheless, in the twisted logic of the NS sect, this egalitarian conception is radically distorted in order to introduce an ideology of discrimination: between the ordinary believer and the Daishōnin, as well as the successive high Priests of the NS lineage.

What strange mental process has she internalized, that she should enthusiastically support such a shockingly feudal hierarchical relationship between master and slave! I would call this mentality – "slavish self-abasement".

– You mean in other words, that it is not only not an authentic teaching of Nichiren Buddhism, but belief in a transcendental person or a mysterious transcendental power is not a teaching of NB at all, don't you?

Matsudo: That's exactly right. Such a belief amounts to slavish self-abasement, the relinquishing of the true self. The important thing to remember is that the Daishōnin had declared himself to be nothing other than an ordinary man. He never claimed that he would become an Eternal Original Buddha, while you and I would remain deluded and foolish ordinary people. It is a natural for us to begin as ordinary people and then to realize the "attainment of enlightenment in this life" by upholding faith in the LS and practicing the Dharma of Nam-myō-hō-ren-ge-kyō. That's why we can change our karma and create value in our own lives.

– that means, that Mrs. Uchida has simply no idea about the meaning of the term "verbal stage of identity" and is misusing the word only in order to promote an ideology of discrimination, doesn't it?

Matsudo: This is just one example. Many passages of the Daishōnin's wirings have been distorted to justify the logic of discrimination.

Self-perfection from the bottom up – The Daishōnin's view with respect to self-realization and the attainment of enlightenment

– You expand on the argument about the "eternal Master Shakyamuni" in the third chapter.

Matsudo: The Daishōnin indeed speaks about the "eternal Master Shakyamuni". As to this Buddha the traditional NS doctrine of "the Eternal Original Buddha" states that there was a perfectly-accomplished Buddha present at the Primordial Origin of the Beginning of the remotest past. And this perfectly-accomplished Buddha appears in our world for spiritual liberation of all beings. This represents a view of "liberation from the top down". Against this view I propose an alternative for understanding self-realization and the attainment of enlightenment, which is powerfully symbolized by the Bodhisattva of the Earth. In this representation, Buddhahood emerges in ordinary people within the Nine Worlds, implying "self-perfection from the bottom up". Clearly, this understanding of the attainment of enlightenment is the exact opposite to that above.

The Eternal Original Buddha is **wholly imaginary**

— I see. With respect to Buddhism, it is generally understood to be quite different from the "revealed religions", such as Christianity or Islam. It rejected the concept of a single all-powerful God and established the Dharma as a universal law. Yet, without much notice being taken of it, the Buddha mutated into an object of worship, in fact performing a role not dissimilar to that of God in Christianity.

Matsudo: Yes, exactly. And moreover, for a long time, we have been quite irritated by proclamations of the existence of this Eternal Original Buddha. "Nichiren" has been deified in a way not dissimilar to how "Christ" has been deified. In Germany, this problem did not concern us very much. With respect to the phrase: "At the beginning there was a perfectly accomplished Buddha" the article quoted above continues quite seriously that: "The idea about an Original Buddha of the remotest past is a matter relevant only to the mystical domain and is hardly to be grasped". Yet, this is illogical mystification: our natural reason clearly cannot conceive in any coherent way an existence such as an Eternal Original Buddha.

No, we can't understand it. As it is a deified transcendent Buddha, it is actually nothing other than a figment of the imagination. It is a "theology" which essentially contradicts the fundamental assumptions of the "Buddha Dharma".

As long as the doctrine of the existence of such an eternal Buddha is accepted and propagated, and my criticism is a profoundly Buddhist one, my assertion that the Daishōnin was nothing other than a great ordinary man who struggled as an ordinary human being on behalf of other ordinary human beings, will never be forgiven by the doctrinally orthodox.

The Buddha of the Latter Day of the Law is a Bodhisattva of the Earth

— You mean, "When a Buddha stops being an ordinary person, he is no longer a Buddha", don't you?

Matsudo: Yes, in the Buddhism of the Daishōnin there are no buddhas other than the bodhisattvas of the Earth. Consequently, it makes a great deal of difference as to whether you enter into nirvana and cease to be an ordinary person and become a Buddha, or whether you remain as an ordinary person and manifest your Buddha nature that works as wisdom to create real value in your daily life. It is the latter, which is the most fundamental idea with respect to "attaining Buddhahood or realizing enlightenment". The second chapter of my book "The Theory of the Ordinary Person as True Buddha" particularly considers this difference in understanding with respect to the concept of "Buddha".

One view had been taught prior to the compilation of the Lotus Sutra. According to this provisional teaching, one should cast aside all desires and attachments binding one to this Sahā World, so that one can progress from the level of an ordinary human being (Nine Worlds) towards the level of a fully-enlightened being (Buddha World). In this way, one will cease to be an ordinary human being and become a Buddha, an enlightened being free from the sufferings in this Sahā World. For the Daishōnin, this implies that you an ordinary person have misguidedly sought to become a transcendent Buddha, a being which cannot possibly exist.

An alternative is that Buddhist practice by an ordinary human being activates Buddhahood within (Buddha World), which then manifests in the body of an ordinary human being (Nine Worlds). The essential difference between these two views is the difference between "becoming a Buddha" and "opening up to Buddhahood".

— SG has been teaching such an understanding, yet at the same time the doctrine of the Eternal Original Buddha has been dominant also, hasn't it?

Matsudo: That's right. It is because SG was then a lay organization of NS, as such it was not permitted to innovate with respect to NS doctrine and practice. However, subsequently SG was "excommunicated" by NS and became an independent, spiritually liberated organization. From that time on, it has been essential for SG to proclaim clearly and vigorously a humanistic NB doctrine, a religion for the whole world.

Not a person but the Dharma alone should be the object of worship – Practicing to gain "immediate enlightenment" in order to "attain Buddhahood in this lifetime"

— What is Chapter 4, entitled "The Dharma body of Nam-myō-hō-ren-ge-kyō", all about?

Matsudo: In short, I seek to stress the idea that the foundation of Buddhism is not a person who should be worshipped but the Dharma which should be practiced. Among other things, it is for me very important that we understand that "Nam-myō-hō-ren-ge-kyō is the Mystic Law inherent in all ordinary people". In other words, because the Dharma of Nam-myō-hō-ren-ge-kyō represents the Law of all life in our very own body, so we are naturally able to activate our enlightened life by chanting Daimoku.

So, there is no need to become something else. Just as we are, in our present existence, we can activate the Mystic Law inherently within and thereby manifest our enlightened life. The Daishōnin discovered this Dharma and made it manifest in the form of the Gohonzon, the object of devotion. The Dharma is the foundation, not a Buddha or any other person. Given this, a Buddha, whether Shakyamuni or Amida, could only realize the Mystic Law within their own lives as ordinary human beings. That is, according to the Daishōnin, they only manifested their Buddha nature which is inherently within their own bodies, i.e. by practicing the Dharma of Nam-myō-hō-ren-ge-kyō as ordinary human beings.

Consequently, we also can manifest in our own ordinary body Nam-myō-hō-ren-ge-kyō. From this perspective, asserting that an ordinary person is buddha is a coherent proposition. The Daishōnin also inscribed the Gohonzon in order to give form to and manifest the Dharma of Nam-myō-hō-ren-ge-kyō, which is the source of the attainment of enlightenment for all Buddhas. In contemplating the Gohonzon under this aspect, you will aware of that the Mystic Law of Nam-myō-hō-ren-ge-kyō is inscribed down the center, while at each side are the names of Buddhas, Bodhisattvas and deities. Further, the inscription "Nam-myō-hō-ren-ge-kyō" (the Eternal Mystic Law) = Nichiren (the votary of the LS in the Latter Day of the Law)", should be accepted in the sense as stated by the Daishōnin below:

> The object of devotion is the entity of the entire life of the votary of the LS. ("The object of devotion for Observing the Mind«, p. 760 / OTT p. 142)

In this way, the Daishōnin inscribed the Dharma body of his own enlightenment in the form of the Gohonzon, the Oneness of Buddha and Dharma; however, this Gohonzon also demonstrates nothing other than the form of our own enlightened life. It functions as a mirror reflecting our own enlightenment. The "Unity of Person and Law" manifests as the "law" through the "person".

This manifestation occurs while chanting Daimoku and is expressed as "shining by manifesting the true identity" (*jitaikenshō*), which means that the original Three Bodies of the Tathāgata will manifest through the bodies of ordinary people.

The Daishōnin states that "*Nam-myō-hō-ren-ge-kyō is the Mystic Law originally inherent in all people*". This statement provides the essential foundation for the "Theory of the Ordinary Person as True Buddha".

In many Gosho, there are several references to idea that we are able to activate and develop Buddhahood in a natural way:

> Shakyamuni's practices and the virtues he consequently attained, these two laws of cause and effect are all contained within the five characters of Myō-hō-ren-ge-kyō. If we believe these five characters, we will *naturally* be granted the same benefits which he has.

> (»The Object of Devotion for Observing the Mind«, p. 246 / I. 364)

He explains this meaning further by describing a baby who grows naturally by drinking its mother's milk:

> Question: If a person simply chants Nam-myō-hō-ren-ge-kyō with no understanding of its meaning, are the benefits of understanding thereby included?
> Answer: When a baby drinks milk, it has no understanding of its taste, and yet its body is *naturally* nourished.
> (»On the Four stages of the Faith and Five Stages of Practice« p. 341 / I. 788)

Most important is the idea of "natural growth". Similarly, the Daishōnin stresses this aspect in another Gosho:

> Although I and my disciples may encounter various difficulties, if we do not harbor doubts in our hearts, we will *naturally* attain Buddhahood.
> (»The Opening of the Eyes«, p. 236 / I. 283)

In conclusion: keeping the LS does definitely not have the meaning that either Shakyamuni or the Daishōnin will "save us from above", whereby in their capacity as Eternal Master and transcendent being radically distinct from ourselves, ordinary sentient beings. For we ourselves are endowed with Buddhahood, which we ourselves can open, activate and develop in a very natural way.

— So, you mean, everyone can attain the state of a Buddha?

Matsudo: Yes. Regarding the concept of "attaining the Buddha state" there are two types: "immediately attaining the Buddha state" (Instant Enlightenment) and "realizing the Buddha state in this lifetime". Instant Enlightenment occurs in each moment of practicing the Buddha way and continues throughout the whole of a life time. In this process, you will change naturally, grow and expand all your capacities, as well as deepen your understanding and wisdom.

Consequently, in this way, to uphold the practice of Nam-myō-hō-ren-ge-kyō for the whole of one's life and thereby to carry out "human revolution" means to "manifest the Buddha state in this lifetime".

Striving for spiritual independence – Everyone will grow spiritually like "Nichiren"

— Please talk a little bit more about the difference between Japan and Germany in terms of the religious context!

Matsudo: For the people of Germany, Europe and the United States, Buddhism began with Shakyamuni, who attained enlightenment and preached the dharma. This is radically distinct from Christianity. And that's one reason why many begin Buddhist practice.

Another characteristic aspect is that the Buddhist teachings are considered to be "reasonable"; in fact, ND was convinced of this truth:

> Untampered iron quickly melts in a blazing fire, like ice put in hot water. But a sword, even when exposed to a great fire, withstands the heat for a while, because it has been well forged. [...] Buddhism is reason. Reason will win over your lord. (»The Hero of the World«, p. 1169 / I. 839)

The principle that Buddhist teachings do not contradict natural laws and are logically consistent is also confirmed by the "three kinds of proof", such as documentary, theoretical and empirical proof.

Given the above, the speeches of SGI president Ikeda can be well understood. Currently, it is widely accepted that the authoritarian, feudal style of propagation based on funeral-oriented Buddhism, can no longer be considered appropriate. Further, European people are much more reflectively aware of and engaged with their faith and religion and social issues generally. They are much more used to thinking clearly and logically.

– So, is there any message to the reader?

Matsudo: Now, we are living in the global community close to the beginning of the 21st century. However, Japanese Buddhism has still to step out of the cultural and institutional constraints which had been formed in the 17th century. Buddhism had significance throughout Japanese society generally almost exclusively as "Funeral Buddhism" and this has remained the case to the present. However, in the main, the temple system of support for, as well as the doctrinal system in justification of, "Funeral Buddhism", had nothing to do with what had been taught, spread and established by the founders of the new Buddhist movements of the Kamakura period, such as Dōgen, Shinran and Nichiren.

Currently, Japanese Buddhism has become merely an establishment ideology that has abandoned the true essence of Mahayana Buddhism, i.e. to be radically life affirming. Within this framework, subservient devotees rejoice in discriminatory organizations and practices. The original high religious ideals have been abandoned and deformed institutional and doctrinal systems have been established. People appreciate them as valuable "traditions" and entertain no concern about the contemporary status quo with respect to religious practice. The mentality of the modern Japanese is terrifying to me.

This mentality uncritically regards any tradition as of some value. It has often been said that the Japanese have no clear real self-understanding, but I want to emphasize that Buddhism is a religion which seeks to make each of us spiritually independent. The reason why I am advocating a new understanding of NB and critically raising new questions, is that I wish for SG/SGI to grow strong, in order that it can more effectively promote the ideals of individualism, humanism and pacifism, based on a radical Buddhist philosophy. That is to say, I hope every Nichiren Buddhist will become a "little Nichiren", destined to cast aside the Confucian tradition within Japanese society, which has been historically responsible for repressing the truly independent and creative personality. (End)

Chapter 5
Unfounded and Contentious Criticism from NS

Both »Humanism« and »Innovation« critically dealt with NS's bizarre strident assertions, which claimed to doctrinally define both the "absolute power of the high priest" and the "high priest as representative of the original Buddha". Clearly, the foundation behind these assertions is the "doctrine of Nichiren as the eternal original Buddha". In critically challenging this traditional doctrine of NS, my own "Theory of the Ordinary Person as True Buddha" had been developed. Subsequently, criticisms of my work published by those associated with NS appeared. These included:

- In criticism of »Humanism« (1992), as already mentioned, an anonymous writer "a NS believer volunteer" published an article with the title »A discussion forum: Pointing out the problematic views in Yukio Matsudo's "In search of a humanistic theory of "Nichiren as True Buddha"« in the magazine "Kōfu" in a series of 4 issues, published from June through to September 1993.
- In response to the criticisms raised, I published »Innovation« (1994). Subsequently, Jijō Ōhashai responded with an article "Pointing to contradictions in the theses of Yukio Matsudo", published in the NS periodical magazine the »Dōshin No.6« (August 1994).
- At the "First Guidance Meeting for Head and Deputy Responsibles of Lay believers" on August 24, 1994, and at the "43rd Nationwide Teacher Training Session" on the following day, both of which took place at the head temple Taisekiji, the high priest Nikken referred to my »Humanism« and attempted to counter my "symbolic theory of the Gohonzon".
- Subsequently, in the official magazine of the NS head temple »Dai-Nichiren«, a sustained attack on me began in a series of articles entitled the "Proposals to Break the evil theory of Yukio Matsudo", published between December 1994 and March 1996. These articles written by NS priests were published altogether on 8 occasions, but I only followed the series until March 1995, as I considered continuing debate fruitless[9].

---

[9] The NS publications above are only those which I had been aware of at that time. No doubt more highly-charged opinions about my views can be found on the internet. One example would be: https://www.nst.org/sgi-faqs/the-history-of-the-relationship-between-nichiren-shoshu-and-the-soka-gakkai/6-issuing-counterfeit-objects-of-worship-and-discussion-of-doctrines-and-purposes/

- Consequently, I presented my considered answer to the series in my third book »The Doctrine Controversy of the *Heisei period* – Laughing at the "Refutation" of Nichiren Shōshū« (1995).

Considering the overview above, NS responded somewhat nervously to my series of doctrinal reform proposals. It was clear, reflecting on this series of counterarguments, that one important difference of view existed between us. It is an unfortunate problem that current NS doctrine has been established fundamentally on the pre-LS view with respect to "the guidance of the Buddha". By this I mean, that both Shakyamuni and Nichiren, as well as the high priest, are quite literally worshipped as "saviors" offering salvation to faithful believers through their "Other Power". Yet contrary to this view, I have more persuasively argued that ND upheld a "meditative view of the Essential Section", based on "self-realization as the mode of attaining enlightenment". Consequently, NS teaching can best be characterized as below:

> The doctrine of Nichiren as the Eternal Original Buddha
> ⇒ Faith in the Dai-gohonzon
> ⇒ The ideology of the high priest with absolute power
> ⇒ The believers' radical subordination
> ⇒ and faithful surrender to this system

This scheme shows clearly the structural problem faced by NS on both the doctrinal and the institutional level. To that extent my criticism has become quite cutting and has led me to wholly reject this particular form of faith and practice based on the doctrine of NS.

Chapter 6
The Dai-gohonzon is a Past Forgery

Given this background, I decided to strike at the fundamental NS doctrine that the "Dai-gohonzon is the Sanctuary of the Essential Section". The Dai-gohonzon has been understood as "the soul and life or the very entity of Buddhahood of the Daishōnin". Consequently, it has been erroneously and insistently asserted that: "If you don't accept this foundational doctrine with respect to belief in the Dai-gohonzon as the Sanctuary and even if you chant Daimoku, necessarily you cannot be a Bodhisattva of the Earth nor you will you be able to attain to realization of Buddhahood". Thus, the Dai-gohonzon continues to enjoy a very special place and significance well above the hundreds of other Mandala-Gohonzon which Nichiren had personally inscribed.

The legend of the Persecution at Atsuhara

However, there is no mention whatsoever of the "Dai-gohonzon" throughout the entire extant written works of ND. Consequently, my criticism of the doctrine with respect to the Dai-gohonzon is based exclusively on this fact.

It is asserted that the Dai-gohonzon had been inscribed on October 12, 1279. As documentary proof for this assertion, NS have frequently cited a Gosho claimed to have been written shortly before the inscription and hence the attribution of the above date. This is the following passage found in the Gosho »On Persecutions Befalling the Sage«, which Nichiren had written on Minobu on October 1, 1279:

> Now, in the second year of Kōan (1279), [...] it has been twenty-seven years since I first proclaimed this teaching at Seichō-ji temple. It was at the hour of the horse [noon] on the twenty-eighth day of the fourth month in the fifth year of Kenchō (1253), [...]. The Buddha fulfilled the purpose of his advent in a little over forty years, the Great Teacher T'ien-t'ai took about thirty years, and the Great Teacher Dengyō, some twenty years. I have spoken repeatedly of the indescribable persecutions they suffered during those years. For me it took twenty-seven years, and the great persecutions I faced during this period are well known to you all. (p. 1189 / I. 996)

In the doctrine of NS, it is explained that Nichiren was deeply impressed by some farmers who did not abandon their faith despite severe persecution in the Atsuhara region. This event moved Nichiren to inscribe a special Mandala-Gohonzon for people of the entire world as he attained the "purpose of his advent", some 27 years after the first proclamation of Daimoku on April 28, 1253. In order that it be better understood, I will describe this event in a little more detail below.

After ND's arrival on the mountain of Minobu in May 1274, his disciple Nikkō and other followers undertook a series of harsh *Shakubuku* campaigns in the region of Fuji in Suruga country (in the central part of Shizuoka prefecture). Through these efforts, some priests and laypeople of the Tendai school abandoned their faith and became exclusively devoted to the teaching of ND. However, as a result, the affected Tendai temple, supported by the local authorities, began to threaten, coerce and persecute those who had embraced the new faith.

Consequently, in September 1279, 20 farmers who had embraced the faith were arrested on trumped up charges and taken to Kamakura. The farmers were interrogated under torture in the private residence of *Hei no Saemon-no-jō*, the deputy chief to the Office of Military and Police Affairs of the Kamakura Shogunate. An attempt was made to coerce them into renouncing their faith in the Lotus Sutra but remained firm in their faith. Finally, the three ringleaders of the farmers were executed, and the remaining 17 farmers were forcibly exiled from their home area. This series of events is known as "the persecution at Atsuhara".

At the time of this persecution, Nichiren felt a great compassion and admiration for the firm faith of the farmers, who devoted their lives to the Mystic Law and courageously endured even such unjust and harsh treatment. Consequently, instead of awarding an individual Gohonzon to each person as usual, the legend tells us that Nichiren inscribed the "Mandala-honzon granted to all people in the entire world". It is both the One Great Secret Law and, at the same time, the Dai-gohonzon of the Sanctuary of the Essential Section.

Nevertheless, there are no references to this most important matter in Nichiren's writings at all, and no mention is made even during the persecution at Atsuhara. Further, in essence, NB does not conceivably have such a narrow focus, whereby its universal propagation might converge only upon one Mandala-Gohonzon. Simply worshipping the Dai-gohonzon, a plank made of a wood, to say nothing of such worship's narrow and exclusivistic character, is fundamentally quite contrary to the spirit of ND. Consequently, already in 1995, I had argued that this narrow faith in the Dai-gohonzon should be left behind us for good.

> The pair of NS doctrines consisting of "Nichiren as the Eternal Original Buddha" and "**Faith in the Dai-gohonzon**" is a fabrication of later generations. As long as the NS teachings start from the assumption that the Dai-gohozon is the foundation of NB, then there is a fundamental error of principle. For it is nothing other than an ideology to deify the Daishōnin

and to give justification to Temple Buddhism, a forgery of later generations at the NS head temple. (»Doctrinal controversy«)

The fabricated myth about the Dai-gohonzon

Akihiko Kinbara suspected that the Dai-gohozon would never be confirmed as having been inscribed by ND on October 10, 1279, as it consists of an atypical mandala inscribed on a wooden plank, while its character style argues against its authenticity, as it has features, with respect to character style and the alignment of inscribed names, quite clearly not from this period. In his study, published in »Nichiren and the Honzon legend – On the truth of the plank honzon from the alter in Taisekiji« (2007), he came to the conclusion that the Dai-gohonzon is in fact, with respect to its inscribed form and the style of the characters which constitute the Daimoku, identical to the honzon inscribed on May 9, 1280, and bestowed upon *Nichizen* (?-1331), one of the senior disciples of Nikkō[10]. It therefore must be assumed, that some laypersons from Hokkekō must have constructed a copy of the Nichizen mandala, with the purpose of erecting it as the object of worship in the main hall of Taisekiji, in the period between the 6th Abbot *Nichiji* (tenure 1369-1406) and the 8th Abbot *Nichiei* (tenure 1407-1419). Subsequently, a legend emerged that attributed this mandala directly to Nichiren himself.

Kinbara indeed notes that the Dai-gohonzon is "a special Mandala-honzon in an engraved copy form with authentic features from the Kōan period". However:

> It is false to insist on "the thesis on direct establishment by the founder", "the thesis on the absolute uniqueness of the fundamental honzon" and "the thesis on Nichiren's fulfilling the purpose of his advent". I regard it as a most important agenda to correct these erroneous views and to resolve the related problems on the doctrinal level. (ibid. p. 213)

Kinbara made this constructive proposal in August 2007, seven years before the official announcement of SG to renounce faith in the Dai-gohonzon in November 2014. He had already foreseen the need for a revision of the SG teaching. I don't know what kind of doctrinal direction he was thinking about, but I would like to express my most sincere appreciation for his achievement in conclusively demonstrating that the Dai-gohonzon is not authentic. Consequently, I consider that he has objectively confirmed my own conclusions outlined in my "Thesis on the Dai-gohonzon as a fake", which I made much

---

[10] There have been several critical essays published about the Dai-gohonzon and Kinbara is not alone in his conclusions. Ken Mandara's well-argued study is available in English: »The mandala in Nichiren Buddhism. Special Feature: The 'Honmon Kaidan Dai-gohonzon' of Nichiren Shōshū Taisekiji« (2015). He suggests that the "Dai-gohonzon" could have been produced during the tenur period (1419-1467) of *Nanjō Nichiu* (1409-1482), the 9th Abbot of Taisekiji.

use of in my »Doctrinal controversy« (April 1995), as well as in my subsequent critical argument found in my thesis on "Nichiren as the Eternal Original Buddha".

Chapter 7
An objective assessment of the "Theory of the Ordinary Person as True Buddha"

Incidentally, there are two scholars who have actively appreciated my efforts at critical innovation with respect to NS doctrine: *Fumihiko Sueki*, professor of Buddhist studies, and *Shigeru Nishiyama*, professor of the sociology of religion, both very familiar with NB and its historical development, called the "Hokke movements".

Nishiyama's book review

First, I will consider Nishiyama's book review. In his article entitled »The Self-reliance process and the innovation in religious style – The case of Soka Gakkai in the second period after the war« (1998), he commented as below. He has expressed a valuable insight, so I would like to quote from it at some length.

> Yukio Matsudo (Studied Philosophy and Sociology), Director of the Research in the European Center of the Institute of Oriental Philosophy, published a series of works (on the Honzon and on Nichiren as the Original Buddha) in 1992 and 1994. With respect to the innovations in SG's own religious style, this series of works cannot be ignored. [...]
>
> In his first book »In search of a humanistic theory of 'Nichiren as the True Buddha'« (March 1992) he criticized the NS particular view upheld today by arguing that the Mandala-honzon of the Mystic Law has been reified or objectified as an absolute "thing". Against this mystification he insists solely on the symbolic character of the honzon, which although remaining an object of worship, is considered to be a "self-reflecting mirror", i.e. reflecting the "original truth inherent within" the life of the votaries of the LS in the Latter Day of the Law. This truth is expounded as the form of Buddhahood of the "ordinary person identical with the Buddha". This image is best described as the "object of devotion for observing the mind".
>
> In his next book »The innovation of Nichiren Thought« (March 1994), Matsudo criticizes the traditional NS "doctrine of the Original Buddha in terms of the Original Effect" (Nichiren = Tathāgata of the Wisdom Body at the Original Beginning of Eternity = True Buddha as savior of all people). He reinterprets the meaning of "original Buddha" as "Chanting Daimoku enabled Nichiren himself to manifest the Dharma of Nam-myō-hō-ren-

ge-kyō inherent in his life" (p. 138). Consequently, it implies the self-realization of the original truth inherent in everyone's life and this is in fact the meaning of "true Buddha". Therefore, this universal way to the realization of Buddhahood is not only limited to Nichiren himself but it is also available to anyone who embraces the Mystic Law. In this manner, Matsudo emphasizes this aspect of the Original Cause for his "Thesis on the Ordinary Person as True Buddha". [...]

These above-mentioned works of Matsudo [...] are singular academic papers and do not represent official opinion within SG yet. But it can be said that their significance is paramount for SG since they give scholarly justification to SG's humanistic views about the honzon and the original Buddha [...].

At this point it should be noted that NS published a book in March 1997 under the name of "NS doctrinal study committee on doctrinal studies". [This book presents a collection of several articles critical of Matsudo's "Thesis on the Ordinary Person as True Buddha" and has the title »A new theory of SG and its Essence«.] However, the priests of NS insisted on the "substantial thingness" of the plank mandala, which cannot endure the cycle of change and destruction, as well as the myth of the high priest's inheritance of the "bloodline" against any historical proof. As long as NS continues to rely solely on such unpersuasive arguments, which could be defined as a "seal box theory" (20), it would appear to be difficult to undermine the new theory of Matsudo. (Pp. 136-137)

In footnote (20), Nishiyama defines his own minted term "seal box theory" as "a form of theory deployed as a means to intimidate others by laying a foundation to legitimacy upon a singular piece of "matter" (the mandala made of a wooden plank) and upon the authority of the high priest". The "seal box" is a small decorated box which ordinarily contains seals of identity and medicine and it is usually hung from a belt. This word reminds me of a famous TV program, the "Travel Reports of *Mito Kōmon*". The hero of the stories is the historic *Tokugawa Mitsukuni* (1628-1701), former vice-shogun and retired second lord of the Mito Domain. He traveled in the guise of a retired merchant, accompanied by two samurai servants. An episode typically begins with misfortune and suffering of ordinary people as a result of some injustice perpetrated by a corrupt official, wealthy merchant or gangster. The travelers arrive incognito, discover the injustice and quietly investigate it; and the episode concludes with a brawl in which they are surrounded by a crowd of samurai and gangsters. At this critical moment one of the samurai's servants shows up with the seal bearing the family crest of the Tokugawa Shogunate and shouts: "Step back! Can't you see this crest with your eyes?! This person is the former vice-shogun Mito Mitsukuni!!" After having revealed the true identity another assistant shouts: "You are standing in front a noble and honorable person. Kneel down!" Afterwards, the hero passes judgement upon the villains, and sets things straight with judicious comments and encouragement, and then moves on.

Clearly, this story has many significant aspects, which Nishiyama may have imagined such a scenario when he described the Japanese feudal "authoritarianism" of NS as a "seal box theory".

Sueki's book review

Sueki is a rare for a scholar of Buddhist studies, as he always tries to understand Japanese Buddhist intellectual history in its wider multifaceted, diverse, multilayered context. Regarding Nichiren's thought, he admitted that there is indeed justification for perceiving in his work a "Theory of the Ordinary Person as True Buddha" (see Sueki 2000, p. 198 f.). Given the above, I am truly thankful to him for having given a very positive evaluation of my work.

My work from the early 1990s would appear to have been buried in the past, yet Sueki wrote an article with the title "Secularization and Nichiren Buddhism – On Yukio Matsudo's 'Theory of the Ordinary Person as True Buddha" in a collection entitled »Series Nichiren volume 5: The Contemporary World and Nichiren« (2015, hereafter »Sueki's book review«). My reply to his article has been published in »Lotus Buddhism Studies No. 21« (2015) under with the title "Towards a contemporary reconstruction of Nichiren Buddhism" (hereafter »Reconstruction«). Here, I would like to mention only Sueki's overall evaluation of my thought. For this relates to the essential points outlined found in Part 3 of this book which redefines in some detail the ongoing doctrinal debate. The essential points can be summarized in the following four headings, under which I will include Sueki's comments.

How will the doctrinal controversy develop now that SG has separated from NS?

First, Sueki describes the context after the separation of SG from the NS head temple as follows.

> After that, SG abandoned the traditional teaching and discouraged any interest in that teaching itself. Up until today, it has been radically representing itself as a secular new religious movement. [...] However, from the outset of the breakdown, the doctrinal problems have been largely ignored, and attempts to critically reconstruct the doctrine of NS have been made vigorously closed down. A form of such reconstruction was Matsudo's "Theory of the Ordinary Person as True Buddha". Yet, this is not an official study of Soka Gakkai. [...] From the NS side there were some highly-charged refutations which claimed that *"Matsudo's theory is referred to in several places in Ikeda's speeches"* or *"Matsudo's theory will*

most likely become the central stream of thought underlying the erroneous teachings of SG" (Matsudo 1955, p. 75). Although some such consideration may possibly have occurred, yet the discussion about doctrine simply slumped [...]. (»Sueki's book review«, p. 94)

With respect to the above point, as I noted in »Reconstruction«, SG has been expanding globally since the 1960s, propagating traditional SG doctrines, such as "Faith in the Dai-gohonzon" and the doctrine of "Nichiren as the Eternal Original Buddha". However, at the same time, Ikeda had developed a lay Buddhist orientation decisively towards "humanism and pacifism" and openness towards society and the world. Nevertheless, the latter is clearly inconsistent with the former, and there is no doubt that this intellectual and doctrinal tension was one of the main causes of separation. As I myself had embraced and practiced Nichiren Buddhism exclusively within a Western cultural context, there was absolutely no inhibition as far as I was concerned to critically reassess traditional NS doctrine. Consequently, I endeavored to radically represent a "humanistic Nichiren Buddhism", in order that it might become the doctrinal foundation for SGI, a globally acting lay Buddhist organization.

In this respect, I was indeed able to deepen and develop my own interpretation of Nichiren Buddhism through argument with NS priests. On the other hand, I had the same optimistic feelings as my own "baby-boom generation", who proved enthusiastic and supportive when I had raised doctrinal concerns in order to bring about "innovation" within SG studies. Nevertheless, the senior leaders who had over many years internalized NS doctrine reacted negatively and stifled any doctrinal discussion both at the public and at the private level within SG. After all, essentially SG did not depart from traditional NS teachings even after excommunication and continued to maintain the faith in the Dai-gohonzon until November 2014.

Of course, I regarded the abandonment of faith in Dai-gohonzon as positive and indeed as a necessary requirement if SG was to reject the dogmatic and exclusivistic position peculiar to NS and to embrace a more democratic, universal and humanistic "Theory of the Ordinary Person as True Buddha". I hoped for a more constructive discourse to emerge from within SG. That will be the subject of Part 2 of this book.

Doctrinally Placing the Theory of the Ordinary Person as True Buddha

With respect to the forms of belief within NS and SG, I have made a distinction between the ritual-centered Temple Buddhism, which I characterize as a "Catholic form" and a modern, secular, lay Buddhism based on the Theory of the Ordinary Person as True Buddha, which I characterize as a

"Protestant form" (see Matsudo 2000) Having said that, Sueki commented as follows.

> In the Nichiren system, the dominant tendency is not only the Doctrine of Nichiren as the Original Buddha, which is limited to a certain sect, but also a more widespread interpretation of the salvation type which upholds the Eternal Buddha Shakyamuni as the object of devotion, the honzon. These types form the main current in modern Nichiren studies (Sueki 2015, p. 97).

Against such "religious views of the salvation type", I oppose my "religious view of the self-realization type". Sueki pays attention to this innovative view.

> We should pay a little bit more attention to the Theory of the Ordinary Person as True Buddha, which represents a "self-realization type". In this point of view there is not only the reaffirmation of Original Enlightenment Thought but also a mode of thinking common also to Zen and esoteric Buddhism. Thus, it has the potential to free up NB to stride towards a wider horizon and to open up a way of thinking about Buddhism from a fresh and novel perspective (ibid., p. 98)

An Evaluation of Original Enlightenment Thought

Sueki is a scholar of Buddhist studies who views the so-called "Original Enlightenment Thought" from a multi-facetted perspective, too. This ability has enabled him to properly grasp the significance of my practice-oriented Original Enlightenment Thought, which is grounded in Nichiren's "Original Enlightenment Teaching".

> The 'Theory of the Ordinary Person as True Buddha' affirms the standpoint of ordinary people and asserts that "ordinary people are real-existing true Buddhas" (Matsudo 1994, p. 203). At this point it comes near to the affirmation of the reality of the status quo, as in the sense of Original Enlightenment Thought. However, I dare to say that it indeed has a new face, which revitalizes Original Enlightenment Thought for our contemporary era. It is just as Matsudo states: *"The thought of Original Enlightenment should be denied if it is understood as a philosophical concept that merely asserts the reality of the status quo and makes any Buddhist practice redundant. However, it would also be wrong to deny the validity of any concept related to 'original enlightenment'* (ibid., p. 202)". (Sueki 2015, p. 101)

Gosho considered to be Apocrypha

With respect to a consideration of Original Enlightenment Thought, Sueki makes reference to *Yōrin Asai* (1883-1942), a priest of Nichiren Shū and a professor at Risshō university. He systematized a modern method of authenticating Nichiren's writings, but he also sought to separate Nichiren teachings from any element of Original Enlightenment Thought. Consequently, Sueki characterizes his position as a "philologically oriented literary perspective hostile to any orally transmitted teachings" (ibid., p. 102).

His working method was based on such a premise, and he determined that what matched it were Nichiren's authentic writings while, on the contrary, he regarded those containing elements of Original Enlightenment Thought in the form of orally transmitted teachings as apocrypha (ibid.).

Consequently, as Asai even read »The Object of Devotion for Observing the Mind« as "focusing on Shakyamuni as the Original Buddha",

Such a "thesis on the Ordinary Person as true Buddha" as Matsudo proposes, would imply "focusing on sentient beings" which would as a matter of course be excluded as something heterogeneous within the "Standard Writings" of Nichiren (ibid., p. 103).

There is a very important document that SG inherited from NS, »The Record of the Orally Transmitted Teachings«. Asai regarded it as apocryphal and his disciple, *Kaishū Shigyō* (1907-1968), a priest of Nichiren Shū and professor at Risshō university, confirmed its apocryphal character by detailed analysis in his dissertation. Sueki summarizes this problem as follows.

Philological Criticism regarding a historical document is of great importance. But at the same time, even if it is philologically rejected, it is quite another matter to try to find new value in what has been handed down and revered for a long time even if denied as authentic literature (ibid., p. 104)

Having said that, Sueki selects some examples from »The Record of the Orally Transmitted Teachings« to demonstrate that there is definitely a sense in which the practice of chanting Daimoku is emphasized. Consequently, he evaluates it positively as it is not simply an abstract theory but a most realistic philosophy.

This document has been valued by SG because it contains Original Enlightenment Thought of a very practical character and based on this Matsudo has developed his "Theory of the Ordinary Man as True Buddha". This provides an alternative modern study with very different possibilities to that of a modernized philological criticism (ibid., p. 105).

Sueki highly values »The Record of Orally Transmitted Teachings« because *"it contains a richness of thought which cannot be just excluded as an apocryphal document"*. As the conclusion of his book review emphasizes an interesting point, I would like to quote it just as it is.

This point of view is not limited to the »The Record of Orally Transmitted Teachings« alone. I would stress that it is necessary to reconsider on philosophical grounds the so-called "questionable writings" that have been rejected as inauthentic by philological criticism in the modern period generally. Matsudo's Theory of the Ordinary Man as True Buddha has made a useful start in this direction. Of course, this perspective is not limited only to Nichiren studies, as it also has a wider application, e.g. to the thought and writings of *Shinran* or *Dōgen*, and it should not be neglected as an analytical tool in Buddhist studies generally. As noted at the beginning, when only popular or traditional prejudice trumps reflective philosophical analysis, the very foundation becomes distorted, and such confusion is never a gratifying matter, rather it should be taken as a warning that we are entering a critical situation which demands critical and thoughtful resolution. Once again, this is the reason why clearing out outmoded dogma and a critical reconsideration of doctrine is required as an urgent task (ibid, p. 106).

As a serious acknowledgment of Sueki's warning, I would like from now on to rename my *Theory of the Ordinary Person as True Buddha* (grounded on the *Principle of the Mutual Containment of the Ten Worlds),* both at his suggestion and in respectful dedication to him, as *The Theory of the Instant Enlightenment of the Ordinary Person.*

Part Two

Whither SG's Doctrine of Nichiren as the True Buddha?

Chapter 1
On Organization, Doctrine and the Unity of Master and Disciple

1. Organizational transformation by way of doctrinal change

As a consequence of doctrinal revision in November 2014, SG renounced its previous exclusivistic orientation, which had been grounded upon the narrow and rigid NS-Nichikan doctrine on the unique significance of the Dai-gohonzon. With this revision, conditions are now favorable for SG to abandon its former exclusivistic dogmatism and to develop a more inclusive universal orientation as a world religion.

Incidentally, I can make such a positive prediction with respect to the future development of SGI as I had myself been proposing the abandonment of traditional NS doctrine over a period of more than 20 years ago. This particular doctrine is based both on the doctrine of Nichiren as the Eternal Original Buddha and on the doctrine of the necessity of maintaining exclusive faith in the Dai-gohonzon. Further, this exclusivistic stance became the doctrinal foundation for the hierarchical feudal system, buttressed by such ideologies as the High Priest has an absolute authority derived from his inheritance of the "bloodline of the dharma", that the High Priest is True Buddha, and that the High Priest alone is the Representative of the Original Buddha. As mentioned in the Part One, I had regularly subjected these institutional ideologies to a scathing, radical critique. Indeed, the main reason why I was in a position to view the traditional exclusivistic NS doctrines critically at that time may be because I was able to reflect upon the conflict between SG and NS far more objectively from a detached perspective outside Japan.

From its foundation, SG had inherited traditional NS doctrine and was able to achieve a rapid expansion, having been driven by its fanatical sectarian orientation based on an exclusivistic dogmatism, yet at the same time its fanatical dynamism led to conflict in society more widely. As a religious organization, it internalized a self-righteous ideology, e.g. that "SG / SGI is the only doctrinally orthodox organization promoting the spread of NB for world peace". Its sectarian stance was characterized by the strident castigation and contentious identification of "enemies" under the traditional designation of "slander", meaning thereby the upholding of an erroneous faith inconsistent with and hostile to the true Buddhist teachings. As a result, this sectarian logic was applied not only to NS temples and priests but also to all other Buddhist schools and all other religions. Even within its own organization and within its local groups, any members raising any criticism were regarded as "apostate", viewed as hostile and expelled. This was nothing but the foundation of a cult. Further, special factors, such as an expressly political organization within Japan, compounded the problem, while for SGI outside Japan, its rigid exclusivism was the main reason why SGI could not escape the imputation that it was a fanatical cult unwelcome in society more generally.

In fact, as SG abandoned the doctrine of the necessity of exclusive faith in the Dai-gohonzon which had been the root cause of this exclusivism, it opened a new prospect to overcome its sectarian failings. I published an article about this more positive prospect in Germany (Matsudo 2017). In fact, without such a radical reform of both doctrine and institutions, SG / SGI would never be able to successfully promote *Kōsenrufu*. Consequently, the abandonment of exclusive faith in the Dai-gohonzon at this time has a revolutionary significance for SG history. Further, the doctrine of "Nichiren as the Original Buddha", which will be considered in some detail in this Part, relates not only to one of the fundamental doctrinal problems of SG but also has serious implications which directly relate to the philosophical culture and formal constitution of the SG organization itself.

2. Ambiguity in the master/disciple relationship

With respect to the above, there is one matter more I need to consider. The revision of the doctrinal clause at this time also related to the ideal image of "The Unity of Master and Disciple", which was fraught with emotional difficulties. The unshakable faith in the Dai-gohozon had been the foundation of SG, a doctrine which all three SG presidents had shared from its foundation and which they had thoroughly embraced and practiced. Consequently, some members, especially among the older generation, questioned whether the abandonment of exclusive faith in the Dai-gohonzon might not be a severe betrayal of traditional SG doctrine. Especially for those who regard Ikeda as their unquestioned master and yet remain sensitive to the crucial nature of the doctrinal problem, an emotional dilemma has to be faced. In this context, some have made criticism of Miyata, who is considered one of the key advisors on SG study programs and who remains close to the executive top circle considered to be responsible for promoting a series of radical reforms. As I noted previously, I myself regard these doctrinal changes as necessary and essential measures if SGI is to have a sound future.

At this point, to avoid misunderstanding, I would like to briefly describe my personal encounters with Ikeda. For I consider that my own work to be in direct succession to his "Buddhist Humanism", which is an attempt to construct a radically new systematic understanding of NB.

I first met Ikeda personally in May 1981 when he visited Germany. At that time, I was a member of the executive committee, and he just came over to several of us, who were waiting for the next event. He began talking to us quite spontaneously about something which was obviously on his mind: "To tell you the truth, I have a problem, I am going to give a lecture at the University of Sophia soon, but I am in trouble because of translation difficulties". I replied also quite spontaneously and without hesitation: "There are certainly only a few people who can translate directly from Japanese to Bulgarian, but from German it should be much easier. As I am qualified Japanese-German translator, shall I translate your lecture into German?" Ikeda accepted at once: "I would appreciate that, thanks". That was the day before his departure to Bulgaria, so I had to complete the translation overnight. In fact, during that night while I was working, he called me down to the lobby of the hotel. He appeared anxious and wanted to give me some warm words of encouragement. By the next day, his party had already left the hotel. So, as soon as I finished the work, I drove to Frankfurt airport and handed it to his assistant.

Subsequently, as part of his dialogue with Josef Derbolav (1912-1987), professor of philosophy and education at the university of Bonn, I was assigned to the position of coordinator on the German side[11]. In order to work on the translation and publication of the documents relating to the dialogue, I was invited to Japan to have access to resources at SG headquarters, where I remained for about a month. During that stay, I had several opportunities to attend lunch parties and Gongyō, in a very small private circle with Ikeda. Consequently, these encounters also became precious opportunities to get to know Ikeda closely.

When Ikeda visited Europe again in May 1989, I was involved in the executive committee which organized and supported his visit. At that time, I was working freelance and undertaking SGI responsibilities as the national leader of the Young Men's Division and later of the Youth Division. As well as this, I was writing my Ph.D. thesis in Philosophy, although it took me several years to finish. When Ikeda visited the U.K., I had a chance in Taplow Court, the HQ of SGI U.K., to report to him personally, that I had been awarded a doctoral degree. He was very pleased and later arranged to appoint me Director of Research at the newly established European Center of the Institute of Oriental Philosophy (IOP). I prepared to establish a library related to Buddhism at Taplow Court, held lectures and meetings with invited scholars from several

---

[11] This dialogue was published in Japanese in 1989 and in English in 1992 with the title »The Search for a New Humanity«.

European countries, and I myself participated in academic conferences related to Buddhism and religious sociology throughout Europe and the US. I served in this position for ten years, between 1990 and 2000.

Subsequently, Ikeda visited Germany several times. In May 1994 there was a lunch meeting with him at a Chinese restaurant in the city of Frankfurt. I sat at the table opposite his. As chance would have it, he turned around and talked to me directly: "One of my relatives read your book and told me that its theme is most interesting". Albeit subtly and indirectly he thereby transmitted to me his favorable impression of my book on "The Theory of the Ordinary Person as True Buddha", just recently published in Japan. His encouragement allowed me to feel confident of his support in the midst of the furor occasioned by the fiercely controversial debate on doctrine, which I had to face alone without any organizational support. As I myself was acutely conscious of inheriting and further developing his humanistic approach to NB, I was naturally deeply encouraged by receiving such a "positive response" directly from him.

Here I would like to recount my personal impressions of Ikeda. He is a really kind hearted, caring warm person, as well as being trustworthy. He oversaw my personal development and gave me some concrete opportunities in which to demonstrate my abilities. He also gave me the chance to eat together and to do Gongyo together time after time. And he never abused me by assuming that I would only work pro bono. No, rather, he was attentive to always pay me above the normal rate of remuneration. Consequently, for me, he has been and is a trustworthy mentor, whom I very much admire and to whom I will always be deeply grateful.

So far, I have briefly described some personal encounters with Ikeda. It was my great good fortune and honor to get to know him personally "as an ordinary man" in a very direct manner. Consequently, I felt that I had built a very natural human relationship with him. Conversely, because of this, I myself did not proclaim loudly "the doctrine of the Unity of Master and Disciple", nor did I demand this from other people. Each person is able to read and listen to his lectures and receive his guidance to as a means of deepening his or her faith. Yet, I always remained very uneasy and deeply repelled at times when the "doctrine of the Unity of Master and Disciple" was blatantly abused as a political ideology intended to maintain the hierarchy and status quo within the organization. For example, the name "Sensei" was often used to simply suppress unwelcome questions or reasonable criticism simply by asserting: "Sensei said this and that", "This is Sensei's wish", "We should not bother Sensei" and so on. Some almost screamed out the name and exhibited an attitude and demeanor of total obedience and abject surrender. It is quite abnormal and in fact even dangerous to fanatically worship Sensei as an authoritarian guru. Indeed, outside Japan, this kind of "guru worship" deeply tarnished the reputation of SGI, which was perceived by outsiders as an "Ikeda Cult". As a result, some left the organization. Consequently, I became fearful every time that I heard or read that the "righteous attitude of absolute obedience" was exclusively the "true way of the Master and Disciple" – Yet doesn't this attitude remind one of an authoritarian belief system found elsewhere? This is most frustrating, as what I have learned from Ikeda personally is the exact opposite: i.e. to take care of everyone sensitively and with true affection and to listen to everyone's individual concerns and aspirations, in order that each be encouraged and enabled to truly grow spiritually.

Thus, I consider myself to be in succession to Ikeda's essentially humanistic approach to NB, although I have expanded it by way of a more radical and systematic critique grounded in contemporary Buddhist studies. Against this personal background, the second part will review the present contemporary ongoing debate on doctrine and organization within SG. However, first there is a need to analyze the manner in which Ikeda has modified and subsequently developed away from his previous beliefs with respect to both the Gohonzon and the true Buddha.

Chapter 2
The Gohonzon considered in »The Wisdom of the Lotus Sutra«

1. Time and Eternity, after the abandonment of faith in the Dai-gohonzon

A conversation and reflection on the LS had been initiated by Ikeda, the honorary president of SG, with the three heads responsible for the SG study department. Subsequently, there appeared, in SG's monthly magazine *"Daibyakurenge"*, a series of articles in dialogue published between February 1995 and June 1999. This dialogue was also later published as a series of paperbacks (in English: »The Wisdom of the Lotus Sutra: A Discussion by Daisaku Ikeda, Katsuya Saito, Takanori Endo and Haruo Suda«).

In response to these publications, an anonymous blogger known as "ClearSky" posted a PDF file entitled »Learning about "The Eternal Law" and "The Eternal Buddha" from the "Wisdom of the Lotus Sutra"« on his website in October 2016 (hereafter, just Vol. 1 and 2 with reference to the pager number of the downloaded PDF file). This would appear to be an article concerned to reemphasize the previous traditional view of Ikeda with respect to the Honzon at the time of a radical revision of SG doctrine. I refer to this document as important points in the doctrinal debate are picked up and concisely summarized. It is indeed most convenient to have at hand such a concise overview rather than having to make reference to the several volumes of the paperback edition. Another reason to refer to this document is that it is deeply related to the present context of SG doctrinal studies, including ambivalent reactions from members of SG. ClearSky would appear to belong to a faction within SG, who regard the traditional NS doctrines as the exclusive foundation for all SG doctrinal studies. For this purpose, he has published the document and picked up on those statements from Ikeda that might appear to corroborate his contentions. However, I myself read them differently and I will demonstrate that Ikeda has in fact articulated a radically alternative vision far from traditional NS doctrine.

In any event, currently within SG in Japan, some very critical opinions have been expressed and directed at those at SG-HQ considered to be responsible for the radical doctrinal revisions at and it is this disaffected traditional faction which ClearSky represents. In his "Introduction" he begins by commenting on the above circumstances as follows.

> *The Revision of the Doctrinal Clause of the Constitution of November 2014.*
> Although two years have passed, there are many who accept this revision,

but there are also those who cannot uncritically accept it. I have talked with these members and we have discussed together the reasons for our hesitation. Some of them are outlined below.
- We are confused as it differs substantially from the previous doctrine and policy of SG.
- Does it not also differ from Sensei's guidance given in the past?
- Consequently, we feel a sense of dissonance with respect to the revised constitutional rule.
- As we are still worshipping the Gohonzon inscribed by the priest Nichikan, we cannot yet understand the policy of partial revision of Nichikan's Doctrine.
- The changes seem to have been occasioned by the influence of Professor Miyata of Soka University and consequently we are now most concerned about the future. (ClearSky, vol.1, p. 1)

In this context, his document focuses on the discussion with respect to chapters of the LS like "15 Emerging from the Earth", "16 The Life Span of Tathāgata" and "21 Supernatural Powers of the Tathāgata". Indeed, they are the most important chapters which Nichiren himself considered to be foundational for his own practice of "chanting Daimoku" in front of the "mandala Gohonzon". In this respect, a further consideration is who in fact is the "person" who practices Daimoku.

Reading Clearsky's article or the respective chapters in »The Wisdom of the Lotus Sutra«, one notices that Ikeda is still employing the terms and concepts taken from traditional NS doctrine. This is actually what ClearSky intended to emphasize: the historical fact that Ikeda, like Toda before him, inherited traditional NS doctrine. Yet at the same time, it should be recognized that Ikeda was seeking to go beyond traditional NS doctrine and to introduce "a new humanistic reading of the LS" as a firm foundation for a new humanistic NB.

It is always essential to note the publication date of any writings and speeches by Ikeda and SGI[12]. The dialogue with respect to the LS appeared in a series published between 1995 and 1999. This publication period was relatively brief, immediately after SG separated from NS at the institutional level

---

[12] All publications of SGI before 1991 should be regarded as based on the traditional NS docrine, but this is sometimes the case even after 1991. One of the most popular introductory texts is »Buddha in Daily Life: An introduction to the Buddhism of Nichiren Daishōnin« (1995), written by Richard Causton, former general director of SGI-UK. This still expressly employs NS concepts such as the "Dai-Gohonzon" and "the establishment and completion of the holy place (kaidan) for the Dai-Gohonzon" (Shōhondō). His doctrinal position in another book »Nichiren Shoshu Buddhism: An Introductioin« (1994) is obvious from its title. These two books constitute evidence that NS doctrine had not been comprehensively abandoned within SG until 2014.

in 1991, yet SG maintained its traditional NS faith in the Dai-gohonzon until 2014. This decisive leap at the doctrinal level should be regarded as marking the ultimate separation of SG from NS. Given the above, the dialogue with respect to the LS should be understood as a transitional theory on Attaining Enlightenment and the Object of Devotion. Now, let's examine the debate, following the order as outlined by ClearSky in his article.

2. The Multilayered structure of the discourse

First, it considers the debate focused on the 16th Chapter of the LS. Although those in dialogue acknowledge the intention of the historical Buddha Shakyamuni that "one should solely rely on the Dharma and oneself", the discussion curiously moves in a wholly different direction, i.e. that "he only became enlightened to the Eternal Dharma deep within himself by taking the Eternal Buddha as his master".

> *Honorary President*:   The profound insight that the "Eternal Law -equals- the Eternal Buddha" which Shakyamuni realized as the "eternal great life", all Buddhas have likewise realized. Every Buddha in the past, in the present and in the future, who has attained to this realization exactly like Shakyamuni, has only attained enlightenment as a disciple of a master, i.e. as a disciple of "the Buddha at the Original beginning in the remotest past". This Buddha is the "Wisdom Body at the Original beginning of the remotest past" and the Tathāgata of Nam-myō-hō-ren-ge-kyō. Toda Sensei said: "The life of ND as well as our lives are without beginning and without end. This is called the "Original beginning in the remotest past". There is no beginning and no end. The Great Universe itself is a great life entity". Under the guidance of this great life entity as master, which continues to practice eternally out of great compassion, the "human being, Shakyamuni" became a Buddha while he remained a human being. And at the moment of having become enlightened, he understood that all the Buddhas in the Three Existences (of the past, the present and the future) and Ten Directions of the Heaven became Buddhas only under the guidance of this "Eternal Buddha" by way of the Unity of Buddha and Dharma (Vol. 1, p. 4).

To be frank, the logic of the above is incoherent. Let's sort it out!
1) Shakyamuni Buddha and all other Buddhas became enlightened to the "Eternal Dharma-equals-Eternal Buddha = Eternal Great life".
2) That is, they all attained this under the guidance of a master who is "the Buddha at the Original beginning in the remotest past" = "Wisdom Body of the Original beginning in the remotest past" = "Tathāgata of Nam-myō-hō-ren-ge-kyō" = "the Eternal Buddha as the Unity of Buddha and Dharma".

3) The fact that the life of ND himself and of we ourselves is without beginning and without end is called the "Original beginning in the remotest past".
4) The great life entity that is the great universe itself which is without beginning and without end and which continues to practice eternally out of great compassion.
5) The human being Shakyamuni became a Buddha by taking this great life entity as his master while he remained an ordinary human being.
6) At the moment of attaining enlightenment, all Buddhas understand that they have become enlightened as they have taken the "Eternal Buddha as the Unity of Buddha and Dharma" as master.

Here, Ikeda employs some key terms from traditional NS doctrine, such as "the Original beginning in the remotest past", its "Wisdom body" and the "Eternal Buddha as the Unity of Buddha and Dharma". Yet when we take a closer look at the way he defines these terms, we notice that these traditional terms have been given radically different meanings. Additionally, these new definitions incorporate a diffuse mix of elements. The above points can be further highlighted thus:

(1) The universal phenomenon known as the "Great Life" can be understood to represent "Dharma" in its broadest sense, while it can also be understood in terms such as Buddha nature, the Buddha World or by the doctrine that all life is mutually-endowed with each of the Ten Worlds. Yet why should any of these aspects necessarily imply or include the notion of an eternally existent personal "Buddha"?

(2) The phrase "Eternal Buddha at the original beginning in the remotest past" represents exactly the same concept as found in NS doctrine and presumes that this "master" is ND himself. Further, the doctrine of the "unity of Person and Dharma" is also expressly assumed, which is a key foundation to the doctrine of the Dai-gohonzon.

(3) Moreover, the life theory of Toda is likewise expressly assumed, and it is argued that the essence of all people without discrimination is eternal life, while the phrase "The Origin in the remotest past" is expressly understood to be this cosmic life. In this way, Ikeda seems to imply that Toda had already sought to radically deconstruct the traditional NS understanding of the phrase "Origin in the remotest past" by employing an interpretive matrix drawn from his own "life theory".

(4) The idea that the cosmic life force continues to eternally practice out of its great compassion is both deeply spiritual and contemporary: indeed, confirmation for such an understanding has been claimed by pointing to a variety of meditation practices and to near-death-experiences. As such, this idea can be regarded as an aspect of Buddha-nature or the Buddha World.

(5) "The human being Shakyamuni became a Buddha by taking this great life entity as his master while he remained an ordinary human being": this phrase is a near equivalent to the "Theory of the Ordinary Person as True Buddha", which likewise stresses this aspect of a realization of or awakening to a cosmic life force (Buddha nature mutually-endowed with all Ten Worlds) deep within the body of an ordinary human being.

(6) Further, the "Eternal Buddha as the Unity of Buddha and Dharma" is stressed as the seed or Master of the Mystic Principle of the Original Cause. Accepting that there are different teachings through which the Buddhas have attained enlightenment, the idea that they nevertheless immediately realized the essence or root of that enlightenment points to the principle (expounded by Miao-lo in »The Annotation on *The Words and Phrases of the Lotus Sutra*«, a commentary on one of T'ien-t'ai's three major works): *"Though people appear to have attained enlightenment in the present (under the guidance of Shakyamuni Buddha), the original seed of this fruit (the Dharma of the LS) had been sown a long time ago (in the remotest past before they practiced other teachings)"*.

As mentioned in 1), 5), 6), there is no question that Nichiren himself taught a doctrine in which the Mystic Law is to be understood as the "Sowing of the Seed" (*geshu*), i.e. as the original cause of all the Buddhas.

> The "doctrine of the sowing of the seed and its maturing and harvesting" is the very heart and core of the Lotus Sutra. All the Buddhas of the three existences and the ten directions have invariably attained Buddhahood through the seed represented by the five characters of Myōhō-renge-kyō.
> (»Letter to Akimoto«, p. 1072 / l. 1015)

The doctrine of three periods of the process by which a Buddha leads people to Buddhahood corresponds to the growth and development of a plant. First the Buddha plants the seed of Buddhahood in people's lives, then he nurtures them by helping them practice the Law, and finally he enables them to fully manifest Buddhahood. In this context the seed of Buddhahood is the Mystic Law (Dharma) though it has been sown by a person (Buddha).

Given the above, I am curious as to why Ikeda doesn't talk about the seed in the sense above, as the process for cultivating and practicing the Dharma, but only as the "eternal Buddha as the Unity of Buddha and Dharma"? For this phrase clearly contradicts his subsequent assertion that both the life of ND and the lives of all other ordinary human beings are identical with that cosmic life which alone leads all sentient beings to the attainment of enlightenment? Let's now try to find a solution to these questions.

3. The Gohonzon Understood as a Unity of Buddha and Dharma

Subsequently, Ikeda continues to speak about the inner "Eternal Law - equals- the eternal Buddha", yet ultimately, what he understands this to mean only becomes explicit when he makes reference to the Gohonzon as a Unity of Buddha and Dharma.

> *Honorary President:* [...] The Daishōnin made it possible that we, ordinary people in the Latter Day of the Law, might become one with the "Buddha preaching incessantly in this world" by the practice of chanting the Mystic Law in front of the Gohonzon. It is a Gohonzon understood as the Unity of Buddha and Dharma. The aspect of "person" is the *Tathāgata of the Wisdom Body at the Original beginning in the remotest past*. The aspect of "Law" is the principle of *Ichinen Sanzen in actuality.* Therefore, Toda Sensei also called the *Buddha at the Original beginning in the remotest past* "Mr. Ichinen Sanzen". [...] He said that "the Great Universe is equal to the Gohonzon and that the life of Nam-myō-hō-ren-ge-kyō has always been identical with the Great Universe since the eternal past". And, "When we worship the Gohonzon to welcome and embrace its [enlightened] life into our lives, the power of the Gohonzon which will manifest in our lives is nothing other than Nam-myō-hō-ren-ge-kyō". (Vol. 1, p. 10)

Let's summarize the points.
- The Gohonzon signifies the Unity of Buddha and Dharma as in the phrase "the Tathāgata with the Wisdom Body at the Original beginning in the remotest past – equals- Ichinen Sanzen in Actuality".
- At the same time, the Gohonzon is equivalent to the Great Universe and the life of Nam-myō-hō-ren-ge-kyō.
- When we worship the Gohonzon, we become one with this Buddha.

There remains one aspect of this which is problematic. This is with respect to the assertion that the Buddha embodied by the Gohonzon as the Unity of Buddha and Dharma is radically distinct from us and yet becomes one with us when we worship it. Yet it is difficult to easily comprehend what is in fact meant by the mysterious phrase "becoming one". Does it mean the "Fusion of Actuality and Wisdom"? In other words, does being inspired by the life of the Gohonzon mean that the very life of the Buddha will arise in our own lives? Let's look into this further.

> *Saito:* This "Eternal Law" refers to Nam-myō-hō-ren-ge-kyō while the "Eternal Buddha" means the Tathāgata of Nam-myō-hō-ren-ge-kyō, i.e., the Wisdom Body at the Origin in the Remotest Past, doesn't it?
>
> *Honorary President:* That's right. Nam-myō-hō-ren-ge-kyō is a Law, but at the same time it is a Buddha Body. It is the Unity of Person and Law.

[...] The Buddha at the Original beginning in the remotest past, i.e., the ceaselessly practicing, ever present Buddha without beginning and without end is nothing other than the cosmic life itself. It is ceaselessly practicing and ever present for the salvation of all people, without any moment of rest. This Buddha and ourselves are indeed one, [...]. Buddha Shakyamuni also realized that he himself was one with the "Eternal Buddha". (Vol. 1, p. 11)

The problem here can be outlined as follows.
- Nam-myō-hō-ren-ge-kyō is considered to be the Buddha Body at the Original beginning in the remotest past in the Unity of Buddha and Dharma.
- The ceaselessly practicing, ever present Buddha without beginning and without end is the cosmic life itself.
- To understand ourselves as being one with this eternal Buddha is identical to the realization of Buddhahood.

It is correct, though we will discuss this in Part Three in more detail, to simply understand the concept of the Unity of Person and Law as a mode of Instant Enlightenment. Yet, it is wholly irrational to project back this principle to the Original Beginning in the Remotest Past and thereby give a dimension of "personality" to the cosmic life force. This can be understood only if the significance of ND has been clarified.

4. The meaning of "Revealing the true identity by casting aside the shadow"

This idea is discussed with respect to "the Master of the Mystic Principle of the Original Cause". First, the "Original Cause" is defined as the Principle of the Mutual Containment of the Ten Worlds as described in »The Opening of the Eyes«.

Saito: [...] By breaking through the chain of cause and effect up until now, the fundamental cause for realizing Buddhahood and its effect is revealed. Regarding this doctrine of "Original Cause and Original Effect" it is written in the »Opening of the Eyes«: *"This [doctrine] reveals that the Nine Worlds are all present in beginningless Buddhahood and that Buddhahood is inherent in the beginningless Nine Worlds. This is the true mutual possession of the Ten Worlds, the true hundred worlds and thousand factors, the true three thousand realms in a single moment of life"* (p. 197 / p. 235). As a consequence of Revealing the true identity by casting away its shadow in the Life Span Chapter, the true reality that "the beginningless Buddha World" and "the beginningless Nine Worlds" are interdependent (mutually contained) is revealed. That is why true Ichinen Sanzen is established. (Vol. 1, p. 11)

With respect to the Attaining Enlightenment in the Remotest Past of the Essential Teaching, Nichiren himself understood the "Mutual Containment of the beginningless Ten Worlds" as the mutually-inclusive relationship between "beginningless Buddhahood" and the "beginningless Nine Worlds". Yet this quite definitely is only about the mutual inclusion of life within the Ten Worlds. However, curiously, Ikeda defines this concept as being identical to the "Eternal Original Buddha without beginning and end".

> *Honorary President:* [...] The Daishōnin describes the "Mutual Containment of the Ten Worlds" as taught in the Theoretical Teaching as "Initial Enlightenment" while he describes the same principle as taught in the Essential Teaching as "Originally Existing Enlightenment". Thus, he makes a fundamental distinction between these two teachings. The point here is whether or not you know the "Eternal Original Buddha without beginning and end". (Vol. 1, p. 4)

Ikeda continues;

> *Honorary President:* The purpose of the Essential Teaching of the LS is to reveal the "the Original Buddha without beginning". No, the whole of Buddhism is there for that. But if you do not know that Buddha who represents the root, then you will not know the master of all the Buddhas of the Three Existences, and you will never attain enlightenment. It is like a child who does not know his father and hence "I do not know who I am". The Daishōnin expressed it like this: "*if one fails to become acquainted with the Buddha of the Life Span chapter, one is no more than a talented animal who does not even know what lands one's father presides over*" (»The Opening of the Eyes«, p. 215 / I. 258). (ibid.)

This quotation appears in the section that begins with the sentence: "*When the Eternal Past was revealed, it became apparent that all the other Buddhas were emanations of Shakyamuni*" (p. 214 / I. 256). Thereby, the event of Attaining Enlightenment in the Remotest Past is defined with respect to the principle of "*Ichinen Sanzen planting the enlightenment seeds of all Buddhas*" (p. 215 / I. 258). In other words, from the standpoint of the Essential Teaching in contrast to that of the Pre-LS and the Theoretical Teaching, Nichiren gives primacy to the Eternal Original Buddha Shakyamuni because only this Buddha represents the source of enlightenment of all other Buddhas. If we go a step further and seek an explanation of much deeper significance than the bare literal meaning, Nichiren arguably regards the principle of Ichinen Sanzen based on the Mutual Containment of Ten Worlds as the "seed from which all Buddhas sprout". Yet, rather than reading the above passage in a simple straightforward manner, Ikeda cannot resist once again bringing to the fore the traditional NS concept "the Original Buddha without beginning":

CHAPTER 2

Endo: [...] What Shakyamuni Buddha was enlightened to was actually the "Mystic Law of Simultaneity of Cause and Effect". In order to demonstrate this aspect, he taught "Revealing the true identity by casting aside the shadow", didn't he?

Honorary President: That "Mystic Law of Simultaneity of Cause and Effect" is the life of Nam-myō-hō-ren-ge-kyō Tathāgata being the Original Buddha without beginning". Practicing this Eternal Law is the "Original Cause" and the Buddhahood that will be attained by practice is the "Original Effect". The "Doctrine of Original Cause and Original Effect" is intended to reveal this sole Law. That is also the purpose of "Revealing the true identity by casting aside the shadow". (ibid.)

To give this an equation:

The fact of Shakyamuni's "Revealing the true identity by casting aside the shadow" in the 16th Chapter of the LS
= The "Doctrine of Original Cause and Original Effect"
= The "Mystic Law of the Simultaneity of Cause and Effect"
= The Original Buddha without beginning
= The Life of Nam-myō-hō-ren-ge-kyō Tathāgata

This is with direct reference to the Mystic Principle of the Original Cause and the Daishōnin himself is regarded as the Master of this principle.

Honorary President: [...] In the Essential Teaching, if it is read literally, it is only stated that within the very body of Shakyamuni both the Buddha World (effect) and the Nine Worlds (Cause) are endowed with eternity. But, the "Original Cause", that which has in fact established and made possible this "parallel permanence" [of both the enlightened life state and the ordinary life state within the very life of the Eternal Buddha Shakyamuni] has not been preached. In fact, that Original Cause is the "wonderful Law of the Simultaneity of Cause and Effect". Shakyamuni took this Original Cause as his master, and the one who teaches this law of the Original Cause is the "Master of the Mystic Principle of the Original Cause". "I am the master teaching it" (Gosho p. 863), so declared Nichiren Daishōnin (Vol. 1, p. 16)

Nevertheless, these arguments are still difficult to understand. Aside from the parallel permanence of the beginningless Ten Worlds, the Mystic Principle of the Simultaneity of Cause and Effect might be accepted. Yet it remains unclear whether the master teaching this principle of causality is at one only at the moment of attaining enlightenment in the remotest past or also in the present day. Ikeda quoted just one sentence from the so called »One Hundred and Six Comparisons«, but its meaning becomes much clearer if reference is made to the entire passage.

> A Comparison between the Essence and the Shadow with respect to the Teaching Master and the Sowing of Seeds of Buddhahood by Way of the Lotus Sutra:
> The Wisdom Body is the Essence while Nichiren as the Bodhisattva Jōgyō represents the Shadow. The Life Span Chapter in our secret understanding refers to the Mystic Principle of the Original Cause and by way of a Deeper Reading of the Life Span Chapter represents the Harvesting. I am the master teaching it. (p. 863 / -)

In other words, from the particular NS doctrinal viewpoint of a Deeper Reading and Sowing, the Wisdom Body at the Original Beginning in the Remotest Past represents the true identity of Nichiren, while the Bodhisattva Jōgyō taking part in the Ceremony in the Air, as well as the historical person Nichiren in the Latter Day of Law, represents its Shadow or manifestation. This logic implies a relationship between an absolute truth (or the eternal Buddha) and its manifested forms (or historical Buddha). Nichiren often uses the metaphor of the moon in the heavens and its shadow or its image reflected on the surface of a pond.

In the analysis up to this point, it would seem that Ikeda has made use of basic terms taken directly from traditional NS doctrine, but at a closer look, he would appear to have been seeking to subtly amend their meaning. The most significant difference lies in the question as to which is the true identity of Nichiren himself. Is he only the Wisdom Body at the original beginning in the remotest past or does his original essence and significance have the universal character of radical openness and great compassion to all people without discrimination.

5. Summary of the multilayered structure

In order to clarify, let us distinguish the particular perspective for each level of analysis.

From the viewpoint of life theory

- The life of the Daishōnin and the lives of each one of us are without beginning and without end, which is designated as the "original beginning in the remotest past".
- The Great Life, the Great Universe itself, is without beginning and without end, and it keeps being active ceaselessly out of great compassion.
- The Great Universe being identical to the Gohonzon is the life of Nam-myō-hō-ren-ge-kyō.

The difficulty here is to equate the Great Universal Life to the Law of attaining enlightenment by way of actualizing the Law of Nam-myō-hō-ren-ge-kyō, as well as the character of practice. If we consider our individual life in the entirety of its existence as the direct manifestation of the Great Universal Life, this idea might too closely approach the bad "philosophy of original enlightenment", merely affirming things themselves just as they are, i.e. merely affirming the "status quo" of reality. Likewise, it might be also mistaken for a sort of "Concept about the Manifestation of the Essence of all Phenomena". Consequently, in order to retain the dynamism of the Buddhist "philosophy of sowing", we should always distinguish between the reality of the Nine Worlds and the ideal state of the Buddha World, so that we can activate the latter in our daily life simply by chanting Daimoku. This "dialectical" dual structure of our lives should be stressed. For the *"soku"* (equal) used to define the principle of "The Nine Worlds -equals- The Buddha World" should not merely mean that we, simply as we are in our daily reality, are Buddhas, but rather it implies the principle of transformation through openness to the Buddhahood inherent within us, i.e. within all the ordinary beings in the Nine Worlds.

The Gohonzon viewed as the Unity of Buddha and Dharma

- The Gohonzon represents the Unity of the Buddha and Dharma, the Tathāgata of the Wisdom Body at the Original Beginning in the Remotest Past (Buddha) and the "Ichinen Sanzen in Actuality" based on the principle of the Mutual Containment of the Ten Worlds (Law).
- When we worship this Gohonzon, we become one with this Buddha.

The concept of the "Tathāgata of the Wisdom Body at the Original Beginning in the Remotest Past" implies a primordial or fundamental Buddha rather than simply indicating Shakyamuni in the remotest past. Consequently, it does not seem capable of completely discarding the contentious aspect of "personality". From such a perspective, speech about a universal life, or the relationship between the Great Cosmos and the Gohonzon, is contradictory and philosophically incoherent.

The Mystic Law as the Original Cause

- The doctrine that Original Cause and Original Effect = The Mystic Law of the Simultaneity of Cause and Effect = The Original Buddha without beginning = The Life of Nam-myō-hō-ren-ge-kyō Tathāgata.
- The Daishōnin = The Teaching Master of the Mystic Principle of the Original Cause

If the "Mystic Law of the Simultaneity of Cause and Effect" is identical with the "Original Buddha without beginning" and retains a personal aspect, it would lose its universality as a Law. Rather than accept this essentialist identification of the Mystic Law with the "Eternal Buddha Nichiren", we should hold the view that the Unity of the Person and the Law is actually manifested only when an ordinary person practices the Law, thereby manifesting the attributes of a Buddha. Consequently, the Original Cause should mean the totality of the Nine Worlds while the Original Effect is enlightenment, in that Buddhahood (potential) will thereby be manifested in an ordinary person. If the Mystic Law itself is endowed with the aspect of a particular Buddha, then the Law itself can be embraced by a particular ordinary person.

> Ikeda, while leaving traditional NS teachings as they are, at the same time inherited Toda's life theory and developed NB in a universalizing direction.

6. A Nichiren Buddhist Humanism

With respect to the dialogue referred to in Part 1 concerning "The Life Span Chapter", the participants are reviewing the historical development of Theravada, Mahayana and the LS. In this context, they are also speaking about "humanism" in contrast to "authoritarianism". In the first period after Shakyamuni's death, Buddhists devoted themselves to the teachings left behind, yet Buddhism was changing through the process of institutionalization. The Buddha became deified as a sacred person radically distinct from the reality of daily life characterized by suffering, as the Buddha had been liberated from the cycle of rebirth within the Six Worlds. Meanwhile, Mahayana Buddhism developed a faith in the Buddhas and Bodhisattvas, beings endowed with great supernatural powers, who have vowed to liberate all beings from suffering. At this point, an interesting idea is raised, that in fact, the Lotus Sutra was an attempt by its compilers to discard a pernicious ideology or a "dehumanization of religion" by way of an "escape from reality" and, consequently, that the LS itself is emblematic of "a battle to humanize Buddhism" (ibid., p. 8).

> *Honorary President:* When the people had forgotten the "human-Buddha", Buddhism strayed from the "human way of life". "The way of master and disciple" has gone. The result is the corruption of Buddhism and authoritarianism. (ibid., p. 9)

Here, humanistic Buddhism is characterized as not recognizing any authority other than that of ordinary human beings, cultivating the right way of living as an ordinary human being, and committing to Buddhist practice under the instruction of a master for this sole purpose. In this way, the idea of change and transformation in terms of improving one's life condition becomes paramount.

> *Endo:* [...] When we consider "Manifesting the Essence" from this point of view, it may have the meaning of opening up the "eternal great life" without abandoning the "human Shakyamuni".

Honorary President: To speak in philosophical terms, it should mean: Contemplating "eternity" without departing from "present reality"! Seek "transcendence" as well as "immanence"! Open up to "something cosmic" at "the this very spot"! This is the heart of Manifesting the Essence. (Vol. 1, p. 9)

It is an inspiring and wonderful idea to interpret the concept of Manifesting the Essence in a thoroughly contemporary manner by way of reference to our essential practice. This should mean that we will be awakened to the universal life or the cosmic consciousness when we chant Daimoku before the Gohonzon where we breakthrough the barrier of our small ego (the Nine Worlds). This understanding points also to the concept of participation in the Ceremony in the Air. From this spiritual perspective, we are then truly empowered to create new value in our lives. That is what it would mean to practice the Buddhism of the Mystic Principle of the Original Cause. In fact, Nichiren Buddhism does teach us to go beyond the "small self" (ego) of daily life and to manifest the cosmic "great self" ("the beginningless primordial Buddha" or Buddha-nature). The principle, however, is not limited only to Manifesting the True Identity of the Eternal Buddha, who attained enlightenment in the remotest past. For the meaning of "opening" is also always applied to ourselves in the »Records of the Orally Transmitted Teachings«. A passage is quoted below, taken from the 3rd point of 27 important points found in the Life Span chapter.

> Point Three, regarding the phrase "It has been immeasurable, boundless kalpas *since I in fact attained Buddhahood (Ga jitsu jōbutsu irai)*."
>
> The Record of the Orally Transmitted Teachings says: "I in fact" (*Ga jitsu*) is explaining that Shakyamuni in fact attained Buddhahood in the inconceivably remote past. The meaning of this chapter, however, is that "I" represents the living beings of the Dharma-realm. "I" here refers to each and every being in the Ten Worlds. "In fact" refers to the "Buddha endowed with three bodies without intention". This is what is being called "fact".
>
> "Attained" (*jō*) refers both to the one who attains and to the entity attained. "Attain" means to open or reveal. It is to reveal that the Dharma-realm is the "Buddha endowed with three bodies without intention". "Buddha" (*butsu*) means to realize this fact.
>
> In the word "since" (*irai*), the character "I" (already, or having passed) refers to the past, and the character "rai" (coming) refers to the future. And the present is existing in these two elements "I" and "rai".
>
> The passage is thus saying that I [or the beings of the Dharma-realm] am in fact the revealed Buddha and I am immeasurable and boundless in both the past and the future. It is referring to the principle of a hundred worlds,

> a thousand factors and the three thousand realms in a single moment of life. [...] This is nothing but Ichinen Sanzen in Actuality.
> Now Nichiren and his followers, those who chant Nam-myō-hō-ren-ge-kyō, are the original lords of the Life Span Chapter. (p. 753 / OTT 126)

In this way, once we understand the concept of Manifesting the Essence with respect to our practice of chanting Daimoku, it means that when we chant Daimoku, we will always cast aside the ego and attain the dimension of the higher self. It's amazing!!!

Honorary President: Yes. This principle has enabled us to return to "Shakyamuni as an ordinary human being", who at the same time should be regarded as the "eternal Buddha". Thus, a deep religious insight opened up a profound perspective on the world, that is "more than deification". A new way is opened, in that human beings remain as such and go beyond themselves infinitely. (Vol. 1, p. 9)

Not to deify any Buddhas as transcendent beings,
not to accept any authoritarianism and
to open humanity to infinite dignity and nobility,
such is a Nichiren Buddhism of humanism.

---

7. The Chapter on Emerging from the Earth

What particularly interests me in this part is the question of how the partners to the dialogue are reflecting on traditional NS teachings. At first, they speak about the significance of the Bodhisattvas of the Earth and the meaning of the name "Nichiren". Then, they consider the theory that all the beings appearing in the LS correspond to the Ten Worlds in "the mind of Shakyamuni himself".

Saito: The Eternal Original Buddha of the Life Span chapter is equivalent to the "true self" of Shakyamuni, isn't it?

Honorary President: Yes. The Eternal Original Buddha manifests the "eternal Self" in unity with the eternal Mystic Law. (Vol.2, p. 2)

Does it mean that the Eternal Original Buddha is identical with the "Self" endowed with the Ten Worlds in the sense of "the Law -equals- the Person"?

Suda: The Bodhisattvas of the Earth means "the Bodhisattvas in the heart of Shakyamuni", doesn't it?

Honorary President: They are the "eternal Bodhisattva" inherent in the "eternal Self". It is said also in the »Records of the Orally Transmitted Teachings« that *"Because they are the bodhisattvas inherent in Shakyamuni and the original disciples of the original essence, they were invited to the Ceremony"*. No, they are not inherent only in Shakyamuni. The

Daishōnin says: *"All people are identical to just one person"*. The "eternal Self" of Shakyamuni is the "eternal Self" of all people. Generally speaking, all people are the original Buddha. The Bodhisattvas of the Earth are the "eternal Bodhisattva" inherent in all people. The Daishōnin explains this dimension in »The Object of Devotion for Observing the Mind« as follows: *"Shakyamuni Buddha, who has attained perfect enlightenment, is our own flesh and blood. His practices and the resulting virtues are our bones and marrow"* [p. 246 / I. 365]; *"The Shakyamuni Buddha within our lives is the ancient Buddha since time without beginning"* [ibid.]; *"The Bodhisattvas of the Earth such as Jōgyō, Muhengyō, Jyōgyō, Anryūgyō and the like represent the world of the bodhisattva within ourselves"* [p. 246 / I. 366].

In terms of the Ten Worlds theory, of course, our life consists of Ten Worlds, but now we can affirm the dual structure that the "eternal self" is endowed with the Ten Worlds. This can be expressed as "The Buddha World -equals- The Nine Worlds" in the sense that the Nine or Ten Worlds are included in the essential Buddha World. In addition, this ontological dual structure is held to be not only unique to the Eternal Original Buddha and the historical Buddha Shakyamuni but is likewise exactly the same for the Daishōnin and for all of us. So, how does this relate to the Gohonzon?

Endo: The drama of the Lotus Sutra is also the drama of all people's lives, isn't it? If that is so, is it identical with the LS of the Daishōnin, i.e., the Gohonzon?

Honorary President: The Daishōnin used the stage of the Lotus Sutra called the Ceremony in the Air to manifest his own "eternal Self" in the form of the Gohonzon. Not to mention that his own "eternal self" is "Nam-myō-hō-ren-ge-kyō". It is as is inscribed in the center of the Gohonzon: "Nam-myō-hō-ren-ge-kyō Nichiren".

Saito: It says also in the Gosho: *"I, Nichiren, have inscribed my life in sumi ink, so believe in the Gohonzon with your whole heart. […] the soul of Nichiren is nothing other than Nam-myō-hō-ren-ge-kyō"* [p. 1124 / I. 411]. (ibid.)

Even if we regard the "soul" of the Daishōnin as the "eternal self", there is no doubt that it is Nam-myō-hō-ren-ge-kyō and the Gohonzon represents its expression or manifestation.

Yet "Nam-myō-hō-ren-ge-kyō Nichiren" should not be considered to be exclusively the essence or spirit of the Daishōnin, as though he alone has a "spiritual monopoly". For the principle of the Unity of the Person and the Law must be a principle universally applicable and open to all people, as all people share an identical ontological dual structure with the Daishōnin.
It must be understood to have this universally applicable dimension.

Ikeda's reflections are subtle as he doesn't assert that the Daishōnin alone must be the Tathāgata of the Wisdom Body at the Original Beginning in the Remotest Past. Rather he strives towards a far more universalist understanding of the cosmic life itself.

8. The Chapter on the Tathāgata's Supernatural Powers

Subsequently, the following explanation of the supernatural powers of the Buddha is given.

Honorary President: It sounds like a logical leap, but in conclusion, an admiration and celebration of the merits and benefits of Nam-myō-hō-ren-ge-kyō Tathāgata is to be found in the Unity of Buddha and Dharma. Both the "Shakyamuni who attained enlightenment in the remotest past" and "Bodhisattva Jōgyō" represent the "trace or shadow" of Nam-myō-hō-ren-ge-kyō Tathāgata which is the fundamental Buddha of the cosmos. Nam-myō-hō-ren-ge-kyō Tathāgata is the Buddha without beginning and without end, the cosmic life itself, the fundamental foundation of all Buddhas, and the entity endowed with the original Ten Worlds and their mutual possession. Among those Ten Worlds the "Buddha World" is expounded in the Lotus Sutra in the form of "Shakyamuni from the remotest past" and "Tathāgata Tahō (Many Treasures)", while the "Nine Worlds" of *Nam-myō-hō-ren-ge-kyō Tathāgata* are preached by "Bodhisattva Jōgyō" and the like. They are all Buddhas and Bodhisattvas which deep within their own hearts are the identical to the fundamental Buddha. Therefore, it is no exaggeration to say, that no one can admire *Nam-myō-hō-ren-ge-kyō Tathāgata* enough. Since this Tathāgata is the "master of the source" which gave birth to all Buddhas, this master is also to be praised. (ibid., p. 3)

With these assertions, several important points are made. However, some philosophical assumptions, along with some parts of NS doctrine, remain intermixed with the life theory and the theory of the Ordinary Person as True Buddha.

Nam-myō-hō-ren-ge-kyō Tathāgata
in the Unity of Buddha and Dharma
= The beginningless and endless Buddha
= Cosmic life
= The root of all Buddhas in the Three Existences and
Ten Heavenly Directions
= Originally endowed with the Ten Worlds
= the entity originally endowed with the Ten Worlds and
their Mutual Containment

Consequently, when viewed from the point of view of the master in his function as the source of wisdom to all Buddhas, the Buddha Shakyamuni from the remotest past and the Tathāgata Tahō (Prabhūtaratna) revealed in the LS are Buddhas who in their innermost "heart are identical to the fundamental Buddha", while the Bodhisattva Jōgyō and the like represent the original disciples or bodhisattvas of the fundamental Buddha. Each l of them is a "representation of the trace or shadow of Nam-myō-hō-ren-ge-kyō Tathāgata, that is the fundamental Buddha of the cosmos". Yet this is to speak of nothing other than the dual structure of "The Buddha Word -equals- The Nine Worlds", described above.

Further, the Tathāgata represents the bodily entity, the "supernatural powers" represent the Tathāgata's function or work, while the "source that gave birth to the Tathāgata is Nam-myō-hō-ren-ge-kyō Tathāgata".

Honorary President: Moreover, because the Buddha is at one with the universe, we and all beings are also at one with Nam-myō-hō-ren-ge-kyō Tathāgata. The true reality of our life within the Ten Worlds is Nam-myō-hō-ren-ge-kyō Tathāgata. And the one who taught this to us is Nichiren Daishōnin. Because he is our teacher, he should be regarded as the "lord of the teachings". Consequently, when we recite the Daimoku just as he taught, the voice which chants has a sound like the great roaring of the whole universe itself. (ibid., p. 4)

At first, I felt that Ikeda seemed to have imaginatively represented the traditional doctrine of NS, yet in fact he has made some rather subtle but striking modifications and rectifications to the traditional NS doctrine. Also in the passage quoted above, he asserts that "the true reality of our life within the Ten Worlds is Nam-myō-hō-ren-ge-kyō Tathāgata" and that "we are at one with it".

For Ikeda Nam-myō-hō-ren-ge-kyō Tathāgata is not restricted as to its essence and function only to the Daishōnin.

---

9. The Dharma Body of Essential Entrustment

As the title of this chapter suggests, Shakyamuni Buddha and the other buddhas displayed their supernatural powers to open up a whole universe replete with Buddhas, Bodhisattvas and all other sentient beings, as well as endowed with beautiful flowers and wonderful precious items, the revelation of a unique and wondrous Buddha Pure Land. Then Shakyamuni Buddha in the midst of the assembly spoke directly to Jōgyō, the leader of the Bodhisattvas of the Earth:

> The supernatural powers of the buddhas, as you have seen, are immeasurable, boundless, inconceivable. If in the process of entrusting this sutra to others I were to employ these supernatural powers for immeasurable, [...] millions of asamkhya kalpas to describe the benefits of the sutra, I could never finish doing so. *To put it briefly, all the doctrines possessed by the Tathāgata, all the freely exercised supernatural powers of the Tathāgata, the storehouse of all the secret essentials of the Tathāgata, all the most profound matters of the Tathāgata — all these are proclaimed, revealed, and clearly expounded in this sutra.* (LS, p. 315 f.)

Shakyamuni Buddha entrusts the Bodhisattvas of the Earth with the mission of propagating this great Dharma in our Sahā World full of suffering in the time after his death. Subsequently, this commission will also be given to all other bodhisattvas in the next chapter (which is concerned with the "General Entrustment").

With respect to the so-called "phrases concerning the essential entrustment", marked in italics in the above quotation, T'ien-t'ai had in fact defined them under a schema of "Five-fold Significance", according to which he sought to expound the meaning of the title of the LS at a more profound level. These are as follows:

Phrases of essential entrustment	Fivefold significance of the Sutra
All the doctrines possessed by the Tathāgata	Interpreting the "Name" = the title of the sutra
The storehouse of all the secret essential wisdom of the Tathāgata	Defining the "Body" = the essence of the sutra
All the most profound matters of the Tathāgata	Expounding the "Doctrine" = the essential doctrines for attaining enlightenment
All the freely exercised supernatural powers of the Tathāgata	Explaining the "Function" = the merits and functions of the sutra for saving all beings
All these are proclaimed, revealed, and clearly expounded in this sutra	Judging the "Teaching" = the theoretical dimension of the sutra

Thus, "all dharmas of the Tathāgata" were transmitted directly to Jōgyō and his followers. However, the discussion is centered around the question of whether what is referred to are the teachings of Shakyamuni Buddha or not. On the level of a literal reading of the LS, it is clearly the LS itself which is to be propagated, as the quoted passage is directly followed by the exhortation: *"For this reason, after the Tathāgata has entered extinction, you must single-mindedly accept, uphold, read, recite, explain, preach, and transcribe it, and practice it as directed"* (LS, p. 316). The practices referred to above are consequently known as the "five kinds of practicing the LS as a bundle of scripture".

Yet for Nichiren the Lotus Sutra with its twenty-eight chapters is not that which is to be propagated. With respect to this, the following passage is quoted from the OTT, i.e. from the section "Regarding the Tathāgata's supernatural powers revealed in the Lotus Sutra":

> This Myōhō-renge-kyō is not the Wonderful Law of Shakyamuni Buddha, because, at the time of the entrustment ceremony in this chapter, the essence of the sutra had already been transmitted to the Bodhisattva Jōgyō.
> (p. 770 / OTT 167)

Ikeda explains that our days are the time in which to propagate the Daimoku, it is the time in which the Buddhist Law of Sowing is operative. The Bodhisattva Jōgyō is the "Bodhisattva embodying in his whole body all the properties of the Tathāgata", and he is to be defined as a "Bodhisattva Buddha" (ibid. p. 5). As he is a Buddha in essence, he is distinct from the Eternal Buddha Shakyamuni, who represents the Original Effect which is gained by practicing the Original Cause. The Original Cause that Jōgyō embodies includes the "virtues of effect (Buddha World) in his status as cause (Nine Worlds). Consequently, he represents the dimension of Original Cause in contrast to Original Effect.

Ikeda goes on to refer to the phrase which reveals the profound aspect that the Eternal Buddha Shakyamuni himself once practiced the bodhisattva way in order to attain enlightenment in the remotest past:

> Thus, since I attained Buddhahood, an extremely long period of time has passed. [...] Good men, *originally I practiced the bodhisattva way*, and the life span that I acquired then has yet to come to an end but will last twice the number of years that have already passed. (LS, p. 267 f.)

Indeed, this sentence *"originally I practiced the bodhisattva way"* plays a most significant role if the doctrinal position of ND is to be fully understood. Yet it is strange that Ikeda doesn't focus his analysis on the "Law" but rather on an original Buddha in oneness with the law.

Honorary President: Consequently, there was a "law" because he devoted himself to the practice of it. This would mean that there was a time when the law was operative but without the buddha teaching it. This would lead to the conclusion that there was no "Buddha at one with the universe without beginning and without end".

Suda: Certainly, if a buddha had appeared at a certain time he would not be the "permanently abiding Buddha throughout the three existences of past, present and future".

Endo: The Daishōnin criticized the Buddha Shakyamuni of Initial Enlightenment as a consequence of the logical incoherence of "abiding without origin" and consequently as being like a "rootless grass". Yet the same criticism can be applied to "Shakyamuni from the remotest past" as this eternal Buddha's origin was only at a certain point in the past. Strictly speaking, each concept of attaining Buddhahood merely suggests "being a Buddha abiding in the present without revealing the origin" yet not "originally abiding as a Buddha".

Saito: If a Buddha does not have the characteristics of "original existence" he cannot be said to be the "original Buddha" abiding throughout the three existences. (ibid., p. 6)

The most problematic assumption here is the idea that there wasn't "*a Buddha in oneness with the universe without beginning and without end*" at the very moment when Shakyamuni practiced the Bodhisattva way prior to his attainment of enlightenment in the remotest past. This issue has already been addressed in the previous section with respect to the principle of the "mutual possession of the beginningless Ten Worlds" expounded in »The Opening of the Eyes". This principle is related to the "Doctrine of Original Cause and Original Effect", but it has been interpreted by way of reference to "the eternal original Buddha without beginning and without end". This Buddha was considered by Nichiren Daishōnin as the "teaching master of the Mystic Principle of Original Cause." Yet this view likewise implies simply "*going back to a certain point in the past*".

However, a more profound view emerges from a much deeper reading and reflection – although this will be the main subject considered in Part Three – from this more profound perspective the attainment of Buddhahood in the remotest past is read as identical to "direct sudden or immediate enlightenment representing Ichinen Sanzen based on the Mutual Containment of the Ten Worlds". Even if one might accept the attained effect to be the Buddha state which has been thereby attained in this life, one cannot also thereby demonstrate the "Original Buddha without beginning and without end" (ibid., p. 7). The only reasonable solution to this is to assert the existence of the "*beginningless ancient Buddha*", as Nichiren expresses it in »The Object of

Devotion for Observing the Mind« (p. 246 / 365), that is to say, Original Enlightenment or Buddha-nature is essentially inherent within all our lives. Consequently, we can conclude the present discussion as follows:

> Only Original Enlightenment represents the "Buddha-nature of true cause" that is inherent within all people. There is absolutely no need to assume an eternal and transcendent Original Buddha who is claimed to be more fundamental than Shakyamuni who attained enlightenment in the remotest past.

However, given the above, now the Bodhisattva Jōgyō should be considered to be a "Buddha" (ibid.).

> Bodhisattva Jōgyō
> = the Buddha of the Original Cause
> = the Buddha of the simultaneity of cause and effect
> = the eternal original Buddha without beginning and without end
> = the Tathāgata of the wisdom body at the original beginning in the remotest past
> = Nam-myō-hō-ren-ge-kyō Tathāgata

Nevertheless, to assert that Bodhisattva Jōgyō is the Tathāgata of the wisdom body at the original beginning in the remotest past and, therefore, that he is the master of Shakyamuni in the remotest past would appear to be nothing other than "deification". By contrast, if you wish to understand "the beginningless ancient Buddha" or "originally existing Enlightenment" in terms of "cosmic life", it should mean at most an impersonal Dharma body or wisdom body representing that wisdom by which Buddhahood is attained. It is this which should be considered to be the teaching lord for Shakyamuni. However, as is further expounded in the dialogue, if the term the "original beginning of eternity" is interpreted as the cosmic life considered in a wholly universalistic sense, the term becomes redundant. Further, to retain the term would cause confusion and would be a hindrance to opening up to all people the Buddhism of Sowing which is the Mystic Principle of the Original Cause. Indeed, Ikeda would indeed appear to have intended to reinterpret traditional NS doctrine in this radically distinctive direction, as follows:

Suda: In this context, as discussed up to this point, the term "the original beginning of eternity" no longer implies a "certain remote past time", does it? Rather, it breaks through the whole framework of time and it no longer remains simply as a "calculation with respect to time".

Honorary President: That's right. The "original beginning of eternity" is another name for "life without beginning and without end". It is not a theory about time but rather a theory about life. It points to the truth of the profundity of life, to that cosmic life which itself has continued to actively function or practice without beginning and without end. It is identical with that which is designated the "Tathāgata endowed with the three bodies without intention". [...] It means "originally existing". [...] It means the state of the ordinary man as he is, the state of "originally and permanently existing", and "as it is originally". These states are called "the remotest past" or "the eternal". It is nothing other than "Nam-myō-hō-ren-ge-kyō". It is represented by the Gohonzon. Consequently, every time we worship the Gohonzon, each moment is the "original beginning of eternity in the remotest past". Thus, we live everyday in eternity. Everyday we are able to be replete throughout our whole body with that pure great compassionate life which itself is eternal. Everyday we can make anew that "original beginning of eternity" and our life can represent that "original source of life".

Saito: That's exactly what "the Mystic Principle of Original Cause" means, isn't it?

Honorary President: Indeed, and the "now" is the most important. [...] Consequently, if we seriously commit ourselves to "propagating the Mystic Law of Eternity" (*Kōsenrufu*), then we will ourselves experience "the dawn of the original beginning of eternity" welling up from deep within our own lives. (II-8)

Here, we can note a wonderful re-interpretation of the term "the remotest past" or "the original beginning of eternity". In discussing this term earlier, Ikeda spoke using the traditional NS doctrinal terms such as that Shakyamuni had attained enlightenment in the "remotest past" under the guidance of the master who is the "Buddha of the original beginning of eternity", but here he now expressly states that this is much more profoundly a "concept beyond time" which should be seen as explanatory with respect to a general theory of cosmic life.

The Original Beginning of Eternity
= The Cosmic Life without beginning and without end
= The Tathāgata endowed with the three bodies without intention
= The Ordinary human person just as he or she is
= Original and permanent existence
= Nam-myō-hō-ren-ge-kyō
= The eternal Mystic Law

According to this understanding, it might be said that from deep within our own hearts the cosmic life or Buddha-nature without beginning and without end will well up and be manifested whenever we chant Daimoku before the

Gohonzon. This is because it is exactly the same to or identical with that Mystic Law which Shakyamuni had practiced in the remotest past and therefore it is a Buddhist law characterized by such features as the eternal principle of the simultaneity of original cause and original effect. And in fact, both Toda and Ikeda were speaking about a life theory which can adequately explain the realization of enlightenment by ordinary people. That is,

> The philosophical understanding with respect to the Buddhism of Sowing can be redeployed as the foundation or referent to the beginningless and endless great cosmic life or Buddha nature itself
> without any need to make use of the traditional phrase
> "the original beginning in the remotest past".

10. The Eternal Bodhisattva as Buddha

Subsequently, the discussion turns to the Dharma body which Bodhisattva Jōgyō received from Shakyamuni Buddha. However, it is not the scripture of the "Lotus Sutra consisting of twenty-eight chapters", but rather "Nam-myō-hō-ren-ge-kyō" understood from the perspective of a far deeper reading, i.e. as the Law that he had originally embraced. To establish this truth is indeed the primary objective of the chapter concerning the "Supernatural Powers of the Tathāgata". Consequently, this chapter should be regarded as a so-called "proof document" and as a representation of the relationship between the "trace or shadow" and the original essence.

Honorary President: [...] Regarding the relationship between the "original essence and its shadow", the difference is like that between heaven and earth. In the »One Hundred and Six Comparisons« it is said:

> A Comparison between the Essence and the Shadow with respect to the Entrustment of the essential teaching:
> At the time when I received the Mystic Law at the verbal stage of identity of an ordinary person, the Mystic Law I received was the essence while the bodhisattvas like Jōgyō represent its shadow. The special entrustment at the original beginning of eternity has a meaning identical with the entrustment of the Life Span chapter today. (p. 865 / -)

This text is difficult to understand, but the point being made is that Nichiren Daishōnin has in fact been manifesting the Law of Nam-myō-hō-ren-ge-kyō in his very body as an ordinary person throughout all eternity. From the perspective of the "true essence", the ceremony of entrusting the law to bodhisattvas such as Jōgyō, as depicted in the Lotus Sutra, is characterized as its "projected shadow". The words and phrases of the Sutra are thereby characterized as a paper representation of the law and a scriptural prediction of the mission of the Daishōnin himself which is to propagate the Mystic Law in actuality. To put it in another way: The "Tathāgata Nam-myō-hō-ren-ge-kyō" projected "his shadow" on to a screen known as the Lotus Sutra, in order that the figures of Shakyamuni who attained enlightenment in the remotest past (Buddha World) and Bodhisattva Jōgyō might appear. So, it can be said that the Mystic Law is the "true entity" while the Bodhisattva Jōgyō represents its "shadow". (II-9)

In the »One Hundred and Six Comparisons« Nichiren is described not only as "the teaching master of the Mystic Principle of the Original Cause" and the "great master of the Essential Teaching" but also as the *"Lord of Original Cause and Original Effect who came from the Pure Land of Eagle Peak, from within the Treasure Tower, which is a representation of eternal enlightenment [...] as well as the reincarnation of the Bodhisattva Jōgyō who represents the trace shadow of the true essence as the wisdom body"* (p. 854 / -). It is claimed in this capacity that Nichiren entrusted to Nikkō the "transfer document" which contains his important teachings in summary form. Yet it is beyond doubt that this document is not an authentic writing of Nichiren himself.[13] This document's inauthenticity is also evidenced by the document's dubious philosophical perspective and construction, according to which Nichiren was projected back to the original beginning in the remotest past in order that he could be regarded as "the wisdom body" that subsequently cast his shadow as the Bodhisattva Jōgyō in the Lotus Sutra and as the historical person Nichiren in the Latter Day of Law.

Such a mythological way of understanding reminds us of the central mystery of orthodox Christian faith that there is only "one God in three divine persons" (the Trinity): The Father, the Son (Jesus Christ) and the Holy Spirit. It is believed that Jesus was sent by the Creator God as Messiah who was then crucified to redeem mankind from Original Sin. After his death and burial, he was resurrected and appeared again and subsequently ascended to heaven. Consequently, the doctrine of the "Buddha at the original beginning of eternity in the Unity of Buddha and Dharma" has a striking resemblance with such a personified God in Heaven. Such a mystery characterizing the person of Nichiren cannot be considered to be in any way authentically Buddhist and in fact rather represents the advent of a speculative mythology.

---

[13] The term "the original beginning in the remotest past" (*Kuonganjo*) appears exclusively in the two transfer documents of NS: »The Mystic Principle of the Original Cause« (*Hon'inmyō shō*) and »The One Hundred and Six Comparisons« (*Hyakurokka shō*). This phrase is central to the reasoning which seeks to give justification to the Doctrine of Nichiren as the Eternal Original Buddha. In this connection Miyata has confirmed that this doctrine can't be found in the writings of the first four abbots from the founder Nikkō up to the 4th abbot Nichidō (1283-1341) (see Miyata's articles on Nichiu and Nikkō).

In contrast, there is little problem in speaking of an eternal cosmic life without beginning and without end, i.e. when understood from the perspective of a cosmic life theory. For from this perspective, an adequate and universal explanation can be given both for the source of life and for we ourselves, as well as for the life and thought of the Daishōnin.

Yet an understanding such as "My life is identical with the cosmic life" would appear to very nearly approach the Vedantic concept of "Tat Tvam Asi" (You are that), interpreted to mean that the principle of an unchangeable individual "Atman (Self)" is the ultimate reality of the universe or "Brahman". Of course, Buddhism began as a religious and philosophical movement radically critical of the Hindu or Brahmanical substantialist philosophy and the Buddha taught the doctrine of "Anātman (Non-self)". For the Buddha held that if the self is taken to be unchanging and permanent, i.e. if it is characterized as the essential center of a human life or as an unchanging, permanent or eternal soul, then this a fundamentally "wrong view" and indeed the fundamental root and primary source of all illusion and suffering. In contrast, Buddhism teaches that all things have no substantial nature or permanent self and all things are radically dependent on each other. Nothing ever remains permanently as it is. This insight is classically given definition in the doctrine of "Dependent Origination or Arising" (pratītya-samutpāda). Because everything is ephemeral, to cling to anything causes suffering. In other words, all things are empty of intrinsic existence and self-nature, and the way to salvation lies in liberation from emotional and bodily attachment and realizing or attaining to the state of non-self, nirvana. This concept is expressed by the Mahayana doctrine of "Emptiness" (śūnyatā).

The main reason for the Buddhist rejection of the Hindu or Brahmanical principle of individual essence was because of the Buddha's radical rejection of any substantialist metaphysical assertion, which asserted a fixed, unchanging and permanent nature at the root of all dharmas or all reality. Consequently, I consider it to be authentically Buddhist to speak about the self not in such a substantialist sense but rather in the sense of a perpetually changing and interdependent process. Indeed, there is no doubt that our lives are part of nature, i.e. both of mother earth and of the whole universe. All things are physically and actively interlinked and connected. Indeed, actively communicating with each other. Further, on the level of consciousness, we enter a spiritual world which transcends our individual ego when we chant Daimoku or engage in any meditation practice. This spiritual state represents the state of "Non-Self" and this can be also understood as the level of consciousness that is vividly depicted metaphorically as the Ceremony in the Air.

The Mandala honzon represents and manifests the spiritual world as a unity of our individual consciousness and

> the infinite cosmic consciousness, the enlightened world
> which transcends our everyday ego consciousness and
> the space-time dimension itself.

With respect to the above, the most adequate and correct understanding is quite simple: The Mystic Law was entrusted by the eternal Buddha Shakyamuni via Bodhisattva Jōgyō to Nichiren; or, conversely, that Nichiren himself discovered the Dharma body of the Buddhism of Sowing at the attainment of Buddhahood in the remotest past and subsequently propagated it in his capacity as a reincarnation of Bodhisattva Jōgyō. For the Buddhism of Sowing in the Latter Day of the Law represents the practice of chanting Daimoku in order that we, ordinary human persons, may realize Instant Enlightenment. Concerning the status of the Daishōnin, he is surely "the Teaching Lord and the True Buddha in the Latter Day of the Law" who has taught and propagated this practice, but he nevertheless doesn't need to be deified as an "Original Buddha of eternity". No, on the contrary, such a mythological deification would radically discount all the suffering and joy that Nichiren endured and experienced in his ordinary human life, as well as radically detracting from the greatness and sublimity of Nichiren's own achievement in his historical struggle to propagate the Mystic Law. As Ikeda himself highlighted it in section 6 "A Nichiren Buddhist Humanism", we should return to "Nichiren, as a human being" if we seek to "establish a new Buddhist Humanism". The humanist theory of the ordinary person as true Buddha and of life theory are logically consistent with each other, yet both contradict the Doctrine of Nichiren as the Eternal Original Buddha. Indeed, if the term "the original beginning of Eternity" remains closely linked to traditional NS doctrine, we should reject it as an incoherent and incomprehensible concept, unsuited to our contemporary age. Further, the term "the Tathāgata of the wisdom body at the original beginning in the remotest past" should also be discarded, as it assumes a primordially actually existing (individual and personal) Buddha at the beginning of eternity. Nevertheless, where the law is characterized or defined as the "eternal Mystic Law", this would be in accord with Nichiren's teaching as it points directly to the law of attaining Buddhahood that can be found by a more meditative deeper reading of the Life Span chapter of the LS itself.

11. The Theory that Every Ordinary Person is a True Buddha

Further on, Ikeda interprets the essential entrustment given by the Buddha Shakyamuni to the Bodhisattva Jōgyō as meaning more generally the essential entrustment given by the Buddha World to the Nine Worlds. If so understood, it also implicitly includes an assertion of the universally applicable theory that "every ordinary person is a true Buddha". For it means that no Buddha can exist apart from the Nine Worlds of an ordinary human person or that no Buddha can actually exist other than as a Bodhisattva. In other words, there is no Buddha who is not a "Bodhisattva Buddha". This particular view is arrived at by reasoning with respect to the "principle of the simultaneity of cause and effect in that the virtues as effects are contained in the actions presenting the causes. This principle represents the enlightened character of the fundamental Buddha of the universe" (II-9).

> *Honorary President:* I am saying that a brilliantly illuminated Buddha exists only "in a dream". It does not actually exist. To tell the truth, the only really existing "Buddha" is a quite ordinary person who is actually practicing the life of the original beginning of eternity at every moment. There is no "Buddha" apart from being "a human being". A Buddha considered to be beyond a human being" is a fake. It is an expedient means. Therefore, it is imperative for every one of us to live as a human being, to go on the "the noble road" as a human being. The crowning of the road can also only be attained as a human being. That person is the "Buddha". The Lotus Sutra is teaching this truth, and the representation of the significance of this transformation into such a Buddhist humanism is to be found in the ceremony of "entrustment to the Bodhisattva Jōgyō" in the chapter concerning the supernatural powers of the Tathāgata. (ibid.)

Here, Ikeda is talking about a radically "humanistic Buddhism". In an identical way to "the enlightened character of the fundamental Buddha of the universe", we ordinary persons (of the Nine Worlds) practice the Mystic Law of the Simultaneity of Cause and Effect so that we may manifest an enlightened character, in so far as we are "activating the life of the original beginning of eternity at every moment". However, in order to give adequate expression to this enlightened state of life manifested by ordinary persons in contemporary times, there is no need to use the term "the life of the original beginning of eternity". Rather isn't it just sufficient to talk about the eternal cosmic life without beginning and without end?

12. Transcending the Philosophy of Original Enlightenment

The dialogue then returns to the theme of the "manifestation of Shakyamuni's true identity". Ikeda calls this event as depicted in the Sutra "the factual manifestation", yet by way of contrast he prefers the term "the theoretical manifestation" as an alternative to "the manifestation of the Tathāgata with wisdom body at the original beginning of eternity". Further, he interprets the manifestation in the Life Span Chapter as "Shakyamuni's personal manifestation of the essence" within his own human life, while the "manifestation viewed from the perspective of a deeper reading" is given a more universal meaning (ibid.).

> *Honorary President:* It means a manifestation on the level of the entire universe. It is about the whole manifestation of all people of the Ten Worlds from ordinary man to Buddha. [...] The true intention of the Life Span Chapter lies in the revelation of the perfect "eternal Buddha (with the wisdom body at the original beginning in the remotest past)". This "eternal Buddha" is at one with the Mystic Law without beginning and without end. It is the great life of the universe itself and represents the Unity of the Buddha and Dharma.
> *Endo:* That means, all creatures in the universe are, just as they are, "eternal Buddha".
> *Honorary President:* All lives are originally Buddha. This is the proclamation of the Life Span Chapter. The Lotus Sutra is seeking to awaken all to this truth.
> *Saito:* If I may be permitted to summarize the key point of our discussion as follows: the manifestation from the perspective of a literal reading refers to the circumstances of "Shakyamuni as an individual person", yet the manifestation from the perspective of a deeper reading represents that of "all Dharma realms (Ten Worlds)". (II-10)

The argument as developed here is difficult to understand as two distinct elements of meaning are somewhat intermixed. I will attempt to unpick them in order to get a clearer view.

The Aspect based on the Philosophy of Original Enlightenment:
> All people of the Ten Worlds
> = Ordinary people just as they are
> = The great life of the universe

The Aspect based on the Doctrine of the Eternal Original Buddha:
> Eternal Buddha with the wisdom body
> at the original beginning of eternity
> = at one with the Mystic Law without beginning and without end
> = The Unity of the Buddha and Dharma

The first aspect reminds us of the way of thinking found in »The Record of the Orally Transmitted Teachings«. An example of this way of thinking can be found in the following passage:

> Point One, concerning Chapter Sixteen, The Life Span of the Tathāgata of Nam-myō-hō-ren-ge-kyō
>
> The Record of the Orally Transmitted Teachings says: The title of this chapter deals with an important matter that concerns Nichiren himself. This is the transmission described in the Supernatural Powers chapter. The Tathāgata is Shakyamuni Buddha or, more generally speaking, all the Buddhas of the ten directions and the three existences. More specifically, it refers to the original entity eternally endowed with the Three Bodies without Intention.
>
> Now it is the understanding of Nichiren and his followers that, generally speaking, the Tathāgata refers to all living beings. More specifically, it refers to the disciples and lay supporters of Nichiren. This being the case, the term "eternally endowed with the Three Bodies without Intention" refers to the votaries of the Lotus Sutra in the Latter Day of the Law. The honorable title of the Three Bodies without Intention is Nam-myō-hō-ren-ge-kyō. [...]
>
> Speaking of the chapter as a whole, the idea of gradually overcoming illusions is not the ultimate meaning of the Life Span chapter. You should understand that the ultimate truth of this chapter is that ordinary mortals, just as they are in their original state of being, are Nam-myō-hō-ren-ge-kyō. (p. 752 / OTT 123)

> Point One, concerning the supernatural powers of the Tathāgata of Nam-myō-hō-ren-ge-kyō
>
> The Record of the Orally Transmitted Teachings says: This Myōhō-renge-kyō is not the Wonderful Law of Shakyamuni Buddha, because, at the time of the transfer ceremony in this chapter, the essence of the sutra has already been transmitted to the Bodhisattva Jōgyō. [...]
>
> These supernatural powers are the Daimoku, *Nam-myō-hō-ren-ge-kyō*, that Nichiren and his followers are now chanting. [...]
>
> The Tathāgata refers to all living beings, as has already been explained in the section on the Life Span Chapter. (p. 770 / OTT 167)

On the one hand, under the theoretical aspect, »The Record of Orally Transmitted Teachings« is replete with Original Enlightenment Thought in that all ordinary persons, just as they are, are the Tathāgata endowed with the three bodies without intention. Yet on the other hand, under the factual aspect, it also makes reference to an idea of mediation by way of the practice of chanting the Daimoku. Consequently, to stress it once again, if you simply insist that the actual world just as it is would represent the manifestation of originally existing enlightenment, this idea might be regarded as nothing other than an ideology for affirming the status quo. To avoid such a misunderstanding, you need to maintain a dualism between the Nine Worlds and the Buddha World and to mediate it by way of the character "*soku*" (-equal-) which represents the principle of transformation. Consequently, the practice of chanting the Daimoku is the means by which Buddhahood can be activated in the Nine Worlds. In fact, this is the actual meaning of the dialectical principle of "The Nine Worlds -equal- the Buddha World".

Regarding the doctrine of the eternal original Buddha, such related terms as "the original beginning in the remotest past" and "the Tathāgata of the wisdom body" are especially made use of in the NS transfer documents like »The Mystic Principle of the Original Cause« and »The One Hundred and Six Comparisons". In addition to the above quoted passage on the "Essential Entrustment at the original beginning of eternity" (p. 865 / -), the latter document contains two significant passages:

> Comparison between the Essence and the Shadow with respect to the Teaching Lord of the Lotus Sutra and the Sowing of the Seed:
> The wisdom body is the essence while Jōgyō Nichiren represents its shadow. Our secret Life Span Chapter means the Mystic Law of the Original Cause which deeply underlies and is found in the depths of the Life Span Chapter which describes the Harvesting of the Fruit. I am its teaching master. (p. 863 / -)

> Comparison between the Essence and the Shadow with respect to the Teaching Lord in the three domains of the present and the Sowing of the Seed:
> "There is no equal to me below heaven and on this earth" at the original beginning of eternity. This phrase refers to me, Nichiren. The remotest past is the essence while the present day represents its shadow. The Nichiren who is permanently dwelling in the three existences benefits ordinary people in their verbal stage of identity. (ibid.)

Likewise, »The Mystic Principle of the Original Cause« emphasizes the doctrinal position from the perspective of deep reading and meditation as described in "The teaching of One Heart and the Dharma World, the doctrine found in the depths of and underlying the 'Life Span' Chapter, the true Essential Teaching of the Tathāgata of the Wisdom Body, and the Nam-myō-hō-ren-ge-kyō of the eternal Ichinen" (p. 871 / -). This Buddhism of the Mystic Principle of the Original Cause proclaims Nichiren to be the Eternal Original Buddha. Further, the following assertions are also made by way of comparison between Tendai's Meditation based on the Theoretical Teaching and Nichiren's Meditation based on the Essential Teaching:

> Tendai posits that the difference between the superior and the inferior part is to be found within the Lotus Sutra while Nichiren considers the entire Sutra to be a shadow.
> Tendai inherited to the domain of the Physical Body while Nichiren embraced a deeper understanding found in the depths of the Life Span Chapter.
> Tendai practiced the *threefold contemplation in a single mind* and Ichinen Sanzen based on the Wisdom Body emanating from the Physical Body while Nichiren without hesitation at once chants the Mystic Law that originally and naturally belongs to the Wisdom Body at the Original Beginning of Eternity. (p. 875 f. / -)

The NS-Nichikan Doctrine was ultimately established by taking the "theory of Nichiren as the Eternal Original Buddha" proclaimed in these transfer documents to be fundamental and thereby grounding faith in the Dai-gohonzon as a Unity of the Buddha and Dharma. However, today, we know that these transfer documents and the Dai-gohonzon are in fact the pious forgeries of later generations of believers subsequent to Nichiren's own death. More negatively, these teachings have been misused in order to establish the authoritarian structure of NS institutions. Consequently, we need to exclude these particular NS doctrines from any truly humanistic understanding of Nichiren Buddhism.

Summary

We have explored the four different philosophical elements which Ikeda expounded in his discourse »The Wisdom of the Lotus Sutra« in the late 1990's. This particular context can be best understood as a time in which he intended not to immediately discard traditional NS doctrines, but to gradually reconstruct a new doctrinal perspective for SG. Consequently, some of these philosophical and doctrinal changes have proved to be transient, evidence of an attempt at reconstruction. Each should be considered in the following order:

Traditional NS doctrine
»»» Theory of Cosmic Life
»»» Original Enlightenment Thought
»»» Theory of the ordinary man as true Buddha

In the "Afterword" ClearSky gave his opinion with respect to any further doctrinal revision facing SG in the future:

- The change of doctrine as a consequence of constitutional revision is continuing. There are rumors that the fundamental significance of the Personal Object of Worship (Nichiren as the Eternal Original Buddha) is to be downplayed or discarded, there will be further review of some of Nichikan's traditional doctrines, as well as anticipated changes with respect to the "Gosho". Is it now the time when each one of us should seriously think about what exactly SG teaching should be?
- The revision to the doctrinal clause of the constitutional rule was allegedly pushed through by the influence of Professor Miyata of Soka University. At least, so far as can be understood from his statements (especially from the lecture he gave to the conference of the Japan Association for Religious Studies in 2015) and from articles posted on his home page, he has surely been in a position to influence the Study Department of SG.
- Foremost amongst many academic theses proposed by Miyata, attention should most be given to his "denial of Nichiren as the Original Buddha". He constructed his academic thesis beginning with a presupposition that "the Daishōnin never declared himself to be the Original Buddha". Of course, he should be free to construct his own academic thesis, yet if his understanding is to be accepted doctrinally within SG, it should be carefully examined. Above all else, it should be explained in a sufficiently persuasive manner, in order to be properly understood and accepted by the SG membership more widely.
- With respect Miyata's paper, Suda, the former deputy director of the SG Study Department, reacted by submitting an article entitled "Raising Questions about Miyata's Thesis – A Reflection on the Doctrine of Nichiren as True Buddha". It should be recommended reading. Suda's article considers the Doctrine of Nichiren as the Original Buddha from a multi-angled deeply-learned perspective. This article presents a crucial opportunity to rediscover a doctrinally acceptable perspective on the Daishōnin. (II-14)

Given this background, I will now track the Miyata/Suda controversy and make my own comments on it.

Chapter 3
Comments on the Miyata/Suda Controversy

In this chapter I will deal with the controversy provoked by Miyata's article (27-09-2015) and Suda's reply (14-09-2016). In fact, Suda both raised questions about Miyata's conclusions and expounded his own views in a systematic order, presented in seven points.

Consequently, I will seek to follow this order of debate as a means by which to give my own considered opinion on each of the articles. In brief, my conclusion is that Miyata has attempted to advance a modernizing position in order to discard traditional NS Nichikan doctrine, while Suda has sought to reaffirm a conservative stance in order to defend and maintain traditional doctrine.

1. Can the Believers of all other Nichiren sects also obtain merit by faith in any "honzon of the essential teaching"?

Miyata understands SG's abandonment of faith in the Dai-gohonzon as a means of correcting "the traditional, exclusivistic and self-righteous claim that merits and benefits can be obtained only by faith in the Honzon of the High Sanctuary". He has fully understood the dialectical necessity and progression towards "universalization", a required characteristic of any contemporary global religion. Yet Suda firmly opposes any such progressive tendency by falling back on a deeply traditional standpoint, i.e. "that SG members gain merit only through the bloodline of correct faith" and quotes the following passage in support of his contention:

> Even embracing the Lotus Sutra would be useless without the heritage [or bloodline] of faith.
> (»The Heritage of the Ultimate Law of Life«, p. 1338 / I. 218).

Yet this is disingenuous. The context of the passage is a discussion about an attitude to faith which has nothing to do with the requirement of institutional affiliation. That is to say, ND is speaking about the "bloodline of faith" as it relates solely to the pure practice of the Mystic Law, i.e. independent of any institutional or organizational considerations. The true sense of the above passage becomes clearer if we quote the whole section from which the passage has been taken:

> Be resolved to summon forth the great power of faith and chant Nam-myō-hō-ren-ge-kyō with the prayer that your faith will be steadfast and correct at the moment of death. Never seek any other way to inherit the ultimate Law of life and death. Only then will you realize that earthly desires are equal to enlightenment, and that the sufferings of birth and death are equal to nirvana. Even embracing the Lotus Sutra would be useless without the heritage of faith. (ibid.)

In addition, Suda gives justification for his position by stating that *"Soka Gakkai never accepted that the faith and doctrines of other Nichiren sects (such as Nichiren Shū of Minobusan-kuonji or Nakayama-Hokekyōji) were authentic or orthodox and indeed considered that such sects promoted false or heterodox teachings"* and further that *"Once we change this strict attitude, it would mean betraying members who have been practicing their faith in accordance with all previous guidance received from the Soka Gakkai leadership"*. He is describing the highly charged emotional dilemma faced by many SG members, yet on the other hand, he is seeking justification for a deeply conservative stance by way of "retrospective argumentation".

Soka Gakkai has been firmly based up until now on the doctrine of the "bloodline of faith" whereby the only correct or orthodox faith is represented by this bloodline which has its foundation in »The Heritage of the Ultimate Law of Life«. »An Introduction to Buddhist Study«, published by the SG Study Department in 2015, further elaborates as follows:

Nichiren Daishōnin has clearly shown that the bloodline [or heritage] for attaining Buddhahood is not the exclusive possession of a particular person, but rather it is open to all people. In »The Heritage of the Ultimate Law of Life« the Daishōnin states that "Nichiren has been trying to awaken all the people of Japan to faith in the Lotus Sutra so that they too can share in the heritage for attaining Buddhahood" (p. 1337 / II. 218). In the Buddhism of Nichiren Daishōnin, all talk about the "bloodline" culminates in the conclusion that the definition of 'faith' is as expressed in the phrase 'the faith of the bloodline' (p. 1338 / II. 218) (»An Introduction to Buddhist Study«, p. 318)

Nevertheless, it is self-contradictory to claim that SG alone is holding to *"the bloodline of the correct faith"* while at the same time Suda seeks to stress the Daishōnin's conviction that *"the bloodline [or heritage] for attaining Buddhahood [...] is open to all people"*. For, as a matter of fact, this "bloodline of faith" necessarily must be open to all those who chant Daimoku faithfully. We gain further support for this fundamental understanding from the same Gosho »The Heritage of the Ultimate Law of Life«:

> All disciples and lay believers of Nichiren should chant Nam-myō-hō-ren-ge-kyō with the spirit of *many in body but one in mind* [*itaidōshin*], transcending all differences among themselves to become as inseparable as fish and the water in which they swim. This spiritual bond is the basis for the universal transmission of the ultimate Law of life and death. Herein lies the true goal of Nichiren's propagation. When you are so united, even the great desire for *widespread propagation* [*Kōsenrufu*] can be fulfilled.
> But if any of Nichiren's disciples disrupt the unity of many in body but one in mind, they would be like warriors who destroy their own castle from within. Nichiren has been trying to awaken all the people of Japan to faith in the Lotus Sutra so that they too can share the heritage of attaining Buddhahood" (p. 1337 / II. 218).

To repeat once again, the heritage or bloodline of faith refers to everyone who chants Daimoku faithfully and this is the deep foundation to that spiritual fellowship which transcends particular organizational or doctrinal issues. We should all recognize the fact that it is open to all believers of any temple affiliation or from any Nichiren school. For everyone who chants Daimoku should undoubtedly be considered to be a disciple of Nichiren, a votary of the Lotus Sutra, and as such a Bodhisattva of the Earth. This fundamental fact remains ever true on the level of faith and practice and is independent of any institutional affiliation. If we share this fundamental understanding, we are all encouraged to mutually respect each other and to work together for Kōsenrufu.

> Now, no matter what, strive in faith and be known as a votary of the Lotus Sutra, and remain my disciple for the rest of your life. If you are of the same mind as Nichiren, you must be a Bodhisattva of the Earth. […] There should be no discrimination among those who propagate the five characters of Myōhō-renge-kyō in the Latter Day of the Law, be they men or women. Were they not Bodhisattvas of the Earth, they could not chant the Daimoku.
> At first only Nichiren chanted Nam-myō-hō-ren-ge-kyō, but then two, three, and a hundred followed, chanting and teaching others. Propagation will unfold this way in the future as well. Does this not signify "emerging from the earth"? (»The True Aspect of All Phenomena«, p. 1360 / II. 385)

Further, by way of aside, the question of the legitimacy and merit of chanting the Daimoku has nothing at all to do with the question of the authenticity of the Gosho »The Heritage of the Ultimate Law of Life". For if the term "the bloodline of faith" is found only in this particular Gosho, the general understanding that those who chant Daimoku will obtain merits and benefits represents the core of Nichiren doctrine and is an understanding found throughout Nichiren's authentic writings. Just to point to some relevant passages:

> The Buddhas of the worlds in the ten directions [...], all are emanations of the one Buddha, Shakyamuni. Therefore, this one Buddha is none other than all Buddhas, and all Buddhas are thus brought together within the two characters of myōhō. For this reason, the benefits to be gained by reciting the five characters of Myōhō-renge-kyō are great indeed.
> (»On Reciting the Daimoku of the Lotus Sutra«, p. 13 / I. 230)

> Shakyamuni's practices and the virtues he consequently attained, these two laws of cause and effect are all contained within the five characters of Myō-hō-ren-ge-kyō. If we believe these five characters, we will naturally be granted the same benefits as he was.
> (»The Object of Devotion for Observing the Mind«, p. 246 / I. 365)

> The five characters of Myō-hō-ren-ge-kyō, the heart of the essential teaching of the Lotus Sutra, contain the benefit amassed through the countless practices and meritorious deeds of all Buddhas throughout the three existences. Then, how can these five characters not include the benefits obtained by observing all of the Buddhas' precepts?
> (»The Teaching, Practice, and Proof«, p. 1282 / I. 481)

Given this guidance of ND, we should seek to correct and indeed abandon and the self-righteous, dogmatic and exclusivistic attitude based upon the traditional NS Nichikan doctrine which SG has internalized up until now.

Further, Suda concedes that all the mandala-honzons that Nichiren himself inscribed, all their copies, and all those inscribed by other priests should be considered to be "*Honmon no honzon*", each embodying Nam-myō-hō-ren-ge-kyō. Yet he still questions "*whether other believers gain benefit by praying and upholding the faith taught at temples such as Kuonji and Hokekyōji. I don't think so*". However, Suda appears to be unaware that he is confusing two different levels of discourse. His doubt might be convincing if directed towards the "faith of other sects", which would include a wide variety of sects worshipping a wide variety of deities. For Nichiren propagated only the sole practice of chanting Daimoku to the Ten Worlds Mandala-gohonzon, but did not encourage (indeed, condemned) the worship of other Buddhas and deities. Yet as SG had officially abandoned its exclusive faith in the Dai-gohonzon, those particular traditional doctrines seeking to legitimate this particular exclusive object of worship need also to be discarded or modified. Consequently, it is odd that Suda himself showed sympathy for the argument in Kinbara's book (2016), as discussed in the previous section "The Fabricated

Myth about the Dai-gohonzon" (see above page 62). We cannot return to the Golden Old Age. Today it is deeply anachronistic and reactionary to speak in such outdated mythological terms as that only SG is in possession of the "correct Gohonzon" and only SG propagates the "correct faith. As was pointed out earlier, such self-righteous and exclusivistic dogmatism is emblematic of a doctrinal foundation destined to foster a dangerous sectarian-orientation throughout the whole body of SG.

2. Is it a failure to make claims with respect to "merits and punishment"?

With respect to the question of "whether or not a believer will be aware of the merit gained by faith", Miyata seeks to investigate this question not only with reference to doctrine but also with regard to the empirical findings of sociology. In fact, in the summer of 2014, I myself carried out a sociological survey by sending out a questionnaire to all members of the German Buddhist Union, asking among other things questions relating to their initial motivation in beginning Buddhist practice, questions about their concrete experiences once they had begun Buddhist practice and questions about the doctrinal aspects of Buddhism which had attracted them. To this survey, which was published in German, entitled »The Fascination of Buddhism – Reasons Why Germans have turned towards Buddhism« (Matsudo 2015), some 578 people responded, including some practitioners of Nichiren Buddhism, Soto-Rinzai Zen, Theravada, Mindfulness and Tibetan Buddhism, as well as those who described themselves as "independent practitioners". I obtained a statistically interesting response, as the differences in practice, as well as culture and doctrine, of each Buddhist school soon became clear. Of course, the subjective basis of this survey was not to objectively evaluate the doctrine and practice of the different Buddhist schools, but rather to analyze what each practitioner was thinking, feeling, experiencing and expecting from Buddhist practice.

I would like to note just some significant points which emerged from the survey's findings, as they would appear to be relevant to the present discussion.

- To the first question which addressed the initial interest in Buddhism, almost half of the respondents sought in Buddhism "assistance in their life " as they were each facing a "life crisis" in the form of a "search for the meaning of life", a "relationship issue", or a struggle with "sickness", or seeking to cope with the "death of a loved one". A further attraction of Buddhism was a positive encounter with Buddhists, either some particular "Buddhist master" or simply "Buddhist friends and acquaintances". Consequently, many Germans had become interested in Buddhism not so

much in an intellectual or theoretical way but rather by way of response to a very personal life crisis or situation.
- After a first contact with Buddhism as a possible solution to a personal life crisis, many became particularly interested in finding inner peace or tranquility. However, the dimension of personal spiritual development and growth became increasingly significant, as this included such considerations as access to enlightenment or a development towards Buddhahood.
- With respect to the "character of the teachings" most of the respondents didn't like a "dogmatic" teaching nor any "idea of God claiming absoluteness". Rather, they were fascinated much more by the idea of „an ethics of personal responsibility", characterized by a positive attitude towards re-creating or transforming their personal life situations.
- Finally, the following question was asked which is relevant to the present issue being considered, i.e. that which concerns the merits or benefit gained by practicing Buddhism: "11. What are your concrete experiences with Buddhism? What in your life has been the most positive or dramatically transformative consequence?" 81% of respondents (468 of 578) acknowledged having experienced a dramatic change in their mental attitude towards their own lives and towards their fellow men. 53% reported having been able to positively overcome such negative feelings as fear, anger or guilt. 73% reported having been able to considerably improve their general mood in daily life, e.g. by becoming more "relaxed" or "more authentic".

Most of the German Buddhists who responded to the questionnaires were much more spiritually and inwardly oriented than SGI members, who have been taught to understand the "merit and benefit of practicing Buddhism" in a more worldly sense. It is generally believed that they chant for a car, a partner, a job, or for success in business and so on. It is just an alternative Buddhist orientation in teaching and practice which I personally find unproblematic, yet I find it essential also to stress the more spiritual dimension which is to be found in Nichiren Buddhism.

Now, independent of all these sociological surveys, Miyata intends only to state that "the monopoly of religious merit by a particular faith must be denied as a matter of fact". Indeed, if you have internalized an exclusivistic dogmatism that your faith alone is correct, you cannot participate in a research survey along with other sects or schools, such as that above. This is because, when compared to other denominations of whatever viewpoint, the absoluteness and the uniqueness of your faith will be relativized and lost.

However, the relativization of one's faith poses a rather different problem to the issue which Suda is addressing: "The thesis of Miyata would lead one to conclude that any religion or school is good as any other as believers will

CHAPTER 3

gain merit indiscriminately"; "The claim of a particular religion that there is no true merit (salvation) apart from its own faith might be denied as not corresponding to the actual truth." Suda remains committed to the exclusivistic position of self-righteous dogmatism which had formerly characterized SG. Thus, he argues:

> Because it is the hallmark of religion to make claims as to the superiority of its own doctrine, it is widely recognized that even the Buddhist scriptures preach the superior merit and excellence of the dharma, as well as threatening punishment of slanderers of the dharma. Among them, the Lotus Sutra that Nichiren proclaimed to be the "king of Sutras" stresses throughout the particular superior merits to be gained by embracing the Sutra and the punishment awaiting those who slander it.

Though Suda's characterization of the sectarian nature of the LS is historically accurate, we still need to differentiate between a personal conviction of the truth of one's own religion as the supreme teaching and a sectarian attitude based on a dogmatic exclusivism, which defames and condemns all other religions and schools. What Miyata is suggesting needs radical correction, for is the latter a sectarian exclusivist attitude condemnatory of all others.

With respect to this, Suda refers to the supplementary phrases inscribed on both sides of the Mandala-honzon referred to above, which state in essence: *"Those who embrace this Sutra will get benefits that are far greater than the Ten Characteristics of the Tathāgata"* and *"Those who trouble the preacher of the Law will suffer by having their heads split into seven pieces."*[14] Miyata had expressed such a relativist view in a previously published paper

---

[14] The first supplemtary phrase is from a commentary of Miao-lo with respect to the praises described in the 23rd chapter of the LS "Previous Actions of the Bodhisattva Medicine King": "Even if a person were to fill the whole major world system with the seven treasures as an offering to the buddha and the great bodhisattvas, pratyekabuddhas, and arhats, the benefits gained by such a person cannot match those gained by accepting and upholding this Lotus Sutra, even just one four-line verse of it! That brings the most numerous blessings of all" (LS, p. 326). The term "The Ten Characteristics of the Tathagata" suggests numerous supernatural characteristics and capacities of a Buddha.

The second supplementary phrase is from a commentary of Miao-lo on the actions of *Kishimojin* (Mother of the demon children) described in the 26th "Dharani" chapter of the LS: *"If there are those who fail to heed our spells and trouble and disrupt the preachers of the Law, their heads will split into seven pieces like the branches of the arjaka tree"* (LS, p. 351).

These supplementary phrases are absent from many other Nichiren's Mandalas, for example they are not found on the so-called "Deathbed-Gohonzon" of 1280 which had been fixed to the wall of the room in the Ikegami brothers' residence where Nichiren lay sick and died.

where he stated that "these supplementary phrases should not be considered to be true from the perspective of the sociology of religion." And he goes on to say:

> In this sense I think Nichiren's assertion is false. Therefore, I propose removing these supplementary phrases from the Mandala. (Miyata 2013)

Miyata's idea is certainly radical, although he has also confused two analytical levels, i.e. he has confused sociological evaluation with the matter of religious faith and value. At first, it seems to be a reasonable assessment when Suda points out that "nobody can hold a doctrine or an object of worship revered by a particular religious tradition as 'erroneous' from the perspective of the sociology of religion in a wholly impartial way."

I myself came to understand the meaning of these supplementary phrases on the Gohonzon only through personal experience as well as through the experience and reflection of my fellow believers. Yet despite a personal conviction as to the validity of this religious experience, I was reluctant to agree to make public the dire consequences which the action of slandering the Mystic Law or rejecting the Gohonzon would cause. For this kind of condemnatory public stance is threatening, and would necessarily cause anxiety or even despair, and appeared to be contrary to the Buddhist spirit of mercy and compassion. Further, the Lotus Sutra was compiled almost 2000 years ago, the era in which the Daishōnin lived was 740 years ago. Yet at the beginning of the 21st century, it was now time to abandon such self-righteous, dogmatic sectarian self-assertion.

3. Matters Relating to Modern Buddhist Studies

With respect to the issue of SG doctrine and modern Buddhist studies, i.e. from the Meiji era (post-1868), Miyata considers the following three matters problematic:

① The fact that the Mahayana Sutras do not represent the directly given or actual teaching of Shakyamuni Buddha himself;
② The difficulty of accepting T'ien-t'ai's traditional classification of the "Five Periods";
③ The significance of a distinction made between the Buddha's era, in which he lived, taught and died, and the period of the Latter Day of the Law, i.e., our own contemporary era.

In short, he suggests that these traditional teachings and doctrines should only be taken into account, if they do not contradict historical fact. With respect to this matter Suda seems to hold a not dissimilar opinion, in that no reasonable person could object to such a suggestion. I will now give my own opinion on these three matters:

① The Mahayana Sutras do not represent the actual spoken teachings of Shakyamuni Buddha

Whether we consider the sutras of the Theravada or the Mahayana, there are no authentic scriptures written by Shakyamuni Buddha himself. Given this, no Buddhist scripture or doctrine represents the Buddha's directly given or actual teaching. However, this is to take an overly philological perspective on the value and significance of the Buddhist scriptures. More fruitfully, Buddhism should be regarded rather as a great philosophical current and a great religious movement to which many wise thinkers and courageous practitioners have contributed, devoting all their passion and lives. Consequently, as Suda has remarked, we should be careful not to "stick too strictly to the letter of the traditional literature".

This has also been the case with the Nichiren Buddhist movement since its first days. One significant dimension is the fact that not all of Nichiren's writings are still extant. A further dimension is that Nichiren Buddhism as a whole can be characterized as a great radical philosophical movement, as well as a strictly religious movement. Of course, the writings are in a certain form, which no doubt reflects how the Daishōnin expressed his thoughts on many occasions to his disciples and lay followers. Further, the Daishōnin developed his own teachings by way of a critical encounter with the Buddhist sutras and commentaries, some of which contain deeper insights than others. After his death, many believers and scholars have made a great effort to understand the Daishōnin's teachings and not a few have elaborated their own interpretative models. Even today we are still floating along on this great radical philosophical and spiritual current.

② "The Five Periods"

This concept represents an attempt at the systematic classification of all the sutras as elaborated by T'ien-t'ai, and in which the Lotus Sutra was held to be the last and the most profound or highest teaching of Shakyamuni Buddha. Clearly, this is not historically accurate: the Buddha simply did not teach the Lotus Sutra "in the last eight years of his life". Nevertheless, this assertion would be correct if we simply tag on one conditional phrase: "according to T'ien-t'ai".

③ "The Latter Day of the Law"

This term traditionally denotes the final period which began 2000 years after the Buddha's passing. This period is traditionally characterized as one in which the Buddhism of Shakyamuni would lose its power to lead all beings to enlightenment as people no longer properly practice or uphold the Buddhist precepts.

> In the Latter Day of the Law those who do not break the precepts are few while those without precepts are many.
> (»The Teaching, Capacity, Time, and Country«, p. 439 / I. 49 f.)

In Japan it was traditionally believed that this decadent and fearful period would start in the year 1052. *Dengyō-daishi Saichō* (767-822), the founder of Japanese Tendai Buddhism and of its head temple *Enryakuji*, had expressly made mention of this period in the »The Candle of the Latter Dharma« written in 801. Current scholarship remains skeptical as to the Saichō's actual authorship of the above treatise, yet Nichiren himself quite understandably considered the treatise authentic, was inspired by it and believed in the traditional doctrine:

> Reading »The Candle of the Latter Dharma« of Dengyō-daishi makes it clear that the year of 801 was 1750 years [after Shakyamuni's passing] and today a further 450 years have passed.[15] Thus, the Latter Day of the Law has already begun. The character of this period is that there are teachings but neither practice nor proof. Therefore, those who practice Buddhism will never attain Buddhahood. (»On Protecting the Land«, p. 46 / II. 106)

However, if you calculate the year of the Buddha's death based on Nichiren's understanding as evidenced by the above passage, you will end up with: 1750 − 801 = 949. This would mean that Shakyamuni Buddha would have died in the year 949 B.C. Further, this calculation as to the date of the Buddha's death had been based upon an earlier Chinese treatise. Yet this conflicted with an understanding found in Southeast Asia that the „Buddhist Era" began around 544 or 543 B.C. Further, today Shakyamuni's life is generally dated from around 563 to around 483 B.C. If we more plausibly take the year of 483 B.C. as the date of the Buddha's passing, that would indicate that the final age of *mappō* had not even begun at the time when Nichiren lived. This historical contradiction is a problem which troubles Miyata. However, the contradiction can be adequately dealt with in the same way as above

---

[15] With respect to this context, Nichiren inscribed on some of his Mandala-honzons an additional phrase, in which the year of his inscription is described as having been so many years "after the Buddha's passing". For example, on the first Mandala-honzon fully endowed with the Ten Worlds, which Nichiren had inscribed three months after he had written »The Object of Devotion for observing the Mind« in Ichinosawa, Sado: *"I was punished on September 12, 1271, [in Tatsunokuchi] and sent in to exile on Sado. On July 8, 1273, I inscribe this. This Great Mandala has never existed anywhere in the entite world in the more than 2220 years since the Buddha's passing. I Nichiren have now manifested it for the first time."*

where T'ien-t'ai's classification of all sutras in the "Five Periods" was considered: it is sufficient simply to tag on a conditional phrase "according to the common understanding of that time".

Of course, "the concept of the final age" can be found as an eschatological idea in many other religions. Indeed, the concept has been used to refer to an ultimate dimension which transcends the mere physical and temporal dimension, ordinarily calculated with disregard to historical fact. For every eschatological concept is normally conceived in the face of a vivid awareness that physical or spiritual crisis (often an apocalypse) is imminent for humanity generally. The end of human history is often conceived distinctly and uniquely, depending on the assumptions of a particular religious tradition. Further, these assumptions are with respect to a religious interpretation of the temporal dimension, rather than a merely physical dimension. For from a religious perspective on human history, a new prophet may be foretold or may appear to urgently proclaim a radical new solution to humanity's quest for salvation during a perceived time of spiritual or physical crisis.

In Nichiren's case, the concept of "our current times", perceived as an age of crisis, has this religious dimension implying an urgent need for a new radical solution to the human quest for liberation or salvation, understood in terms of the attainment of Buddhahood. Further, as he perceived himself to be living in the time at the final age of Shakyamuni's Dharma, he felt it incumbent upon him to urgently proclaim a radical new Dharma which would be powerful enough to lead all people, even those without wisdom or precepts, to enlightenment. Consequently, he took the Dharma which represented the Original Cause of the enlightenment of Shakyamuni Buddha in the remotest past, as the origin and source of all Buddhas.

The matter of authenticity: significant or not?

Miyata has adopted an approach to modern Buddhist Studies which values reference to established historical fact and a technique to establish the authenticity of scripture and other writings usually only by reference to the existence of autographed originals or reliable copies. In contrast to Miyata, Suda makes use of some writings of Nichiren which have generally been considered of questionable attribution or inauthentic. I myself will make use of some Gosho of questionable authenticity, as my judgment will be based more on their philosophical or buddhological content. In this respect, I agree with Suda.

As a matter of fact, neither Buddha nor Jesus Christ left any writings of their own. Consequently, there are no extant writings of the Buddha or Christ: all received scripture is the product and compilation of later generations of believers. However, this obvious historical fact in no way impairs the value of these scriptures or writings to the philosophical and religious movements which they inspired and influenced.

Consequently, we have to make a clear distinction between two separate issues: the problem as to which of Nichiren's "questionable writings" are authentic, as the autographed original or reliable copy made by a direct disciple has not survived; and the question of the way in which later generations have received and further developed Nichiren's teaching. I myself take a position of "creative deconstruction". For Nichiren's thought has been subject to historical modification in accordance with changing times and contexts, often reflecting new ideological or social and political interests, e.g. in an attempt to legitimate a peculiar tradition of a particular temple by way of a radical modification of doctrine. Given this context, we need to discard those adventitious elements which would appear to be extraneous to Nichiren's thought and thereby seek to reconstruct Nichiren's original or authentic understanding by way of critical reflection on his writings. We always need to continue to proceed critically in this way. We should also be careful to avoid any "overly academic one-sided specialization", as well as any "Galapagos evolution of Japan-centrism", something SGI President Ikeda has sought to overcome in making a valuable contribution to the propagation of NB to the world. His achievement has been momentous and should be much valued.

4. The Doctrine of Nichiren as the True Buddha

① *Does such a doctrine lead to the cult of an image?*

In his article entitled »Some Problems with respect to Nichiu's Doctrinal Thought« Miyata critically reconsiders the doctrine of Nichiren as the Original Buddha. He specifically addresses two problematic aspects to the doctrine: one with respect to the doctrine itself and the other with respect to its "socio-political consequences": i.e. first, expressly with the claim that "Nichiren is regarded as a Buddha superior to Shakyamuni", and secondly with respect to consequences or the "possibility that this doctrine continues to expose the overseas SGI movement to the real threat of marginalization as a cult".

Against such an understanding, Suda still holds to the "position of regarding Nichiren as the *Original Buddha* in our times" and defends this view by placing Nichiren in the traditional line of succession of the Four Masters (or Teachers) of the Three Countries, that is, Nichiren is the final successor to Shakyamuni of India, T'ien-t'ai of China and Saichō of Japan.

However, it should be noted that the Japanese term "*Nichiren honbutsu ron*" has a double meaning. This can be confirmed in Suda's extensive work entitled »The New Version: Life and Thought of Nichiren". In section "13

Nichiren honbutsu ron" of the sixteenth chapter "Teaching Activity in Minobu", Nichiren is identified as "the Teaching Lord for our times" (Suda 2016, p. 400). Yet in the section 9 "Manifesting the True Identity" of the eleventh chapter "Persecution at Tatsunokuchi", where reference is also made to Nichikan, Nichiren is regarded as "the Tathāgata of the Wisdom Body at the Original Beginning in the Remotest Past" and "the True Buddha of Sowing for our times". As Suda is also a co-author of the introductory book »The Basics of Study – Understanding Buddhism«, published in 2002 by the SG Study Department, he does not hesitate to refer to this official publication as legitimation for his NS-oriented view. Thus:

> We understand the significance of the persecution which befell the Daishōnin at Tatsunokuchi as an event "in which he opened up his shadow (provisional character) as an Ordinary Man of the Nominal Stage and revealed his true identity (original condition of life) as the Tathāgata of the Wisdom Body at the Original Beginning in the Remotest Past" (»The Basics of Study«, edited by SG Study Department, p. 46). (Suda 2016, p. 206)

Suda sees the basis of Nichiren's life as the necessary requirement for being the Master of our times, as his true identity has its origin in the eternal past and because the human Nichiren is to be regarded as a manifestation of the Eternal Original Buddha. This coupling of two dimensions is an example of the fundamental problem found in the NS Nichikan doctrine. As those currently practicing NB might find it incredible to regard Nichiren Daishōnin as the master for our times (*mappō*), Suda attempts to affirm the traditional view by quoting from a traditional text, i.e. by way of reference to "the four masters of the three countries" (»On the Buddha's Prophecy«, p. 509 / 402), which most believers might accept. For it is consonant with the view that the teaching master will change with the spiritual requirements of each era.

However, for SGI outside Japan (since the 1990s), although the NS doctrines of Nichiren as Eternal Original Buddha and the exclusive faith in the Dai-gohonzon had been left as they are, they had never been discussed openly. As a matter of fact, given the radically different circumstances faced by SGI outside Japan, there were very few opportunities for SGI members to come into contact with temples or priests. New members never heard much about pilgrimage to the NS head temple to worship Dai-gohonzon (*Tozan*) anymore. Consequently, the SGI activities gained a far more "lay Buddhist flavor".

Parallel to this tendency, SGI began to place more stress on the significance of organization and activities for Kōsenrufu under the banner of "the Unity of Master and Disciple". Yet this renewed enthusiasm became so excessive that it only aggravated the pre-existing tendency towards self-righteousness and dogmatic exclusivism. However, this time, at least this unfortunate tendency was primarily directed inwardly, i.e. towards forming a more cohesive and unified organization. Paradoxically, SG/SGI thereby enhanced its pre-existing exclusivist mentality, originally derived from NS institutional culture and structure, characterized by such things as top-down directives; a dualistic confrontation model of benefit and slander, absolute good and evil, friend or foe, conformity or criticism; exclusivistic practice or defamation and exclusion. These patterns of thought and action are characteristics of a cult or sect and are generally regarded as dangerous and harmful to individuals and, consequently, to society as a whole. I personally had got to know many SG / SGI members who asked questions to gain a better understanding or who had expressed critical opinions about the organization and the leaders, but who were then treated as enemy or disruptive elements out of harmony with the organization, who subsequently were excluded as a consequence of malicious rumor. Finally, they became so hurt and disappointed that they stopped being active or felt compelled to leave the organization. Some even gave up practicing NB. This was such a pity! I wonder if such negative tendencies remain present within SG / SGI even now?

For daily life and for society generally, the constitution and activities of SG / SGI on the organizational level is of much more critical importance than theoretical questions about doctrine. For the cult or sect problem is a sociological problem. An authoritarian hierarchical system ordinarily leads directly to such things as: the opaque management of finances and donations, a dogmatic exclusivistic mentality found in both members and executives, the brainwashing with a particularly obsessional and paranoid ideology directed against the beliefs and practices of other Nichiren sects, other Buddhist schools and other religions, and the active discouragement and sometimes suppression of freedom of thought, speech and written criticism. Further conflict has arisen over such problems as internal disaffection and controversial departure from or expulsion from the organization, as well as the tense relationship between overseas SGI and the SG headquarters in Tokyo, especially with respect to the issue of the separation between religion and the state, e.g. with respect to the existence of the political party *New Komeito*. For the existence of a religious organization perceived by outsiders and the state as a cult or sect is frequently related to the question of whether or not the cult or sect poses a real threat to the political, social and cultural order within a particular country. Indeed, this is a primary concern and primary focus of investigation in the field of the sociology of religion.[16]

---

[16] All the problems described above are based on my own personal observation and personal experience, as well as reliable reports from members. With respect to the sectarian character of SGI in Germany, many members suffered and experienced many of the things so described above, e.g. see my article published in Germany entitled »The four-layer model for evaluating a religious community – Illustrated by the example of Sokai Gakkai« (Matsudo 2015).

> Rather than offering up ten thousand prayers for a remedy, it would be better simply to outlaw this one evil.
> (»On Establishing the Correct Teaching for the Peace of the Land«, p. 24 / I. 14)

Given the above, I sincerely hope that with the abandonment of faith in the Dai-gohonzon, the SG / SGI will be able to overcome its sectarian character and develop more fully in a modernizing direction, sincerely thereby embracing a compassionate humanism, a real commitment to tolerance and understanding, egalitarianism, and global peace.[17]

② *Nichiren's own Theory of the True Buddha*

With respect to "the theory of Nichiren as the original or true Buddha", Suda makes implicit use of the theory of the teaching lord for our times, although explicitly upholding the traditional doctrine of Nichiren as the Eternal Original Buddha. Indeed, there is little doubt that Nichiren understood himself to be the teaching lord for our times endowed with the Three Virtues of Sovereign, Master and Parent. However, it is a completely different issue as to whether Nichiren understood himself as such to be "the object of worship, i.e. the honzon in terms of the person", despite reference being made to the following words of Nichiren.

> Devadatta inflicted an injury on Shakyamuni Buddha that drew blood, but when he was on his deathbed, he cried out, "Namu (Devotion)!" If only he had been able to cry, "Namu Buddha (Devotion to the Buddha)!" he would have been spared the fate of falling into hell. But so grave were the misdeeds he had committed that he could only utter the word "Namu" and could not pronounce the word "Buddha" before he died.
> And soon the eminent priests of Japan will no doubt be trying to cry out, "Namu Nichiren Shōnin (Devotion to the Sage Nichiren)!" But most likely they will only have time enough to utter the one word, "Namu!" How pitiful, how pitiful!
> (»The Selection of the Time«, p. 287 / I. 579)

This passage is an illustration of Nichiren's self-understanding, i.e. that he "is working to expose the root of the great slanders against the correct teaching" and "to save them" (ibid., p. 286 / I. 578). Up to this point, he had primarily intended to propagate the universal practice of chanting Daimoku so ordinary people could attain enlightenment, but he never dreamt that his disciples and followers might worship his person as a savior. Consequently, there is an urgent need to radically reevaluate the significance of the theory of

---

[17] I wrote about this new more positive perspective found in SGI in Germany in my article entitled »New Developments within Soka Gakkai« (Matsudo 2017).

Nichiren as the True Buddha from a perspective other than that found in the NS Nichikan doctrine.

③ *The reason why Nichiren should be considered the teaching lord in the Latter Day of the Law (or the True Buddha)*

Nichiren should certainly be considered to be the "teaching master" who propagated the practice of chanting Daimoku or Nam-myō-hō-ren-ge-kyō, yet Suda has over-emphasized the dimension of "True Buddha" found within the phrase "the teaching lord (True Buddha) for in our times". Thus, it is inevitable that an impression is given that he has strikingly failed to refute Miyata's views.

To give an example with respect to the relationship between the Daimoku and the LS itself: an interpretative gap remains.

> Now that we dwell in the time of the Latter Day of the Law, both other sutras and the Lotus Sutra itself are useless. Only Nam-myō-hō-ren-ge-kyō can help us. I dare to say this, but it is not just my intention, but that of Buddha Shakyamuni, Tathāgata Tahō and all Buddhas in the Ten Heavenly Directions as well as that of the numerous Bodhisattvas of the Earth.
> (»Reply to Ueno«, p. 1545 / -)

Taking the latter part of this quotation seriously, Miyata seeks the origin and ground of the Daimoku in the Lotus Sutra itself. Suda rejects this, arguing that "it would be a misunderstanding" and explains further as follows:

> When Nichiren asserts that Nam-myō-hō-ren-ge-kyō is the only great dharma which can save all the people, this doctrinal understanding cannot be grounded in a literal reading of the Lotus Sutra itself nor is it in any way dependent on it. His assertion represents the assertion of an eternal universal truth independent of the existence or character of the Lotus Sutra itself.

This mode of thinking exactly replicates the NS-type of perspective or deeper reading which reaches well beyond the teaching content of the Sutra itself. It runs counter to true understanding and rests on a form of spurious universalization. Is it true that Nichiren's practice of chanting Daimoku ignored the literal contents of the Lotus Sutra itself? Is no meaning to be given to Nichiren's own self-understanding that he was himself the Votary of the Lotus Sutra? Doesn't the traditional lineage of the Four Masters of the Three Countries thereby lose its significance, although Suda himself seeks to emphasize it? He also quotes Nichiren's statement with respect to his own self-understanding:

> My giving myself the name Nichiren (Sun Lotus) derives from my own enlightenment regarding the Buddha vehicle.

> (»Letter to Jakunichibō«, p. 903 / I. 993)

Does it mean, as Suda wants to read it, that "Nichiren attained enlightenment not through studying the sutras like the Lotus Sutra and the teachings of others, but that he realized the fundamental Mystic Law all by himself"? Behind such discourse, I am compelled nevertheless to feel that he remains attached to that particular mode of thought characteristic of NS, expressed in terms of "the Original Beginning of Eternity as the Unique and Independent Essential Teaching when considered from the Perspective of a Deeper Reading".

Further emphasis is given by what appears to be reference to Nichiren's well-known claim that as a youth he obtained great wisdom directly from the Bodhisattva *Kokūzō*:

> From the time I was a small child, I prayed to Bodhisattva *Kokūzō*, asking that I might become the wisest person in all Japan. The bodhisattva transformed himself into a venerable priest before my very eyes and bestowed upon me a jewel of wisdom as bright as the morning star.
> (»The Tripitaka Master Shan-wu-wei«, p. 888 / I. 475 f.)

This event doesn't necessarily mean that "Nichiren attained enlightenment not through studying sutras like the Lotus Sutra and the teachings of others, but by attaining realization of the fundamental Mystic Law all by himself". This episode more plausibly refers to the circumstance that Nichiren gained a deep insight from Kokūzō which subsequently enabled him to judge the relative superiority or inferiority of the received teachings, prior to arriving at his final doctrinal standpoint. Yet Suda still remains inclined to deify Nichiren, e.g. when he remarks that "the Bodhisattva *Kokūzō* is to be regarded as contained in the heart of Nichiren himself as he is a personal expression of that wisdom penetrating the great universe (*Kokūzō*: storehouse empty space)". I personally prefer to see Nichiren as an ordinary human being who devoted his whole life to the Dharma and overcame great difficulties and suffering rather than as a divine savior shrouded in incomprehensible mystery.

④ *The reason why Nichiren revered Shakyamuni Buddha*

In order to propagate the Buddhism of Sowing, there was a need for Nichiren to insist on the superiority of the Lotus Sutra to the pre-Lotus Sutras and the superiority of the Essential Teaching to the Theoretical Teaching of the Lotus Sutra. Consequently, Nichiren held Shakyamuni Buddha to be the Eternal Buddha Shakyamuni. In fact, it is correct, as Suda maintains, that it was not Nichiren's intention to propagate the Lotus Sutra, just as it is, i.e. understood only with reference to its literal meaning. However, once read on a much deeper level, was it Nichiren's intention when propagating a Buddhism of Sowing rather than a Buddhism of Harvesting, to discard the LS itself as no longer useful? Did Nichiren discover the teaching and practice of Nam-myō-hō-ren-ge-kyō independently of the Lotus Sutra itself? As he once declared: "Now we have entered into this contemporary age, both other sutras and the Lotus Sutra itself are useless"?

Consider the example of a scaffold used to erect a pagoda. Nichiren pointed out that the scaffold is torn down once the pagoda has been erected.

> When one is preparing to build a great pagoda, the scaffolding is of great importance. But once the pagoda is completed, then the scaffolding is removed and thrown away. This is the meaning of the passage about "honestly discarding expedient means."
>
> (»Reply to the Mother of Ueno«, p. 1570 / II. 1073)

In this passage Nichiren didn't mean to imply that the Lotus Sutra should be discarded but only that all other sutras should be considered as "expedient means". It is a discourse on the superiority of the Lotus Sutra when considered with reference to pre-Lotus Sutras, rather than a discourse on the significance of the Buddhism of Sowing and the Buddhism of Harvesting.

Further, the Lotus Sutra provided Nichiren not only with the doctrinal foundation of his teaching and practice but also the scriptural basis for his self-understanding as a reincarnation of the Bodhisattva Jōgyō in our times. Thus, Nichiren held the Lotus Sutra to be his scriptural legitimation and he never urged that it should be discarded.

Of course, Nichiren was reflecting and refining his arguments on different levels, as he needed to distinguish, establish and propagate his new teaching in opposition to the many different Buddhist schools of his time. Consequently, we should always be very careful never to confuse the different levels of discourse of which Nichiren was certainly aware. Such an approach is essential to understanding Nichiren's teaching properly. Indeed, it will play a key role in my critical dialogue with scholars from other Nichiren schools in Part Three. An approach which makes clear distinctions with respect to the different levels of Nichiren's teachings will be developed from a radically new multilayered perspective, grounded upon the Fivefold Comparison.

⑤ *Nichiren's intention as represented by the figurative design of the Mandala-honzon*

With respect to the characters "Nam-myō-hō-ren-ge-kyō Nichiren (i.e. including Nichiren's autographed signature)" found at the center of the Mandala-honzon, Suda attempts to highlight "Nichiren's true intention". This particular form might "suggest that Nichiren is the true Buddha (teaching lord) in unity with Nam-myō-hō-ren-ge-kyō". Suda had already speculated in an earlier book that this form suggested the unity of Nichiren and the Law, and this particular form at the very center of the Mandala-honzon, became increasingly prominent, especially on the Mandala-honzon inscribed during the Kōan period, i.e. during Nichiren's period of residence on Minobu (1278-1282). He continues: "this form points to Nichiren as the fundamental Buddha at one with Nam-myō-hō-ren-ge-kyō, i.e. that he is the teaching lord" (Suda 2016, p.426). In brief, such an understanding is no more than an assertion of the traditional doctrine, i.e. an assertion of the doctrine of "the Unity of the Buddha and Dharma" or that "the Eternal Original Buddha -equals- the True Buddha in the Latter Day of the Law". Given the above, I remain perplexed how we would be able to realize Instant Enlightenment in our own lives by chanting and worshipping the Daishōnin himself, as though he were God.

With respect to the "doctrine of the Unity of the Buddha and Dharma" and its relationship to the Daimoku inscribed at the center of the gohonzon, Miyata has raised some interesting questions, and arrived at some significant conclusions, in a recently published article (Miyata 2017). I will summarize here only his conclusions, as they are crucially relevant to the matter currently being considered.

- In order to understand the significance of "Nam-myō-hō-ren-ge-kyō Nichiren" found prominently at the center of the Mandala, already in the time of *Nichiu* (9th high priest of Taisekiji, 1402-1482) this had been interpreted with express reference to the doctrine of the Unity of the Buddha and Dharma. Sub-schools, such as that of Nichirō, Nikō and Nichijō, also made such express reference.
- With respect to the "Doctrine of the Unity of the Buddha and the Dharma" Nichikan in fact actually recognized two different types of Honzon: first, the "Mandala" was regarded as the "Honzon understood as the Person-equals-*the Dharma*" (the Dai-mandala of the Wisdom body of Eternity-equals-Ichinen Sanzen); and secondly, the "**imaginary statue of Nichiren himself**" in the form of a statue taken as the "Honzon understood as the Dharma -equals- *the Person*" (The founder Nichiren of "Ichinen Sanzen -equals- the Wisdom Body").
- **The first SG president Makiguchi considered the object of faith to be the universal law rather than a buddha. Consequently, SG never inherited faith in any image of Nichiren himself representing the dimension of founder worship,** particularly evident in Nichikan's two types of honzon. **Similarly, the second SG president Toda intentionally excluded this dimension of founder worship from SG's liturgy and ritual space.**
- It was the 59th High priest, Hori Nichikō (1867-1957), who discarded the image of Nichiren himself and refocused Nichikan's "doctrine of the Unity of the Buddha and Dharma" exclusively on to Mandala itself. Consequently, since that time the Mandala-honzon has contained within itself

the two dimensions of the "Law = Nam-myō-hō-ren-ge-kyō" and the "Person = Nichiren".
- So, SG never inherited Nichikan's "doctrine of the Unity of the Buddha and Dharma", but only the doctrine formulated by Hori Nichikō in the time of Toda.

The conclusions to Miyata's research are highly persuasive. The central positioning of the characters "Nam-myō-hō-ren-ge-kyō Nichiren" can clearly be held to give emphasis to the claim that Nichiren is the teaching lord for our times, yet he should never be held to be the Buddha at the Original Beginning of Eternity. If Nichiren is held to be the original primordial Buddha and therefore the primordial origin of all Buddhas, then such a conception would be not dissimilar from other conceptions found generally within the "religions of salvation", e.g. Christianity, where Jesus Christ is at once both God and savior. It should be remembered also, that many people from a Christian cultural background become interested in Nichiren Buddhism and embrace its beliefs and practice precisely because it does not demand an acceptance of such a "salvation mythology".

⑥ T'ien-t'ai's understanding of the role of the teaching lord for each age

It must surely be correct to regard Nichiren as the teaching lord for our times, who like the Bodhisattva Fukyō (*Never Disparaging*) gives guidance to deluded and evil people who have established no relationship to Buddhism. Yet they can never be "saved" by an "Original Buddha" but only by their own practice of the "Right Dharma (Mystic Law)". Up to this point, Suda has read this traditional idea into Nichiren's writings. For example, he refers to a commentary of T'ien-t'ai's »The Words and Phrases of the Lotus Sutra«, stating that "between Tahō (the previous Buddha) and Shakyamuni (the present Buddha) a future Buddha will take his seat within the Treasure Tower."

> This "future Buddha" who will take his seat within the Treasure Tower just like Shakyamuni and Tahō is none other than the "Nam-myō-hō-ren-ge-kyō Nichiren" which has been inscribed prominently in the midst of both Buddhas. This characteristic form indicates that both Buddhas serve as assistants to "Nam-myō-hō-ren-ge-kyō Nichiren".

The centrally prominent Daimoku can be surely understood under its varied aspects, but it should never be limited in meaning only with reference to Nichiren. Rather, the Daimoku in the center of Mandala-honzon may be understood to signify the Eternal Buddha Shakyamuni, when each Buddha, Shakyamuni and Tahō, are considered and given their respective roles by the Lotus Sutra itself. However, it may also signify the Tathāgata Nam-myō-hō-ren-ge-kyō himself, as each are considered to represent the two dimensions of objective actuality and subjective wisdom. In this respect, this Tathāgata can be identified with Nichiren, yet it also represents we ourselves, or all who chant the Daimoku before the Gohonzon, as each will thereby manifest his or her own enlightenment immediately and see it reflected on the Mandala-honzon. Consequently, we need to make this multilayered dimension of the Gohonzon very clear and, in fact, this will be the central theme of Part Three.

⑦ Buddhism spreads to the East and then returns to the West: the principle of change in Buddhist teachings

The thought that Buddhist doctrine and teaching masters change with the times is not a surprising idea. In the case of Christianity, the Old Testament based on the Jewish covenant with God, was superseded by the teachings of a new prophet, Jesus Christ, who established a new covenant, reflected in a New Testament. In this case, both the teaching master and the content of the covenant with God have been radically revised and renewed. Subsequently, differing interpretations of the Biblical faith, has led to a profusion of churches and sects.

Similarly, Buddhism has also led to a profusion of differing schools and sects, each distinguished by the Buddhas who are to be worshipped or teaching masters and doctrine. Thus, in principle, a progression from the Buddhism of Shakyamuni to the Buddhism of Nichiren is unproblematic. Indeed, it is a matter of great wonderment and joy that the Buddhism of the sun which illuminates all darkness spreads to the whole world. Consequently, Nichiren Buddhists should work united as one in order to attain the goal of Kōsenrufu.

⑧ Significance of the entrustment to Jōgyō – The idea of the change of teaching master

The Lotus Sutra is a scripture of prophecy that predicted the emergence of the Bodhisattvas of the Earth in the time after the Buddha's passing, entrusted with the mission to propagate the Buddha Dharma. However, the Dharma body which Shakyamuni Buddha entrusted to be propagated is not the Lotus Sutra from the perspective of its literal meaning, but rather it is the fundamental Mystic Law which is to be discovered only by a much deeper, more profound, esoteric reading of the Lotus Sutra.

I myself reject such an esoteric, implicitly exclusivist interpretation, as represented by Suda. The Lotus Sutra is a compilation of diverse written materials, which attained its recognizable and characteristic form within the Mahayana tradition almost 2,000 years ago. The compilers of the Lotus Sutra consciously upheld and promoted the revolutionary idea of the One-Buddha-Vehicle: an idea by means of which they not only understood themselves, but which also had a uniquely transformative impact on the subsequent development of Mahayana Buddhism. The Lotus Sutra is particularly characterized by the vividness of its fantastic, dreamlike imagery and by its narrative which plays out on an immense, cosmic scale. A striking example is the description of the Ceremony in the Air. Further, the Bodhisattvas of the Earth appearing from underground would appear to be central to the compilers understanding of their own unique identity as practitioners of the Mahayana.

Yet Suda appears only to I understand that "the significance of the Lotus Sutra lies in its prophecy of the appearance of Nichiren in the Latter Day of the Law". This interpretation is clearly erroneous: the compilers of the Lotus Sutra could have known nothing whatsoever of Nichiren or Japan in the 13th Century. There is therefore no prediction of Nichiren's particular mission. In fact, quite the contrary: It was only after Nichiren's mission had provoked intense hostility and persecution, and only after he had deeply reflected on how he had managed to endure and overcome the suffering he had faced consequent upon that persecution, that Nichiren expressly identified with the persecutions as described in the Lotus Sutra itself. Subsequently, by a "reading of the Lotus Sutra with his body", Nichiren claimed to be none other than the Bodhisattva Jōgyō. Indeed, it was Nichiren himself who gave the Sutra its significance as that which prophesized his own emergence as the Bodhisattva Jōgyō, not the other way around.

Thus, it is simply not reasonable to claim that there had existed a Buddha at the Original Beginning of Eternity, or that the Lotus Sutra had been compiled for the purpose of predicting his appearance in the Latter Day of the Dharma. Likewise, it is not reasonable to claim that the Mystic Law entrusted to Jōgyō is to be found in the depths of the Lotus Sutra itself. Yet it is reasonable to claim that through his great learning and insight, as well as through his great suffering and compassion, Nichiren himself discovered this most precious jewel. Therein lies his greatness and spiritual dynamism.

With respect to this, Suda refers to Nichiren's assertions that "It is for Nichiren and his kind for today and for our times" and "It is only for us". However, the phrases quoted above more likely indicate that Nichiren had himself undertaken a course of intense creative study in order to properly understand the significance of all the extant Buddhist sutras and commentaries, with the intention of firmly establishing the Buddha Dharma to enable all ordinary people to attain Buddhahood. Consequently, it is clearly not the case, that nothing of the teaching and practice which Nichiren established was hidden in any of the sutras and commentaries he had so intensively studied.

At this point, with respect to the issue of "Nichiren = Jōgyō", Miyata holds the position that Nichiren self-consciously identified with his role as "envoy" entrusted by the Eternal Tathāgata Shakyamuni. Suda rejects such a view,

Chapter 3

instead he considers a Bodhisattva of the Earth to be none other than a "Bodhisattva Buddha" bearing the Mystic Law deep within his own life, i.e. as "a Buddha of the Original Cause". Consequently, the entrustment made to Jōgyō, necessarily required a ceremony for the legitimation of a teaching master for the Latter Day of the Dharma. In order to demonstrate this, Suda quotes the following from Ikeda's »The Wisdom of the Lotus Sutra«:

> *Honorary President:* The entrustment ceremony in the chapter "Supernatural Powers of the Tathāgata" represents in short that "the teaching master of the Mystic Principle of the Original Effect" entrusted the mission to propagate to "the teaching master of the Mystic Principle of the Original Cause". It represents a great transformation from a Buddhism which focused on an ideal image of a great Buddha with extraordinary characteristics (Effect) to a Buddhism which focuses on the practice for attaining Buddhahood by ordinary people (Cause). It is a transition to a Buddhism which dwells perpetually within the everyday reality of all people.

Do these two seemingly different perspectives contradict each other, i.e. Nichiren considered to be the envoy of the eternal Tathāgata Shakyamuni, and Nichiren considered to be the teaching master of the Mystic Law of Original Cause and the true Buddha for the Latter Day of the Law? I think that they are not inconsistent if one considers them as two complimentary dimensions when viewed from two different perspectives, i.e. from a philological perspective and from a meditative perspective.

⑨ *Gosho of undetermined authenticity*

All gosho which are not autographed by Nichiren himself or copies made by Nichiren's disciples, Miyata considers to be apocryphal and consequently he reconstructs Nichiren's thought only with reference to gosho that are definitely authentic. Suda represents an alternative position: "as a matter of course gosho which are clearly apocryphal should be excluded, but gosho which are only of doubtful authenticity should nevertheless be considered significant, although of undetermined authenticity". I agree.

Nevertheless, I take a different position when Suda goes too far and states that "if one extends the scope of investigation to include gosho of undetermined authenticity one will get acquire further documentary support for the thesis that Nichiren regarded himself as the Original Buddha". For if one does include gosho of undetermined authenticity, it is far more likely that one acquires further documentary support not for Suda's claim but rather for the doctrine of the Ordinary Person as True Buddha based on the Mutual Containment of the Ten Worlds. Yet I wonder if this interpretation has been especially disliked and marginalized since the beginnings of Nichiren Buddhism, as it is clearly contrary to a faith based on worship of the Eternal Shakyamuni

Buddha or the founder Nichiren himself, as well as clearly contrary to the cult of other deities with the purpose of obtaining worldly benefits for devotees, historically established by temples. I am surely not the only one who senses an unfortunate sectarian or political ideology lurking behind the "authenticity question".

Further, when determining the authenticity of gosho based on philosophical considerations, I myself would accept »The Record of the Orally Transmitted Teachings« as it is addressed to "Nichiren's disciples and lay followers". However, we should not consider the transfer documents of NS, i.e. »The Mystic Principle of the Original Cause« and »The One Hundred and Six Comparisons«, as equally significant, as both make use of a particular term "the Original Beginning of Eternity" and regard Nichiren himself as a uniquely exalted or deified person. Of course, for me, Nichiren's intention was to proclaim a universally oriented Buddhism which seeks to activate the Buddhahood of all ordinary people, not to establish a cult for his own worship.

⑩ The Heritage of the Doctrine of Nichiren as the Original Buddha within the Nikkō lineage

In his article entitled »Some Problems with the Teachings of Nichiu« (2009), Miyata concluded as a result of his research that the "doctrine of Nichiren as the Original Buddha is characteristic of Taisekiji polemics and apologetics generally" but the doctrine was unknown both to Nichiren himself, to Nikkō, and to Nikkō's senior disciple, *Mitsui Nichijun* (1294-?). This doctrine had only emerged in a copy of »The Mystic Principle of the Original Cause«, annotated by the 6th high priest *Nichiji* (? – 1406) and was only given clear articulation and further elaboration by the 9th high priest *Nichiu* (1402-1482). Critically reconsidering the "Doctrine of Nichiren as the Original Buddha", Miyata focuses primarily on the problem of the idea of the "Three Bodies at the Original Beginning of Eternity = the Buddha of the Mystic Principle of the Original Cause = Nichiren as the Original Buddha".

Assuming the Mandala-honzon to be at One with Buddha and Dharma, as well as representing in the aspect of the Person, conceived with reference to the doctrine of Nichiren as the Original Buddha, Suda contends that these ideas had in fact already been elaborated by Nichiren himself and were subsequently upheld consistently by the Nikkō lineage. In support of this contention, he asserts that Nikkō may have entitled Nichiren the "Blessed Buddha", "Blessed Dharma Lord", and he may have conducted memorial services before a portrait image of Nichiren. Consequently, he may have abandoned the idea of Shakyamuni as the Original Buddha. Further, Suda considers that with respect to the style of his copying the Mandala, unlike Nichiren's other senior disciples, Nisshō (1236-1323) and Nichirō (1245-1320), Nikkō identified himself as "Nichiren's disciple" and considered Nichiren to be the True Buddha of our times at one with Nam-myō-hō-ren-ge-kyō. Yet all the above merely demonstrates that Nikkō deeply revered Nichiren as founder and not that he considered him to be in some sense "the True Buddha and the Teaching Lord for our times". In this respect, I myself would have no problem.

The only matter I am deeply critical of is the Doctrine of Nichiren as the Eternal Original Buddha. In order to reject the conclusion of Miyata that this doctrine only emerged some time after Nichiren's death, Suda can cite only one passage from Nichijun's writings.

> Also in the »Oral Transmission of The Mystic Principle of the Original Cause« which has been regarded as written by Nichijun, there is one sentence which clearly represents the Doctrine of Nichiren as the Original Buddha: "Nichiren Daishōnin who taught the Mystic Principle of the Original Cause [as hidden in the depths of the LS] interpreted *'originally I practiced the bodhisattva way'* as being identified with "the Wisdom Body at the Original Beginning of Eternity'" (ibid. p.83).

However, Miyata considers this document to be apocryphal as it includes a reference to "Nichiren Shū" which didn't exist in the 14th Century. Suda tries to answer this by claiming there is insufficient evidence for this assertion. Yet apart from this authenticity problem, we cannot easily perceive any reference to the "Doctrine of Nichiren as the Eternal Original Buddha" made by either Nichiren himself or Nikkō. Consequently, it is not legitimate to deify Nichiren in this sense as the personal dimension of the object of worship and devotion.

It is true that The Teaching Lord of our times proclaimed and disseminated the Buddhism of Sowing for realization of Buddhahood by all ordinary people. Yet a person-focused devotion clearly conflicts with this universal dimension of the Law.

5. Is worship of a Buddha statue to be accepted?

Nichiren generally encouraged the erection and worship of statues of Shakyamuni Buddha as a compliment to the worship of the Mandala-honzon. He encouraged both Toki Jōnin as well as Shijō Kingo and his wife to erect such statues, as is evident from his extant letters to them. Miyata considers these to be exceptional cases, reflecting Buddhist ritual norms and the Buddhist understanding of the time. It thereby represents a perspective whereby the primacy of the Essential Teaching of the LS is stressed, by way of comparison to the Theoretical Teaching of the LS and to other provisional sutras. I agree with this view. However, Suda argues that Nichiren encouraged others to pray only to the Mandala-honzon as their object of worship.

In the period of writing »The Object of Devotion for Observing the Mind« [1273 in Ichinosawa, Sado] Nichiren was ambiguous, but he clearly stated in »Questions and Answers on the Object of Devotion« [1278 in Minobu] not to see Shakyamuni Buddha as the object of worship (That is, he denied the doctrine of Shakyamuni as the Original Buddha). From this perspective we must say that Miyata is misreading the true intention of Nichiren when he states that »The Object of Devotion for Observing the Mind« makes reference to both the Mandala-honzon and statues of Shakyamuni Buddha as objects of worship. Given Nichiren's actual behavior and the teachings as presented in the scriptures, the Mandala-honzon should be only the legitimate object of devotion in the teaching of Nichiren and there is nowhere any encouragement to erect statues of Shakyamuni Buddha as objects of devotion.

Nevertheless, it seems odd even to me that Miyata considers that »The Object of Devotion for Observing the Mind« contains doctrinal support for both the use of the Mandala-honzon and the use of statues of Shakyamuni Buddha. Further it remains a mystery to me as to why Suda considers the Gosho "includes some phrases expressly referring to the doctrine of Nichiren as the Original Buddha". I will leave further comment on this until Part Three, but this Gosho should be considered as a guide to and an explanation of "the Object of Devotion enabling all people to realize Buddhahood in our times". In this respect, the doctrine of Shakyamuni Buddha as the Original Buddha makes no sense. Up to this point, I share the view of Suda, but we differ as to the reasons we have for holding the view that Nichiren's Mandala alone should be considered to be the legitimate object of devotion, the Gohonzon. Here it is enough to point out that there is a fundamental difference in our understanding of the unique significance of the Gohonzon.

Without the Mandala inscribed with characters it is not possible to express the principle that all things in the Ten Worlds including human beings are subsumed in the Mystic Law and the doctrine of the Unity of Nam-myō-hō-ren-ge-kyō and Nichiren.

I can share this view with Suda, i.e. to consider the Mandala endowed with the Ten Worlds as the ideal means to give expression to the enlightened state of life based on the principle of the Mutual Possession of the Ten Worlds and Ichinen Sanzen. Yet it is not meant to be a focus of worship of the Daishōnin himself, under the aspect of the Unity of the Buddha and Dharma. For it is actually because "Nichiren as well as his disciples and lay followers" by chanting Daimoku can all see their own enlightened state of life reflected in the Gohonzon, in terms of "the Unity of the Person and the Law".

CHAPTER 3

6. Can an academic theory alone be a sufficient foundation for doctrinal understanding?

It is true, as Suda has pointed out, that the various academic disciplines are becoming increasingly fragmented and that cumbersome debate is perpetuated throughout the closed fields of expertise, thereby becoming isolated from the common sense of the general public. Further, this "academic one-sided specialization" will aggravate a further tendency: i.e. for specialists of religious thought to ignore the experiential and spiritual dimension of believers themselves when predominantly considering religious scriptures. Such an academic approach to study is artificial and may lead only to dry self-satisfied erudition. Further, turning the eye towards the Japanese context, the scholars working within the area of Buddhist studies should take care to avoid a tendency characterized as "Galapagos evolution", i.e. that they consider Japanese development in isolation from the rest of the world. This is sometimes derided as "what is considered common sense in Japan is considered bizarre by the rest of the world".

Although Suda seeks to force Miyata's academic research into a category of this kind, I personally find many of his articles often insightful and valuable, regardless of whether they have been published in the journals of academic associations. Of course, part of his approach and some of his conclusions I cannot agree with. But this is true for every published article or book. After all, each of one of us has to consider, reflect and formulate his or her own thought from a particular perspective. Especially with respect to the study of Nichiren Buddhism, if we are faithful practitioners, our own religious experience will provide us with an important foundation upon which to seek a deeper understanding of NB. In this respect, we will always be in search of a more adequate understanding of Nichiren's thought that might deepen and enrich our experience of practice. Consequently, I remain personally appreciative of both Miyata's and Suda's contributions and their sincere efforts to advance our understanding. For each has certainly provided me with an opportunity to deepen my own understanding and formulate my own views.

7. Can one's own judgment be the standard for everything?

In fact, Miyata has a tendency towards a relativistic rationalism. Indeed, his remarks below are quite radical:

> Buddhism has originally the characteristic of multilingualism. If the Mandala does not need to be sanctified, it may be enough just to convey the universal message of salvation. In this case, the Mandala would not need to be written in Sino-Japanese characters. Although Nichiren held

the recitation of the 2nd and the 16th chapter of the Lotus Sutra as an essential practice, there is nevertheless no requirement to recite these Chinese scriptures in the Sino-Japanese pronunciation. (»About the Gosho "Questions and Answers on the Object of Devotion"«, Miyata 2013)

His remarks remind me of MBSR (Mindfullness Based Stress Reduction) which is currently in vogue throughout the developed world. This form of meditation practice was developed by Jon Kabat-Zin (1944-today), an American Professor Emeritus of Medicine at the University of Massachusetts Medical School, and it has been become very popular because it functions as a technique for wellness, health care and therapy on both the mental and physical level. Similarly, all Buddhist religious and institutional elements have been removed from the meditation practices of the Vietnamese Zen monk, Thich Nhat Hanh (1926-today). Mindfulness techniques are applied today not only in private centers but also in some medical centers and hospitals. With respect to the actual method of chanting Daimoku before the Mandala, it is not clear how far particular Buddhist and Japanese cultural elements might be omitted if it is to function effectively for wellness and health care. In the future, Nichiren's Mandala might also be represented by way of a three- or four-dimensional holograph, incorporating all the beings of the Ten World modelled as concrete figures.

However, Miyata admits that he himself has had no mystical experiences and is unable to easily understand mysticism. Consequently, I don't think it is reasonable to accuse him of arrogance in the way that Suda does. Personally, I have never had such an impression of Miyata when we exchanged opinions at conferences held by the Institute of Oriental Philosophy (IOP) in Tokyo.

Another matter is with respect to the statement of Miyata in his article »About "The Protection of the Land"«: "I do not like any portrayal of Nichiren as a religious man with double standards" (Miyata 2000). Suda criticizes this remark by stating: "It is not appropriate or sufficient to judge the humanity of a religious man and his teachings by the criterion of personal like or dislike". I do not find this particularly problematic. For every one of us reflects and makes judgements often only on the basis of personal and subjective preference. The important thing to remember is that some doctrines Nichiren proclaimed openly while other doctrines he revealed only to some of his disciples. This is what Miyata characterizes as a "double standard" or "esoteric". Yet for me Nichiren didn't have merely double standards, but much more than that he had multiple standards which gives a multilayered structure to his teachings. As I have already indicated above, I will return to this subject in Part Three.

Contrary to Miyata, I highly value the mystical religiosity in Nichiren's thought. This is because Nichiren's deep wisdom, compassion and love can never be based on merely rational considerations. Behind his articulated understanding, his behavior and his practice, he most certainly must have been in constant contact and communion with the vast dimension of universal life and cosmic consciousness. This kind of communion was certainly not limited only to a mode of inward experience, but he must also have often felt himself deeply engaged with the great universe itself. There is definite significance in the fact that Nichiren frequently communed with the sun, the moon and the stars. One such event took place at Tsukahara, where he had been taken after arriving on Sado on November 1. 1271, and where he had been confined in a small dilapidated hut surrounded by abandoned and exposed corpses:

> In the yard around the hut the snow piled up deeper and deeper. No one came to see me; my only visitor was the piercing wind. »The Great Concentration and Insight« and the Lotus Sutra lay open before my eyes, and Nam-myō-hō-ren-ge-kyō flowed from my lips. My evenings passed in discourse with the moon and stars on the fallacies of the various schools and the profound meaning of the Lotus Sutra. Thus, one year gave way to the next.   (»The Actions of the Votary of the Lotus Sutra«, p. 916 / I. 771)

Such sentences might be read as examples of a distinctive Nichiren literary preference for poetic hyperbole or dramatic paranoia, but I take them much more seriously and wish to cherish them as an intensely emotional and deeply spiritual expression of Nichiren's whole heart. Now, let's imagine the scene:

> At night you sit down alone in a hut in a vast field. There is no Neon lamp, no smart phone or PC. You look at the myriad of stars and the moon glowing in the crystal-clear sky. You feel yourself to be wrapped around by the vast, limitless, great universe itself. In that moment, you begin to chant Daimoku and you feel completely fused with the cosmos. You are overwhelmed by a deep love and compassion. Then, you look up to the moon and stars and talk to them about the doctrinal superiority of the Lotus Sutra or Nam-myō-hō-ren-ge-kyō. This is only because you are completely filled with a great compassionate intention to help all suffering people attain true happiness. Thus, you are determined to propagate the teaching and practice of Nam-myō-hō-ren-ge-kyō.

Similarly, Nichiren must have felt himself wrapped around by the great universe of infinite space and eternal time. This is the spiritually enlightened world of Ichinen Sanzen which is intimately and deeply related to the cosmic consciousness itself (Buddhahood, the enlightened state of life, the cosmic life). And this leads directly to the world of Nichiren's Mandala-honzon.[18]

In this way, Nichiren seems to have felt himself to have been involved in the natural world and the vast universe itself since his childhood and he lived always in direct communion with the cosmic consciousness. I wonder whether this feeling of fusion with the universe represents the source of that unique mystical religiosity or spirituality found within Nichiren Buddhism. For this represents a spiritual dimension of cosmic consciousness far beyond the everyday ego, i.e. it represents the very source of wisdom and compassion. Consequently, the practice of chanting Daimoku opens up our narrow-closed heart to this spiritual, cosmic dimension deep within our own ordinary lives.

Summary

In conclusion, Suda is still seeking to provide arguments in support of the NS Nichikan teaching, but with the unfortunate result of an enforced reading of the gosho from a perspective which is completely alien to that of Nichiren himself. Such traditional doctrines as "Nichiren as the Eternal Original Buddha" simply cannot be found in the thought of Nichiren or Nikkō. Nevertheless such doctrines helped to promote a pre-modern authoritarian organizational structure and legitimated an exclusivistic religious mentality still widespread today. Both NS and SG have been deeply affected by such an unwholesome doctrinal tendency, and as it is the primary source of a militant exclusivistic sectarianism, such doctrines should be abandoned. However, to consider Nichiren to be the Master of the Teachings of the Buddhism of Sowing for our times remains legitimate. In this respect, when we talk about "Nichiren as the True Buddha", the term "True Buddha" should simply mean an actually existing human being endowed with the characteristics of Buddhahood, which he himself can activate. In fact, this is the meaning of the principle of the "Ordinary Person -equals- Buddha" or the "Instant Enlightenment".

Thus, Nichiren Daishōnin is our master with respect to Buddhist teachings, who has established the Buddhism of Sowing in order to enable us to manifest an enlightened state of life. In order that we can understand what this actually means for us, he provided us with the example of his own extraordinary life and profound practice. He overcome not only extremely difficult circumstances and transformed negative relationships into positive ones, but he gave encouragement to all out of his great compassion and deep understanding. We are called to follow this eternal Buddhist master. And I would

---

[18] We have used this scene to illustrate the spiritual dimension of the Mandala-honzon and NB generally in the Book NB 3.0 (2016).

define his fundamental teaching as the "Instant Enlightenment of ordinary people".

However, backed up by his modern philological research Miyata goes well beyond the traditional NS teaching in an attempt to arrive at a radically new interpretation with respect to the history and philosophical background of Nichiren Buddhism. Yet his conclusions should not be uncritically accepted. As he ignores all elements of Original Enlightenment in Nichiren's thought, his mode of interpretation of the gosho leaves me with the impression that his reading is somewhat shallow and is drily philological. There are obvious pitfalls to the use of a method which considers only authenticated autographs as relevant to an interpretation of Nichiren's life and thought: in this way, a rather lifeless unpersuasive portrait of Nichiren emerges. Further, if we never consider the philosophical context and never engage with such ideas as Original Enlightenment, Buddhahood or Buddha nature, we remain perpetually moored at the philological level of the Essential Teaching and we will never progress from a form of faith focused on the worship of the Eternal Buddha Shakyamuni. In this case, we will have thereby excluded from consideration the more profound philosophical principle of attaining Buddhahood, expressed in such phrases as "for all ordinary people in our times" or especially "for Nichiren and his disciples and lay followers". This matter will be addressed further in Part Three.

Let's summarize the conclusions of this chapter:

> Suda remains at the comparative level with respect to the superiority of Sowing against Harvesting, yet he is stuck in traditional NS teaching.
> Miyata accepts at the comparative level the superiority of the Lotus Sutra with respect to the pre-Lotos Sutras but in actuality returns to a doctrinal position not dissimilar to that of Nichiren Shū.
> I propose a third or Middle Way with respect to Nichiren's teaching.

Additional remarks on the present revised version

With respect to the pervasive understanding, partially represented by Miyata, that only Nichiren's authenticated writings should be considered relevant to any respectable academic assessment of Nichiren's thought, there are some aspects of the debate which I previously overlooked. Consequently, I would like to comment on them for this revised version.

In his article entitled »Concerning 'Questions and Answers on the Object of Devotion'« (Miyata 2013), Miyata concluded:

> I am cautious of including all these suspect materials into any accepted canon of Nichiren's Writings, although I am against any scholarly approach to limit Nichiren Buddhism only to Nichiren's autographed or otherwise authenticated work and only those ideas which are arguably extracted from it. As there are many aspects to his thought which Nichiren himself did not clarify, it was only natural for Nichiren's followers to seek to provide answers to those matters which had remained problematic at the time of Nichiren's death. I consider such efforts highly laudable even though some followers may have developed an understanding of Nichiren's thought more likely based on their own faith which was then projected back on to Nichiren himself in order to resolve and legitimate solutions to particular doctrinal problems, something often observed within the framework of any religion.

Nevertheless, Miyata introduced a clear distinction between "Nichiren's own thought" and "Nichiren Buddhism as a religious tradition". As to the former, he employs a strict method in only making reference to Nichiren's writings which have been established as authentic. As to the latter, he does adopt a more flexible attitude.

This understanding is also evident in his comments on my interpretation of Nichiren.

> I have exchanged comments and opinions with Matsudo several times, who had been my colleague previously at the Institute of Oriental Philosophy. While I adopt a "Slim Nichiren Theory" which limits an understanding of Nichiren thought to the authenticated writings, Matsudo adopts a "Fat Nichiren Theory" which considers it legitimate to have regard to other writings generally considered to be not strictly authenticated. By doing so, Matsudo is exploring the possibility of a contemporary understanding of Nichiren thought based on his theory of the "Ordinary Person as True Buddha". Although I cannot agree with the claim that this theory is based on Nichiren's own thought, nevertheless I consider that his theory has validity if considered to be firmly based on the doctrines of Nichiren Buddhism whose ultimate source is in the thought of Nichiren himself. (addition of Sep. 28, 2011)

Miyata has well understood my own standpoint. Of course, I myself never seek to reconfigure the Nichiren's own thought in an arbitrary manner, thereby simply ignoring the questionable authenticity of some of the problematic writings. For I seek to make an effort to get as close as possible to the actual thought of Nichiren himself. Yet at the same time, I am seeking to go well beyond the traditional doctrinal understanding of Nichiren thought developed in the Kamakura period during the 13th century, as I am seeking to develop and expand on that traditional understanding to make Nichiren thought relevant to the contemporary world of the 21st century.

Consequently, I completely agree with Miyata's acceptance of SG's view on the affirmation of the Mandala-honzon as the legitimate object of worship. Further, with respect to practice for our current age, I affirm the "superiority of the Law to the Person" and that the practice of chanting Daimoku is in actuality the manifestation of that Unity of Law and Person.

In conclusion to PART TWO, I would like now to consider SG's Study Department's most recent guidance on Nichiren Buddhist doctrine, by way of a focus on the major principles and significant terms.

Chapter 4
Comments on the SG Study Document

1. Some terms and definitions found in the SGDB

On the SG official website SOKAnet the "Search of Study Terms" is available, copyrighted thus: "© 2017 SokaGakkai (Japan) All Rights Reserved"[19]. I don't know about the circumstances which led to the change of contents, although currently, this version should be considered the latest on the official teaching of SG. Consequently, I have tried to search for the most significant terms related to the discussion in Part Three. I will list them in summary form. For non-Japanese SGI members or for other Nichiren Buddhists, I will also compare each Japanese definition with the respective English version given in "The Soka Gakkai – Dictionary of Buddhism" (hereafter SGDB)[20]. I will begin with the term "*Hosshaku-kenpon*".

Hosshaku-kenpon: Revealing the true identity by casting aside its shadow, or according to SGDB: Casting off the transient and revealing the true

> This term represents the idea of opening up the provisional character or identity in order to lead people towards the revelation of an original or more profound identity. ① Using this term T'ien-t'ai explained that in the Life Span Chapter the historical Shakyamuni Buddha cast off his provisional identity as the Buddha who attained enlightenment for the first time under the Bodhi tree and revealed his true identity as the Buddha who had attained enlightenment in the remotest past. ② Further, applying this principle to Nichiren Daishōnin, he cast off his transient status as an ordinary person burdened with karma and suffering and, while remaining an ordinary human being, revealed his original, true identity as a Buddha possessing infinite wisdom and compassion (Tathāgata with the Wisdom body at the original Beginning of Eternity).

---

[19] http://k-dic.sokanet.jp/
[20] http://www.nichirenlibrary.org/en/dic/Appendix/J. Important terms are listed in "Appendix J – Terms and Names in Japanese". There you can select any term, for example, you can find an explanation of the term "*Hosshaku-kenpon*" if you click the English translation of the entry word "*casting off the transient and revealing the true*". Where necessary I have amended these English terms and definitions for this book.

Although Nichiren's true identity is defined by the traditional NS term in parentheses, its significance would appear to have been changed by the wording "a Buddha possessing infinite wisdom and compassion while remaining an ordinary human being".

The English version gives a rather similar definition and seems to be a direct translation of the original Japanese text. Only the term for Nichiren's true identity is given as "the Buddha of limitless joy" (*jijuyūshin*) which has not followed the traditional NS term "the original beginning of eternity (*kuonganjo*)". Though reference to Nichikan is clearly made, the definition in a general sense remains rather detached from it. In addition, there is no particular entry word for a definition of this term in the SGDB.

In both the Japanese and English versions, an implicit reference to both the traditional term and to Nichiren is made, yet the significance of Nichiren's identity seems to have been changed. Indeed, this change in significance is for me rather ambiguous. Let's examine this matter further.

Kuonganjo jijuyūhōshin nyorai: The Tathāgata of the wisdom body of limitless joy at the original beginning of eternity

> The eternal Buddha who has realized the most fundamental Law and receives and uses its benefits freely. The "Eternal Beginning of Eternity" (*kuonganjo*) doesn't mean a particular distant point in the past but suggests an eternal source. The "Self-enjoyment or Reward or Wisdom Body (sambhogakāya)" (*jijuyūhōshin*) is also called the "Self-enjoyment Body" (*jijuyūshin*) meaning the "body which receives and utilizes the benefits" as a result of realizing the Law. This is a fundamental Buddha full of mercy and wisdom, inherent within all life.

"*Kuonganjo*" had been defined with a double meaning in the dialogue on »The Wisdom of the Lotus Sutra« in the late 1990's. One meaning was given as "Nichiren as the Eternal Original Buddha", the master of Shakyamuni Buddha, who had attained enlightenment in the remotest past, and thus the term signified a more primordial time. The second meaning reflects the definition given earlier above, with a more universal sense *"it doesn't mean a particular distant point in the past but suggests an eternal source"*.

The *"Jijuyūhōshin"* or *"Jijuyūshin"* means *"a fundamental Buddha full of mercy and wisdom, inherent in all life"*, which is close to the concept of "Buddha nature" or the "Buddha World" (the enlightened state of life). Thus, the Wisdom Body is understood more as a universal, inherent principle rather than any particular Buddha. In that case, does the concept of "Revealing the true identity by casting off its shadow" mean that Nichiren manifested his state of life in the sense of "Ordinary Person -equals- Buddha"?

Nichiren Daishōnin

1222 - 1282. He devoted his life to the vow of Kōsenrufu or the propagation of the Law, as proclaimed in the Lotus Sutra. He manifested the fundamental Law of attaining Buddhahood for all people by inscribing it in the form of a Gohonzon and established the chanting of Daimoku as the essential practice for oneself and others. In this way, he opened up the way for ordinary people to attain Buddhahood in the Latter Day of the Law. For these reasons we respect and believe in Nichiren Daishōnin who is our teaching lord and the true Buddha endowed with the three virtues.

Though I agree with this basic understanding, I would like to make one amendment: "He opened the way for ordinary people to attain Buddhahood in our times by establishing the fundamental Law for attaining Buddhahood by the chanting of Daimoku as the essential practice for oneself and others and by manifesting this Law in the form of the Gohonzon." Anyway, this understanding of Nichiren corresponds to the doctrinal standpoint of "the theory of the Ordinary Person as True Buddha" which I have been advocating for a long time. So far, it is not at all unreasonable to regard Nichiren as "the true Buddha in our times". However, I want to stress this aspect of Teaching Master, by underlining the fact that the Daishōnin was able to teach the way to the realization of Instant Enlightenment by all ordinary people as both he and we have an identical ontological dual structure, i.e. "ordinary person - equals- Buddha".

Further, within this explanation is an overview of the Daishōnin's life. The following description seems to be especially important.

The Daishōnin wrote many important writings on Sado island. In particular, in »The Opening of the Eye« (page 186) written in February 1272, he makes it clear that he himself is the "votary of the Lotus Sutra" in the Latter Day of the Law, who practiced as predicted in the Lotus Sutra and is the true Buddha endowed with the tree virtues of sovereign, master and parent " in order to save the people of the Latter Day of the Law. Further, in »The Object of Devotion for Observing the Mind« (page 238), written in April 1273, the Daishōnin explained that the honzon of Nam-myō-hō-ren-ge-kyō should be embraced by the people of the Latter Day of the Law as the means of attaining Buddhahood.

According to the traditional NS Nichikan doctrine, »The Opening of the Eyes« has been explained as "a writing for manifesting *the Person* dimension of the honzon" while »The Object of Devotion for Observing the Mind« represents "a writing for manifesting *the Law* dimension of the honzon". There would appear to be no significant difference between the traditional understanding and the new explanation.

Let's check this point with the entry word "The honzon of the essential teaching".

Honmon no Honzon: The object of devotion of the essential teaching

> The Mandala-Gohonzon is the means by which the fundamental Law of Nam-myō-hō-ren-ge-kyō for people's attaining Buddhahood is manifested. One of the Three Great Secret Laws, representing the aspect of meditation of the three types of Learning – precepts, meditation, and wisdom. The "Essential Teaching" here doesn't mean that of the Lotus Sutra taught by Shakyamuni Buddha under the aspect of a theoretical reading, but rather Nichiren Daishōnin's own "Unique and Independent Essential Teaching under the Aspect of a Deeper Reading". The Mandala-Gohonzon is the object of worship that represents the Buddha's state of life which the Daishōnin realized in his own life and, therefore, the Law aspect of the object of worship. On the other hand, because Nichiren Daishōnin is the Buddha embodying Nam-myō-hō-ren-ge-kyō, he represents the Person aspect of the object of worship. Since Nam-myō-hō-ren-ge-kyō contains all the benefit amassed through the countless practices and meritorious deeds of Shakyamuni Buddha, embracing the Gohonzon embodying this Mystic Law corresponds to the practice of meditation for attaining Buddhahood. In this way the benefit will be opened up and manifested in order to attain enlightenment. This principle is called "Embracing the Gohonzon is in itself observing one's own mind".

This series of explanations does not seem to differ from the conventional NS Nichikan teaching, does it? "The *Unique and Independent Essential Teaching under the Aspect of a Deeper Reading*" means nothing other than Nam-myō-hō-ren-ge-kyō, the core teaching hidden in the depths of the words of the Life Span chapter in the essential teaching of the Lotus Sutra. "*The Buddha embodying this Mystic Law*" is Nichiren Daishōnin, representing the Person aspect of the object of worship. The Mandala-honzon is "*the object of worship that represents the Buddha's state of life which the Daishōnin realized in his own life and, therefore, the Law aspect of the object of worship*".

At this point, in a conventional way, both aspects can be unified as "the Gohonzon in the Oneness of Buddha and Dharma". However, there is no such entry word in the Japanese version while the conventional explanation for this "Oneness of the Person and the Law" is still found in the English SGDB. In the case of this revised Japanese version the relationship between the two aspects of the Mandala-honzon has become rather unclear. Should we worship the Daishōnin alone as Buddha? Or does the Mandala-honzon represent the life state of the Daishōnin as Buddha? If it is so, that means nothing other than the unity of the Person and the Law, doesn't it? However, no explanation is given.

So again, let's see the entry word "Gohonzon".

Gohonzon: The object of Devotion

In stating that "there is multi-significance to the Gohonzon of Nam-myō-hō-ren-ge-kyō which Nichiren Daishōnin inscribed", a number of aspects are explained. The essential points are summarized below:

- The Mystic Law representing the original cause for attaining Buddhahood actually means Buddha nature or the Buddhahood that all people are endowed with.
- The Daishōnin realized the Mystic Law and established not only the practice of chanting Daimoku but also the Mandala-honzon embodying his own enlightened state of life.
- In the center of the Gohonzon is inscribed "Nam-myō-hō-ren-ge-kyō Nichiren", representing the aspect of "the Unity of person and law".
- Therefore, "we can open up and manifest the Buddhahood inherent in our own lives as ordinary people just like the Daishōnin".
- In that sense, the "Gohonzon functions like a clear mirror reflecting our own Buddhahood in actuality".
- The Gohonzon represents the principle of Ichinen Sanzen based on the Mutual Containment of the Ten Worlds. The Daishōnin manifested "the life state of a Buddha opened up in the body of an ordinary person" in actuality which is reflected on the Gohonzon. This is called the Ichinen Sanzen of Actuality.

Though the Daishōnin may be regarded as the true Buddha for our times and be venerated as the object of devotion in terms of the Person, the important consideration here is that we, just like the Daishōnin, can open up Buddhahood within our own lives based on the principle of the ordinary person as Buddha. In this sense, the Gohonzon has the significance of being a clear mirror reflecting our own enlightened state of life.

Finally, let's check the definition of the Mystic Law itself from this perspective.

Nam-myō-hō-ren-ge-kyō

Likewise, in this item "some important aspects are explained". These can be listed as follows, while I extract and summarize only the important points which have not been mentioned above.

- Nam-myō-hō-ren-ge-kyō is a fundamental Law pervading the whole universe and all life. Shakyamuni realized this Law within his own life and was called Buddha. Based on the Lotus Sutra, the Daishōnin made

it clear that the fundamental Law which the Buddha realized for liberating all beings from the root cause of all suffering and opening up to all beings the way to happiness is none other than Nam-myō-hō-ren-ge-kyō.
- Nam-myō-hō-ren-ge-kyō is a universal Law which all people are endowed with and it is an eternal Law pervading the three existences of past, present and future.
- *Renge*, the lotus flower, has a dual-significance: it remains unstained even when growing in a quagmire, and it symbolizes the principle of the Simultaneity of Cause and Effect as both the petals (cause) and the seed pods (result) grow at the same time.
- The Daishōnin realized and then revealed and made clear that the fundamental law referred to in the Lotus Sutra is manifested in his own life and it is none other than Nam-myō-hō-ren-ge-kyō. We venerate the Daishōnin in his capacity as the true Buddha in the Latter Day of the Law, the era filled with confusion and suffering. Nam-myō-hō-ren-ge-kyō is the Buddha's life itself and therefore the Daishōnin embodies the fundamental law which pervades the whole universe and all life.
- Originally, each one of us is also Nam-myō-hō-ren-ge-kyō itself. When we believe and practice it, the power and function of the Mystic Law will at once appear.
- The Daishōnin inscribed his own enlightened life as a mandala, and he established the Gohonzon for us, ordinary people, in order to practice and thereby embody Nam-myō-hō-ren-ge-kyō and to attain Buddhahood just like the Daishōnin. In this way we are able to open up and manifest the Mystic Law inherent within each of us and attain the state of the Buddha's enlightened of life.

Several explanations about the Mystic Law of Nam-myō-hō-ren-ge-kyō are provided, but they can be summarized under two important aspects.

> *"Nam-myō-hō-ren-ge-kyō is the Buddha's life itself which the Daishōnin embodies and is the fundamental law pervading the whole universe and all life"* and *"the Daishōnin inscribed his own enlightened life on a mandala"*.

> *"Originally, each of one of us is also Nam-myō-hō-ren-ge-kyō itself"* and *"he established the Gohonzon for us, ordinary people, in order to practice and thereby embody Nam-myō-hō-ren-ge-kyō and to attain Buddhahood just like the Daishōnin"*.

According to these definitions, the Daishōnin is considered to be the true Buddha for our times who already embodies the enlightened state of life. For this reason, he should be revered as the object of worship in terms of the Person. On the other hand, we can attain the same enlightened state of life as the Daishōnin by chanting the Mystic Law symbolizing the principle of the simultaneity of cause and effect, that is, the ordinary person -equals- Buddha. This particular definition is close to the doctrinal position which I have been advocating for a long time: "the theory of the ordinary person as true Buddha based on the Mutual Containment of the Ten Worlds". However, the first definition still represents a conventional view with respect to the Daishōnin in that it gives the impression that the Mystic Law of Nam-myō-hō-ren-ge-kyō is only identical to his own life. In order to avoid a deifying mystification of the Person, the Mystic Law must necessarily have a universal significance. Thus, it is absolutely essential to make a clear distinction between the Law and the Person. The Unity of the Person and the Law will be manifested only when we chant Daimoku.

2. The basic doctrinal concepts used in SG Silent Prayer

Some parts of SG silent prayer section were changed in November 2015. Let's check the changes made with respect to the Gohonzon and the Daishōnin.

By way of comparison, first we will take a look at the older version which was identical to the traditional Taisekiji version found in "The Liturgy of Nichiren Shōshū".[21]

Second Prayer - Offering to the Dai-Gohonzon

I express my sincere devotion to the **Dai-gohonzon** - the soul of the Juryo chapter of the Essential Teachings and the Supreme Law concealed within its depths, the fusion of the realm of the Original Infinite Law and the inherent wisdom within the **Buddha of Kuon Ganjo**, the manifestation of the Buddha of Intrinsically Perfect Wisdom, the eternal coexistence of the Ten Worlds, the entity of Ichinen Sanzen, **the oneness of the Person and the Law**, and **the Supreme Object of Worship of the High Sanctuary**. I also express my heartfelt gratitude for Its beneficence and pray that Its profound benevolent power may ever more widely prevail.

Third Prayer - Offering to Nichiren Daishōnin and the Successive High Priests

I express my sincere devotion to **the Founder of True Buddhism**, Nichiren Daishōnin, the boundlessly compassionate Buddha who revealed **the True Cause of Original Enlightenment**; who possesses the Three Enlightened Properties, and **whose Three Enlightened Properties comprise His single being**; whose beneficence transcends the Three Existences; and

---

[21] Quoted from the link on "The Liturgy of Nichiren Shoshu", Nichiren Shoshu Head Temple Taiseki-ji edition (p. 33-34):
https://de.scribd.com/doc/34254294/The-Liturgy-of-Nichiren-Shoshu

who possesses the Three Virtues of sovereign, teacher, and parent. I also express my heartfelt gratitude for His beneficence and pray that His profound benevolent power may ever more widely prevail.

Thus, the conventional silent prayers practiced in NS represent wholly traditional NS Nichiren doctrine on the Dai-gohonzon and Nichiren as the true and original Buddha who is embodied on the Dai-gohonzon in the Oneness of the Person and the Law. In contrast to this older version, the new revised SG silent prayers are much simplified.[22]

> In expressing my faith in the Gohonzon of Nam-myō-hō-ren-ge-kyō, the essence of the Lotus Sutra, I offer my profound gratitude and appreciation.
>
> In expressing my faith in Nichiren Daishōnin, the true Buddha in the Latter Day of the Law, I offer my profound gratitude and appreciation.

"In expressing my faith in" is my translation of the Japanese wording "Doing *Namu*" that sounds very peculiar. Anyway, the new silent prayers still stress the two aspects of the Mystic Law and the Person (Buddha) as the objects of devotion. They are explained clearly in the entry "For new members" as follows:

> (The meaning) The basic SG teaching is to venerate Nichiren Daishōnin as the true Buddha in the Latter Day of the Law, to believe in the Three Secret Laws in that the fundamental law of Nam-myō-hō-ren-ge-kyō has been embodied in a concrete manifest form, and to chant Daimoku is for the sake of one's own practice and for the instruction of others toward the Gohonzon. The Daishōnin often taught in the gosho that Nam-myō-hō-ren-ge-kyō representing the fundamental law is the "the essence of the Lotus Sutra" and is manifested in the form of the Gohonzon. Therefore, when we express our faith in "the Gohonzon of Nam-myō-hō-ren-ge-kyō, the essence of the Lotus Sutra", we offer our profound gratitude and appreciation, and we swear to practice faith in the Gohonzon as the foundation of our lives. In addition, we venerate Nichiren Daishōnin as the "true Buddha in the Latter Day of the Law" who inscribed the

---

[22] At this point, the traditional prayer to the *Shoten Zenjin* (heavenly gods and benevolent deities) was completely omitted. Regarding the new English version of the SG gongyō see, for example: http://chantforhappiness.blogspot.de/2015/12/ revised-silent-prayers-for-sgi-members.html.
The corresponding English Silent Prayers state now:
I offer my profound gratitude and appreciation to the Gohonzon, which embodies Nam-myoho-renge-kyo, the essence of the Lotus Sutra.
I offer my profound gratitude and appreciation to Nichiren Daishōnin, the Buddha of the Latter Day of the Law.

Gohonzon, we offer our profound gratitude and appreciation, and we swear to practice our faith in direct communion with the Daishōnin.

What is meant by the "the fundamental law" can be better understood with reference to the following definition of the purpose of the Gohonzon in the entry "What is gongyō?".

"The Gohonzon" represents his own life as the Buddha whereby Nichiren Daishōnin, the true Buddha, was enlightened to Nam-myō-hō-ren-ge-kyō, the fundamental law pervading the whole universe and all life. Believing in the Gohonzon, when we recite the Sutra and chant Daimoku, the life state of Buddhahood originally inherent in our own lives will appear. Thus, our lives will be polished by persisting with the practice of Gongyo day by day.

To summarize the main points:
- Nam-myō-hō-ren-ge-kyō is the fundamental Law pervading the whole universe and all life.
- Nichiren Daishōnin was enlightened to this Law.
- He manifested the enlightened life of the true Buddha in the concrete form of the Gohonzon.
- We take a vow to maintain our faith focused on the Gohonzon and in expressing our devotion to the Gohonzon of Nam-myō-hō-ren-ge-kyō, the essence of the Lotus Sutra.
- At the same time, we venerate Nichiren Daishōnin, who inscribed the Gohonzon, as the true Buddha of the Latter Day of the Law, we offer our profound gratitude and appreciation, and we take a vow to maintain our faith in direct communion with the Daishōnin.
- In addition, in chanting Daimoku with faith in the Gohonzon, the highest life state inherent in us appears. Thus, our lives will be polished.

So far, because these explanations are for beginners, we may disregard the finer points, so it can be basically said that the new version of SG teaching expresses the position of "the theory of the Instant Enlightenment of the ordinary person". At least, it is oriented in this doctrinal direction.

Summary

No matter how long I consider the definitions of Buddhist terms given by the SG Study Department in 2017, the definitions of the basic terms are still ultimately derived from the NS Nichikan teaching, e.g. *"Unique and Independent Essential Teaching under the Aspect of a Deeper Reading"* or "the Original Beginning of Eternity". However, the basic doctrines of "Nichiren as the Eternal Original Buddha" and "The Dai-gohonzon as the Supreme Object of Worship of the High Sanctuary" have been discarded. Instead, the new revised SG teaching gives me the impression that the "theory of the ordinary person as true Buddha" based on the principle of "ordinary person -equals- Buddha" has become generally accepted.

However, with respect to "Nam-myō-hō-ren-ge-kyō" and the "Object of devotion", the new definitions given by the SG Study Department remain somewhat opaque and ambiguous. They lack a systematic articulation and clear definition. Consequently, this situation is further confirmation of the necessity to act on my proposal to further clarify and radically redefine the doctrine and practice of Nichiren Buddhism. To that end, in Part Three I will propose a "multilayered perspective based on the Meditative Viewpoint with respect to the Essential Teaching for our times". This multilayered approach will enable us to classify the main interpretative patterns found in Nichiren Shōshū and Nichiren Shū, and to systematize each set of teachings, including my own analytical standpoint, in order to undertake a systematic comparison.

Part Three

The Theory of the Ordinary Person as Buddha based on the Principle of the Mutual Containment of the Ten Worlds

Introduction

I have been very much inspired by the in-depth treatment, from a variety of perspectives on a wide range of issues related to Nichiren and the Lotus Sutra, found in the articles and reviews which have been published in »Lotus Buddhism Studies No. 21« (October of 2015), as well as in the subsequent issue (May of 2016). Especially with those articles dealing with such matters as the comparative evaluation of *the Essential and Theoretical Sections of the Lotus Sutra*, with *the attainment of Buddhahood* and on with *the object of devotion*. Indeed, I have felt impelled to reformulate my own basic principles in the light of insights gleaned from these two magazines. As issue No. 23 (December of 2016) has only just appeared as I write, I will also refer to it where necessary. It is my intention to develop a new perspective on Nichiren thought, without the use of cumbersome terminology and abstruse speculation on philological and historiographical issues, as well as avoiding all sectarian and ideological presuppositions with respect to doctrinal history. This should permit me to focus primarily on the central doctrinal problems associated with "Daimoku" and "honzon".

However, if I simply state that my fundamental position amounts to "a theory of the ordinary person as true Buddha", some might be misled it to concluding that it is no more than a novel version of *the medieval Tendai philosophy of original enlightenment*. In order to avoid this unfortunate assumption, I will therefore seek to emphasize the dynamics of praxis itself and its dialectical relationship to self-understanding and enlightened life. In other words, the "theory of the ordinary person -qua- Buddha" is based on the fundamental principle of the "Nine Worlds -qua- Buddhahood". Yet the transformation denoted by "-qua-" is consequent upon the concrete practice of chanting Daimoku. For it is only then that the ordinary person will manifest in his or her own life that particular quality of enlightened life. Consequently, the theory of "the ordinary person -qua- Buddha" is firmly based on *the principle of the Mutual Containment of the Ten Worlds*. This is synonymous with "the theory of the immediate or Instant Enlightenment of the ordinary person".

Any attempt to provide rational justification for one's own thesis inevitably tends towards complexity, given that one is faced with a whole series of analytical problems and an abundance of detailed sources, as well as with the previous reflections of others. Consequently, for clarity, I will begin by summarizing my conclusions to the matters considered in Part Three.

- Nichiren doctrine is rich in meaning and has a multilayered structure. By way of organization and to emphasize its contemporary significance, I have designated the heart of Nichiren's teaching as the "Meditative Essential Teaching for our times". From that I develop a "four-fold or quadruple comparative method", basically following the traditional four-fold comparison: 1) the Lotus Sutra contra the pre-Lotus Sutras, 2) the Essential Section contra the Theoretical Section of the Lotus Sutra, 3) the Sowing contra the Harvesting within the Essential Section and 4) the chanting of Daimoku as the meditative practice of Instant Enlightenment for our times.

- The last comparison represents the most profound insight of Nichiren, as I understand it. For this signifies nothing other than the "theory of the ordinary person -qua- Buddha" or the "theory of the Instant Enlightenment of the ordinary person".
- The seven characters of "Na-m(u)-myō-hō-ren-ge-kyō" signify the "practice of chanting Daimoku" itself. This is the practice of the five characters of "Myō-hō-ren-ge-kyō", the Mystic Law for the immediate enlightenment of all beings based on *the principle of the Mutual Containment of the Ten Worlds*.
- Nichiren considered that this practice represented "original cause -qua- original effect" and is identical to "the Attainment of Enlightenment in the remotest past" as described in the Life Span Chapter of the Essential Section, and he declared it to be the practice of the original cause for all buddhas in the three existences.
- Consequently, Nichiren's own practice is nothing other than the practice of chanting Daimoku as transmitted to Jōgyō, and in this capacity he inscribed *the Mandala-honzon of Ichinen Sanzen based on the principle of the Mutual Containment of the Ten Worlds*.
- The principle is universal so that we, the ordinary people of today, can also attain the enlightened state of life by chanting the Daimoku of seven characters.
- The Mandala-honzon represents *the object of devotion for observing or manifesting Buddhahood* (Buddha World) in an ordinary body within the Nine Worlds. Thus, it represents the principle of the Instant Enlightenment of ordinary people.

As Nichiren's doctrine takes into account a variety of viewpoints on the significance of the Lotus Sutra, the Mandala-honzon can likewise be understood from a multilayered perspective. Consequently, an analysis and classification of the multilayered structure of NB is the primary task of Part 3.

Discarding the dogma of authenticity

Primarily, since I will emphasize the aspect of the activation of Buddhahood by ordinary people today, the doctrine of "Instant Enlightenment based on the Mutual Containment of the Ten Worlds" will play the central role. This presupposes *the doctrine of original enlightenment*. i.e. that Buddhahood or Buddha nature is inherent in our own lives. In order to activate this potential and to attain to an enlightened state of life, it is necessary to practice by chanting Daimoku. Thus, the doctrine of the "ordinary person - qua- Buddha" never depends on the absurd idea that we are, just as we are, Buddha. The preposition "-qua-" always implies a dialectical relationship of actual transformation in that we, ordinary people, activate the Buddhahood inherent in our own lives. It is a dynamic process by way of which we can improve our personal circumstances and modify our karmic tendencies. We will never remain in a static situation, rather we are challenged to grow.

Given the above, NB has a new radical orientation, for the relationship between "ordinary person" and "buddha" is reversed. It is no longer a primary concern of the practitioner, as with traditional Temple Buddhism, to worship Buddhas and Bodhisattvas and to participate in such ritual-focused religious concerns as funeral or memorial ceremonies. Thus, in contrast to a priest or temple-focused form of Buddhist practice, our main concern in practicing NB is to activate Buddhahood and to manifest it in our own everyday life. In fact, such a focus can be found in many gosho which implicitly or explicitly make reference to the doctrine of original enlightenment. Indeed, for this reason, such gosho have frequently been unfairly dismissed as apocryphal or of questionable authenticity. Yet to my mind, these writings are a rich and wonderful resource, containing the most precious gems of wisdom found anywhere in Nichiren's thought. For they represent the most profound insights of Nichiren himself and brilliantly reflect his ultimate teaching and intention.

With respect to dogmatic "authenticity-centrism", Hiroshi Kawasaki, NB researcher, took a radical critical stance : *"Whichever of Nichiren's original writings have survived until today is purely accidental"*; *"If one takes only the surviving original writings into consideration, it is not possible to fully understand Nichiren's thought as it changed with the times"*; *"We cannot get an overall picture without the use of non-autographed copied manuscripts and by considering them to be authentic"* (21: 99).[23] I completely agree.

Further, with respect to Nichiren's autobiographical writing entitled »The Actions of the Votary of the Lotus Sutra«, Kawasaki considered all relevant non-autographed copied manuscripts, as well as all other relevant manuscripts and literature in great detail. Then, based on his philological and historiographical research, he arrived at an interesting conclusion: *"Although*

---

[23] hereinafter, the source of quotation from the Japanese magazine »Lotus Buddhism Studies « is indicated simply by the issue number and page number (e.g. 21: 99). Any kind of titles of honor or is omitted as usual in an academic discourse.

this writing might be considered to be non-apocryphal, it nevertheless contains a lot of additional information, detail and modes of often dramatic expression, which might still remain of great value to posterity" (23: 160).
This means for us today:

> Unless it is a writing in Nichiren's own hand
> and no matter what kind of manuscript it otherwise is,
> we can never deny the possibility that it might contain
> additions, corrections, and misunderstandings which are
> attributable to later generations of editors or copyists.

With respect to the philosophical dimension, convinced that *"Nichiren began from the esoteric Buddhist teachings"* (21: 81), Toshiyuki Ishizuki, a historical-oriented researcher, greatly valued the "esoteric mystical experience reflected in Nichiren's thought" (21: 82). He points out: *"This aspect represents that opaque mystical part of Nichiren's teaching which had been wholly discarded from the Nichiren Shū doctrine which had subsequently been authorized and handed down to posterity"* (ibid.). I fully agree with this.

Likewise, I feel rather encouraged by the criticisms raised by Jūdō Hanano with respect to the research tendency *"to exclude all writings lacking an original autograph [...] and eliminating medieval Tendai teaching and all esoteric Buddhist thought from Nichiren's writings"* (21: 190).

Further, Makoto Ozaki clearly states, especially highlighting the varied interplay of ideas and the overall complexity found in all examples of reflective or discursive thought.

> In the case of philosophical literature, a wide variety of ideas are compounded and constitute the whole. Therefore, it is a short-sighted and superficial methodological approach to raise only one idea as a standard by which criteria are established in order to judge the truth or falsehood of a particular writing. By doing so, the whole complexity of a philosophical or Buddhist idea would be thereby unduly simplified (23: 260).

The above criticism had been raised as an objection to the view that those gosho which Ozaki was willing to consider to be of use in establishing the authentic teaching of Nichiren were in fact apocryphal, e.g. »The Entity of the Mystic Law«, »The Mystic Principle of the Original Cause« and »One Hundred and Six Comparisons«. Generally, I personally welcome any use of non-authenticated writings in so far as they are philosophically coherent and consistent with Nichiren's own authenticated works.

In other words, it is a legitimate interpretive device to draw out the theoretical and practical implications of what Nichiren intended to say to posterity, as long as any conclusions are clearly annotated, explained and conceptually well-organized. In this sense, there can be no doubt that Nichiren thought includes a doctrine of original enlightenment, but it is nevertheless

INTRODUCTION

essential to consider with great discrimination exactly what kind of Original Enlightenment thought is being implied. For example, in »The Actions of the Votary of the Lotus Sutra«, it is necessary to examine the content of the Gosho very carefully, as both Original Enlightenment thought and alternative modulations on that thought appear in the same Gosho.

I have mentioned already that Sueki places great value on »The Record of the Orally Transmitted Teachings«, given its highly philosophical content even though it is usually considered to be apocryphal (see above page 68). I also consider this Gosho to be not simply a fabrication without any legitimate foundation, but rather as a record which Nichiren's disciples carefully compiled by systematically rearranging Nichiren's lectures on the Lotus Sutra.

For example, as I noted with reference to the matter of the Buddhist sutras and the Bible (see above page 119 f.), neither the Buddha nor Jesus Christ left any autographed writings. That is to say, there is no authentic writing received from either of these founders. Yet given this, should all the extant sutras and scriptures thereby be regarded as the pious forgeries of later believers, i.e. that they are all apocrypha? The problem of authenticity with respect to the received sutras and scriptures is relevant not only to Mahayana Buddhism, where many have questioned whether they can be considered to be directly related to the actual teachings of the historical Shakyamuni Buddha, but indeed also both to the Theravada sutras themselves and the Bible itself. Are all the philosophical and religious reflections of so many wise believers over a period of several hundred or thousands of years to be discounted as worthless? Conversely, any system of thought naturally changes as it is handed down and modified over time. During this process of transition, *"a particular ideological background tends to coalesce"* (23: 260), as Ozaki has correctly pointed out.

Consequently, the attempt to exclude particular ideas from Nichiren thought, such as "the theory of the ordinary person as Buddha based on the Mutual Containment of the Ten Worlds", might in fact be taken to represent a partisan doctrinal stance based on a sectarian ideology which seeks to defend a faith, ritual, priest and temple focused form of NB. This highlights a fundamental principle: was NB established in order that believers worship a Buddha as an external savior or was NB established in order that we might activate that Buddhahood inherent within our own lives?

Against this background, Hanano developed his theory that Nichiren's teaching itself inherently contains esoteric and medieval Tendai teachings. For this reason, he was motivated to accept as legitimate sources for the reconstruction of Nichiren thought those gosho which have widely been considered to be apocryphal, e.g. »The Real Aspect of the Gohonzon«, »The Teaching, Time, Capacity and Country«, »The True Aspect of All phenomena«,

»On Practicing the Buddha's Teachings«, »On Establishing Correct Meditation«, »The Teaching, Practice, and Proof«, »Critical Consideration« of all the Buddha's Teachings«, and »The Three Great Secret Laws« (Hanano 2012). I would like to express my sincere gratitude for his efforts.

In addition, I feel some sympathy with Hiroshi Kanno's remarks: *"in the light of today's situation, it is becoming necessary that we revitalize Nichiren's thought in a contemporary manner"* (21: 183). Given this encouragement, I have myself sought to reconceptualize Nichiren thought in order to make it contemporarily relevant, and any success in which I owe to the research of scholars currently working in the field of Nichiren Buddhist studies. In other words, I have been *"seeking to rebuild Nichiren Buddhism so that it can be effectively practiced throughout contemporary global society"* in order *"to forge a radical religious individualism characterized by radical self-responsibility"* (21: 154). This is an attitude which I consistently maintain.

Philosophical evaluation of the non-authenticated writings

In the argument developed below, I don't begin from any preconceived religious position or sectarian doctrinal viewpoint. I will take Nichiren's writings at face value, without any extraneous interpretive considerations. In this way, I will develop a theory of the ordinary person as inherently Buddha. As justification for my theory, I will primarily rely upon the "authentic gosho", but I will permit myself to draw upon "unauthenticated gosho" as long as they seem to be philosophically consistent with Nichiren's original thought. For they will serve as additional justification for my theory. This means that I don't rely on unauthenticated writings in order to establish my theory itself, rather I rely on them only during the process of argumentation, whereby I cite them as an additional support. Incidentally, this methodological approach is consistent with that recommended by Shinjō Suguro (1925-2012), a priest of Nichiren Shū and professor at Risshō University.

> I think that a good methodology should be to designate the non-authenticated gosho as auxiliary materials, to consider the Shonin's thought first with reference only to the basic materials, and to use the auxiliary material only in so far as they do not contradict the basic materials. This methodological approach seems to me to be the most appropriate (Suguro 1998).

Chapter 1
The Process of Formation of the Three Principles for Realizing Buddhahood

1. Elucidating the Multilayered Character of Nichiren's Teachings

Let's begin with the main subject. Kanji Tamura, Professor of Buddhist Studies at Risshō university, performed a useful service in systematically categorizing the most significant gosho, e.g. under such headings as "gosho focused on the Essential Section", "the Three Great Secret Laws of the Essential Section", "Significance of the Daimoku", etc. (21: 17-58)[24]. This categorization is extremely useful, and I will make use of it. However, when such a system of categorization is used it can become rather arbitrary, with gosho simply listed together without any thought of detailed analysis or adequate justification by way of citation, etc. Consequently, I am rather anxious as to whether gosho may have been simply listed under category headings, which do not adequately reflect the richness and variety of the material to be found in each gosho.

For it is certainly true when Tamura notes that *"Nichiren Shonin never developed a completely consistent teaching which was, from the beginning to the end, logically consistent and formulated in a harmonious and unified manner"* (21: 13). This ambiguity is probably related to Nichiren's shifting perspective and emphases in his discourse as he reacted to criticism or altered circumstances. Nevertheless, Nichiren loudly proclaimed the superiority of the Lotus Sutra to the pre-Lotus Sutras and the superiority of the Essential Section to the Theoretical Section within the Lotus Sutra itself.

Further, while maintaining the position of the superiority of the Essential Section to the Theoretical Section, Tamura goes beyond this comparative level by admitting that *"we can find some evidence that Nichiren considered that the Daimoku itself surpasses both the teaching of the essential and Theoretical Sections of the Lotus Sutra"* (21: 62). Consequently, we need to proceed using a comparative method of evaluation: i.e. considering either the depth or shallowness of a particular teaching, as well as the superiority and inferiority of the various teachings. In this way, we will elucidate the multilayered character of Nichiren's teaching. If we never undertake such a task,

---

[24] Tamura quotes from the »Showa Standard« (SS), which is usual for scholars of Nichiren Shū, but in this book I will quote mainly from »the Soka Gakkai version«, noting each page number.

we are compelled to surrender to chaos, simply admitting to a fundamental incoherence or confusion, or at least a dissonant admixture of contradictory elements, in the thought of Nichiren. Consequently, we would ourselves be thrown into a situation which Nichiren warned against, i.e. uncritically allowing a variety of objects of devotion and promiscuously accepting miscellaneous forms of practice or belief in and offering worship to a whole range of Buddhas, Bodhisattvas or deities.

2. The Difference in Nichiren's Teaching before and after the Sado Exile

In elucidating the particular character of NB, a *"distinction between teachings before and after the Sado exile"* should be the first marker. There have been a variety of hypotheses as to the demarcation point, but following Kawasaki (21: 123), I would take the "persecution at Tatsunokuchi" as the point of transition. This is because Nichiren himself took this event as declaratory for his radically new self-understanding that he himself was indeed the only true Votary of the Lotus Sutra, as he later recorded:

> On the twelfth day of the ninth month of last year [1271], between the hours of the rat and the ox [11:00 p.m. to 3:00 a.m.], this person named Nichiren was beheaded. It is his soul that has come to this island of Sado.
> (»The Opening of the Eyes«, p. 223 / I. 269)

Based on this radically new self-understanding, Nichiren made a clear distinction with respect to his own teachings:

> As for my teachings, regard those before my exile to the province of Sado as equivalent to the Buddha's pre-Lotus Sutra teachings.
> (»Letter to Misawa«, p. 1489 / I. 896)

The Dual Identity of the Tendai Monk and the Bodhisattva Jōgyō

So, what changed fundamentally before and after Sado? Hanano together with Yutaka Takagi points out that Nichiren throughout his life always thought of himself partly as simply *"being a Tendai monk"* (23: 55-57). Before Sado Nichiren might be considered to be a Tendai monk of "heterodox reformist tendency", who had established *"a group within the Tendai school for promoting the practice of Daimoku"* (23: 67). Consequently, Tendai monks gathered around Nichiren, and with them he established a place to provide a series of "Tendai Daishi Lectures" which also served as a place of meeting. These group meetings, which focused on the study of Tendai doctrine, began around the year 1265 and continued each year up to year before Nichiren's death. Hanano believes after Sado Nichiren changed his focus: from henceforth, the practice of Daimoku was promoted with express reference to his radically new self-understanding and that he was himself identical with Bodhisattva Jōgyō. Thus:

> With Nichiren we must be aware of these two dimensions: the "Tendai Monk Nichiren" who established the Tendai Daishi Lectures and the "Bodhisattva Jōgyō Nichiren" who practiced shakubuku in order to propagate the Buddhism of Sowing. (23: 57)

The Dual Practice of Chanting Daimoku and Meditation on Ichinen Sanzen

On the occasions when he gave the Tendai Daishi Lecture, Nichiren lectured on T'ien-t'ai's »Great Concentration and Insight« (23: 55). This fact reminds us once again as to how important the "doctrine of observing the mind" (*kanjin*) was to him. Taking an example from the period before Sado, there is in »The Ten Chapters« written in May 1271 a prescription which recommends both "Daimoku Chanting" and "Meditation on Ichinen Sanzen". Thereby, Nichiren found the real meaning of Ichinen Sanzen only in the Essential Section:

> There are ten chapters in T'ien-t'ai's »Great Concentration and insight". [...] It now states that setting up the right practice in accordance with the mystic understanding is right contemplation, with its ten objects and the ten kinds of meditation methods, as expounded in chapter seven. This is the heart of the Essential Section. Ichinen Sanzen is derived from this chapter. [...] Although the source of Ichinen Sanzen lies in the Ten Aspects of Suchness which open up to the One Buddha Vehicle, the real meaning is found only in the Essential Section. [...] The Essential Section can be read just as it is written if the true meaning of the words are to be understood.
> (p. 1274 / -)

The doctrine of contemplation which Nichiren adopted is Ichinen Sanzen, but he held in mind that this method of meditation should be practiced while chanting Daimoku.

> Following the true and perfect practice, we should constantly recite Nam-myō-hō-ren-ge-kyō. What we should bear in our heart is this method of meditation on Ichinen Sanzen. This is however the understanding of a wise person. For lay believers in Japan let them exclusively chant Nam-myō-hō-ren-ge-kyō. The "name" has the virtue to inevitably reach the "essence". [...] All Buddhas such as Amitabha and Shakyamuni practiced this method of Concentration and Insight as the cause by which they attained

> Buddhahood. That which they were always humming was Nam-myō-hō-ren-ge-kyō. (ibid.)

That is to say, as a matter of doctrine, the ordinary people of our time should practice both the method of meditation of Ichinen Sanzen and chant the Daimoku, as these are the practices which cause the enlightenment of all Buddhas. Nichiren had been propagating the practice of chanting Daimoku from the beginning of the proclamation of his new teaching, yet what is understood by the other practice of contemplation?

In »The Opening of the Eyes« written in February of 1272 on Sado, Nichiren stated that the doctrine of Ichinen Sanzen is the principle for attaining Buddhahood and that this jewel is wrapped in the Lotus Sutra.

> Only the T'ien-t'ai doctrine of Ichinen Sanzen can be considered the path to Buddhahood. As to this Ichinen Sanzen we don't have the slightest idea. Nevertheless, among all the sutras preached by the Buddha during his lifetime, the Lotus Sutra alone contains this jewel of Ichinen Sanzen. [...]
>
> Although I and my disciples may encounter various difficulties, if we do not harbor doubts in our hearts, we will as a matter of course attain Buddhahood. (p. 234 / I. 282)

Again, in »The Object of Observing the Mind« written in April 1273 on Sado, Nichiren described the actual character of this jewel, which should be given to the ordinary people of our time.

> The Lotus Sutra, especially its Essential Section, is intended primarily for those people living after the Buddha's passing, and the Buddha entrusted it firstly to the Bodhisattvas of the Earth. [...]
>
> In the middle and latter part of the Middle Day of the Law, Bodhisattva *Kannon* was reborn as Nan-yüeh, and Bodhisattva *Yakuō* (Medicine King) as T'ien-t'ai. Keeping the Theoretical Section to the fore while keeping the Essential Section in the background, they fully revealed the meaning of Ichinen Sanzen in terms of the One Hundred Worlds and the Thousand Factors. Though they expounded in principle of the Mutual Containment of the Ten Worlds, they did not practice the five characters of Nam-myō-hō-ren-ge-kyō in actuality, nor did they establish the Object of Devotion based on the Essential Section. This is just because the time was not right for propagation, although some Buddhists already had the actual capacity.
>
> Now, in the beginning of the Latter Day of the Law, [...] the Bodhisattvas of the Earth have appeared in this world for the first time solely in order to bring the medicine of the five characters of Myō-hō-ren-ge-kyō to ignorant ordinary people. (p. 253 / I. 375)

Thus, Nichiren declared that the Bodhisattva Jōgyō would appear in our time and establish "the Object of Devotion based on the Essential Section" which is to be conferred on all ordinary people. Consequently, a real change can be seen in Nichiren's self-understanding, a transition from "a Tendai monk chanting the Title of the Lotus Sutra" to "a reborn Jōgyō chanting the five characters of Nam-myō-hō-ren-ge-kyō in actuality" (Hanano 23: 67). However, even if there was a change in the significance of "Nichiren's self-understanding and position", there was no change at all with respect to the practice of chanting Daimoku. It should be remembered, that Nichiren consistently held "chanting Daimoku" to be the most essential practice after the first proclamation of his teaching.

Thus, the fundamental transition point before and after Sado is this radical change in Nichiren's self-understanding and express self-identification as "the votary of the Lotus Sutra, the reincarnation of Jōgyō". And it was with this self-understanding that Nichiren inscribed the Mandala-honzon manifesting all the Ten Worlds. In order to explain these two essential matters Nichiren wrote two of his major works on Sado: »The Opening of the Eyes« and »The Object for Observing the Mind".

By prescribing the Gohonzon as the most essential object of faith and devotion, Nichiren provided the very basis for the standardization of his teachings in the form of the Three Great Secret Laws. Having considered the circumstances before and after Sado, we may conclude the following:

When Nichiren publicly proclaimed the practice of chanting Daimoku as
the essential practice at Seichōji Temple in 1253,
he began the propagation of "his own teaching".
When he inscribed the Mandala-honzon manifesting
the Ten worlds on Sado in 1273, he founded "his own school".

In other words, at the time of proclamation of chanting Daimoku at Seichōji, there were as yet neither doctrinal foundations nor the Three Great Secret Laws, which became the practical and ritual foundations for formation of a distinctive sect or school (see the discussion in 21: 111-113).

3. The essential consistent focus on the multiple significance of the Daimoku

Even if there is a significant difference in Nichiren's self-understanding and teaching before and after Sado, there is no doubt that the essential practice of NB is the "Daimoku" and that he devoted his whole life to propagating it. Nichiren would recall this in his last years, in December 1280, on Minobu.

> In the last 28 years from April 28, 1253, until today, I, Nichiren, have been active with the sole mission of putting the seven or five characters of Myō-hō-ren-ge-kyō into the mouth of all the people in Japan. This effort

is made with compassion like a mother who puts milk into the mouth of her baby. (»The Admonishing the Great Bodhisattva Hachiman«, p. 585 / -)

To practice the chanting of Daimoku by oneself and to propagate that practice among other people and thereby achieve Kōsenrufu, this duty is expressly advocated in »The True Aspect of All Phenomena« written in May of 1273 on Sado.

> Among those who propagate the five characters of Myō-hō-ren-ge-kyō in the Latter Day of the Law, there should be no discrimination between men and women. Were they not Bodhisattvas of the Earth, they could not chant the Daimoku. At first only Nichiren chanted Nam-myō-hō-ren-ge-kyō, but then two, three, and a hundred followed, chanting and teaching others. Propagation will unfold in this way in the future as well. Does this not signify "emerging from the earth"? That the entire Japanese nation will chant Nam-myō-hō-ren-ge-kyō at the time of Kōsenrufu, is as certain as aiming an arrow at the earth which cannot miss its target.
> (p. 1360 / I. 385)

With respect to the term "Daimoku", this is given significance in various ways throughout the Gosho. Further examples of its use are given. Some examples of usage are given here: *"the seven or five characters of Myō-hō-ren-ge-kyō"* (»The Admonishing of the Great Bodhisattva Hachiman«), *"the five or seven characters of Myō-hō-ren-ge-kyō"* (»The Daimoku of the Lotus Sutra«), *"the seven characters of Nam-myō-hō-ren-ge-kyō—which is the heart of the twenty-eight chapters of the Lotus Sutra"* (»How Those Initially Aspiring to the Way Can Attain Buddhahood through the Lotus Sutra«). However, in the »The Object of Observing the Mind« we are given some rather different designations such as : *"the five characters of the Mystic Law"*, *"the five characters of Nam-myō-hō-ren-ge-kyō, the heart of the Essential Section of the Lotus Sutra"*, *"the five characters of Nam-myō-hō-ren-ge-kyō"*, *"the five characters of the Daimoku"*, *"the actual practice of the five characters of Nam-myō-hō-ren-ge-kyō"*.

Consequently, Nichiren designates the term "Daimoku" by way of "five characters", "seven characters" or "five or seven characters", as he also frequently designates the seven characters of Nam-myō-hō-ren-ge-kyō itself as "five characters". It will be necessary to elucidate the ambiguity of the term "Daimoku" further, yet as a beginning it is valid to note:

> "To propagate the five characters of Myō-hō-ren-ge-kyō" means
> "to propagate the seven characters of Nam-myō-hō-ren-ge-kyō,
> which is the practice of chanting the Daimoku
> of Nam-myō-hō-ren-ge-kyō.

In a similar manner, we can note a variety of significations as to what should be offered to the Gohonzon, such as : *"the entire body of the Lotus Sutra and the Daimoku"* (»On Reciting the Daimoku of the Lotus Sutra«), *"the Daimoku of the Lotus Sutra and the Master of the Teaching of the Lotus Sutra"* (»Questions and Answers on the Object of Devotion«), *"Shakyamuni, the Master of the Teaching of the Essential Section"* (»On Repaying Debts of Gratitude«, and so on. Given this ambiguity of expression in Nichiren's writings, with respect to the question of what the object of devotion and worship should be, three different perspectives have developed in terms of "Person (Buddha)", "Law (Dharma)", and the "Unity of the Person and the Law".

In order to resolve these questions, it is essential to pay attention to the context of the discourse and to consider the interpretive perspective. For this is to discern the multiple-layered significance of both the Daimoku and the Gohonzon themselves, yet at the same time, this will elucidate the fundamental teaching of Nichiren Buddhism itself.

4. The three fundamental principles for realizing Buddhahood in our time

Chanting Daimoku remains the essential practice

Nichiren's thought is such that at first sight, as Tamura has pointed out, *"Nichiren Shonin didn't appear to reveal a wholly logical or balanced teaching, which was harmonious and consistent from beginning to end"* and that even in each of his autographed writings *"contradictions, improbable leaps in logic, and multi-valent or ambiguous ideas are to be found"* (21: 13). This certainly suggests *"a dynamic and vital teaching"*, as well as indicating *"a process of reading the Sutra as an actual prophecy predicting his own emergence, as well as providing further legitimation for his own self-understanding in the light of his unique experience of persecution"* (21: 14).

However, I do not believe that Nichiren's fundamental doctrinal stance was only gradually arrived at. For example, beginning on April 28, 1253, he immediately criticized the practice of Nenbutsu from a perspective based fundamentally upon the superiority of the Lotus Sutra and thus proclaimed the essential practice of chanting Daimoku. Thus, from the start this proclamation was provocative, indeed radically contrary to the common understanding and accepted traditions of the religious establishment of his time. He would have known that he would be condemned and persecuted, as the Lotus Sutra predicts. Nichiren clearly needed a compass to navigate through the storm he provoked. Consequently, he must have already arrived at a fundamental conviction that the essence of his teaching could be relied upon to provide an unshakable foundation for his turbulent mission to disseminate his radically innovative form of practice.

Indeed, it is implausible that his fundamental doctrinal stance had not been arrived at prior to the time of advocating the "the seven characters of Nam-myō-hō-ren-ge-kyō as the practice for our time". For it would have been inconceivable and irresponsible to publicly proclaim a radical new teaching without a firm doctrinal foundation. So, let's review Nichiren's starting point.

The three principles for establishing the practice of Daimoku

There is little doubt that Nichiren consistently held the Lotus Sutra to be foremost amongst all the Sutras in accordance with the "doctrine of Attaining Enlightenment in the Remotest Past" as revealed in the Life Span Chapter of the Essential Section. Already in his early work, written at the age of 39, »On Reciting the Daimoku of the Lotus Sutra« (1260), Nichiren emphasized that:

> The two characters of *Myō-Hō* of the Daimoku contain within them the heart of the Lotus Sutra, namely, the doctrine of Three Thousand Realms in a Single Moment of life (*Ichinen Sanzen*) set forth in the Expedient Means chapter, and the doctrine of the Buddha's attainment of enlightenment in the far distant past (*Kuonjitsujō*) set forth in the Life Span Chapter. (p. 13 / II. 229)

As noted above, already in the period before Sado, Nichiren understood the significance of the Mystic Law in relation to the principle of "Attaining Enlightenment in the Remotest Past" = "Ichinen Sanzen". For the Mystic Law itself represents the source of all enlightenment which brings forth all Buddhas.

> One Buddha represents all Buddhas, and all of them are included in the two characters of the Mystic Law. Therefore, the merit of chanting the five characters of Myō-hō-ren-ge-kyō is great and immense. We should chant the Daimoku of the Lotus Sutra in knowing that the Mystic Law has the function of opening up to enlightenment all other Buddhas and all other sutras. (ibid.)

To emphasize once again, chanting the Mystic Law is the direct way for realizing Buddhahood, because it contains the principle of "Attaining Enlightenment in the Remotest Past = Ichinen Sanzen" and the function of opening up to enlightenment and bringing forth all buddhas.

Even in his later years on Minobu (1278, aged 57), this fundamental attitude is evident., Thus:

> Truly, the doctrine of Ichinen Sanzen as revealed by the Attainment of Enlightenment in the Remotest Past was [...] preached in the Life Span Chapter within the Essential Section. This jewel of Ichinen Sanzen was

> wrapped around with the five characters of the Mystic Law, which is as indestructible as a diamond, and bequeathed to us the poor people of the Latter Day.   (»Reply to Ōta Saemon-no-jō«, p. 1016 / -)

In this passage, Nichiren advances one step further and interprets the Attainment of Enlightenment in the Remotest Past as representing the doctrine of Ichinen Sanzen. Although claiming that "Shakyamuni" himself had wrapped this jewel of Ichinen Sanzen around with the indestructible five characters of the Mystic Law and then bequeathed it to the people of the Latter Day, in actuality it was Nichiren himself who had bequeathed this jewel.

In December 1277 (aged 56), Nichiren looked back on the first public proclamation of his teaching and described the Dharma Body of the Mystic Law in some detail.

> On April 28, 1253, I, Nichiren, for the first time clearly enacted the transmission of the large carriage drawn by a white ox, which means the One Vehicle of the Lotus Sutra. [...] The doctrine of Ichinen Sanzen, the event of the Attainment of Buddhahood in the Remotest Past, and the doctrine of Immediate Enlightenment, which are both taught only in the Lotus Sutra.   (»The Large Carriage Drawn by a White Ox«, p. 1543 / I. 723)

Further, the foundation of Ichinen Sanzen is the principle of the Mutual Containment of the Ten Worlds.

> It was stated in the sutras [preached before the Lotus Sutra] that none of the bodhisattvas as well as human and heavenly beings could attain the way. This is only because in such sutras *the principle of the Mutual Containment of the Ten Worlds* is never expounded, nor is it taught that *the Buddha in reality gained enlightenment in the inconceivably remote past*. [In contrast to them, however,] in the Lotus Sutra [both these doctrines] are clearly set forth.   (»On the Protection of the Nation«, p. 74 / II. 146 f.)

> The doctrine of Ichinen Sanzen is hidden in the depths of the Life Span Chapter of the Essential Section of the Lotus Sutra. [...] The Great Wise Master T'ien-t'ai alone embraced it and kept it ever in mind. *The doctrine of Ichinen Sanzen begins with the concept of the Mutual Containment of the Ten Worlds.*   (»The Opening of the Eyes«, p. 188 / I. 220)

> When Shakyamuni Buddha prepared to preach at the place where he had gained enlightenment, the various Buddhas made their appearance in the ten directions, and all the great bodhisattvas gathered around. [...] All begged the Buddha to preach. But the World-Honored One did not reveal a single word concerning the doctrines that hold that persons of the Two

> Vehicles can attain Buddhahood, or that he himself had attained enlightenment countless kalpas in the past, nor did he set forth the most vital teachings of all, those concerning Ichinen Sanzen and Immediate Enlightenment. There was only one reason for this: the fact that, although his listeners possessed the capacity to understand such doctrines, the proper time had not yet come. And he also expounded *the doctrine of Ichinen Sanzen, explaining that all the Nine Worlds have the potential for Buddhahood and that Buddhahood contains all the Nine Worlds.*
>
> («The Selection of the Time«, p. 256 / I. 538)

I will summarize each point of this section.
- Nichiren discovered the foundation for the superiority of the Lotus Sutra in *the Attainment of Enlightenment in the Remotest Past* as revealed in the Life Span Chapter of the Essential Section.
- This event represents the fundamental, original character of enlightenment as described in terms of *"the doctrine of Ichinen Sanzen hidden in the depths of the 'Life Span' chapter of the Essential Section".*
- The doctrine of Ichinen Sanzen is founded upon *the principle of the Mutual Containment of the Ten Worlds* which means *"that all the Nine Worlds have the potential for Buddhahood and that Buddhahood contains all the Nine Worlds".*
- And finally, the doctrine of Ichinen Sanzen based on the doctrine of the Mutual Containment of the Ten Worlds theoretically expresses the fact of "Immediate Enlightenment", whereby Buddhahood is manifested in your own life just as you are.

Throughout his life, Nichiren upheld
the "**Three Major Principles of the Mutual Containment of
the Ten Worlds, Ichinen Sanzen, and Immediate Enlightenment**"
as the foundation of his teaching for
realizing Buddhahood in the Latter Day of the Law.

- Nichiren claimed that these "**Three Major Principles for Realizing Buddhahood**" had been revealed in the description of the events of "Attaining Enlightenment in the Remotest Past" found in the Life Span Chapter. These events continue into the present as the **prototype** for the attainment of enlightenment by all Buddhas in the three existences as well as for each of one of us, the ordinary people of the present.

In so far as we understand Ichinen Sanzen in terms of the principle of Instant Enlightenment based on the principle of the "The Nine Worlds as Buddhahood and Buddhahood as the Nine Worlds", we don't need to have regard to a whole list of cumbersome categories and scholastic debates, e.g. as expounded in the writings of T'ien-t'ai. These complex classifications and explications are in fact based on the concept of Initial Enlightenment, i.e., attaining enlightenment by discarding and overcoming all attachment and desire and gradually extinguishing all negative karma through a succession of positive rebirths. For example, the doctrine which classifies the bodhisattva's way into 52 stages will no longer be valid. For the Ten Worlds are no longer to be considered as ten distinct and separate regions, but rather as ten distinct but inter-related and mutually-contained states found within our own lives. They are constantly changing from one life state to another throughout the course of our daily life, i.e. they are mutually interconnected and form a dynamic process, while Buddhahood itself is found inherent within each of our own lives.

> In Nichiren's teaching, the most significant dimension lies exclusively in the radical dualistic distinction made between the Nine Worlds (the ninefold ontological dimension of the ordinary person) and the Buddha World (The Buddhahood inherent within all life), and the activation and manifestation of Buddhahood in the ordinary life of each person (Instant Enlightenment).

Given the above, for the term "the Mutual Containment of the Ten Worlds" I will from now on use a simplified variant "the Tenfold Life Structure"

5. The starting point of Nichiren's teaching

Nichiren did not limit the doctrine of *the Tenfold Life Structure* only to the event of Attaining Enlightenment in the Remotest Past in the Life Span Chapter, for he considered it as emblematic of the universal potential for attaining enlightenment by everyone. Further, from the start, Nichiren focused on this principle as an absolute requirement for Instant Enlightenment.

From the age of twelve, Nichiren studied and practiced the esoteric teachings. In this early period long before the public proclamation of his own teaching, he had a mysterious experience and recalled it as follows.

> [As a youth,] it once happened that I, Nichiren, received great wisdom from the living Bodhisattva *Kokūzō*. I prayed to this bodhisattva to become the wisest person in Japan. The bodhisattva must have taken pity on me, for he presented me with a great jewel as brilliant as the morning star, which I tucked away in my right sleeve. Thereafter, on perusing the entire body of sutras, I was able to discern the essential difference between the superior and the inferior teachings among the eight schools as well as of all the scriptures. («Letter to the Priests of Seichōji«, p. 893 / I. 650)

As historical background, it should be noted that Seichōji temple was founded by a wandering monk in 771 A.D. for worshipping the statue of Bodhisattva *Kokūzō*. This bodhisattva is, as the Sanskrit name Ākāśagarbha suggests, associated with "the great empty space of the universe" implying limitless compassion and wisdom. He is also associated with "the morning star" as its manifestation and with a precious "jewel" symbolizing boundless wisdom. Later in 836, as the monk *Ennin* (794-864) had visited the temple, Seichōji became a temple of the Tendai school.

Although Nichiren later criticized Ennin for his introduction of esoteric elements into the teachings of the head temple of the Tendai school, Nichiren himself seems to have been devoted to the esoteric practice associated with the Bodhisattva *Kokūzō*, reciting his mantra ceaselessly for several weeks. This particularly strict esoteric practice was supposedly established by the founder of the Shingon school, *Kūkai* (774-835), with the aim of enhancing or expanding the capacity for memory and knowledge.

To return to our present theme, although it is not clear what kind of insight Nichiren received from *Kokūzō* at the time of *"fulfilling his most heartfelt desire"*, we can catch a glimpse of it in his early work »The significance of immediate enlightenment for the body of the precepts« (1242). He was only aged 21 when he wrote it and it is the earliest extent authenticated Gosho.

> The body of the precepts which the Lotus teaching reveals is the entity of the precepts related to the principle of the Buddha's cause and the Buddha's effect. (SS, p. 8 / -)

> The immediate enlightenment manifested by the Dragon Girl is that immediate enlightenment manifesting the 32 characteristics of a buddha without changing the animal body of a snake. (ibid., p. 9/ -)

> The Mystic Law is characterized by the fact that the Ten Worlds are mutually contained in each other. [...] What the Lotus Sutra intends to reveal is that the attainment of enlightenment in one world means the attainment of enlightenment in each of the other Ten Worlds. Though the pre-Lotus Sutra teachings speak of buddhas, they are not really existing buddhas, because they are considered to be distinct from the Nine Worlds [of the ordinary person]. Likewise, these Nine Worlds are considered to be distinct from Buddhahood. Against such a view, what the Lotus Sutra intends to teach is that the ordinary person is in truth a Buddha, because he is endowed with the Ten Worlds. Likewise, Buddhahood itself is considered to be endowed with the Ten Worlds. (ibid., p. 10/ -)

That is to say:

CHAPTER 1

> Already in his youth, Nichiren discovered the "Body of the Precepts of Immediate Enlightenment" as revealed in the Lotus Sutra and conceived "the theory of the ordinary person as Buddha" based on the principle of "the Tenfold Life Structure = Immediate Enlightenment".

Incidentally, this theory of the youthful Nichiren has frequently been considered as inauthentic, as this early Gosho is rich in esoteric symbolism. Yet, as Hanano points out, the Seichōji Temple where Nichiren studied and practiced belonged to the Tendai esoteric lineage and it was where Nichiren was himself initiated into the esoteric doctrines of the Tendai sect. His practice which related to the Bodhisattva *Kokūzō* was apparently a kind of esoteric discipline. Above all, aged 17, Nichiren was permitted to make a copy of the »Collection of the Orally Transmitted Teachings« which was supposedly the work of *Chishō* (814–891), the fifth abbot of the head temple of the Tendai school, and which was a key source of the Tendai Philosophy of Original Enlightenment. Nichiren's copy is extent today in its original autographed form. Subsequently, Nichiren visited Kamakura for further study in order to gain a more profound understanding of the esoteric teachings of the Tendai lineage: his efforts led him directly to write »The significance of immediate enlightenment for the body of the precepts« (see Hanano 23: 44).

At this point, Nichiren held to the doctrinal standpoint that the Lotus Sutra and Shingon shared the same teaching of Ichinen Sanzen, but that with respect to the practice of Immediate Enlightenment Shingon was superior to the Lotus Sutra due to the esoteric practice of the sign (mudra) and the use of mantras. Yet this standpoint would later be radically reversed as Nichiren firmly upheld the superiority of the Lotus Sutra over the Shingon esoteric teachings subsequent to his years of study on Mt. Hiei.

Thus far, we can note that three doctrinal elements had been admixed with the principle for the attainment of enlightenment which the youthful Nichiren sought:

> Nichiren's theory of the ordinary person as Buddha in the sense of Instant Enlightenment based on the Tenfold Life Structure
> = the Tendai esoteric view of immediate enlightenment
> + the Tendai doctrine of the Mutual Containment of the Ten Worlds
> + the theory of the ordinary person as Buddha
> in line with the concept of Original Enlightenment

6. The early form of the theory of the ordinary person as Buddha

The principle of the dual structure of life as a universal condition for attaining enlightenment

With respect to the theory of the ordinary person as Buddha, Nichiren first expounded it systematically in his early work »The Meaning of the Sacred Teachings of the Buddha's lifetime". This work was written in 1258, aged 37, in the period between the public proclamation of his teaching in 1253 and before the submission of his major work »On Establishing the Correct Teaching for the Peace of the Land« in 1260. This early work is, as the title suggests, an overview over the teachings of Shakyamuni Buddha based on T'ien-t'ai's classification into the Five Periods and the Eight Teachings. By such means, the aim is to demonstrate the superiority of the Lotus Sutra. Nichiren explains the doctrine of Ichinen Sanzen and refers also to the Three Disciplines of Precept, Meditation and Wisdom, which much later were to become the fundamental foundation for the Three Great Secret Laws.

What interests us most at this stage, is that Nichiren expounds the Tenfold Life Structure as the universal precondition for attaining enlightenment, without directly referring to the Attainment of Enlightenment in the Remotest Past as revealed in the Life Span Chapter. His particular perspective on this opaque passage is as follows:

First, Nichiren interprets the significance of each of the five characters of Myō-Hō-Ren-Ge-Kyō according to T'ien-t'ai's »The Profound Meaning of the Lotus Sutra". Then, he proceeds to assert that the Mystic Law means the principle of "the Mutual Containment of the Ten Worlds". This principle does not require a "practice to gain enlightenment over a period of countless kalpas" nor the practice of the six pāramitās of a bodhisattva. *"Because of the practice of the Mystic Law we are already bodhisattvas who have attained to all six pāramitās"*. In addition, Nichiren interprets that aspect of the Mystic Law which has the significance of "keeping the precepts". Because of its key significance I will quote the passage:

> The Sutra [of Immeasurable Meanings] states: "Although [those who practice this sutra] have not yet been able to practice the six pāramitās, these will of themselves manifest before them". Thus, *we do not observe even a single one of the precepts, yet we are to be regarded as upholders of the precepts.*
>
> (»The Meaning of the Sacred Teachings of the Buddha's lifetime«, II. p. 401 / II. 57)

Then, Nichiren expounds the Mystic Law in relation to Ichinen Sanzen. Referring to "volume five of T'ien-t'ai's »The Great Concentration and insight«", he interprets the factors which compose Ichinen Sanzen, such as "Ten

Worlds", "One Hundred Worlds", and "Three kinds of Realm". At the end of this analysis he quotes the phrase which states that *"These three thousand realms are all found in one heart, in a single moment of life"*. He continues, following the commentary of Miao-lo:

> The Great Master Miao-lo comments: "You should understand that one's life and its environment at a single moment encompasses the three thousand realms. Therefore, when one attains enlightenment, one puts oneself in accordance with this fundamental principle, and one's body and mind at a single moment pervade the entire realm of phenomena."
> (p. 402 / II. 60)

Nichiren uses this quotation along with others later in »The Object of Devotion for Observing the Mind« (p. 247 / I. 365). Thus, he appears to have inherited this particular understanding of Ichinen Sanzen in its relation to enlightenment. Thus far, this quotation illuminates the doctrine of Ichinen Sanzen based on the Tenfold Life Structure, which represents the principle for the activation of Buddhahood and that every one of us can very naturally do the same "in accordance with this fundamental principle".

The Complementarity of self-power and other-power

At this point, I will follow Nichiren's discourse with respect to his assertion that the practice of the Mystic Law leading naturally to the realization of Buddhahood is a matter neither of self-power nor of other-power. First, we will assert once again, that the idea of Buddhahood inherent within our own lives forms a fundamental premise of Nichiren Buddhism.

> Now in the teachings of the Lotus Sutra, people are certainly *self-empowered*, and yet they are *not self-empowered*. This is because one's own self, or life, at the same time possesses the nature of all living beings in the Ten Worlds. Therefore, *this self has originally been in possession of one's own realm of Buddhahood and of the realms of Buddhahood possessed by all other living beings*. Thus, when one attains Buddhahood one does not take on some new or "other" Buddha identity.
> Again, in the teachings of the Lotus Sutra, people are certainly *other-empowered*, and yet they are *not other-empowered*. The Buddhas, who are considered separate from us, are actually contained within our own selves, or the lives of us ordinary people. Those Buddhas manifest the realms of Buddhahood of all living beings *in the same manner as we do*.
> (p. 403 / II. 62)

Given his fundamental premise, with regard to "self-power", Nichiren states that in a sense one is able to realize enlightenment as one is originally endowed with universal Buddhahood. This capacity is not dependent on the different factors of self-power in terms of one's personal abilities or one's length of practice. It is rather that one simply manifests that Buddhahood already inherent in one's own life, so that one does not become a "new Buddha" in the sense of becoming a Buddha by discarding all the characteristics of an ordinary person.

Yet with regard to "other-power", Nichiren asserts that any other Buddha upon which one might rely is not distinct from that Buddhahood with which one is already endowed. Consequently, since one is already endowed with the capacity to activate it oneself, one does not need to rely on the capacity of others (see id.).

Thus, the quotation above suggests a very radical reinterpretation of the significance of the distinction between "self" and "other".

The "self" used in the sense of "self-empowerment" refers not only to everyday consciousness or simply to the "ego" (with six different types of consciousness, the Nine Worlds), but also to the essential entity of the Ten Worlds, the "Self" (the 9th consciousness, the cosmic life).

That is to say, on the one hand, we do practice on the basis of our own egoistic self-awareness, determination and activities; yet on the other hand, Buddhahood itself can be only be realized by activating the Self or the cosmic life inherent in the Nine Worlds. This is precisely the meaning of the ambivalent phrase *"people are certainly self-empowered, and yet they are not self-empowered."* Thus far, this Self appears to the Ego as that "Other" transcending the Ego. But this other existence is somehow different to the transcendent Buddhas who are supposed to exist external to ourselves. Rather, it is inherent to one's own life. Therefore, this relationship is paradoxically expressed as *"people are certainly other-empowered, and yet they are not other-empowered"*.

Consequently, we practice the Mystic Law neither through self-power only nor through other-power only, but rather by way of cooperation between each of the powers. This actually means a natural way of practice in accordance with the principle of Ichinen Sanzen based on the Tenfold Life Structure, as it is said *"we will as a matter of course attain Buddhahood"* (»The Opening of the Eyes«, p. 234 / I. 282). Given this context, it is a persuasive argument that we cannot ourselves attain to enlightenment through our own wisdom but rather only *"through faith alone"*, as in the case of Shariputra (see »Letter to Niike«, p. 1443 / I. 1030). Chanting Daimoku should therefore be grounded upon a *"faith representing the wisdom of the Buddha in order to activate Buddhahood"* (Ishindaie).

Chanting Daimoku enables us to activate Buddhahood in a very natural way because this practice is

> in accordance with the ontological structure of life.
> It is neither self-power nor other-power alone,
> but a cooperation of each.

Realizing the enlightenment of ordinary people based on the tenfold life structure

Immediately following the passage quoted above, concerning self- and other power in »The Meaning of the Sacred Teachings of the Buddha's lifetime«, Nichiren goes on to consider the possibility "for an ordinary person to realize Buddhahood based on the tenfold life structure".

> In the sutras preached prior to the Lotus Sutra, *the principle of the Mutual Possession of the Ten Worlds* is not stated. Therefore, if one wishes to attain Buddhahood, one must necessarily reject the Nine Worlds, since they are not contained in Buddhahood.
>
> And hence these sutras declare that one must invariably wipe out evil and put an end to earthly desires in order to become a Buddha, since they do not recognize the ordinary person as in part a Buddha. In other words, human and heavenly beings and evil persons must wipe out their own existence before they can become Buddhas. This is what the Great Teacher Miao-lo has termed the *"Buddha based on the practice of hating and cutting off the Nine Worlds."*
>
> Therefore, persons who follow the pre-Lotus teachings hold the view that when the Buddha takes form in the Nine Worlds, this simply represents a manifestation of his incomparably wonderful supernatural powers of transformation. They do not talk about the fact that *these Nine Worlds appear in a Buddha's life as it is originally endowed with them.*
>
> Thus, if we inquire into the truth of the matter, we will find in the pre-Lotus sutras a provisional type of Buddha and there is no way in which an ordinary person living in such a reality might have realized Buddhahood. *When one wishes to attain Buddhahood by cutting off earthly desires and rejecting the Nine Worlds, there can in fact be no Buddha who exists separate from the Nine Worlds, and therefore there cannot be any actual ordinary person who has realized rebirth in the Pure Land.* (p. 403 / II. 62)

I will summarize the main points of the passage quoted above.
- First, in the pre-Lotus Sutra teachings a Buddha is considered to be a transcendent entity above the ordinary person and represents "the view of becoming a Buddha after extinguishing the Nine Worlds." Nichiren criticizes this view by pointing out the logical incoherence of *"eliminating the evils and cutting off the desires"* and of *"a Buddha cut off from the Nine Worlds"*.

- Nichiren himself held the view that a Buddha is inherently endowed with the body of an ordinary person and does not cast it off.
- Thus, he could only conclude that *"there can in actuality be no Buddha who exists apart from the Nine Worlds, and therefore there cannot be any actual ordinary person who has attained rebirth in the Pure Land"*. Nichiren is consistently adamant in expressing the view that a Buddha who is not also an ordinary person cannot exist in actuality and that there is no other way to "become a Buddha" than by activating the Buddhahood inherent within the life of an ordinary person.

In seeking the way to the attainment of Buddhahood for himself, Nichiren would seem to have arrived at a particular view based on the principles of the Mutual Containment of the Ten Worlds and Ichinen Sanzen. For "his approach to the study of the Buddhist teachings appears to have been by application to the circumstances of his own particular personal situation" which became emblematic of Nichiren's particular mindset and can be seen also in his whole manner of reading the Lotus Sutra itself. This mindset has been called "bodily reading". Additionally, Nichiren made a great effort to discover the most appropriate and effective Buddhist teaching for the "salvation" of all the ordinary people of our time.

7. The early theory of Instant Enlightenment based on the principle of Eternal Realization

Manifesting the Buddhahood inherent within the ordinary person

We will next consider Nichiren's subsequent early work »On the Protection of the Nation« (1259, aged 38), which was written in the year following »The Meaning of the Sacred Teachings of the Buddha's lifetime". This work represents a systematic refutation of the *Jōdo-Nenbutsu* school established by Hōnen (1133-1212), predominantly by way of comparison between the true and the provisional teachings. The point of interest in this gosho is that Nichiren stresses the superiority of the Lotus Sutra, when compared with the pre-Lotus Sutra teachings, primarily because of its understanding that the attainment of Buddhahood is based on the Tenfold Structure of Life "to manifest one's own Buddhahood through opening it up in all the Nine Worlds."

> The sutras preached in the forty and more years before the Lotus Sutra contain no mention of the Mutual Containment of the Ten Worlds. Without enunciating this principle, nobody gets to know Buddhahood within himself. And if one does not know it in one's own heart, no other Buddhas will appear outside of oneself. [...] Ordinary people likewise fail to understand the Mutual Possession of the Ten Worlds and thus are unable to manifest that Buddhahood which is inherent within them. [...]

> *But once one has arrived at the Lotus Sutra, the Buddhahood existing within the Nine Worlds is now revealed.* Hence the bodhisattvas, persons of the Two Vehicles, and ordinary people in the Six Paths of Existence can for the first time after the forty and more years see their own Buddhahood. Now for the first time the Buddhas and bodhisattvas and persons of the Two Vehicles appear [in their actual existing forms]. Now for the first time persons of the Two Vehicles and bodhisattvas are able to attain Buddhahood, and ordinary people too are for the first time able **to be reborn in the Pure Land**. (p. 67 / II. 138)

To be able to see their own Buddhahood attained by opening it up within their own body, that is Nichiren's theory on the realization of Buddhahood by ordinary people based on the Tenfold Life Structure.

A pitfall of the autographed-centered view

Miyata refers to the passage quoted above in an article yet interprets it in a very narrow-minded spirit stating: "*At first, Nichiren sets a doctrinal limit on the discourse of attaining Buddhahood by the principle of the Mutual Containment of the Ten Worlds. Then, he sets a further limit to allow ordinary people no enlightenment but merely rebirth in the Pure Land*" (Miyata 2000). As a consequence of this peculiarly restrictive interpretation, he has missed the crucial significance of the Tenfold Life Structure. The reason for this failure lies in his philological stance characterized as "true autographed centrism".

Miyata reviewed all the writings which were supposed to have been written in the same period as the treatise »On the Protection of the Nation«. This treatise once existed on Minobu and is thereby regarded as an authentic writing of Nichiren. In contrast, there are several writings which include some particular terms related to the *Tendai Philosophy of Original Enlightenment*, such as "three bodies in a body" and "the Tathāgata of original enlightenment" as well as "the concept of the superiority of the ordinary person to a Buddha". Miyata regards all these scriptures as apocryphal and as alien to Nichiren's own thought.

Yet, starting with these presuppositions, Miyata assumes that there would be no such elements in the gosho »On the Protection of the Nation« as it is an authentic writing. Consequently, he perversely overlooks the most important understanding represented by this writing with which we are currently concerned. For the meaning of the passage quoted above is in brief: "Arriving at the Lotus Sutra, the ordinary people of the Nine Worlds will come to know the Tenfold Life Structure and will be enabled thereby to manifest their own Buddhahood. Because they open the Buddhahood inherent within the Nine Worlds, they perceive their own Buddhahood. In this way they realize Buddhahood and will be reborn in the Pure Land, too." This is nothing other than the theory of the ordinary person as true Buddha in the sense of opening that Buddhahood inherent within one's own life. And this theory presupposes the very concept of "Original Enlightenment".

This World of Suffering where the Eternal Buddha resides

Although in the passage quoted above the critique is with reference to a comparison between the Lotus Sutra and the pre-Lotus Sutras, Nichiren subsequently goes on to consider the "Attainment of Enlightenment in the Remotest Past", or simply, the "Eternal Realization" as revealed in the Life Span Chapter of the Essential Section.

> The Life Span Chapter, which is the heart and core of the twenty-eight chapters of the Lotus Sutra, states: "I have been abiding constantly in this Sahā World". And it states: "I am always here". And again: "This, my land, remains safe and tranquil".
>
> If we go by these passages, then the perfect Buddha of Eternal Realization is here in this world. Why would we wish to abandon this land and seek to reborn elsewhere? Therefore, practitioners of the Lotus Sutra should think of the place where they are as the pure land. Why worry about trying to go somewhere else?
>
> Hence it is stated in the Supernatural Powers chapter: "Wherever the sutra rolls are preserved, [...] you should know that such places are practice halls." [...]
>
> Those who have faith in and practice the Lotus and Nirvana sutras should never seek any other place. *The place where those who have faith in these sutras are is the pure land.*
>
> (»On the Protection of the Nation«, p. 71 / II. 134 f.)

It should be noted here, that two levels of reality are depicted which interpenetrate. In other words, "our world of suffering" is at the very same time also the world where the "perfect Buddha of Eternal Realization" is abiding. Consequently, the place where we practice the Lotus Sutra will thereby manifest as the Buddha's pure land. However, this Eternal Buddha doesn't abide in the actuality of our daily life in a concrete form such as a human being. So, in what form is he present in our world of suffering?

The clue can be found in the next passage, which will also be used in a further discussion that will be developed later.

> Kāshyapa and the other monks have for the first time realized *the everlasting Buddha nature* [represented by] *the attainment of enlightenment in the remotest past* as preached in the Lotus Sutra. (ibid., p. 74 / II. 146)

If any person other than the Eternal Buddha himself could realize *"the everlasting Buddha nature represented by this Eternal Realization,"* this would suggest that Nichiren had already clearly conceived individual practice and a particular mode of Eternal Realization in terms of a universal possibility of attaining Buddhahood in a manner which is open to everyone. This particular reading of the Life Span Chapter transcends a mere literal reading and represents a more profound contemplative insight. The concept of universal "Buddha nature" is also articulated later with respect to the "beginningless Ten Worlds", e.g. as "Buddhahood without beginning" (»The Opening of the Eyes«), and "Shakyamuni abiding within our own heart" which suggests the *"primordial Buddha without beginning"* (»The Object of Devotion for Observing the Mind«).

> In both the periods before and after Sado,
> Nichiren considered the Eternal Buddha Shakyamuni not only
> as a particular exceptional person but also as an expression of
> a universal ceaselessly abiding or eternal Buddhahood.

Consequently, given this context, the dual structure of reality is made manifest and the actual world of suffering where we live our daily lives is at the same time an enlightened world, just as the dual structure of our life as an ordinary person (of the Nine Worlds) is also Buddhahood. This means that "this secular world of suffering" and "the sacred world of nirvana" are intimately connected to each other in the mode of "immanence as transcendence". Viewed from this perspective, any Buddha pure land which presents a projection beyond this actual world of suffering is revealed to be only a provisional land which does not exist in actuality. It is just the same with any imaginary buddha, bodhisattva or deity.

The dual Structure of Original Enlightenment

We have considered two early works in order to understand Nichiren's particular understanding of the foundation of his own teachings, as found in »The Meaning of the Sacred Teachings of the Buddha's lifetime« (1258) and »On the Protection of the Nation« (1259). We have noted that the concept of the dual structure of life and land, expressed in the phrase "the Mutual Containment of the Ten Worlds", plays a very significant role in Nichiren's teaching on the Mystic Law.

As well as these authenticated writings there are many other writings from this period, which have been considered to be apocryphal or "undetermined" simply because they are rich in elements of Tendai Original Enlightenment Thought. One of them deals directly with the subject considered here and is entitled »On the Ten Dharma Worlds« (1259). Miyata regards this writing as apocryphal while I myself see in it an important dimension with which to gain a much deeper understanding of Nichiren's teaching.

For in this Gosho, which examines the superiority of the LS amongst all other Buddhist teachings, Nichiren makes use of "the Fourfold Comparative Criteria" of (1) the pre-Lotus Sutra teachings, (2) the Theoretical Section of the Lotus Sutra, (3) the Essential Section of the LS, and (4) "Contemplation" (*kanjin*). However, he himself takes his stance on the ultimate "*contemplative viewpoint of the Essential Section of the Lotus Sutra*" (p. 420 / II. 163) and arrives at the conclusion that the Eternal Buddha alone is the "perfect Buddha." This relationship is indicated at the outset as follows.

> Reviewing all the teachings of the Buddha, no perfect Buddha can emerge unless firmly grounded on the Essential Section of the Lotus Sutra and the wisdom of Contemplation. In this case, actual ordinary people can never hope of attaining enlightenment based only on the provisional teachings. (»On the Ten Dharma Worlds«, p. 418 / II. 159)

The term "the perfect Buddha", as noted above, is exactly the same term as found in the phrase "the perfect Buddha of Eternal Realization" (»On the Protection of the Nation«) and indicates the realization of Buddhahood by actually existing ordinary people who can activate and manifest the eternal Buddha-nature from deep within their own lives.

In interpreting this Eternal realization, Nichiren also introduced a view of Instant Enlightenment based on Ichinen Sanzen. Buddhahood cannot be realized by any gradual practice to gain enlightenment over a period of countless kalpas, which would be required if one tries to extinguish all desires. Only the dharma which enabled the perfect Buddha can bring forth the enlightenment within "the actually existing ordinary person". Thus, for Nichiren the attainment of Buddhahood based on the Dual Life Structure is Instant Enlightenment based on Ichinen Sanzen. Consequently, it is philosophically coherent to assert "*the Mutual Possession of the Ten Worlds as it appears to one who has been in a state of Original Enlightenment from the beginning*" by way of contrast to "*gaining enlightenment for the first time*" (ibid., p. 421 / II. 166).

As to the term "eternal or ceaselessly existing Buddha nature" which appears in the Gosho »On the Protection of the Nation«, it is also found in »Cloth for a Robe and an Unlined Robe« (1275) as follows:

> Though there is only one unlined robe, when it is presented as an offering to the Lotus Sutra, it is offered to all 69,384 characters of the sutra, each of which is a Buddha. These Buddhas have [...] received a revelation [Eternal Realization] of the immeasurable life span which is their life, *the*

> *eternal or ceaselessly existing Buddha nature* which is their throat, and the wonderful practice of the single vehicle which is their eyes. (p. 970 / II. 602)

The phrase *"the eternal or ceaselessly existing Buddha nature* which is their throat"* is taken from a phrase of Miao-lo who had already used the term "eternal or ceaselessly existing Buddha nature" in his »Annotations on 'The Words and Phrases of the Lotus Sutra". This indicates that such phrases like "the eternal and ceaselessly existing Buddha nature" and "Buddhahood without beginning" are synonymous with "Original Enlightenment". Thus, it is not the case that Nichiren only became aware of these concepts for the first time when reflecting upon Tendai Original Enlightenment Thought. For in using a concept like Original Enlightenment and asserting a theory of the ordinary person as true Buddha, Nichiren never falls into the philosophical trap of simply affirming and legitimating the status quo as he does not simply assert a wholly monistic world view.

Rather, he makes a clear dualistic distinction between the Nine Worlds (the ordinary person and the world of suffering) and the Buddha World (the enlightened Buddha and the Buddha's pure land), between blind ignorance and enlightening wisdom, and so on. For behind this world and all phenomena, Original Enlightenment is presupposed to be the fundamental dimension of the world and all life.

Further, this fundamental quality of enlightenment can only be activated and brought to manifestation through the Buddhist practice of chanting the Mystic Law. Consequently, the activation of Daimoku power works to transform all negative characteristics into positive ones, or all suffering into joy and happiness.

Chanting Daimoku has two aspects:
(1) **Immediate Enlightenment** which activates the Buddhahood
Inherent within our own lives at each moment and,
based on that,
(2) **the development of Buddhahood in this very lifetime**
which is a continuous dynamic process for transforming our karma, improving our condition of life and fulfilling one's own deepest desires throughout the whole of one's life.

In order to be more easily understood in our own times, Buddhahood can better be defined by such terms as "cosmic life" or "pure consciousness" in distinction from "ego consciousness," or by "Higher Self" in contrast to the "everyday ego consciousness", as they have been used in our book series Nichiren Buddhism 3.0 (2016) and NB 3.1 (2017).

The everyday ego within the Nine Worlds is replete with the Three Ways of Desire, Karma and Suffering, while the Higher Self or the non-local, unlimited cosmic consciousness (equivalent to the 9th consciousness) is able to transform these Three Ways into the Three virtues of Dharma body, Transcendent Wisdom and Liberation. Thus, we live within such a dual life structure and we can activate the Higher Self in order to transform all difficulties and transform our karma so that we may realize a happy and meaningful life.

> Both the world of suffering and our condition of life has a double structure consisting of the Nine Worlds of delusion and suffering
> and
> the Buddha World of compassion and wisdom.
> Chanting Daimoku means to activate this enlightened nature within our lives in the reality of our own daily life and thus, to transform the sufferings of birth and death into nirvana and the sufferings of desire into enlightenment.

8. The case of the dragon girl

The immediate enlightenment of the dragon girl as prototype

Above we have considered Nichiren's early writings such as »The Significance of Immediate Enlightenment and the Body of Precepts « (1242), »The Meaning of the Sacred Teachings of the Buddha's lifetime« (1258), »On the Protection of the Nation« (1259) and »On the Ten Dharma Worlds« (1259). These works strongly indicate that Nichiren had conceived as prototype "Instant Enlightenment based on the Dual Life Structure" and subsequently he discovered this basic principle as the "Eternal Realization" found in the Life Span Chapter of the Lotus Sutra. In other words, to use more ordinary terminology,

> Nichiren first considered the fundamental basis of his teachings to be "the Three Major Principles of the Mutual Containment of the Ten Worlds, Ichinen Sanzen, and Immediate Enlightenment"
> in order to proclaim it as the principle for the realization of Buddhahood for all ordinary people in the Latter Day of the Law.
> Subsequently, he developed a doctrinal position from the standpoint of a Contemplative Reading in order to advocate the superiority of the teaching based on "Shakyamuni's attaining enlightenment in the remotest past" as revealed in the Life Span Chapter of the Lotus Sutra.

The three major principles forming the basis of Nichiren's teaching, he upheld consistently throughout his life. As a typical example, consider the case of the "dragon king's daughter." The concept of "attaining enlightenment immediately" contains a double meaning of "remaining in one's own present form" and "at once instantly" and this can only be adequately explained by reference to the principles of Ichinen Sanzen which are based on the Dual Life Structure.

> When the dragon king's daughter attained Buddhahood, this does not mean simply that one person did so. It reveals the fact that all women will attain Buddhahood. In the various Hinayana sutras that were preached before the Lotus Sutra, it is denied that women can ever attain Buddhahood. In the Mahayana sutras other than the Lotus Sutra, it would appear that women can attain Buddhahood or be reborn in the pure land. But they may do so only after they have changed into some other form. *Because it is not based on the doctrine of Ichinen Sanzen, any attainment of Buddhahood or rebirth in the pure land remains in name only and not in reality.* The dragon king's daughter represents "one example that stands for all the rest". When she attained Buddhahood, it opened up the way to attaining Buddhahood for all women of later ages.
> (»The Opening of the Eyes«, p. 223 / I. 269)

The Instant Enlightenment of the dragon king's daughter represents a prototype for the attainment of enlightenment by all women.

Referring to this passage, Keijin Mamiya, Professor of Buddhist Studies at Minobusan university, considers the case of the dragon king's girl. He explains *"Nichiren's principle of salvation"* for women, as *"there is no need for a woman to become a man"* because *"at this moment of embracing the five characters of the Mystic Law, that is, chanting the Daimoku, the woman realizes enlightenment immediately just as she is"* (22: 15). He summarizes his conclusion with the following equation:

Embracing the five characters of the Mystic Law
= The immediate enlightenment of chanting Daimoku
= Realizing the Buddhahood of Ichinen Sanzen (ibid.)

I wholly agree with his conclusion. Likewise, I consider the "Daimoku" which Nichiren proclaimed as "the practice of chanting Daimoku". And this is the meaning of "Nam-myō-hō-ren-ge-kyō in Actuality", in that the Three Major Principles of the Dual Life Structure, Ichinen Sanzen, and Instant Enlightenment will thereby be fulfilled and manifested in actuality.

The dragon girl represents the prototype for all women's immediate enlightenment

As Nichiren had conceived in his youth the doctrine of Instant Enlightenment based on the Dual Life Structure of the ordinary person as Buddha, he consistently maintained this position. In his later years in 1280, first in July, he explained to the lady. *Myōichinyo* "a comparison of the exoteric and esoteric Buddhist teachings on immediate enlightenment" in »The Doctrine for Attaining Buddhahood in One's Present Form (Reply to Myōichinyo)« (p. 1255 f. / I. 1052 f.), and then in October, he sent another letter (»Reply to Myōichinyo (The Attainment of Buddhahood in Principle and in Its Actual Aspect)« (p. 1260 f. / -) as a supplement to his view as follows.

> All the well-known scholars in society recognize the vital importance of the doctrine of "attaining Buddhahood in one's present form" [or "immediate enlightenment"]. My disciples and followers in particular, then, should set everything else aside and give their attention to this single doctrine. The teachings I have spoken of in various places over a period of twenty-seven years, from 1253 to the present, 1280, are numerous, but *fundamentally my intention has been this one alone.* (p. 1260 / -)

As rationale for this doctrine, Nichiren points to the immediate enlightenment of the eight-year-old dragon king's daughter found in the 12th "Devadatta" chapter. The LS depicts her quite vividly in two scenes at a Dharma assembly with the Buddha:

1) In reply to a question from the Bodhisattva *Chishaku* (Wisdom Accumulation), Manjushri speaks about "the palace of the dragon king Sagara in the great ocean" where he carried out his mission to propagate the "the Law of the single [Buddha] vehicle". The daughter of the dragon king was one of the innumerable beings he converted and brought to the attainment of enlightenment. However, the Bodhisattva *Chishaku* expresses doubt about the attainment of enlightenment by the eight-year-old dragon king's daughter. In fact, he expresses a conventional understanding that one must practice austerities over a period of countless kalpas.

> Bodhisattva Wisdom Accumulated said, "When I observe Shakyamuni Tathāgata, I see that for immeasurable kalpas he carried out harsh and difficult practices, accumulating merit, piling up virtue, seeking the way of the bodhisattva without ever resting. [...] Only after he had done that was he able to complete the way of enlightenment. I cannot believe that this girl in the space of an instant could actually achieve perfect enlightenment". (LS, p. 226)

2) The second scene begins with the sudden appearance of the dragon king's daughter emerging from the dragon palace in the sea before the Buddha. This time, Shariputra expresses his doubts, again representing a traditional understanding about the attainment of enlightenment. They are actually two widely held prejudices found among Buddhists at that time.
(1) That women would never be able to attain Buddhahood.

(2) That one requires immeasurable kalpas in order to practice austerities in order to attain enlightenment.

> [After the dragon girl recited verses of praise with the words "having heard his teachings, I have attained enlightenment…"]
> Shariputra said to the dragon girl, "You suppose that in this short time you have been able to attain the unsurpassed way. But this is difficult to believe. Why? *A woman's body is soiled and defiled, not a vessel for the Law.* […] How could you attain the unsurpassed enlightenment? The road to Buddhahood is long and stretches far. *Only after one has spent immeasurable kalpas pursuing austerities, accumulating deeds, practicing all kinds of paramitas, can one finally achieve success.* Moreover, a woman is subject to *the five obstacles.* First, she cannot become a Brahma heavenly king. Second, she cannot become […] (LS, p. 227)

Then, in order to dispel these prejudices and doubts, the dragon king's daughter had demonstrated her virtuosity. First, she presented a precious jewel to the Buddha.

> The dragon girl said to Bodhisattva Wisdom Accumulated and to the venerable one, Shariputra, "I presented the precious jewel and the world-honored one accepted it—was that not quickly done?" They replied, "Very quickly!"
> The girl said, "Employ your supernatural powers and watch me attain Buddhahood. It will be even quicker than that!"
> At that time the members of the assembly all saw the dragon girl in the space of an instant *change into a man and carry out all the practices of a bodhisattva*, immediately preceding to the Spotless World of the south, taking a seat on a jeweled lotus, and attaining impartial and perfect enlightenment. With the thirty-two features and the eighty characteristics, he expounded the wonderful Law for all living beings everywhere in the ten directions.
> At that time in the Sahā World the bodhisattvas and arhats, the gods, dragons, and others of the eight kinds of guardians, human and non-human beings, all from a distance saw the dragon girl become a buddha and preach the Law to all human and heavenly beings in the assembly at that time. Their hearts were filled with great joy and all from a distance paid reverent obeisance. Immeasurable living beings, hearing the Law, understood it and were able to reach the level of non-regression. (LS, p. 227 f.)

At first sight, there might appear to be a contradiction when the dragon girl transforms herself firstly into a man and demonstrates her attainment of enlightenment by way of a series of performances. Yet she had already attained enlightenment in the palace of dragon king under Manjushri's guidance as he has already spoken about this event. So, she is now confronted with the above-mentioned prejudices that *only a man can attain enlightenment through the practice of various austerities*. Given this context, this scene can best be understood as a dramatic attempt to dispel the prejudices of many in the assembly by the undermining of their conventional expectations.

The doctrine of immediate enlightenment in actuality as expounded in the Essential Section

Nichiren refers to the fantastic example of the dragon girl as an assurance for the immediate enlightenment of all ordinary women. At the same time, this example further enhanced his conviction that the doctrine of Immediate Enlightenment is the foundation of his teachings.

> First of all, the case of the dragon girl should serve as a rationale for *the doctrine of the Immediate Enlightenment taught in the Lotus Sutra*. The "Devadatta" chapter says: "this girl could in the space of an instant actually achieve perfect enlightenment". [...]
> The Great Teacher Dengyō says: "The performing dragon girl didn't carry out countless kalpas of austere practice nor did the audience. There was no practice requiring countless kalpas for either party. Due to the power of the Lotus Sutra they realized Buddhahood immediately", and so on.
> (»Reply to Myōichinyo«, p. 1261 / -)

Moreover, instead of an endless practice seeking Initial Enlightenment, this kind of Immediate Enlightenment takes Eternal Realization as its prototype based on the Dual Life Structure and Original Enlightenment. The ordinary people of the actual world can manifest Buddhahood instantly without ever changing their physical form.

> In addition, there are two kinds of the concept with respect to Immediate Enlightenment in the Lotus Sutra, the ideal concept of the Theoretical Section and the *proactive one based on the Essential Section*. Because this latter type is able to *bring about Immediate Enlightenment without changing the actual status of a person as they originally are,* it designates our fleshy body as *the Tathāgata endowed with the Original Three Bodies. This doctrine cannot be found expressly in any other teaching of the Buddha*. T'ien-t'ai's »Words and Phrases of the Lotus Sutra« says: "This has been kept secret and has not been transmitted in any other teaching", and so on. (ibid.)

Consequently, Nichiren stresses that this *"doctrine of Immediate Enlightenment in actuality as taught in the Essential Section of the Lotus Sutra"* can be found neither in the pre-Lotus Sutra teachings nor in the Theoretical Section of the Lotus Sutra. However, strictly speaking, it is also not expressly evident even in the Life Span Chapter if it is read only on the literal level. For Nichiren does seem to have been aware of the radically innovative nature of his proclamation "to chant Daimoku for the realization of the Three Major Principles of the Dual Structure of Life, Ichinen Sanzen, and Immediate Enlightenment".

So, in summary:
- In his early years, Nichiren conceived the doctrine of Original Enlightenment in terms of a dual life structure, including a doctrine of Immediate Enlightenment taken from the esoteric teachings of both the Shingon and Tendai schools.
- Subsequently, he found a paradigm for these major principles in the Eternal Realization depicted in the Life Span Chapter and aimed at a theoretical foundation to legitimate the innovative practice of chanting Daimoku from the perspective of both a literal and a contemplative reading of the LS.
- Thus, it was only natural that his doctrinal orientation toward Original Enlightenment, such as in the theory of the ordinary person as Buddha based on the Dual Life Structure, was evident in his early works. Further, radically rereading the LS and especially the Essential Section, he had need to forcefully proclaim the Essential Section's superiority over all the pre-Lotus Sutra teachings, as well as over the Theoretical Section of the LS itself.
- In the period after Sado, in the light of his self-understanding as none other than a rebirth of the Bodhisattva Jōgyō, he inscribed the Mandala-honzon as the object of meditation in a concrete representational form, thereby making visibly manifest the Three Major Principles for realizing Buddhahood.
- Chanting Daimoku to the Mandala-honzon, therefore, represents a concrete practice for all ordinary people of our times to enable them to realize Instant Enlightenment. For this reason, in his later years, the theory of the ordinary person as Buddha comes once again into the foreground. For this particular practice represents Nichiren's ultimate teaching, i.e. the doctrine of Instant Enlightenment of Ichinen Sanzen based on the Dual Life Structure.

The particular practice of "chanting Daimoku before the Gohonzon"
is intended for all people in our own times
so that they may attain the Instant Enlightenment
of Ichinen Sanzen based on the Dual Life Structure in each moment.

At this point, with respect to the translation of the term *"sokushin jōbutsu"* it should be mentioned that I would prefer the wording of "Immediate or Instant Enlightenment" to the literal translation of "attaining Buddhahood in one's present form" which WND favors. The former suggests the realization of Buddhahood immediately, just here and now. The latter is more redolent of the particular significance given to the concept in the LS as understood by *Dengyō* who considered Instant Enlightenment to be something which could only be attained sometime in the future.

Chapter 2
The Multiple Structure of Nichiren's Comparative System

1. The multifaceted and multilayered character of Nichiren's comparative system

Nichiren advocated a unique and radically innovative teaching, based on the Essential Section of the LS. Further, his teaching was no longer limited to the Lotus Sutra itself nor focused exclusively on a Tendai doctrinal understanding. Rather his teaching was derived from an innovative interpretation of the esoteric teachings and the Original Enlightenment Thought of his time. Against this background, Nichiren's innovative teaching was in fact multifaceted and multilayered. Consequently, as noted above at the beginning of the previous chapter, Tamura applies the system of "comparison between the Essential and the Theoretical Section", but this criterion in itself is not sufficient to satisfactorily elucidate Nichiren's distinctive multifaceted system. For example, he regards the Daimoku "as the five characters of the Mystic Law representing the heart of the 'Life Span' chapter as well as at the same time being the Daimoku of the entirety of the Lotus Sutra itself" (21: 62). Although Nichiren frequently moves between these two different viewpoints, he never himself treats each viewpoint in parallel or considers them to be identical on an interpretive level. For otherwise they would contradict each other and lead to a confusion in understanding. Indeed, each suggests a particular understanding from a distinctive viewpoint. The "daimoku (title)" of the entirety of the Lotus Sutra represents a comparative understanding of the superiority of the LS over and against the pre-Lotos Sutras, while the Daimoku of the Mystic Law represents a comparative understanding of the superiority of the Essential Section over and against the Theoretical Section of the LS.

An analogy would be with a cylinder. When observed from above it appears as a "circle", yet when observed from the side it appears as a "rectangle". But if observed from a diagonal angle, the whole of the "cylinder" can be observed. From this perspective, the whole cylinder corresponds to Nichiren's ultimate perspective, i.e. Nichiren's innovatory perspective on "the seven characters of chanting Daimoku".

In fact, Nichiren's reasons for inscribing the Mandala-honzon and recommending its use as a focus of devotion, far surpass any straightforward comparison between the Theoretical and the Essential Sections of the LS. For to be understood, they must be viewed from a more profound level: i.e. not from a mere literal reading but rather from a deeper contemplative reading of the Essential Section of the LS. Consequently, in order to delineate the multifaceted character of Nichiren's teaching, especially the multilayered character of Nichiren's rational justification of the paramountcy of the practice of Daimoku before the honzon, it is first necessary to consider Nichiren's comparative system for the classification of the variety of Buddhist teachings.

2. Classification in terms of shallow / deep, superior / inferior, offering / receiving, and primary / secondary

Nichiren himself needed to develop his own comparative system for the classification of the variety of Buddhist teachings, in order to justify his particularly exclusivistic stance as to the superiority of the Lotus Sutra over all other schools. He took up this task assiduously from his earliest period of study and continuously until his death, leaving a considerable volume of writings.

First, let's begin by considering the kind of doctrinal problems Nichiren faced in his early proclamation period, i.e. shortly after his proclamation of Daimoku (in 1253, aged 32). While at first he worked very much within the traditional doctrinal classification system of *Tendai Hokke* Buddhism, Nichiren was also developing his own system.

A representative example for an overview of the classification system as a whole would be »Questions and Answers on the Various Schools« (1255, aged 34). In this letter, supposedly addressed to *Sanmibō Nichigyō*, a priest-disciple of his, Nichiren gives detailed instructions on how to refute the doctrines of the ten major Japanese Buddhist schools of his time.

This writing begins with the question of how to consider the Tendai Lotus School and notes that the commentaries of T'ien-t'ai, Miao-lo and Dengyō have been used as *"a bright mirror to aid in the understanding of its doctrines"* (p. 375 / II. 10). The categories used to classify the teachings and the criteria for assessment are especially important, as can be seen in the short passage quoted below.

> If one cannot distinguish between passages that depend on criteria pertaining to the *four teachings of doctrine* and the *four teachings of method* and those that depend on criteria pertaining to *the five periods*, or between *a lenient interpretation* and *a strict interpretation*, then we would have to say that [though one claims to be a follower of the Tendai Lotus school] one is grossly ignorant of the doctrines of that school. (ibid.)

Amongst other criteria, T'ien-t'ai established the "Three Standards of Comparison" representing the three different ways in which the superiority of the Lotus Sutra can be asserted over all other sutras and the way in which the

superiority of the Essential Section of the LS can be asserted over the Theoretical Section of the LS. They are:
1) the viewpoint with respect to people's capacities for attaining Buddhahood through a particular sutra.
2) The viewpoint with respect to the process of teaching and propagation, from the initial planting of the seed of Buddhahood within people's lives until the final harvesting of its fruit, the attainment of Buddhahood.
3) The viewpoint with respect to the original relationship between master and disciple.

Under the first standard of comparison all the Buddha's teachings are also classified into "Five Periods":
(1) The period of the Avatamsaka (*Kegon*) Sutra
(2) The period of the Āgama (*Agon*) Sutras
(3) The introductory Mahayana sutras (*Hōdō*) such as the Amida, Mahāvairochana, and Vimalakīrti sutras.
(4) The period of the *Prajnā-pāramitā* (*Hannya*) and
(5) The period of the Lotus Sutra and the Nirvana Sutra (*Hokke-Nehan*)

Further, they are all classified into two categories according to both doctrine and the method of introduction on to the Buddhist way:
1) The Four Teachings of Doctrine:
(1) The Tripitaka teaching, which consists of the three divisions of the Buddhist canon—sutras, rules of monastic discipline, and doctrinal commentaries—and corresponds to the Hinayana, or pre-Mahayana, teachings.
(2) The Mahayana focusing on the non-substantiality of all things.
(3) The advanced Mahayana taught particularly to bodhisattvas, which enumerates the fifty-two stages of bodhisattva practice spanning innumerable *kalpas*.
(4) The Perfect Teaching, revealing that all people can attain enlightenment by practicing the threefold truth (Non-substantiality, Temporary Existence, and the Middle Way).
2) The Four Teaching Methods:
(1) The Sudden Teaching, by which the Buddha preached directly from the perspective of his own enlightenment without preparing his disciples.
(2) The Gradual Teaching, by which the Buddha expounded his teaching only gradually, in order to develop his disciples' capacity so that they might understand his higher teachings.
(3) The Secret Teaching, in which the Buddha taught in such a way that each person could understand according to their own individual capacities, thereby receiving different benefits from his teaching while being unaware of any differences.
(4) The Explicit Indeterminate Teaching, as above, yet each is aware of the different benefits received from the teaching.

There are two further ways of interpreting the words and phrases found in the sutras and commentaries.
1) By way of "lenient interpretation", i.e. by way of a more inclusive interpretative method, e.g. as found in the Four Teachings Doctrine, where there are two distinct types of "Perfect Teaching", yet you might nevertheless consider the Perfect Teaching taught in the pre-Lotus Sutras as of equal benefit to that taught in the Lotus Sutra itself, and consider that both lead to the attainment of Buddhahood.
2) By way of "strict interpretation", i.e. by way of a far harsher exclusivistic interpretive method, e.g. when inquiring into the essential meaning of the teachings. In such a case, only the Lotus Sutra itself is accepted as the paramount Perfect Teaching, due to the dialectical relationship, yet essential unity, between the three different aspects of the truth.

With respect to the LS teaching, there are in fact two distinct perspectives from which to view all other teachings, which can be understood in terms of the two different functions of the character "Myō" (the Mystic Entity):
1) "The relative function of the Mystic Entity". This serves to evaluate all other teachings in comparison to the LS and casts aside those which are inferior or provisional.
2) "The integrative function of the Mystic Entity". This can be best understood by way of a quotation given by T'ien-t'ai from Nāgārjuna (ca. 150–250): *"When the various waters enter the sea, all alike then have one salty flavor"*. In this example, all other teachings, once discarded, can nevertheless be regarded as part of the LS teaching, which serves as that great ocean which to integrates them. This integrative function is called "The Opening up and Merging of the teachings".

> We come next to a consideration of *the absolute* myō, which is the doctrine with respect to the opening up and integration of all teachings. By this time the teachings presented in the sutras preached prior to the Lotus, i.e. the provisional teachings, had been cast aside as in themselves no longer beneficial, yet they are now all merged into the great ocean of the Lotus Sutra. Therefore, since these provisional teachings of the pre-Lotus sutras merge into the great sea of the Lotus Sutra, there is no longer anything undesirable about them. All are blended into the single flavor of *Nam-myō-hō-ren-ge-kyō* because of the inconceivably wonderful function of the great ocean of the Lotus Sutra. Hence there is no longer any reason to distinguish them by distinct names such as the Nenbutsu school, the Precepts school, the Shingon school, or Zen school, as has been done in the past. (p. 377 / II. 12)

It is noticeable that Nichiren specifically refers to *"the single flavor of Nam-myō-hō-ren-ge-kyō"* and not simply to Myōhō-Renge-Kyō, the Lotus Sutra.

This is most likely because in the thirteenth century Japan there were, in addition to the six major Buddhist schools, such as well the Tendai- and Shingon schools, new religious movements such as Jodo, Zen and Shingi Ritsu. In order to refute the doctrines of all these established schools and emerging sects, it was clear that the classification system of all the Buddhist teachings which had developed in China between the sixth and eighth centuries would no longer be sufficient. Consequently, Nichiren had to develop a new comparative classification system which would go beyond the traditional classification system for establishing the superiority of the Lotus Sutra. The *"single flavor of Nam-myō-hō-ren-ge-kyō"* therefore suggests that it was his intention to make a radical reassessment of all extant teachings from the ultimate perspective of the "practice of chanting Daimoku".

> We can observe that Nichiren utilizes the integrative function of both Opening up and Merging the teachings when he proclaims that the Mystic Law represents the original cause for bringing forth all Buddhas.

Yet, although the Lotus Sutra was considered to be a great ocean with a single flavor, *"ordinary people in the world today as well as the followers of the Tendai school"* nevertheless continued to embrace the practice of Nenbutsu and the esoteric practices of Shingon (see id.). In fact, given its doctrinal stance which tolerated and accommodated a plurality of doctrines and practices, the Tendai Lotus school at Mt. Hiei had itself been not only much influenced by Shingon esoteric teachings but also permitted monks practicing either Nenbutsu or Zen meditation to reside together.

Given these circumstances, it was Hōnen who was first provoked to discard all other sutras (other than the "Amida sutras"), as well as the LS itself, by proclaiming the exclusive practice of reciting the Nenbutsu, thereby expressly rejecting what he perceived as an overly-tolerant doctrinal pluralism within the Tendai tradition. For this reason, at least with respect to his public pronouncements aimed at a radical restoration of the authentic Tendai Lotus school, Nichiren saw his mission to be that of a radical reformer, determined to return Tendai to what he considered to be its pristine authentic doctrine, cleansed of all extraneous doctrinal influences.

Consequently, he especially targeted Hōnen's exclusive faith in Amida, as powerfully witnessed to in his major writing »On Establishing the Correct Teaching for the Peace of the Land« (1260). For Nichiren felt compelled to radicalize his doctrinal stance by forcefully emphasizing the superiority of the Lotus Sutra over and against all the pre-LS teachings.

> So long as one thinks of it as a single body of water which is like the great ocean, there is no harm in following one's own inclinations, going along with the teachings of a particular Buddha or bodhisattva, and continuing

> to intone whatever names one has in the past. Consequently, by way of such reasoning, people go on following their own inclinations and intoning the Nenbutsu or carrying out Shingon practices just as before.
>
> If one applies a tolerant interpretation with respect to this matter, one may perhaps view it in this way. But if one applies a strict interpretation, one can only say that such reasoning will most certainly lead one to fall into hell. (p. 377 / II. 12 f.)

At that time, by radicalizing his doctrinal stance over and against all other schools, Nichiren seems to have already elaborated his incisive critique over and against all other schools. Nenbutsu he regarded as a teaching that *"leads one to fall into hell"*. Zen, he considered like all doctrines reliant upon a *"transmission outside the sutras, independent of words or phrases"*, as *"something handed down by a heavenly devil"* (ibid., p. 378 f. / 16 f.).

Later, Nichiren's powerful critique over and against all other schools became popular under the slogan of the "Four Admonitions":
1) "Nenbutsu leads to the hell of incessant suffering,"
2) "Zen is the invention of a heavenly devil,"
3) "Shingon will lead to the ruin of the country," and
4) "Ritsu is a traitor to the nation."

3. The Practice of Nenbutsu leads to the hell of incessant suffering

That Nenbutsu leads to the hell of incessant suffering was for Nichiren not just a theoretical problem but it was a matter of the most urgent significance in actuality. In 1264 Nichiren dealt with this matter in detail in two Gosho, »The Superiority of the Daimoku to the Invocation of Amida's Name« and »Why Contemporary Nenbutsu Practitioners Are Destined for the Hell of Incessant Suffering«.

Nichiren's Reaction to the new exclusive teaching of Hōnen

Above all, Nichiren was concerned about Hōnen's Nenbutsu doctrine, especially with Hōnen's particular criteria for judging the efficacy of a teaching or a mode of practice, as outlined in his major work »The Nenbutsu Chosen above All« (1198). For there Hōnen had concluded that all teachings and practices other than his own would be too difficult and no longer efficacious for all people of lesser capacities in the Latter Day of the Law. Consequently, instead of the goal of attaining enlightenment in this actual world, he proclaimed "an easy practice of reciting Amida's name for rebirth in his Pure Land".

Yet this posed a serious problem for Nichiren, as Hōnen's exclusivistic demand that *"the four words 'discard, close, ignore, and abandon'"* should be applied to all the sutras other than those sutras exclusively concerned with rebirth in Amida's Pure Land, also meant the complete rejection of the Lotus Sutra itself, which Nichiren considered to be nothing other than *" slander of the Law"* (see p. 105 / II. 294 f.). It is for this reason, that Nichiren consistently admonished and harshly criticized the doctrine and practices of the Jodo school.

Further, Nichiren had to develop new criteria in radical opposition to Hōnen's system for selecting an appropriate practice, in order to establish a new standard by which a teaching should be judged, as it was necessary that a teaching should meet certain criteria:

> Those who hope to spread the teachings of the Buddha must take into consideration certain factors, namely, *the teaching* to be spread, *the capacity* of the people, *the time*, *the country*, and *the sequence* in which the teachings are propagated. (»Why Present-Day Nenbutsu Practitioner Are Destined for the Hell of Incessant Suffering«, p. 109 / II. 297)

We will return later again to Nichiren's "Five Guides for propagating Buddhism". For now, we can see that:

In order to challenge Hōnen's slander of the Lotus Sutra, which consisted in Hōnen's exclusive selection of the Nenbutsu as the only efficacious practice for people of lesser capacities in the Latter Day,
Nichiren was compelled to introduce an alternative teaching and practice that would likewise be exclusive
yet based on his own doctrinal standard.

The Mystic Law itself led Amida Buddha to enlightenment

Amida Buddha has fulfilled his original Bodhisattva vow to reside in his Pure Land in the West and into which he will welcome all Nenbutsu practitioners at the moment of their death. Thus, did Hōnen claim that all those who recite the name of Amida Buddha, *Namu-Amida-Butsu*, will be reborn in the Western Pure Land. With such hopes, many people thereby became devotees of "Nenbutsu only".

Yet for Nichiren, the Pure Land sutras are merely provisional Mahayana teachings which *"had not yet revealed the truth"*, as stated in the Sutra of Immeasurable Meanings.

> The true cause that allows one to leave this land of impurity and gain rebirth in the Pure Land is none other than the Lotus Sutra.
> (»The Superiority of the Daimoku over Amida's Name«, p. 112 / II. 999)

The Mystic Law alone constitutes the true cause as it alone represents "the true cause which brings forth all Buddhas".

> When Amida Buddha was still an ordinary mortal, it was through practicing the five characters of Myō-hō-ren-ge-kyō that he was able to attain Buddhahood. It is nowhere stated that he gained perfect enlightenment by reciting Namu-Amida-butsu. Myō-hō-ren-ge-kyō is that which opens up, and Namu-Amida-butsu is that which has been opened up.
> (ibid., p. 115 / II. 1003)

For Nichiren the Mystic Law is the true cause of enlightenment for all Buddhas. Yet as Hōnen taught that one should *"discard, close, ignore, and abandon'"* even the LS itself, necessarily all Nenbutsu practitioners are destined for the Hell of Incessant Suffering as *"slanderers of the true Law"*.

The Slander of the Law leads to falling into hell

The decision to embrace a particular teaching has practical consequences for actual life. Consequently, Nichiren placed a high value on "empirical proof". In this particular case, he made a comparison between the Daimoku and the Buddha's name with respect to *"the blessings to be gained"* (p. 111 / II. 997). The most crucial criterion in this regard is how one dies. There are several relevant factors, e.g. whether in presenting a peaceful countenance as though in sleep or whether exhibiting a crazed state of mind due to suffering. The "slander of the true Law" has particularly serious consequence in this respect. Contrary to the claims of Nenbutsu practitioners, Nichiren gave examples of many cases where Nenbutsu masters and lay believers *"had been unable to achieve what they had hoped for"* (p. 112 / II. 1000). These cases amounted to "real proof" as to the consequences of slandering the true Law.

> Furthermore, is it not understandable that present-day much revered leaders of the Nenbutsu sect and their eminent lay supporters, persons who have surely not committed the ten evil acts or the five cardinal sins, yet at the moment of their death, should be so afflicted by grave afflictions such as outbreaks of hideous sores, or when on their deathbed they should fall into a crazed and disordered state of mind. [...]
>
> For it was the practitioners of the Lotus Sutra [...] of whom he predicted that not one person in a thousand would be saved. And yet we have received reports that such practitioners in most cases confront death in a state of right mindfulness.   (»Why Present-Day Nenbutsu Practitioners Are Destined for the Hell of Incessant Suffering«, p. 106 / II. 291)

Consequently, for Nichiren how one dies was particularly important. As *Myōhōni*, one of his lay believers, had written to him about the death of her husband (1278), Nichiren replied:

> In your letter you write that your husband chanted Nam-myō-hō-ren-ge-kyō day and night. You say that when the time drew near he chanted twice in a loud voice. And that his complexion was whiter than it had been in life, and that he didn't lose his looks.
>
> (»The Importance of the Moment of Death«, p. 1404 / II. 759)

Nichiren quotes passages referring to a variety of states or signs that emerge at the time of one's death. For example: *"Those whose faces are pink and white, and whose features retain their proper shape, are reborn in the realm of heavenly beings"*. Such features suggest *"immediate enlightenment"*, realizing principles like *"earthly desires are equal to enlightenment"* and *"the sufferings of birth and death are equal to nirvana"* (p. 1045 / II. 760).

By contrast, Nenbutsu practitioners exhibit the features which belong to *"those with a dark complexion at the moment of death who will fall into hell"* (ibid.).

4. Witnessing to the pervasion of hell throughout the whole of society

If the slander of the True Law is the primary reason for falling into hell, empirical proof can be established by observation of the complexion and behavior of a dying person at the time of death, yet also by insightful consideration of observed conditions throughout a whole society more generally. The True Dharma brings peace and happiness to a country, bad law leads to retribution by pushing people into an abyss of misery and suffering, which provokes wars and natural disasters throughout a country. Nichiren was not just a Buddhist scholar nor just a humble monk, for he was also a great visionary who saw how the Buddha's Pure Land is actually of this earth. In other words, Nichiren was not merely engaged in the classification of the Buddhist sutras and commentaries. For he sought proof of the truth of his teaching by its consistency with the circumstances of actual life.

> In judging the merit of Buddhist doctrine in a comparative manner, I, Nichiren, believe that the best standards are those of *reason* and *documentary testimony*. And even more valuable than these two kinds of proof are *the evidence of actual fact*.
>
> (»Three Tripitaka Masters Pray for Rain«, p. 1468 / I. 599)

Consequently, in »On Establishing the Correct Teaching for the Peace of the Land« (1260), Nichiren linked theoretical speculation to a description of the natural disasters and sufferings which afflicted the people.

> In recent years, there have been unusual disturbances in the heavens, strange occurrences on earth, famine and pestilence, all affecting every

> corner of the empire and spreading throughout the land. Oxen and horses lie dead in the streets, and the bones of the stricken crowd the highways. Over half the population has already been carried off by death, and there is hardly a single person who does not grieve. (p. 17 / I. 6)

Thus, for Nichiren, the tragic condition of the country represented further empirical proof that he lived in the Latter Day of the Law. He refers also to the calamity of invasion from without and the calamity of revolt within. And in fact they later took the form of two Mongolian military incursions into Japan in 1274 and 1281, as well as in the form of a civil war in 1272 which rocked the power of the Kamakura Shogunate. The fact that many of Nichiren's prophecies appeared to have been fulfilled he always considered to be further empirical confirmation of the truth of his teaching. In a similar way, Nichiren Buddhism is primarily motivated by a vision and an active desire to achieve peace and tranquility in every society throughout the world.

Indeed, the idea of "Establishing the Correct Teaching for the Peace of the Land" has become increasingly important for the contemporary world. In particular, with respect to religion and peace or war, the rise of a dogmatic and exclusivistic Islamic fundamentalism is increasingly becoming a threat globally. The "Islamic State" (IS) is repeatedly violating the most fundamental of human rights and is actively seeking to advance its religious & political ends by the most obscenely cruel means, including wanton destruction, plunder, enslavement, rape, slaughter and terrorist attacks which target the innocent. These criminal activities are expressly pursued in the name, of Allah, and outrageously justified as "jihad" or "holy struggle". Allegedly in accord with the demands of both the Koran and the Hadith, believers are compelled to pray five times a day, women to wholly cover their bodies with black cloth, including their faces. There are patrols by the religious police, denunciations are encouraged against people who do not observe the imposed harsh moral and religious rules, while those arrested are brutally punished, e.g. by amputation for theft, or stoning for adultery. What an irrational, inhuman and cruel state this is! There is an outright brutal theocratic ideology, denying all dignity, freedom and equality to human life. Without a doubt, such a cruel religious & political system, policed by a fundamentally inhumane system of belief and law, is certain empirical proof of falling into hell.

5. The age of miscellaneous forms of faith and practice

In the age of Nichiren, several "new" Buddhist movements arose alongside the traditional "old" Buddhist schools, further extending the variety of folk beliefs which already flourished. At the beginning of the Gosho »On Establishing the Correct Teaching for the Peace of the Land«, as well as describing the catastrophic social reality of his day, Nichiren also graphically depicted

CHAPTER 2

the religious context. I will quote the passage below and then give some additional explanation.

> All the while, putting their whole faith in the phrase that "the name of *Buddha Amida* is a sharp sword to cut off carnal desires", some people are intoning the name of this lord of the Western Pure Land; others are reciting the Sutra of the *Tathāgata Medicine Master* of the Eastern Land believing his vow to "heal all ills". Or some are paying homage to the wonderful words of the *Lotus Sutra* which says, "His illness will be wiped out and he will know neither old age nor death". Moreover, others, relying upon the sutra passage that reads, "The seven disasters will instantly vanish, and the seven blessings will instantly appear," conduct ceremonies at which a hundred priests expound the *Prajñā-pāramitā Sutra* on a hundred preaching platforms. There are those who follow the *Shingon* esoteric teachings and conduct prayers by filling five colored jars with water to drive out evil spirits. Others devote themselves entirely to *seated meditation* and try to perceive the emptiness of all phenomena as clearly as the moon. Some write out the names of the seven guardian spirits and paste them on a thousand gates, others paint pictures of the five mighty bodhisattvas and hang them over ten thousand thresholds, and still others pray to the heavenly gods and earthly deities in ceremonies conducted at the four corners of the capital and on the four boundaries of Kamakura.
>
> (p. 17 / l. 6)

Both the people and the authorities sought to meet so many different needs by means of a variety of religious rituals and prayers.

> But despite all these efforts, they merely exhaust themselves in vain. Famine and epidemics rage more fiercely than ever, beggars are everywhere in sight, and scenes of death fill our eyes. Corpses pile up in mounds like observation platforms, and dead bodies lie side by side like planks on a bridge.
> (ibid.)

Faced with this mixture of a wide variety religious beliefs and practices and with prayers being offered to a whole host of Buddhas, bodhisattvas and deities, Nichiren admonished the Shogunate to fundamentally reorient its religious policy away from indulgence towards what he perceived as Hōnen's slander towards the True Dharma. For reciting the Nenbutsu for Nichiren meant nothing other than discarding the Lotus Sutra in favor of the Amida Sutras, as well as rejecting Shakyamuni Buddha in favor of Amida Buddha. Consequently, Nichiren wished the Shogunate to cease its religious indifference and over-indulgence.

> If people favor what is only incidental and forget what is primary, can the benevolent deities be anything but angry? If people cast aside what is

> perfect and take up what is biased, can the world escape the plots of demons? Rather than offering up ten thousand prayers for remedy, it would be better simply to outlaw this one evil. (p. 24 / I. 14)

In addition to his admonitions against the Nenbutsu, Nichiren was compelled to proclaim his own radical doctrinal stance in sharp contrast to all the other established sects and the new popular schools. And in seeking to complete this task, it became clear that the traditional Tendai system for classifying and evaluating the Buddhist teachings was simply inadequate. For Nichiren was forced to go far beyond the traditional Tendai doctrinal understanding if he was to establish a radically new system for the comparative evaluation of all existing Buddhist teachings.

6. The Daimoku and Honzon of the Essential Section for our current time

In »On Reciting the Daimoku of the Lotus Sutra« (1260, aged 39), at the same time as admonishing against the practice of Nenbutsu, Nichiren forcefully argued for the superiority of the practice of Daimoku in a systematic way. Initially, he assents to the "perfect teaching" of the Lotus Sutra in line with Tendai's comparative evaluative system for classifying the Four Teachings with respect to doctrine. Yet we can already observe a desire to surpass the mere comparative evaluation of the pre-LS teachings to the LS and to press on further towards a clear comparative evaluation of the significance of the Theoretical and the Essential Sections of the LS.

> In comparison to the Essential Section of the Lotus Sutra, there is no doubt that the Perfect Teaching of the pre-Lotus Sutra and that of the Theoretical Section of the Lotus Sutra are both to be regarded as inferior. [...] When this approach [of the four teachings on doctrine] is used, the perfect teaching of the pre-Lotus Sutras is classified with what the Immeasurable Meanings Sutra calls a teaching which requires many kalpas of religious practice in order that enlightenment can be attained. (p. 12 / II. 227)

In other words, from the perspective of the Essential Section, Nichiren considers each of the perfect teachings as the "teaching requiring many kalpas of practice in order that enlightenment can be attained", i.e. as a means of Initial Enlightenment, but not as a means to the "direct way", i.e. to "immediate, supreme and perfect enlightenment".

Immediately thereafter, Nichiren himself, by way of a question-and-answer-format, described the most appropriate form of practice firmly grounded in the "Essential Section of the Lotus Sutra for the Latter Day of the Law".

CHAPTER 2

> Question: For persons who place their faith in the Lotus Sutra, what is the proper Object of Devotion, and what rules are to be followed in acts of worship, and what kind of practice is to be carried out on a daily basis?
> Answer: First, with regard to the Object of Devotion, one should inscribe the eight volumes of the Lotus Sutra, or one volume, or one chapter, or simply *the daimoku [title] of the Sutra*, and make that the object of devotion, as is indicated in the "Dharma Teacher" and "The Supernatural Powers" chapters of the Sutra. And those persons who are able to do so further should write out the names of the Tathāgata Shakyamuni and the Buddha Tahō, or fashion images of them, and place these to the left and right of the Lotus Sutra. And if they are further able to do so, they should fashion images or write out the names of the Buddhas of the ten directions and the bodhisattva *Fugen* (Universal Worthy) and the others.
> As for the rules to be followed in worship, one should always *sit upright in front of the Object of Devotion*. Once one leaves the place of practice, however, one is free to walk, stand still, sit, or lie down as one wishes.
> As a daily practice, one should chant the Daimoku, Nam-myō-hō-ren-ge-kyō. [...]
> Since we live in an age when there are many foolish people, *practicing the meditation of Ichinen Sanzen* cannot be pushed into the foreground. However, if there are persons who wish to do so, they should learn this practice and carry it out. (p. 12 / II. 228)

By this point, Nichiren had envisioned the prototype of the Three Great Secret Laws in terms of "the Honzon", "the Daimoku", and "the place of practice", all in relation to the Essential Section.

Nichiren represents the Dharma body or the essence of the Essential Section as directly related to Eternal Realization. That is to say, to practice the five characters of the Mystic Law by chanting Daimoku is thereby to manifest that very same Mystic Law in one's own life.

> The two characters of myō-hō of the Daimoku contain within them the heart of the Lotus Sutra, namely, the doctrine of three thousand realms in a single moment of life (Ichinen Sanzen) as set forth in the Expedient Means chapter, and the doctrine of the Buddha's attainment of enlightenment in the far distant past (Kuonjitsujō) as set forth in the Life Span Chapter. [...]
> All Buddhas are emanations of the one Buddha, Shakyamuni. Therefore, [...] they are all brought together within the two characters of myō-hō.
> For this reason, the benefits to be gained by reciting the five characters of Myō-hō-ren-ge-kyō are great indeed. All the Buddhas, all the daimoku of the various sutras, are opened up and merged in the Lotus Sutra. Taking

> note of this opening up function of the Mystic Law, one should recite the daimoku of the Lotus Sutra. (p. 13 / II. 228)

Nevertheless, how can one truly understand the idea that the Mystic Law serves the function of opening up all the variety of Buddhas and all the variety of doctrines?

7. A doctrinal heritage which transcends the Eight Teachings

With respect to the superiority of the Daimoku when compared to the titles of all other sutras, in his later writing »This Is What I Heard (Reply to the Lay Priest Soya)« (1277, aged 56), Nichiren gives a clear answer. He explains that every sutra begins with the words "This is what I heard" in order to signify what is the essence as expounded in the entire sutra. When Nichiren quotes from any work of T'ien-t'ai, we should note that Nichiren frequently makes reference to or quotes from Miao-lo, the sixth patriarch of the T'ien-t'ai school. In order to counter the rise of the Hua yen school (*Kegonshū*), Miao-lo himself sharpened T'ien-t'ai's comparative evaluation systems such as the "Five Periods and Eight Teachings" and thereby made an important contribution to a radical doctrinal reconstruction of the School. And Nichiren himself received Miao-lo's doctrinal understanding that the Lotus Sutra itself transcended all the Eight Teachings.

> In the first volume of [T'ien-t'ai's] »The Words and Phrases of the Lotus Sutra« we find a passage that states, "The word 'this' [of 'This is what I heard'] indicates the essence of a doctrine heard from the Buddha". And the first volume of [Miao-lo's] »The Annotations on 'The Words and Phrases of the Lotus Sutra'« states, "If 'this' is not the teaching that surpasses the eight teachings, then how can it be considered the teaching of this [Lotus] sutra?"
>
> The *Kegon* Sutra begins: "The Great and Vast Buddha Flower Garland [*Mahā-vaipulya-buddha-avataṃsaka*] Sutra. This is what I heard". [...] What does "this" indicate in these and all other sutras? It refers to the title of each sutra. When the Buddha expounded a sutra, he put a title to it, revealing its ultimate principle. [...]
>
> However, those who listen to the titles of such provisional sutras are unable to realize *the benefit of perfect enlightenment* that arises from the teachings of [ichinen Sanzen based on the Tenfold Life Structure and so on].
>
> The sutras other than the Lotus Sutra do not expound this ultimate doctrine, and so their followers are like *ordinary persons at the stage of being a Buddha only in theory*. The Buddhas and bodhisattvas who appear in

> those sutras do not reach *the stage of hearing the name and words of the truth* in the practice of the Lotus Sutra, let alone *the stage of perception and action*, for they do not even chant the Daimoku. This is why the Great Teacher Miao-lo stated in »The Annotations on 'The Words and Phrases of the Lotus Sutra'«: *"If 'this' is not the teaching that surpasses the eight teachings, then how can it be considered the teaching of this [Lotus] sutra?"*
>
> The titles of the various other sutras fall within the Eight Teachings. These titles are like the meshes of a fishing net, while the title of the Lotus Sutra is like the main cord of the net that gathers all the meshes of the eight teachings together.
>
> *Nam-myō-hō-ren-ge-kyō* is not only the quintessence of the Buddha's lifetime teachings, but also the heart of the Lotus Sutra, its body, and its ultimate principle. (p. 1057 f. / I. 859 f.)

Let's summarize the main points taken from the above quotations.
- The title of each sutra expresses the quintessence of the teaching expounded within it.
- The titles of all sutras other than the Lotus Sutra can be understood by way of reference to the Eight Teachings while the title of the Lotus Sutra transcends the Eight Teachings as it represents the quintessence of all the teachings of the Buddha taught during his lifetime. The LS can therefore be understood by way of an analogy as the main cord which gathers together all the other meshes of a fishing net.
- The reason for this is that the title of the Lotus Sutra is to be practiced in our current time as the "seven characters of Nam-myō-hō-ren-ge-kyō", which embodies the principle of Ichinen Sanzen based on the Tenfold Life Structure.
- In other sutras and commentaries as well as in the doctrines of the other schools this "benefit of perfect enlightenment" is not expounded. In other words, only the title of the Lotus Sutra represents the original cause for attaining Buddhahood by all Buddhas and by all people. It is the Dharma Body and the practice for the attainment of Immediate Enlightenment as understood by the phrase "the ordinary person as Buddha".
- Consequently, the Daimoku is proclaimed for all ordinary people at *the stage of Buddhahood in theory*. Yet when they hear the Daimoku, they attain to the *nominal stage of identity*. When they chant Daimoku, they attain to *the stage of observation of the truth*. Nevertheless, these different stages of attainment reflect a rather theoretical understanding. This is because there is no gradual progression in attainment when one takes up the practice of chanting Daimoku, for this practice is identical with and nothing other than the attainment of Buddhahood at the stage of an ordinary person.

Chapter 3
Nichiren's own system of critical evaluation

1. The Five Principles of Propagation

As Nichiren depicted graphically in his writing »On Establishing the Correct Teaching for the Peace of the Land«, he was faced with "miscellaneous forms of faith and practice", including many new Buddhist schools. Consequently, he was compelled to develop a new system for evaluating all the Buddhist teachings, which also legitimated his own radical innovation in doctrine, essential if the propagation of his own teaching was to be successful in the 13th-century Japan. For this purpose Nichiren started to formulate his own "Five Guides to Propagation", as already referred to in writings such as »Why Contemporary Nenbutsu Practitioners Are Destined to Fall into the Hell of Incessant Suffering« (1264; see above page 169) and »What It Means to Slander the Law« (1262 or 1272?; p. 453 / 259). Further, Nichiren's criteria are also expounded systematically in »On Teaching, Capacity, Time, and Country« (1262). In brief, this writing considered the factors relevant to propagation as below (p. 438-442 / l. 48-53):

Teaching	The Law as to when the Lotus Sutra should be propagated
Capacity	With respect to the people (who although they slander the Law nevertheless establish a relationship to it)
Time	in the Latter Day of the Law
Country	in Japan, a country which is solely suited to the Mahayana Sutras, and from amongst which it should be dedicated exclusively to the Lotus Sutra)
Sequence of propagation	after the Mahayana has been established.

We know that Nichiren later changed the last criterion of "the sequence of propagation" to that of "the national master". There had already been a hint of this change in the Gosho now being considered.

> If one propagates the Buddhist teachings strictly with reference to the five guides outlined above, then one would surely become *a national master of Japan*. (p. 440 / l. 50)

Chapter 3

A national master is a Buddhist master of great wisdom, who knows the correct teaching which will save the nation from falling into the hell as a consequence of slandering the law.

In this sense, a more detailed Five Guides to Propagation is found in »On the Five Guides to Propagation (A letter to the lay priest Soya)« (1275, aged 54). This Gosho at the beginning outlines its main subject as follows:

> Just as one searches for a potent medicine to cure a critical illness, there is nothing as effective as the essential Law for the salvation of those who have committed the cardinal sins or have slandered the Law.
> In the category of *times* there are three periods such as the Former, the Middle, and the Latter Days of the Law. In the category of *teachings* we have Hinayana and Mahayana, the partial and the perfect teachings, the provisional and the true, and the exoteric and the esoteric. In the category of *countries* there are two types of central and peripheral countries depending on the geopolitical position. In the category of the people's *capacity* to understand the teachings, there are differences depending upon whether the person has already committed the cardinal sins or has not done so, and whether the person has already slandered the Law or has not done so. In the category of *teachers* there are ordinary teachers and sage teachers; persons of the two vehicles and bodhisattvas; bodhisattvas of other worlds and bodhisattvas of this world; and bodhisattvas of the theoretical section and bodhisattvas of the essential section.
> (p. 1026 / 540)

We don't need here to consider Nichiren's complex selection, evaluation and categorization process for each particular aspect. What is most significant, is his assertion that one should "consider *the five characters of daimoku as the means of sowing the seed of Buddhahood*" (id., p. 1027 / 542).

Of greater interest, is the fact that Nichiren utilizes these Five Principles of Propagation as a narrative mode by which he can clearly define his doctrinal stance. A typical example is the following passage from »The Object of Devotion for Observing the Mind)«, where Nichiren highlights the five categories by the use of parentheses:

> At the dawn of the Latter Day [*time*] evil people who slander the correct teaching [*capacity*] would fill the land [*country*], so Shakyamuni Buddha [...] summoned the multitude of great bodhisattvas from beneath the earth [*teacher*]. He entrusted them with the five characters of Myō-hō-ren-ge-kyō [*teaching*], the heart of the "Life Span" chapter, for the enlightenment of all people throughout the entire world.   (p. 250 / I. 370)

This narrative pattern can be found in »The Selection of the Time« where Nichiren likewise highlights the aspect of time.

> I, Nichiren [teacher], have already successfully attempted to refute all these evil doctrines [of Nenbutsu]. There is no doubt that our present age corresponds to the fifth five-hundred-year period [time] described in the Great Collection Sutra, when "the pure Law will become obscured and lost." But after the pure Law is obscured and lost, the great pure Law of Nam-myō-hō-ren-ge-kyō [teaching], the heart of the Lotus Sutra, will widely spread throughout the entire world [country] just as the name of Amida is now chanted by the mouths of the priests, nuns, laymen, and laywomen [capacity] in Japan. (p. 258 / I. 540)

In this passage, Nichiren already envisions "kōsenrufu" (wide propagation) in terms of propagation throughout the entire world, not just throughout Japan.

In addition to the above quotations, a further passage should be taken into account in order to highlight the content of the "teaching" which should be propagated. With respect to the dragon girl, I already quoted from the »Reply to Myōichinyo« (1280), which asserts the "immediate enlightenment of the essential section" as the central doctrine of Nichiren's teaching (see above page 186). In this gosho, Nichiren emphasizes the difference in circumstances which are to be considered when propagating a particular teaching.

> First of all, you should take the dragon king's daughter as proof of the validity of the *"doctrine of immediate enlightenment"*[25] as expounded in the Lotus Sutra. [...]
> Moreover, there are two versions of this doctrine found in the Lotus Sutra. The theoretical section of the sutra expounds the "immediate enlightenment" in principle, and *the essential section* expounds it in actuality. This explains that one can attain Buddhahood in one's present status as an ordinary person, without changing one's individual characteristics. That is why one's physical form, just as it is, is the Tathāgata endowed with the original and everlasting three bodies. [...]
> Furthermore, there are two times or periods when the Lotus Sutra is spread. They are the time when Shakyamuni was in the world and the Latter Day of the Law. Likewise, there are two teachings that are put into practice. In the Buddha's lifetime, it was the pure and perfect teaching, the sutra of the single true teaching. And now, *the Latter Day after the Buddha's passing, is the time when the essential section alone will spread.* [...]

---

[25] The English translation in the WND is the *"doctrine of attaining Buddhahood in one's present form"* (891) which resembles far more the concept of *"Sokushin jōbutsu"*, so designated by Dengyō. The "doctrine of immediate enlightenment" is synonymous with this, yet a basic difference lies in whether one can attain Buddhahood in one's present form in actuality *instantly* or not.

> *Nichiren* has truly been given this time. How could I possibly not spread the essential section, which perfectly suits the age? There is a vast difference between the essential section and the theoretical section in terms of the *capacity* of the people, the *doctrine*, and the *time* of its spreading. [...] In the Latter Day of the Law, the age of conflict, the Bodhisattvas of the Earth will appear and spread Nam-myō-hō-ren-ge-kyō, the heart of the essential section. [...]
> The essential section is the true doctrine that makes immediate attainment possible.
> (p. 1261 f. / II.891 f.)

In this passage, Nichiren make his position much clearer than in his early works and his position can be summarized as follows, with reference to the Five Principles of Propagation as well as to the passage quoted above:

Teaching	Nam-myō-hō-ren-ge-kyō, the heart of the Lotus Sutra, the true doctrine of "immediate enlightenment expounded in the essential section" should be propagated
Capacity	for people who have already committed the cardinal sins and have slandered the Law
Time	in the Latter Day of the Law, the time of conflict and after the pure Law of Shakyamuni Buddha has been obscured and lost
Country	in Japan replete with evil people and slander
Master	Nichiren, the Bodhisattva of the Earth who is the eternal disciple entrusted by the (eternal) Buddha Shakyamuni with the mission of propagating the Law for attaining Buddhahood.

2. The National Master of the Latter Day

As noted above, Nichiren began to understand the "sequence of teachings" to be one of the Five Principles for Propagation as elaborated in his early work »The Teaching, Capacity, Time, and Country«. Subsequently, he placed less significance on this principle and emphasized the role of the "national master". In fact, this early work had already explicitly highlighted the necessity for *"a national master of Japan"* who would propagate the correct Buddhist teaching as required by the Five Principles. Consequently, Nichiren's own self-understanding seems to have developed as a consequence of his reading the Lotus Sutra experientially, i.e. with direct reference to his own extraordinary life. This work was written in 1262 during his exile on the Izu peninsula (May 1261 – February 1263), i.e. following the attack on his place of abode in Matsubagayatsu (August 1260), a month after he had presented »On Establishing the Correct Teaching for the Peace of the Land«.

> The fourth volume of the Lotus Sutra states, "Since hatred and jealousy toward this sutra abound even in the world when the Tathāgata is present, how much more will this be true after his passing?" [...] And the sixth volume reads, "Never hesitating even at the cost of their lives." [...] When I examine these passages, I know that, if I do not bring forth these three enemies of the Lotus Sutra, then I will not be *the votary of the Lotus Sutra*. And yet if I do so, I am almost certain to lose my life. (p. 442 / l. 48)

Here, Nichiren identified himself as the "votary of the Lotus Sutra in the Latter Day" who would read the Sutra with his body. This particular self-understanding by way of "bodily reading" compelled Nichiren to interpret the events of his own life as having been foretold in the Lotus Sutra itself. Consequently, Nichiren's "bodily reading" was a particular mode of "empirical proof", whereby particular passages in the Sutra could be read as "prophecy" for the appearance of Nichiren himself in the Latter Day, who has himself been entrusted with the mission to propagate the Mystic Law transmitted to Jōgyō in the form of the Three Great Secret Laws.

This particular way of reading the Sutra is characteristic of Nichiren and always informs his understanding of the Sutra itself. Indeed, it was an understanding which not only demanded of and applied to himself alone, but also demanded of and applied to his disciples as well. For example, at the same time that Nichiren was almost beheaded at Tatsunokuchi several of his followers were arrested and imprisoned. On his way to exile on the island of Sado, Nichiren sent a letter to his senior disciples who had been imprisoned.

> Tomorrow I am to leave for the province of Sado. In the cold tonight, I think of what it must be like for you in prison, and it pains me. Admirable Nichirō, because you have read the entirety of the Lotus Sutra in both body and spirit, you will also be able to save your father and mother, your six kinds of relatives, and all living beings. Others read the Lotus Sutra with their mouths alone, in word alone, but they do not read it with their hearts. And even if they read it with their hearts, they do not read it with their bodies. It is reading the sutra with both one's body and mind that is truly praiseworthy!
> Since the sutra teaches that "the young sons of heavenly beings will wait on him and serve him. Swords and staves will not touch him and poison will have no power to harm him," certainly nothing untoward will befall you. When you are released from prison, please come as quickly as you can. I am eager to see you, and to show you that I too am well.
> (»Letter to Priest Nichirō in Prison«, p. 1212 / l. 204)

Thus, despite being carried away as a captive to the remote island of Sado, Nichiren retained an unshakable conviction in the face of persecution, and likewise rained a profound love and concern for his disciples. This was emblematic of his unique personal charm and charisma which attracted many people.

Nichiren sharpened his self-identification as the master of the country in his writing »The Opening of the Eyes« written at Tsukahara, his first place of abode while in exile on Sado. This important writing is primarily concerned with the following understanding:

> There are three categories of people that all human beings should respect. They are the sovereign, the teacher, and the parent. (p. 186 / I. 220)

By asking the question: "Is Nichiren not the votary of the Lotus Sutra?", he highlights the proof required if the "prophecy" of the LS is to be considered to have been fulfilled, i.e. that the votary of the LS would be attacked, persecuted and slandered. Nichiren concludes:

> I, Nichiren, am sovereign, teacher, and father and mother to all the people of Japan. (p. 237 / 287)

For if Nichiren has demonstrated that he is indeed the "votary of the LS in the Latter Day", he should thereby be regarded as the "lord of the teachings equipped with the Three Virtues of sovereign, teacher, and parent."

In the above writing, the Five Principles for Propagation are deployed to provide a framework for the overall structure of his argument. The subjects can be summarized as follows.

Teaching	The Mystic Law of Ichinen Sanzen expounded in the essential section
Capacity	ignorant and slanderous people
Time	the Latter Day of the Law, the time of conflict filled with the Three Types of Powerful Enemies (of arrogant laypeople and priests as well as false sages)
Country	Japan, the country of slandering the Law
Master	Nichiren, the votary of the LS, the lord of the teachings with the three virtues of sovereign, teacher and parent

According to traditional NS teaching, this writing is considered to reveal the true identity of Nichiren as the "object of worship in terms of the Buddha". We do not need to go so far. It is sufficient that we be satisfied with

Nichiren's own self-identification as the master of the teachings in the Latter Day. Further, Nichiren's particular self-understanding can also be found in other writings, such as »The Letter of Petition from Yorimoto« (1277), a petition which Nichiren wrote on behalf of Shijō Kingo to address a dispute between Shijō Kingo & his lord, Ema. Indeed, given this official context, this writing gives formal expression to Nichiren's own self-understanding as to his position in Buddhist history.

> Considering what the Sutra states, the Sage Nichiren is *the envoy of the Tathāgata who attained enlightenment in the remotest past, the manifestation of Bodhisattva Jōgyō, the votary of the essential section of the Lotus Sutra, and the great master in the fifth five-hundred-year period* [following the Buddha's passing]. (p. 1156 / I. 807)

Further, this self-understanding suggests the image of a "bodhisattva buddha", i.e. a bodhisattva who is enlightened in his essence, as described in the Lotus Sutra. Consequently, the leader of the Bodhisattvas of the Earth should be deeply revered and admired as the master of the teachings by the whole nation. Yet clearly Nichiren himself did not demand that he be worshipped as the sole Buddha in the Latter Day.

3. The Fivefold Comparison

In addition to question of who is the teaching master of the nation in the Latter Day, the »Opening of the Eyes« also considers which type of teaching is to be propagated.

> There are three types of teachings that are to be studied. They are Confucianism, Brahmanism, and Buddhism. (p. 186 / I. 220)

Nichiren considers each of these teachings step by step in order to attain to the highest teaching by way of a critical method following the Fivefold Comparison[26]. This system for critically evaluating the teachings by way of five steps is an important innovation which Nichiren required in order to demonstrate the superiority of his own doctrine when considered against all other teachings extent at his time.

1) *Buddhism is superior to non-Buddhist teachings.*

Buddhism is more profound than other religions as it teaches the causal law of life that penetrates the three existences of past, present, and future.

2) *Mahayana Buddhism is superior to Hinayana Buddhism.*

Hinayana Buddhism (Theravada) is for a limited number of people such as those of the two vehicles (*shravaka* and *pratyekabuddha*), who aim at per-

---

[26] See http://www.nichirenlibrary.org/en/dic/Content/F/47#para-0

sonal liberation by eliminating all earthly desires. In contrast, Mahayana Buddhism is the teaching for bodhisattvas who seek to t lead all people to enlightenment, without any distinction.

3) True Mahayana is superior to provisional Mahayana.

The third level of comparison refers to the division of all the teachings of Shakyamuni Buddha: in the first forty-two years of his preaching life after his enlightenment at the age of thirty and in the last eight years of his life when the Lotus Sutra was traditionally supposed to have been taught.

In the pre-Lotus Sutra teachings, according to T'ien-t'ai's system of classification, the people of the two vehicles, women, and evil persons are precluded from any possibility of attaining enlightenment; in addition, Buddhahood can be attained only by advancing through the progressive stages of bodhisattva practice conducted throughout incalculable *kalpas*. In contrast, the Lotus Sutra teaches direct access to the enlightenment for everyone who embraces the Sutra.

4) The essential section of the Lotus Sutra is superior to its theoretical section.

The theoretical section takes the form of preaching by Shakyamuni who is still viewed as having attained enlightenment for the first time during his lifetime in India. In contrast, the essential section reveals Shakyamuni's true identity as the eternal Buddha since the remotest past, symbolizing the ever-present Buddhahood inherent in all beings.

5) The Buddhism of sowing is superior to the Buddhism of the harvest.

Nichiren elaborated this comparison based on the three-phase process of sowing, maturing, and harvesting. The teaching which focuses on the process of sowing the seed for the attainment of Buddhahood is characterized by universality in that it is applicable to all people.

Below we will consider only the last three comparative steps within the Mahayana teachings.

The superiority of the Lotus Sutra in comparison to the pre-Lotus Sutra teachings

At this comparative level, Nichiren states the most important reason for considering the LS to be superior to the pre-LS teachings: with reference to the two doctrines that are found only in the LS and nowhere in the pre-LS teachings:

> The chief difference lies in the fact that the Lotus Sutra teaches that persons of the two vehicles can attain Buddhahood, and that the Buddha Shakyamuni in reality attained enlightenment at an inconceivably distant time in the past. (p. 191 / I. 226)

Further, Nichiren elaborates as to how these two particular teachings depicted in the metaphorical language of the LS should be understood in the language of Buddhist doctrine.

> These [pre-Lotus] sutras have two flaws. First, because they teach that the Ten Worlds are separate from one another, they fail to remove their provisional character and they do not reveal the doctrine of Ichinen Sanzen expounded in the theoretical section. Second, because they teach that Shakyamuni Buddha attained enlightenment for the first time in this world, referring only to his provisional aspect, they fail to reveal the attainment of enlightenment in the remotest past as expounded in the essential section. These two great doctrines are the core of the Buddha's lifetime teachings, and the very heart and marrow of all the sutras.
>
> (p. 198 / I. 235)

First, the reason why the pre-Lotus Sutra teachings are regarded as provisional teachings is explained by considering them from the unique perspective of the Lotus Sutra. The pre-LS represent a variety of teachings appropriate to the different capacities of those of Two Vehicles and those on the way of the Bodhisattva. Yet the Lotus Sutra reveals that their provisional character is a consequence of the Buddha's use of "Expedient Means", in order to lead all of them to the One Buddha Vehicle which alone can open to them the Buddha's wisdom. In this part of the theoretical section, they are assured of attaining to enlightenment by completing the Bodhisattva Way as described in the LS, and the prophecies are accompanied by reference to details, such as the Tathāgata's names, time, place, and Buddha land. Further, this assurance is also given to evil people and women who were traditionally considered to be unable to attain Buddhahood due to their inherent lack of capacity. Thus, the doctrine of the "true aspect of all phenomena", as expounded in the "Expedient Means" chapter, provides a universal foundation for the equal possibility of attaining to enlightenment, as all people without distinction are intrinsically endowed with the same "ten factors of life".

What is more, the pre-Lotus Sutra teachings describe "a gradually progressing practice requiring an inordinate length of time of many kalpas by means of which all desires are cut off and the human body discarded". Yet for Nichiren, the attainment of Buddhahood cannot be achieved by means of this kind of practice, but only through an immediate enlightenment which activates the eternal Buddhahood originally inherent within the ordinary human being. Shakyamuni's revelation of his having attained enlightenment in the remotest past, as expounded in the essential section, symbolizes the original or eternal source for the true attainment of enlightenment. Thus:

CHAPTER 3

> *Nichiren's doctrine of Ichinen Sanzen* is founded on both the theoretical principle of "ten factors of life" and the essential principle of Shakyamuni's revelation of having attained enlightenment in the remotest past. That's what amounts to "the core of the Buddha's lifetime teachings".

The superiority of the essential section in comparison to the theoretical section

Ichinen Sanzen is a doctrine that T'ien-t'ai and Miao-lo formulated by reflecting on the states of being considered through the focus of the practice of meditation. This doctrine is essentially grounded on the principle of "ten factors of life" and gives expression to the equality of each of the aspects of the ten worlds. Consequently, T'ien-t'ai's Ichinen Sanzen represents merely an elucidation of the enlightened state of life on a theoretical level. In distinction from T'ien-t'ai's "Ichinen Sanzen of the theoretical section" Nichiren elaborated his radical concept of "Ichinen Sanzen of the essential section" which is grounded upon Shakyamuni's own eternal enlightenment. Nichiren designated this the *"true doctrine of Ichinen Sanzen"*.

> The "Expedient Means" chapter, which belongs to the theoretical section, expounds both the doctrine of Ichinen Sanzen and the doctrine of the possibility for those of the two vehicles to achieve Buddhahood. It thus gets rid of one of the two errors found in the earlier sutras. However, so long as the Buddha's true identity is not revealed, *the true doctrine of Ichinen Sanzen* cannot be manifested while the attainment of Buddhahood by persons of the two vehicles remains uncertain. Such teachings are like the moon seen in water, or rootless plants that drift on the waves.
> (p. 197 / I. 235)

The reason why both doctrines of the theoretical section remain nothing more than beautiful ideas is because of the concept of initial enlightenment. To speak more precisely, Nichiren considers all teachings other than the eternal realization in the Life Span chapter as teachings grounded merely on the concept of initial enlightenment.

> Even the fourteen chapters that form the essential section, all of them excluding the two chapters of "Emerging from the Earth" and "Life Span", retain the view that the Buddha first attained enlightenment in his present lifetime. (p. 198 / I. 236)

From the perspective of a contemplative reading of the essential section for the Latter Day

One may ask a simple question: Why is it so that only an eternal realization which reveals the true identity of Shakyamuni Buddha can alone make manifest the true doctrine of Ichinen Sanzen? The reason for that is that Shakyamuni broke free from a provisional view of initial enlightenment and thereby manifested "beginningless Buddhahood". Nevertheless, we need to pay careful attention to Nichiren's particular way of reading this story. For Nichiren moves well beyond literal meaning and interprets the story from his own unique perspective.

> When we come to the essential section of the Lotus Sutra, then the view with respect to the Buddha's initial enlightenment is demolished. Likewise, the effects of the four teachings are demolished, and consequently their causes are also demolished. Thus, the cause and effect of the ten worlds as expounded in the earlier sutras and the theoretical section of the Lotus Sutra are wiped out, and those as expounded in the essential section are revealed. This is exactly *the doctrine of original cause and original effect*. In that case, the nine worlds are all present in *beginningless Buddhahood* and Buddhahood is inherent in *the beginningless nine worlds*. This *true* principle of the mutual containment of the ten worlds constitutes the true hundred worlds and thousand factors and thus *the true doctrine of Ichinen Sanzen*, the true three thousand realms in a single moment of life. (p. 197 / I. 235)

In the first part of the above passage, Nichiren breaks down the false view that one can attain to enlightenment at some point and for the first time in one's life. For all the Buddhas at once are uncovered as being merely provisional and without substance at the moment when Shakyamuni Buddha reveals his true identity as the eternal original Buddha as described in the Life Span chapter.

> They are manifestations of this eternal Buddha which are like the fleeting reflections of the moon in the heavens, which float on the surfaces of various large and small bodies of water. (p. 197 / 236)

If they represent a provisional result, their cause likewise is uncovered to be provisional and false.

In the latter part, Nichiren speaks about the causality of the ten worlds as revealed by the eternal realization, which represents *"the doctrine of original cause and original effect"* and "the mutual containment of the *beginningless ten worlds"*.

However, more strictly, Shakyamuni's "attainment of enlightenment in the remotest past" implies an initial enlightenment at a particular point in the remotest past, so "eternity" has a beginning in the "inconceivable remote past". Yet in fact, the concept of "Buddha nature" had not been elaborated at the time of the compilation of the LS (ca. the 2nd Century), as the concept of "Buddha nature" was first developed only in the Mahayana »Nirvana Sutra« (ca. the 4th Century), which states that *"all beings are endowed with Buddha nature. The Tathāgata is everlasting and not subject to any change."* This is the reason which led to the inclusion of both the Lotus Sutra and the Nirvana Sutra into the last period of T'ien-t'ai's system of classification of Five Periods and Eight Teachings.

As further support for this, Nichiren regarded Shakyamuni's realization of eternal enlightenment as being an initial enlightenment, as can be seen in his writing »On the Errors of the Eight Schools«, completed in February 1272, at the same time that »The Opening of the Eyes« was written. In speaking about the doctrine of the mutual containment of the ten worlds and Ichinen Sanzen, Nichiren quotes the following passage from Miao-lo's »Annotations on "The Great Concentration and Insight«:

> "Taking the view of the theoretical section, after having accomplished the innumerable practices for 'countless kalpas' under the guidance of the *Buddha Daitsūchishō* [as described in the 7th chapter of the Sutra], Shakyamuni finally achieved 'wonderful enlightenment' at the place of practice [under the bodhi tree]. However, taking the view of the essential section, [the passage where the Buddha says] *'originally I practiced the bodhisattva way'* suggests that he practiced for 'countless kalpas' before he in fact attained original Buddhahood, thereby achieving 'wonderful enlightenment'." (p. 160 / II. 424)

From this quotation it would appear that Nichiren inherited this understanding with respect to the eternal realization as described in the Life Span chapter from T'ien t'ai and Miao lo. Consequently, the statement, *"originally I practiced the bodhisattva way,"* indicates the practice which is the "cause of enlightenment" while the statement, *"it has been immeasurable, boundless [time] since I in fact attained Buddhahood",* indicates the "effect of enlightenment." This implies that Nichiren was aware that if the meaning of the text is taken literally, the story of Shakyamuni's eternal realization can be understood as a conventional view of initial enlightenment which reflects the understanding at the time of the compilation of the Sutra. Yet in »The Opening of the Eyes« he nevertheless interpreted this story as indicating the *"doctrine of Ichinen Sanzen based on the principle of the mutual containment of the beginningless ten worlds"*. In so doing, Nichiren went well beyond a literal interpretation of "the essential section taught during the time of Shakyamuni's life".

> The doctrine of Ichinen Sanzen is hidden *at the bottom of the text* in the Life Span chapter deep within the essential section of the Lotus Sutra. Nāgārjuna and Vasubandhu were aware of it but did not bring it forth into the light. Our wise master T'ien-t'ai alone embraced it and kept it ever in mind. The doctrine of Ichinen Sanzen begins with the concept of the mutual containment of the Ten Worlds. (p. 189 / I. 223)

Thus, Nichiren clearly states that "the true doctrine of Ichinen Sanzen based on the mutual containment of the beginningless ten worlds" has been *"hidden at the bottom of the text in the Life Span chapter"*.

With respect to the above passage, Miyata gives his own interpretation (see Miyata 2017, p. 35 f.), according to which the *"bottom of the text in the Life Span chapter"* refers to the eternal realization. Thus, he considers this aspect of effect to be amongst the Three Mystic Principles which T'ien-t'ai classified with reference to the Life Span chapter as found in his »The Profound Meaning of the Lotus Sutra«:
- the "mystic principle of the true cause" is based on the sentence *"originally I practiced the bodhisattva way"*,
- the "mystic principle of the true effect" is based on the sentence *"since I in fact attained Buddhahood"*, and
- the "mystic principle of the true land" is based on the sentence *"Ever since then I have been constantly in this* Sahā *world, preaching the Law, teaching and converting"*.

Miyata is convinced that Nichiren had quoted the *sentence of the mystic principle of the true effect* which is found immediately before the passage which begins with the sentence *"When we come to the essential section of the Lotus Sutra, then the view of Buddha's initial enlightenment is demolished"* (p. 197 / 235).

Yet the sentence of the mystic principle of the true effect is in fact quoted by Nichiren merely with respect to the manifestation of Shakyamuni's true identity which breaks through the conventional view of initial enlightenment. Consequently, what is *"hidden at the bottom of the text in the Life Span chapter"* is definitely not the event of eternal realization (true effect) itself, but rather the principle of Ichinen Sanzen hidden beneath this true effect. This is Nichiren's own unique doctrine representing a further development of T'ien-t'ai's doctrine of Ichinen Sanzen, i.e. it is "true Ichinen Sanzen" based on the dual structure of life.

Nichiren states with respect to causality, that the causality of the ten worlds as revealed by the eternal realization necessarily must be the "doctrine of the true cause and the true effect" which manifests the "principle of the mutual containment of the beginningless ten worlds." However, there is a leap of logic here: as explained above, Shakyamuni's eternal realization signifies in actuality an initial enlightenment achieved at a point in the remotest past, as it is grounded on a view that the Buddhahood can be achieved by discarding the ordinary human body replete with a multitude of earthly desires. Yet Nichiren moves well beyond a literal reading of the narrative concerning the eternal Buddha Shakyamuni by interpreting the same narrative in terms of the "doctrine of Ichinen Sanzen based on the mutual possession of the beginningless ten worlds". At this point, in order to explain the leap of logic, a new perspective must be introduced which focuses on the "significance hidden at the bottom of the sentence". From this deeper perspective

> "the doctrine of the true cause and true effect" can be reinterpreted as "*the doctrine of the true cause **-equals-** true effect*".

In other words, when Shakyamuni attained enlightenment for the first time at some point in the remotest past and if in fact he awakened to "beginningless Buddhahood", then this initial enlightenment actually signifies original enlightenment. Thus, from a more profound and much deeper meditative perspective, any "attainment of enlightenment" never signifies the realization of Buddhahood by discarding the human body (i.e. discarding the nine worlds), but original enlightenment itself (the true effect) which is inherent in *the beginningless nine worlds* of the ordinary person (the true cause). Likewise, the body of the ordinary person which represents the precondition for actual existence in this world is contained within *beginningless Buddhahood*. To summarize:

> From a more profound and much deeper meditative perspective Nichiren understood the story of "Shakyamuni's attainment of enlightenment in the remotest past" in terms of "immediate enlightenment" represented by a dialectic, e.g. "the true cause as true effect", "initial enlightenment as original enlightenment", and "the nine worlds as Buddhahood".
> This is what Nichiren intended to represent in »The Opening of the Eyes« by use of the phrase "the true doctrine of Ichinen Sanzen grounded on the true principle of the mutual containment of the ten worlds."

So far, the perspective of a deeper contemplative reading has been contrasted with the perspective of a literal reading, yet they each should be understood to be two differing I levels of interpretation rather than radically contradictory perspectives. As noted more than once above, the Daimoku is the heart of the Lotus Sutra and signifies Shakyamuni's eternal realization on the level of a literal reading of the Life Span chapter. Yet on a more profound

& much deeper contemplative reading, it is the practice of chanting the Daimoku which actually manifests the *Three major principles for realizing the "Immediate Enlightenment" of Ichinen Sanzen based on the mutual containment of the ten worlds*. This Dharma body and its practice is the direct way of realizing Buddhahood which Nichiren intended to transmit to all of us in our current times. And it was with this intention, that Nichiren elaborated his own system for the critical evaluation of the Buddhist teachings. We should refer to this foundational perspective for critically determining the "received tradition beyond the Eight Teachings" as the "Contemplative Viewpoint of the Essential Section for the Latter Day."

> From this perspective Nichiren re-reads Shakyamuni's eternal realization by maintaining that it was by the practice of chanting the daimoku which manifested his realization of the Three Major principles. In this case, the chanting of daimoku which Shakyamuni practiced as an ordinary person represents the "Original Cause" while his immediate enlightenment corresponds to the "Original effect". As the Mystic Law embodies the principle of "Original Cause – equals-Original Effect", practicing this Law always manifests the aspect of the "Unity of Person and Law".

The superiority of Sowing in comparison to Harvesting

From the Contemplative perspective of the Essential section for the Latter Day, Nichiren upheld the superiority of the Essential section in comparison to the Theoretical section, in order to draw forth the "fundamental principle for realizing the Immediate Enlightenment of Ichinen Sanzen". Of course, he then needed to establish a particular or essential practice in order to manifest this principle in a very concrete form. With respect to this, the aspect of Original Cause he considered far more fundamental when compared to Original Effect and he maintained that it is nothing other than the Mystic Law, characterized by the simultaneity of cause and effect, yet now understood as the "mutual containment of the ten worlds without beginning". That is, the Original Cause contains or is identical to Original Effect. Apart from emphatically emphasizing the wonderous effect of attaining enlightenment itself, it is this simultaneity of cause and effect which is the matter of utmost importance. Consequently, it leads to the necessity of demonstrating the superiority of Sowing to Harvesting.

In this context, in »The Opening of the Eyes«, Nichiren considers the "three-phase process of sowing, reaping and harvesting". Yet at the same time, this perspective provides a foundation for doctrinally establishing the superiority of the Lotus Sutra over all other sutras. For Nichiren argues that this process for attaining Buddhahood is simply not available in other teachings, such as those of Shingon, Kegon and so on. Consequently, although they might assert the doctrine of immediate enlightenment, there assertion merely represents "an expectation of harvesting [the fruit of Buddhahood] while being ignorant of the seed" and is therefore futile.

> The various schools argue with one another, each claiming that its sutra contains *the true seeds of enlightenment*. [...] These seeds of enlightenment are the doctrine of *Ichinen Sanzen* as expounded by T'ien-t'ai.
> The seeds of enlightenment for the various Buddhas described in [...] various Mahayana sutras do all converge upon the one doctrine of Ichinen Sanzen. And the Great Master T'ien-t'ai was the only person who was capable of perceiving this doctrine. [...]
> The Mahāvairochana Sutra of the Shingon school contains no mention of the doctrines such as the possibility of the two vehicles' enlightenment, Shakyamuni's eternal realization in the distant past, and Ichinen Sanzen.
> (p. 215 / l. 259)

By referring to the distinctive discourse of the LS when considered against all other teachings such as Shingon and Kegon, Nichiren emphasizes the "doctrines such as the possibility of the two vehicles' enlightenment, Shakyamuni's eternal realization in the distant past, and Ichinen Sanzen", grounded in both the Theoretical and the Essential sections of the LS. For these doctrines are related to the "seeds of the Lotus Sutra", which signify the Original Cause of the eternal Buddha, thus of all Buddhas.

In another Gosho, a similar assertion is made. In the »Letter to Akimoto« (1280), Nichiren states:

> The doctrine of the sowing of the seed and its maturing and harvesting is the very heart and core of the Lotus Sutra. *All the Buddhas of the three existences and the ten directions have invariably attained Buddhahood through the seeds represented by the five characters of Myō-hō-ren-ge-kyō*. The reciting of the words Namu-Amida-butsu are not the seeds of Buddhahood, nor can the mantras of Shingon or the five precepts act as such seeds.
> (p. 1072 / l. 1015)

Once again, by referring to the distinctive discourse of the LS when considered against all other teachings, Nichiren emphasizes the doctrine of Ichinen Sanzen as the sole seed of enlightenment. If a comparison is made between the Essential section and the Theoretical section of the LS, this particular doctrine itself becomes a matter to be examined much more closely. Nichiren speaks of the two different types of the doctrine of Ichinen Sanzen, most clearly in the Gosho »The Treatment of Illness« (1282).

> There are two ways of observing the [state of being described as] Ichinen Sanzen. One is theoretical, and the other, actual. What T'ien-t'ai and Dengyō practiced was theoretical, but what I practice now is actual. Because this practice is superior [to the other one], the difficulties provoked by it are much more severe. The others' is the Ichinen Sanzen of the Theoretical section, while mine is that of the Essential section. These two are as different as heaven is from earth. (p. 998 / I. 1115)

The *Ichinen Sanzen of the Essential section* represents the superior doctrine which Nichiren delineated by way of contrast to all the pre-LS teachings and to the Theoretical section of the LS itself. However, this is still not the actual doctrine which Nichiren intends to propagate for all people in the Latter Day. For the "Essential section" represents the LS and signifies the LS as expounded by Shakyamuni Buddha (in accordance with the conventional understanding in Nichiren's time). Consequently, it is necessary to take one further step and to make a final distinction between "the literal reading for the Buddha's time" and "the deeper contemplative reading for the Latter Day". Nichiren could not remain within the framework of the LS itself, although it remained essential to him, for he needed to establish a practice which would be the means to the realization of "the supreme principle of instant enlightenment" for the people of the Latter Day. Thus, the practice of chanting daimoku would gain a further more profound and far deeper significance once Nichiren established the distinctive object of devotion for observing the mind, i.e. as the means to activate original enlightenment. The necessary requirement for and the essential form of this Mandala-honzon can only be understood from the perspective of the superiority of Sowing when contrasted with Harvesting. This was to be Nichiren's most important purpose in writing »The Object of Devotion for Observing the Mind to be Established in the Fifth Five-Hundred-Year Period after the Tathāgata's Passing«.

4. The doctrine of Ichinen Sanzen and the object of devotion

We can reconstruct Nichiren's reasoning with respect to the doctrinal foundation for his Mandala-Honzon mainly by reference to his major work »The Object of Devotion for Observing the Mind«.

We can begin with the passage which best expresses the conclusion that Nichiren selected the Buddhism of Sowing as the optimal practice for the Latter Day.

> As regards the essential section, it is exclusively appropriate for the people at the dawn of the Latter Day of the Law. On the surface, the Buddha seems to have preached this teaching for the enlightenment of the people

Chapter 3

> of his own day; they thereby had the seeds of Buddhahood planted in their lives in the remotest past and had been nurtured in the previous age of the Buddha Great Universal Wisdom Excellence and in their own day through the [pre-Lotus Sutra] teachings and the theoretical section. Then with the essential section he brought his followers [...] finally to the stage of perfect enlightenment.
>
> In actuality, however, the essential section bears no resemblance whatsoever to the theoretical section. The Three Parts of preparation, revelation, and transmission related to the essential section are intended entirely for the beginning of the Latter Day of the Law. *The essential section of Shakyamuni's lifetime and that which is appropriate for the beginning of the Latter Day are both pure and perfect* [in that both lead directly to Buddhahood]. *Shakyamuni's, however, is for the harvest, and this is for the sowing.* The core of his teaching is one chapter and two halves [before and after the Life Span chapter], and the core of mine is the five characters of the daimoku alone.
>
> (p. 249 / I. 369)

Here, the "essential section" is focused on Shakyamuni's eternal realization. Through this revelation the disciples understand that they had been cultivated ever since the remotest past up until the Buddha's lifetime. Consequently, Nichiren regards the essential section as the means by which Shakyamuni's disciples harvest the fruit of enlightenment. Yet the people of the Latter Day have had no such relationship to Shakyamuni Buddha back to the remotest past and therefore the essential section of the LS has no meaning for them. For the people of the Latter Day require that the seed of enlightenment, i.e. the Mystic Law of Ichinen Sanzen, should now be sowed, as it is this sowing which had led not only to the realization of the eternal Buddha Shakyamuni himself, but to enlightenment of all other Buddhas and Shakyamuni's disciples.

The seed of enlightenment is always the same perfect Law,
but a distinction can be made between those people who received it
in the past and those people who have received now or
will receive it in the future.
The Life Span chapter and two halves around it
were preached for the people of Shakyamuni's own time,
i.e. it signifies the harvesting of the fruit.
The people in the Latter Day require that
the same seed of the perfect Law now be sowed.

Consequently, for the people of the Latter Day, Nichiren considers that only the Mystic Law representing the Original Cause of Shakyamuni's eternal realization is appropriate.

> *Shakyamuni's practices and the virtues he consequently attained are all contained within the five characters of Myō-hō-ren-ge-kyō. If we embrace and believe in these five characters, we will naturally be granted the same benefits as he was.* (p. 246 / I. 365)

The Daimoku therefore represents both the practice of the original cause and the practice for the original effect of Buddhahood, as chanting daimoku transfers instantly all the benefits and virtues of a Buddha.

> The Mystic Law embodies the principle of the simultaneity of cause and effect and doesn't require any long-term process of ripening or maturing up to the harvest.

Further, Nichiren makes it clear that those who practice the Mystic Law in the Latter Day don't become a Buddha or some transcendent or supernatural being. Such fantasies, as well as those historical characters depicted in the Buddhist sutras now gain a purely symbolic significance with respect to our own actual life.

> Shakyamuni Buddha, who has attained perfect enlightenment, is our own flesh and blood. The benefits and merits resulting from his practices are our bones and marrow. [...]
> The Shakyamuni Buddha within our lives is *the primordial Buddha endowed with the three bodies since time without beginning*, revealed more than numberless major world systems dust particle kalpas ago. [...]
> The bodhisattvas Jōgyō [and the others] represent the world of the bodhisattva within ourselves. The Great Master Miao-lo says: "*You should understand that one's life and its environment at a single moment encompass the three thousand realms. Therefore, when one attains the Buddha way, one puts oneself in accord with this fundamental principle, and one's body and mind at a single moment pervade the entire realm of phenomena.*" (p. 247 / I. 365 f.)

By re-interpreting the ten worlds in the sense of the ten states of life contained within our own life, i.e. from the perspective of a more profound and far deeper contemplative reading, the eternal Buddha Shakyamuni is understood to be *the primordial Buddha since time without beginning*. Consequently, we are able to manifest the instant enlightenment of Ichinen Sanzen based on the mutual containment of the beginningless ten worlds. Given this, the environment in which we live our lives will itself be transformed into an "everlasting pure land". And this enlightened life and enlightened world are intrinsically related to the characteristics of the ten worlds mandala which Nichiren was to inscribe.

Chapter 3

> Shakyamuni Buddha [transmitted] the five characters of Nam-myō-hō-ren-ge-kyō, the heart of the essential section of the Lotus Sutra, [...] only to the great bodhisattvas [...] by summoning them from beneath the earth and preaching the eight chapters. *This true object of devotion* is inscribed as follows:
> The treasure tower dwells in the air above the Sahā world governed by the original Buddha; Myō-hō-ren-ge-kyō is in the center of the tower and to its right and left side both Shakyamuni and Tahō Buddha are seated. They are flanked by Shakyamuni's assistants, the four bodhisattvas, led by Jōgyō, [...]
> Even though statues and paintings have been made of these [different forms of] Shakyamuni Buddha during the last two millennia, the Buddha of the "Life Span" chapter is still not present. *This Buddha statue* will appear only in the Latter Day of the Law. (p. 247 f. / I. 365 f.)

The *"five characters of Nam-myō-hō-ren-ge-kyō, the heart of the essential section of the Lotus Sutra,"* means the practice of the Mystic Law of eternal realization, which was transmitted to the Bodhisattva Jōgyō. In like manner, Nichiren was to inscribe the ten worlds mandala as the object of meditation embodying this Mystic Law.

To summarize:

- Nichiren asserts that the "Chanting of Daimoku" or the Mystic Law represents the Dharma body of Shakyamuni's eternal realization. This practice is for all people in the Latter Day in order that they can realize the same supreme principle of instant enlightenment, legitimated by the doctrine of Ichinen Sanzen based on the mutual containment of ten worlds.
- Nichiren first began to proclaim and propagate the practice of chanting daimoku to realize instant enlightenment and later inscribed the ten worlds mandala representing this realization.
- Nichiren himself was authorized to construct this Object of Observing the Mind in his capacity as Bodhisattva Jōgyō, who had been entrusted with this mission by Shakyamuni Buddha during the Ceremony in the Air.
- Consequently, this unique, never before revealed "Buddha of the Life Span chapter", "this Buddha statue" therefore appeared for the first time only in the Latter Day of the Law.
- Therefore, the Buddhas, Bodhisattvas and all other beings inscribed on the mandala, represent the ten worlds or ten states of being in our very own life.
- As the ten worlds mandala represents eternal realization, this realization will occur in our very own life each time we chant daimoku before this mandala.

Additionally, from the perspective of the superiority of Sowing to Harvesting, there is a threefold significance with respect to all persons who practice the Mystic Law and thereby realize the supreme principle of instant enlightenment.

> The Dharma body which the eternal Buddha practiced, which Jōgyō Nichiren embodied, and which we practice today, are all consistently the same Mystic Law.

Further, the Daimoku of the Essential section does not require any long-term process of gradual development, from its first sowing through maturation to harvesting. For when we practice, we directly access the Mystic Law of Shakyamuni's eternal realization. In this respect, confirmation can be found in Nichiren's writing »The One Hundred and Six Comparisons« e.g.: *"Now, I, Nichiren, chant daimoku which the eternal Buddha Shakyamuni practiced"*, and *"The Right Dharma that Shakyamuni practiced in the remotest past is the right seed of enlightenment. [...] Nichiren's practice is exactly the same which has been transferred from the remotest past."* (p. 862) It is therefore also correct to regard Nichiren as the Master of the Teachings of the Mystic Principle of the Original Cause.

Nevertheless, reversing the direction by projecting Nichiren back to the primordial beginning in the remotest past is erroneous. In such a case, Nichiren is assumed to be *"the original Tathāgata endowed with the wisdom body"* who appeared in the Latter Day as *"the reincarnation of the Bodhisattva Jōgyō"*. In this capacity Nichiren would thereby be regarded as *"the Great Master of the Essential section"* (p. 854). These factors are the basis upon which the NS-Nichikan doctrine of "Nichiren as the Eternal Original Buddha" has been erroneously constructed. And it is a fundamental misunderstanding.

Chapter 4
From the perspective of a Contemplative Reading of the Essential Section for the Latter Day

1. Nichiren's own system of critical evaluation of the Essential Section

At first, at the beginning of his revivalist movement, Nichiren was compelled to proclaim the superiority of the Lotus Sutra amongst all other sutras. Subsequently, he was able to develop and disseminate his supreme doctrine of immediate enlightenment based on his radical novel reading of the Essential Section of the LS. As a result, he has left behind a multifaceted and multilayered assortment of teachings. Consequently, it is necessary that we now reconstruct his teaching in a systematic manner.

With respect to Nichiren's own critical evaluation system, we have already referred to two systems which he elaborated: the *"Fivefold Comparison"* as found in »The Opening of the Eyes« (see above page 210) and the *"Fourfold Rise and Fall"* or the Fourfolde Comparative Criteria as found in the writing »On the Ten Dharma Worlds« (see above page 180). Given the above, when considering Nichiren's intention to proclaim the ultimate superiority of the Buddhism of Sowing, we need to consider only three levels of comparison:
1) the LS considered against all other sutras and schools,
2) the Essential Section considered against the Theoretical Section in the LS itself, and
3) the doctrine of Sowing considered against the doctrine of harvesting.

However, this last criterion which considers the superiority of Sowing against Harvesting still remains on the level of a literal reading, as the essential teaching has been only interpreted from the perspective of a "contemplation on the Essential Section". In other words, as we already noted in reference to »The Object of Devotion for Observing the Mind«, Nichiren re-understood the literal significance of the Ceremony in the Air and its participants from a perspective of a Contemplative Reading in order to elucidate the particular characteristics and form of the Mandala Honzon. Given his original intention, this task was also necessary in order to enable us to realize Instant Enlightenment. Conversely, in order to achieve Buddhahood in this world of suffering in actuality, Nichiren systematically categorized all of the above teachings of the Buddha, thereby critically evaluating each category of teaching. In actuality, as chanting Daimoku before the Mandala is the exclusive practice which Nichiren sought to establish as his ultimate goal, his profound vision and intention provided the parameter within which he constructed his system for the comparative evaluation of the Buddha's teachings.

> The actual practice of chanting Daimoku before the Mandala Honzon represents the actual manifestation of the superiority of Sowing considered against Harvesting, as well as the fundamental basis for Nichiren's critical reasoning.

As considered above, Nichiren's starting point was the theory of the Immediate Enlightenment of Ichinen Sanzen, grounded upon the Tenfold Life Structure. Indeed, it is clear that all his efforts were focused on establishing an appropriate practice with respect to it. So far, his comparative evaluation system has been considered solely as the tool for this doctrinal foundation, as well as a means of theorizing with reference to the Buddhist literature.

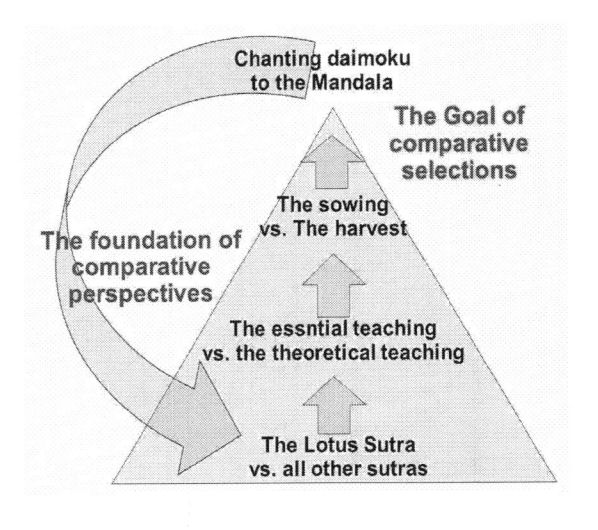

- Chanting daimoku to the Mandala
- The Goal of comparative selections
- The sowing vs. The harvest
- The foundation of comparative perspectives
- The essntial teaching vs. the theoretical teaching
- The Lotus Sutra vs. all other sutras

As noted above, Nichiren himself recalled that when he embarked on philosophical study as a youth his determination and effort had been rewarded as *"the living Bodhisattva Kokūzō presented me with a great jewel as brilliant as the morning star"* so that *"I was able to discern the essential difference between the superior and the inferior teachings among the eight schools as well as discern how all the scriptures should be related throughout the Buddhist canon"* (see above page 169). Thus, we can summarize Nichiren's doctrinal starting point and his final doctrinal standpoint as follows:

- We considered Nichiren's ultimate doctrinal standpoint with reference to a "contemplative reading of the Essential Section for the Latter Day" and this perspective allowed us to posit the "practice of chanting Daimoku for realizing the supreme doctrine of Instant Enlightenment based on the three major principles".
- Following the traditional terminology found with respect to the doctrinal system for comparative evaluation, we consider Nichiren's ultimate doctrinal standpoint to be from "the perspective of a more profound and far

deeper contemplation" (*found in the depths of the text*) when compared to "the perspective of a literal reading" (*merely on the surface of the text*).
- For Nichiren, this ultimate doctrinal standpoint served as a tool or the radical perspective with which to deconstruct the Ceremony in the Air for the Latter Day. To put it another way, it enabled Nichiren to break through from the "enlightened world of the other side" into the "suffering world of this side".
- Thus, by his inscription of the Mandala Honzon, the Ceremony in the Air actually takes place at the very moment of chanting Daimoku before it. Eternal Realization is thereby attained here and now.

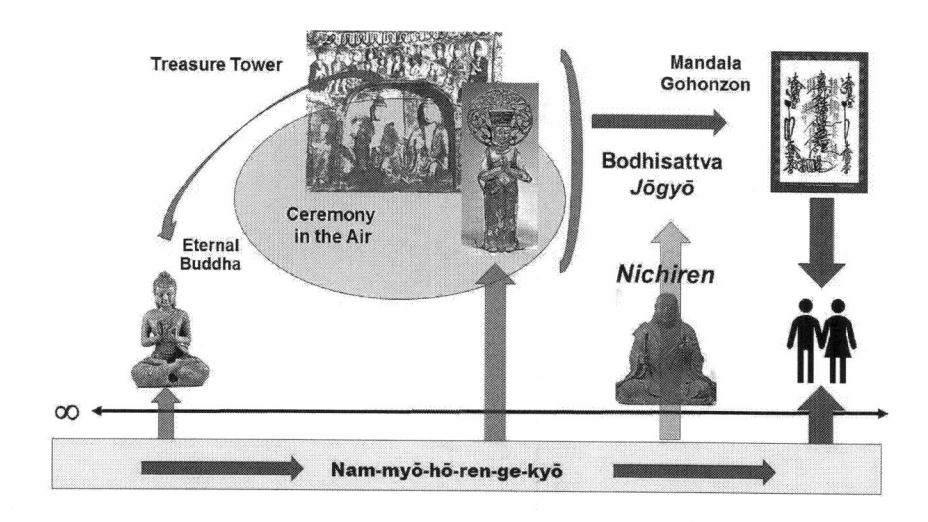

- Further, Nichiren could not be satisfied by simply interpreting the Sutra at a theoretical level. It was absolutely necessary that he himself functions as a mediator or as a bridge enabling the "enlightened world of the other side" to break through into the "suffering world of this side". And in fact, this was Nichiren's fundamental intention: to make manifest and thereby make available the actual to all the Original Enlightenment of Shakyamuni Buddha himself in the form of a Mandala. For this purpose, Nichiren sought to provide both scriptural and experiential evidence that he was indeed the "votary of the Lotus Sutra in the Latter Day" and the actual "rebirth of the Bodhisattva Jōgyō".

2. The Five Guides to Propagation based on a Contemplative Reading of the Essential Section for the Latter Day

Nichiren began with T'ien-t'ai's Fivefold Comparison as a reference point. However, he had to develop his own system of comparative evaluation in order to confront the teachings of the dominant Buddhist schools of his time. One such development is his Five Guides to Preparation, which provides an orientation in which to distinguish not only the doctrinal superiority of his teaching, but also to give an answer to the question of who should be the teaching master of the nation. To once again briefly highlight these principles:

> In Japan [country] replete with evil people and slander [capacity] and in the time of conflict [time], the Mystic Law representing the doctrine of Ichinen Sanzen in Actuality [teaching] should be propagated by the votary of the LS [master].

We focus now on the aspect of the master and the teaching, which can be encapsulated as follows:
- ➤ The "master" should be someone who knows and propagates the Right Dharma and should be established empirically, i.e. by carrying out his mission as the votary of the LS as prophesized in the LS. He is *the teacher of the Mystic Principle of the Original Cause, the national master endowed with the three virtues of sovereign, master and parent.*
- ➤ The "teaching" should be that of the Law for the realization of Buddhahood by all people and this teaching should be selected by using the system of comparative evaluation, i.e. the *"Fivefold Comparison"* and the *"Fourfold Rise and Fall"*
  - The doctrine which Nichiren propagates is not the LS itself, but rather the Mystic Law (Five characters) embodying the Three Major Principles for the realization of enlightenment by all the people in the Latter Day. As a concrete manifestation of the Mystic Law, Nichiren propagates the practice of chanting Daimoku (Seven characters).
  - This teaching has been selected from a perspective of a Contemplative Reading of the Essential Section for the Latter Day which transcends a literal reading of the Sutra. That indicates that Nichiren didn't arrive at this teaching simply with reference to the comparative classification system of T'ien-t'ai and Miao-lo, which was only a step by step approach to demonstrate the doctrinal superiority of the LS.
  - As the doctrine of "the Mystic Law -equals- Chanting Daimoku" is established in the Essential Section, Nichiren proclaimed this as the fundamental reason for concluding that the LS is superior.

- In doctrinal confrontation with other schools, Nichiren insisted on the superiority of the LS in comparison to all other teachings and further proclaimed the LS's essence as "the title of the Lotus Sutra". Yet in actuality, his criticism was derived from his doctrinal understanding of the particular significance of the Daimoku of the Essential Section.
- This means that we need to pay attention to this much deeper significance when Nichiren speaks of the "title of the LS, Myō-hō-ren-ge-kyō". For he employed this term as understood as the "Daimoku of the Essential Section of the LS for the Latter Day, Nam-myō-hō-ren-ge-kyō".
- Consequently, Nichiren consistently employed a dual doctrinal standard: that which represented the conventional doctrinal understanding of the *Tendai Hokke* school and that which represented his own particular doctrinal understanding, as based on his own system of comparative evaluation.

3. Some characteristic features of Nichiren's system of comparative evaluation

Nichiren's own systems of comparative evaluation should be seen as serving as the means of attesting to the Buddhism of Sowing, which is represented by the chanting of the Daimoku of the Mystic Law. Consequently, as already discussed, we should characterize Nichiren's ultimate perspective as derived from his standpoint on a Contemplative Reading of the Essential Section for the Latter Day, and this can be observed by reference to some particular characteristics.

Nichiren begins with a rehearsal of the ways in which the Essential Section is superior to the Theoretical Section.

> Remember this with respect to the Theoretical and Essential Sections of the Lotus Sutra: Which is shallow, and which is profound, which is superior, and which is inferior, which is tolerant, and which is strict, and which is subordinate, and which is primary, for each can only be judged in accordance with the time and the people's capacity. [...]
>
> In the beginning of the Latter Day of the Law, only the Essential Section should spread, but even so, *the Theoretical Section should not be discarded*. Nowhere in the entire Lotus Sutra do we find a passage suggesting that we should discard the first fourteen chapters, which comprise the Theoretical Section. [...]
>
> *In the present period the Essential Section is primary, while the Theoretical Section is subordinate.* But those who discard the latter, saying it is not the way to enlightenment, and believe only in the former, have not yet

> understood the doctrine which reveals Nichiren's true intention. For they have a completely distorted view. (p. 989 / I. 978)

The above is a quotation from Nichiren's writing »On Establishing the Four Bodhisattvas as the Object of Worship (Reply to Toki)« (1279), the authenticity of which is not yet certain as neither autographed original nor authenticated copy made by his disciples is extent. Nevertheless, this letter deals with very significant issues which later became problematic among the Nichiren branches, especially the question of whether a Nichiren Buddhist should recite the Expedient Means chapter or not, and whether the Essential Section should be regarded superior to or equal to the Theoretical Section. Such confusions have originated with Nichiren himself as he had left a body of teachings both multifaceted and ambiguous, as well as a multilayered system of comparative evaluation. The answer which Nichiren gave in this writing is to state that one should neither cast away nor refuse to recite the Theoretical Section just because it is doctrinally subordinate to the Essential Section. Nichiren thereby expressly considers that any failure to understand the subtlety of the distinction he himself makes amounts to a distorted point of view.

To illustrate the significance of a multifaceted way of viewing, I will use again the example of a cylinder (see above page 189). When observed from above it appears as a "circle", yet when observed from the side it appears as a "rectangle". Now, two parties cannot reach an agreement as to what characterizes a cylinder if each of them insists on simply one defining characteristic, such as a circle or a rectangle. However, if it is realized that a cylinder represents the ultimate purpose, and even if a circle might be considered superior to a rectangle from a particular perspective, it is imperative not to cut off the rectangle as a cylinder consists of both of a rectangle and a circle. Thus, if a cylinder is considered with respect to its ultimate form, both a rectangle and a circle are shown to be coherent parts of a cylinder.

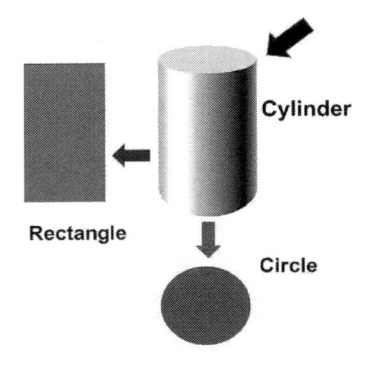

Although Nichiren's subsequent writing »Understanding the Meaning of 'The Object of Devotion for Observing the Mind'« (1275), likewise addressed to *Toki*, is also uncertain as regards its authenticity, it nevertheless provides an answer to the question as to whether Nichiren's disciples should recite the Theoretical Section.

> According to your letter, the lay priest *Kyōshin*, basing himself on a passage in »The Object of Devotion for Observing the Mind« in which I said that the Theoretical Section fails to lead to enlightenment, now wonders if we should not cease to read the Theoretical Section entirely. But this is an erroneous view, one that I myself have never expounded.
> (p. 972 / II. 604)

This example is a revealing insight into the difficulties which even his senior disciples and lay followers had in grasping the essence and arriving at correct understanding of Nichiren's teachings. In this case, Nichiren's lay follower *Soya* misunderstood the passage in »The Object of Devotion for Observing the Mind« which states:

> All the teachings other than the "One Chapter and Two Halves" are Hinayana in nature and erroneous. Not only do they fail to lead to enlightenment, but also they lack the truth. (p. 249 / I. 369)

Nichiren corrected such a misinterpretation as follows.

> To be sure, I have in many places and on many occasions written that the Theoretical Section should be abandoned. But, this does not refer to the part that we at present read [and recite]. By that I just meant to break with the Theoretical Section as taught in past times by the Tendai school of Mount Hiei. Even though this might still [be practiced] as T'ien-t'ai and Dengyō taught, *now that we have entered the Latter Day of the Law, they are as useless as following last year's calendar.*
>
> And this is even more so when we consider that, beginning with Jikaku, the doctrines [expounded on Mount Hiei] have confused the distinction between Mahayana and Hinayana and between provisional and true teachings, and are comparable to a serious slander of the Law. Such doctrines could have no value even in the Middle Day of the Law, much less now in the Latter Day! (ibid.)

Does this mean that the Theoretical Section of the LS has a different significance depending on the time? No, the question doesn't seem to be directly related to the aspect of time. By declaring that the Theoretical Section should be abandoned, Nichiren doesn't mean that this particular part of the LS itself should be discarded, Nichiren is rather making an assertion from a perspective based on the comparative superiority of the Essential Section. Consequently, for Nichiren it is problematic and erroneous to place the Theoretical Section in the foreground while ignoring the Essential Section. And this is consistent with the above quotation taken from the writing »On Establishing the Four Bodhisattvas as the Object of Worship (Reply to Toki)". To sum up:

> In the present period the Essential Section is *primary*, while the Theoretical Section is *subordinate*. (p. 989 / I. 978)

Further, Nichiren considers this problem with more informed historical awareness than the Tendai school at Mt. Hiei. For Tendai had developed a doctrinal position based on the Theoretical Section's doctrine of Initial Enlightenment, thereby regarding all Buddhist teachings as having the same value on theoretical level. Consequently, Tendai *"confused the distinction between Mahayana and Hinayana and between the provisional and true teachings."* This was for Nichiren *"comparable to a serious slander of the Law and had no value even in the Middle Day of the Law, much less now in the Latter Day!"* (ibid.)

But by considering the Theoretical Section solely from the perspective of a Contemplative Reading of the Essential Section for the Latter Day, Nichiren disregards the literal meaning of the Sutra and focuses on the doctrine of Ichinen Sanzen which T'ien-t'ai had established by putting the Theoretical Section in the foreground. However, Nichiren's own doctrine of Ichinen Sanzen deploys both teachings of the LS as indispensable components. We can most easily understand their significance by referring to the »Orally Transmitted Teachings« as one chapter expressly considers this matter: "The issue that all the Twenty-eight chapters of the Lotus Sutra are Nammyō-hō-ren-ge-kyō" (p. 794 / OTT 221). Thus, the second chapter should not read literally, but as *"Nam-myō-hō-ren-ge-kyō Hōbenpon Daini"*. It is the same with the 16th chapter that should be read: *"Nam-myō-hō-ren-ge-kyō Nyoraijuryōhon Daijūroku"*. This is exactly how Nichiren reads the Lotos Sutra in the Latter Day of the Law.

A further problem is addressed in the writing »Understanding the Meaning of "The Object of Devotion for Observing the Mind"«, i.e. the criticism that there is an apparent contradiction when Nichiren cites the pre-Lotus sutras in support of his argument while at the same time he urges that they be discarded:

> You also state that a teacher of Kitakata has criticized me, saying: "Although Nichiren urges us to cast away the sutras preached prior to the Lotus Sutra because they represent a period when the Buddha had 'not yet revealed the truth,' in his »On Establishing the Correct Teaching for the Peace of the Land« he cites the pre-Lotus sutras to support his argument, thus contradicting his own line of reasoning." (p. 972 / II. 605)

Nichiren gave a following answer to clarify this seemingly contradiction:

> I have commented concerning this matter many times in the past. Generally speaking, the sacred teachings of the Buddha's lifetime may be divided into two general categories, those which function as the main chord

> of the net, and those which represent the net's finer meshes. First, the main chord of the net signifies the teaching that leads to the attainment of Buddhahood, that is the Lotus Sutra. Then, the finer meshes refer to the sutras preached prior to the Lotus. These sutras embody teachings that do not lead to the attainment of Buddhahood. [...]
> But the doctrines other than that pertaining to the attainment of Buddhahood that are set forth in the provisional teachings are not mere empty preachings, because they act as the finer meshes of the Lotus Sutra.
> (ibid.)

This answer also highlights a comparative evaluation, which stresses the superiority of the LS when considered against all other teachings. Thus, Nichiren considers the teachings to be placed in a hierarchical order, like a pyramid, with the Lotus Sutra as the supreme teaching at the apex. Or once again using the example of a cylinder, which is formed of a circle and a rectangle but where each of them in itself does not form a complete cylinder. Nevertheless, neither a circle nor a rectangle can be discarded or eliminated from the complete form of a cylinder, as they serve a necessary function in any coherent description of a cylinder.

However, Nichiren also applies the image of a scaffold used as a support when constructing a tower. In fact, Nichiren uses this example in several of his writings. In »Nenbutsu and the Hell of Incessant Suffering« (1255), for instance, he expressly describes Nenbutsu as being like a scaffold to the LS.

> Those who persistently cling to the Nenbutsu after the Lotus Sutra has been preached are thus like persons who, after the tower has been erected, cling to the scaffold and make no use of the tower. How could they fail to be guilty of not honoring the builder's wishes? (p. 98 / II. 25)

Further, in »Reply to the Mother of Ueno« (1280) Nichiren states.

> Suppose that one is building a great pagoda. [...] And when the pagoda is completed, one then removes the scaffolding and discards it, leaving the pagoda in place. Now the scaffolding represents *the various other sutras*, and the great pagoda, the Lotus Sutra. When the Buddha preached *the other sutras,* he was in effect erecting a scaffolding in preparation for the preaching of the Lotus Sutra. In the same manner as the sutra says, "*honestly discarding expedient means,*" all people who would have faith in the Lotus Sutra should first cast aside and fling away the Namu-Amida-butsu invocation based on the Amida and other sutras. (p. 1570 f. / I. 1073 f.)

In WND I: 1074 English terms such as *"the various other sutras"* and *"the other sutras"* are found. But in the Japanese original text, the corresponding phrase says, *"all the Buddha's life teachings"*. Does it make any difference? Yes, it does a lot. Nichiren is writing here from the perspective of "the Lotus

Sutra beyond the Eight Teachings". Yet while the LS can be represented by the pagoda soon to be built, nevertheless Nichiren doesn't simply mean one of the Buddha's life teachings in comparison to the other sutras taught prior to it. For Nichiren always bears in mind *the LS of the Latter Day*.

Although a cursory glance might give the impression that Nichiren had a preference for the LS over all other teachings, that would be mistaken as Nichiren would also consider the LS itself to be an inferior teaching. So, the question is, which level of comparison did it reflect, and in which period did this writing emerge? In »The Teaching for the Latter Day (Reply to Ueno)« (1278), Nichiren radically asserted that the LS should be cast off in the Latter Day.

> Now, in the Latter Day of the Law, both the Lotus Sutra and the other sutras are no use. Only Nam-myō-hō-ren-ge-kyō [has the power to lead to enlightenment. ...] To mix other practices with this Nam-myō-hō-ren-ge-kyō is a grave error. A lantern is useless when the sun rises. How can dew-drops be beneficial when the rain falls? Should one feed a newborn baby anything other than its mother's milk? No additional medicines are needed with a good medicine. (p. 1545 / I. 902)

If we take this statement literally, we may get the impression that the LS has really no significance in current times. However, the context is one of cautionary warning against the unfortunate practice of mixing various practices with chanting *"at the moment of death"* in seeking *"to be reborn in the Pure Land"*, as *"Nam-myō-hō-ren-ge-kyō is the heart of the Lotus Sutra and like the soul of a person"* (ibid.). Nichiren never tolerated any lazy compromise when it came to an issue of life and death. Thus, Nichiren was here addressing an actual urgent need, something well beyond mere doctrinal discourse.

And certainly, in the strictest sense, the primary and only correct practice for all ordinary people to attain Instant Enlightenment in the Latter Day is by chanting Daimoku, which as an actual practice is beyond mere doctrinal study of the LS. However, in fact, Nichiren consistently upheld a fundamental standpoint grounded upon the superiority of the LS with respect to all other sutras, as well as consistently reciting the LS including the Expedient Means chapter. Thus, Nichiren never had any thought of discarding the LS itself. He never could abandon the LS, as the most fundamental level of comparison, i.e. that between Sowing and Harvesting, he had constructed from a very particular interpretation of the LS itself. For Nam-myō-hō-ren-ge-kyō always itself refers both to the LS and to the practice of chanting Daimoku and both are directly related to Shakyamuni's Eternal Realization.

To summarize:
- At the level of comparison between the LS and all other sutras, the pre-Lotus sutras should be discarded as inferior teachings. However, when

considered from the perspective of *"absolute myō"*, which represents the function of "opening up", all the other teachings can also be utilized in support of the ultimate Law which leads to the attainment of Buddhahood.
- On the level of comparison between the Essential Section and the Theoretical Section of the LS, the Theoretical Section should never be discarded even though it is to be considered an inferior teaching. For Nichiren's doctrine of Ichinen Sanzen consists of the Ten factors of Life expounded in the Theoretical Section, although it is likewise grounded upon Shakyamuni's Eternal Realization, which is represented by the principle of the Mutual Containment of the Ten Worlds as expounded in the depths of the Essential Section.
- On the level of comparison between Sowing and Harvesting, the "Mystic Law -equals - Chanting Daimoku" and therefore is the essential or paramount practice, while the recitation of the LS itself within a liturgical framework should be considered only an auxiliary practice.

4. The seed which brings forth all Buddhas is the Mystic Law

As illustrated above, Nichiren elaborated a system of comparative evaluation which is multifaceted and multilayered. The meaning of any particular doctrinal statement, even if at first sight only implicitly, nevertheless can be most fully understood from the perspective of his ultimate doctrinal standpoint. As an example of this, we will now consider the significance of the three comparative levels from the perspective of "a Contemplative Reading of the Essential Section for the Latter Day".

With respect to this, on all the comparative levels of his discourse, Nichiren consistently represents the chanting of the Mystic Law as the "seed which brings forth all the Buddhas" and, consequently, the true and original cause by which all people attain to Buddhahood.

> All Buddhas are emanations of the one Buddha, Shakyamuni. Therefore, [...] *they are all brought together within the two characters of myōhō.*
> For this reason, the benefits to be gained by reciting the five characters of Myō-hō-ren-ge-kyō are great indeed. All the Buddhas, all the daimoku of the various sutras, are opened up and merged in the Lotus Sutra. Taking notice of *this opening up function of the Mystic Law*, one should recite the Daimoku of the Lotus Sutra.
> (»On Reciting the Daimoku of the Lotus Sutra«, p. 13 / II. 228)

> Amida, Shakyamuni, and all the other Buddhas, when they were creating the cause for the attainment of enlightenment, invariably fixed their minds on the practice of concentration and insight, and *with their mouths they invariably recited Nam-myō-hō-ren-ge-kyō.*
> («On the Ten Chapters of 'Great Concentration and Insight'«, p. 1274 / II. 378)

> The Buddha revealed that he had attained enlightenment countless kalpas in the past [...]. The doctrine of ichinen Sanzen [can be explained by the principle of the Mutual Containment of the Ten Worlds in this way so that] the Nine Worlds which are each endowed with the potential of Buddhahood and Buddhahood is endowed with the Nine Worlds.
> Thus, a single word of this *"kyō* (Sutra)" is as precious as a wish-granting jewel, and a single phrase [of myō-hō-ren-ge-kyō] is *the seed of all Buddhas.*
> («The Selection of the Time«, p. 256 / I. 538)

> All Buddhas of the three existences, too, attain Buddhahood by virtue of the five characters of Myō-hō-ren-ge-kyō. They represent *the Mystic Law which is the reason why the Buddhas of the three existences appear in the world and, at the same time, enables all living beings to attain the Buddha way.* You should take notice of these matters thoroughly and, on the path of attaining Buddhahood, chant Nam-myō-hō-ren-ge-kyō without arrogance or attachment to biased views. («How Those Initially Aspiring to the Way Can Attain Buddhahood through the Lotus Sutra«, p. 557 / I. 887 f.)

In all these writings Nichiren speaks of the "title of the Lotus Sutra" or "the Mystic Law" (*Myōhō*), yet he more specifically means "chanting Daimoku - equals - Nam-myō-hō-ren-ge-kyō". Consequently, such phrases should be read and understood only by reference to a "contemplative reading of the Essential Section for the Latter Day". This is even the case with Miura, who, albeit reluctantly, has to *"admit that the significance of the Daimoku transcends both the Essential and the Theoretical Section"* (21: 62).

5. The Fourfold interpretation level of the Buddhism of Sowing

By way of a beginning to a consideration of the theoretical foundation for Daimoku and Honzon, I would like to highlight four "perspectives of discourse" or "levels of interpretation". Further, "the ultimate standpoint from a contemplative reading of the Essential Section for the Latter Day" is consistently applied to each level of interpretation. Practically, this standpoint can be formulated as "Daimoku -equals- Chanting the Daimoku of the Essential Section for the Latter Day". Thus, when I speak of Nichiren's own system of comparative evaluation, I will always add the conditional phrase "for the Latter Day" in order to distinguish Nichiren's own system from that of T'ient'ai.

A. the Perspective of the superiority of the LS for the Latter Day

This perspective is with respect to the superiority the Lotus Sutra being in comparison to all other sutras and teachings. More profoundly, this perspective is grounded upon the superiority of the Daimoku or the chanting of the Daimoku of the Essential Section for the Latter Day. Thus, this necessitates a radical affirmation of Daimoku as an exclusive practice, including harsh criticism of all other schools, in radical contrast to the inclusive and tolerant attitude of the Japanese Tendai school.

B. the Perspective of the superiority of the Essential Section for the Latter Day

This perspective is with respect to a view on „the Essential Section of the Buddha's lifetime", which can be characterized as superior to the Theoretical Section and all other teachings. On this level of interpretation, Nichiren takes part of the content of the Sutra literally, yet he also considers it to have a more profound meaning, for it already contains an interpretation when viewed from a perspective of the Daimoku of the Essential Section for the Latter Day.

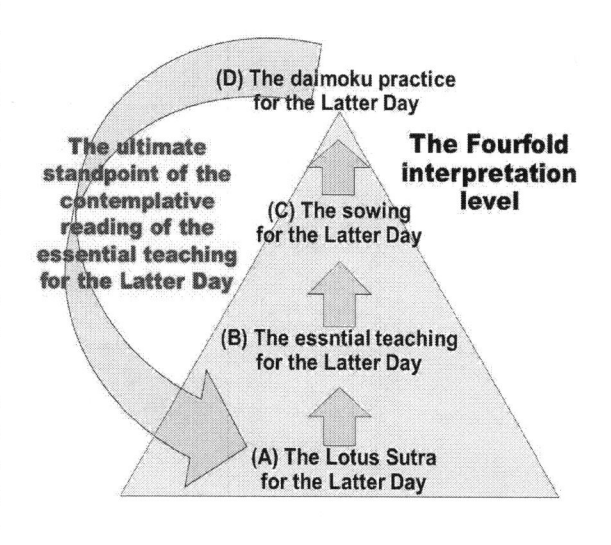

The ultimate standpoint of the contemplative reading of the essential teaching for the Latter Day

(D) The daimoku practice for the Latter Day

(C) The sowing for the Latter Day

(B) The essntial teaching for the Latter Day

(A) The Lotus Sutra for the Latter Day

The Fourfold interpretation level

We can observe this type of transformative reading most typically in »The Object of Devotion for Observing the Mind« which had been written to explain the inscription of the Mandala Honzon. Although the subject is related to "*the doctrine of Contemplation*" (»The accompanying letter to the thesis on "The Object of Devotion for Observing the Mind«, p. 255 / -), the interpretation given is from the perspective (B), which is also illuminated by " the perspective of a contemplative reading of the Essential Section for the Latter Day" (D). Consequently, each perspective is conjoined. To give an example, the Shakyamuni Buddha who attained enlightenment in the remotest past represents a Buddha of Initial Enlightenment as the Sutra describes, yet on the level of interpretation "from the depths of the sentence" Nichiren reads it as "Original Enlightenment without beginning and end".

As already considered, the "doctrine of original cause **and** original effect" as defined by Nichiren in »The Opening of the Eyes« should rather be understood as the "doctrine of original cause **-equals-** original effect" (see above page 217). For Nichiren reads the story of Shakyamuni's Eternal Realization from the particular perspective of that which is appropriate for the Latter Day, given the significance of the doctrine of Instant Enlightenment in accord with such dialectical principles as "original cause -equals- original effect", "Initial Enlightenment -equals- original enlightenment" and "the Nine Worlds -equals- Buddhahood". And it is only by means of such reinterpretation, that Nichiren can speak of *"the true doctrine of Ichinen Sanzen based on the true principle of the Mutual Containment of the Ten Worlds"*.

For example, the quotation below highlights Nichiren's particular mode of reinterpretation whereby the eternal Buddha Shakyamuni is to be understood universally as that eternal Buddhahood which is found within each one of us.

> The Shakyamuni Buddha within our lives is *the primordial Buddha endowed with the three bodies since time without beginning*, revealed more than numberless major world system dust particle kalpas ago.
> (»The Object of Devotion for Observing the Mind«, p. 247 / I. 365)

This, as I have already pointed out, is an example of "the work of universalization for the Latter Day", e.g. to interpret the eternal Buddha Shakyamuni as "the primordial Buddha since time without beginning" or "the everlasting Buddha nature", or to interpret Shakyamuni's Eternal Realization in terms of the the supreme doctrine of "Instant Enlightenment" which consists of the Three Major Principles for realizing enlightenment, i.e. "Immediate Enightenment", "Ichinen Sanzen", and the "Mutual Containment of the Ten Worlds".

C. the Perspective of the Buddhism of Sowing for the Latter Day

In the Essential Section, as well as revealing Shakyamuni's true identity as the Eternal Buddha, there is a revelation of another crucial matter, i.e. "The Entrustment of the Law to the Bodhisattva Jōgyō". This matter goes well beyond any exegesis of the Sutra itself and specifically relates to Nichiren's own true identity revealed through his actions in the Latter Day of the Law. More particularly, Nichiren undertook the propagation of the practice of chanting

Daimoku, which provoked influential persons within the political and Buddhist establishment to subject Nichiren to harsh persecutions, which he managed to endure and overcome before finally inscribing the Ten Worlds Mandala Honzon while in exile on Sado. And by this time, Nichiren had begun to identify himself as the reincarnation of the Bodhisattva Jōgyō, who had inherited the Mystic Law as the Buddhism of Sowing and had inscribed and manifested it in the form of the Object of Devotion for Observing One's Mind. All Nichiren's efforts and suffering had been for the sole purpose of inaugurating the Buddhism of Sowing, by which all of us would be led to realize the supreme principle of Instant Enlightenment in Actuality in the Latter Day.

Although each perspective is derived from the Essential Section, I would like to make a distinction between "(C) The Perspective of the Buddhism of Sowing for the Latter Day" which relates to Nichiren's own self-identification and "bodily reading" from "(B) The Perspective of the superiority of the Essential Section for the Latter Day" which relates to the Eternal Realization of Shakyamuni Buddha.

D. the Significance of Daimoku practice for the Latter Day

To introduce Nichiren's fourfold level of discourse, I would summarize as follows:

(B) The Mandala Honzon is a depiction of the Ceremony in the Air, as such it is a representation of "the enlightened world".
(C) Nichiren established a particular form of practice, i.e. chanting Daimoku before the Ten Worlds Mandala Honzon.
(D) When we carry out this practice, we manifest Eternal Buddhahood in while remaining an ordinary person who is endowed with the Ten Worlds which are mutually contained within each other.
At the same time, "the enlightened world" of the Essential Section of the LS manifests in this actual "world of suffering".

Every effort made by Nichiren was in order that we might realize Buddhahood and lead happy and fulfilled lives. Consequently, on the level of discourse (D), the concept of the "ordinary person -equals- Buddha" is in the foreground and particularly emphasized. The three levels of (B), (C), and (D) can also be expressed doctrinally as:

(B) From the perspective of "the contemplative reading of the Essential Section for the Latter Day", Nichiren reinterprets Shakyamuni's Eternal Realization revealed in the Ceremony in the Air as the prototype for a universal doctrine of immediate enlightenment.

(C) The Mystic Law which Shakyamuni practiced in the remotest past represents the Three Major Principles of "the Mutual Containment of the Ten Worlds", "Ichinen Sanzen", and "Immediate Enlightenment".
Nichiren was entrusted with propagating this Mystic Law and established it in the form of the practice of chanting Daimoku.
Nichiren inscribed the supreme doctrine of Instant Enlightenment based on the Three Major principles in the form of the Ten Worlds Mandala Honzon.

(D) Chanting Daimoku before this Gohonzon, this supreme doctrine of Instant Enlightenment will be realized in the actual body of an ordinary person.

6 The four-layered dimensional structure of the Gohonzon

We have seen that the Three Major Principles for the Instant Enlightenment of ordinary people is consistent in all four levels of interpretation:

$$(A)=(B)=(C)=(D).$$

Thus, with respect to the form of the Gohonzon, the significance of the Daimoku is emphasized by its being inscribed at the center.

Further, there are four-layers or dimensions to the Gohonzon which correspond to the four levels of interpretation.

(A): *The basic layer*

The Daimoku in the center of the Mandala Gohonzon signifies that the chanting the Daimoku is to practice and realize the Mystic Law. This should be considered to be the practice of the Mystic Law *"for all people in order that they realize the Buddha way"*, as well as the practice which "brings forth all Buddhas of the three existences". Thus,

- **the Daimoku at the center** manifests the universal truth that everyone who chants Daimoku will realize the supreme principle of the Instant Enlightenment of Ichinen Sanzen based on the Mutual Containment of the Ten Worlds.
- Consequently, the Daimoku always signifies the enlightened state of life in terms of **the Unity of the Person and the Law**.
- In fact, the whole mandala manifests the enlightened world of Ichinen Sanzen.

Grounded upon this universal basic layer, the following three layers should be understood always by reference to **"the Person"** who manifests Instant Enlightenment by chanting Daimoku.

(B): *The primordial layer*

The Eternal Buddha Shakyamuni practiced and realized the supreme doctrine of Instant Enlightenment based on the three major principles of the Mutual Containment of the Ten Worlds, Ichinen Sanzen and immediate enlightenment.

(C): *The Intermediate layer*

Nichiren, the teaching master of the Latter Day practiced the chanting of Daimoku, the Mystic Law which he was entrusted with. By so doing, he manifested Instant Enlightenment in the form of "an ordinary person as Buddha". This functions as a mode of mediation whereby we are enabled to break through into the enlightened world of the primordial Buddha which is without beginning.

(D): *The surface layer*

We, the ordinary people of the Latter Day in this "world of suffering", chant the Mystic Law of Sowing before the "enlightened world of the other side" depicted in the Gohonzon.
- We all realize the supreme doctrine based on the Three Major Principles.
- Buddhahood will manifest both in body and mind as well in our surrounding environment. Consequently,
- we can observe the depiction of our own Immediate Enlightenment in the Gohonzon itself.

The Gohonzon functions as a mirror
reflecting our own Immediate Enlightenment.

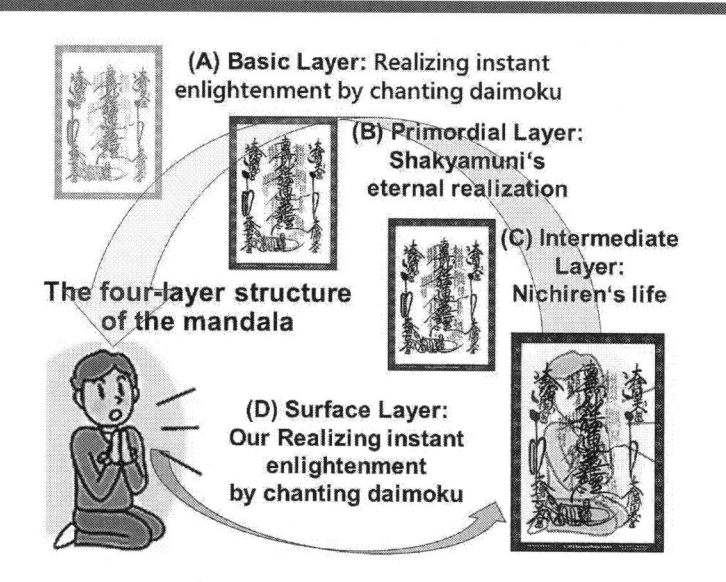

The four-layer structure of the mandala

(A) Basic Layer: Realizing instant enlightenment by chanting daimoku

(B) Primordial Layer: Shakyamuni's eternal realization

(C) Intermediate Layer: Nichiren's life

(D) Surface Layer: Our Realizing instant enlightenment by chanting daimoku

The "fourfold level of interpretation for the Buddhism of Sowing" and the "four-layered dimensional structure of the Gohonzon" should not be understood as a doctrinal method for establishing the superiority of a certain doctrinal standpoint but rather as the means by which the characteristics and significance of a particular teaching is elucidated. In fact, they provide a useful framework with which to understand Nichiren's thought in its multifaceted and multilayered form. Further, I will deploy this framework of understanding in support of my own innovative theory, with the intention of thereby demonstrating its consonance with Nichiren's own doctrinal understanding.

In the previous chapters I have discussed that Nichiren began with the doctrine of "immediate enlightenment" and the concept of the "ordinary person as Buddha" which is based on the principle of the Mutual Containment of the Ten Worlds". Now, I would like to consider the matter of the "Three Great Secret Laws" which represent the ultimate intention of Nichiren's teachings. In this way, we shall I surely gain a more complete understanding of Nichiren's ultimate intention.

Chapter 5
The Honzon of the Essential Section

1. The Three Great Secret Laws of the Essential Teaching

Two references to the concept while on Minobu

Concerning Nichiren's particular intention in inscribing the Honzon, the object of devotion or worship, there are a variety of opinions. Even if we disregard forms of the Honzon other than Nichiren's Ten Worlds Mandala, there are still three different aspects in terms of which its significance can be understood, i.e. in terms of the "Person (Buddha)", the "Law (Dharma)" or the "Unity of Person (Buddha) and Law (Dharma)".

Interestingly, Nichiren specifically refers to the Three Great Secret Laws only after having retired to Mt. Minobu and, curiously, in the two writings which are quoted below, where Nichiren expressly describes the Honzon as being "the teaching lord Shakyamuni".

First, to quote from »On Repaying Debts of Gratitude« (1276).

> Question: What form does [the correct teaching that was not propagated even by T'ien-t'ai and Dengyō] take?
>
> Answer: First, Japan and the other countries throughout the entire world should all *make the Shakyamuni Buddha of the Essential Section their object of devotion*. In that case, the Shakyamuni and Tahō who sit together in the Treasure Tower, all the other Buddhas, and the Four Bodhisattvas headed by Jōgyō, will act as assistants to this Buddha. Second, there is the sanctuary of the Essential Section. Third, in Japan, China, India, and all the other countries of the entire world, every person, regardless of whether wise or ignorant, will set aside other practices and chant Nam-myō-hō-ren-ge-kyō.   (p. 328 / l. 735)

Similar reasoning is to be found in »On Receiving the Three Great Secret Laws« (1282), although in a much more particular form. The Three Great Secret Laws are given as "the object of devotion" (*Honzon*), the sanctuary (*Kaidan*), and the five characters of the *Daimoku* as revealed in the depths of the Life Span Chapter, i.e. that which *the Buddha practiced at the moment of attaining enlightenment*" (p. 1021 / II. 984). Further, the Three Great Secret Laws are also defined as the very Dharma which Shakyamuni Buddha transmitted to the Bodhisattva Jōgyō, encapsulated in the Four Phrases found in the Supernatural Powers chapter[27].

Nichiren defines the Honzon as:

> The object of devotion as set forth in the Life Span Chapter is *Shakyamuni Buddha, the lord of teachings, endowed with the original and natural three bodies*, who since the beginning [of the remotest past] has had deep and abiding affinities with this land of ours. (p. 1022 / II. 986)

With respect to the Daimoku, Nichiren states.

> The Daimoku that I, Nichiren, chant today in the Latter Day is different from that of earlier ages. This Nam-myō-hō-ren-ge-kyō encompasses both practice for oneself and for others. Its five characters have the "Fivefold Significance of Name, Body, Doctrine, Function and Teaching." (ibid.)

With respect to the high sanctuary, Nichiren intends that this should be built with the sanction of the state as the Altar for Mahayana Precepts ordination had been established by Dengyō at Enryakuji on Mt. Hiei. However, such a construction would necessarily presuppose that Kōsenrufu has been realized by way of a union between the Buddha Dharma and state power.

> The most fitting site will be sought out, one resembling the pure land of Eagle Peak, and the sanctuary will be established there. We have only to wait for the proper time for this. This is what is meant by *the precept of Law in actuality*. This will be a sanctuary not only where the people of the three countries of India, China, and Japan, and all the inhabitants of Jambudvīpa, will come to receive the precept of the Law that enables them to repent and wipe out offenses, but also where the great heavenly kings Brahmā and Shakra will descend to take part in the ceremony. (ibid.)

Nichiren states in these two writings that the "lord of teachings Shakyamuni" is to be understood as the *"lord of teachings Shakyamuni endowed with the original and natural three bodies"*. Such a representation can be regarded as synonymous with the concept of *"the primordial Buddha endowed with the three bodies since time without beginning"* (»The Object of Devotion for Observing the Mind«). Thus, it is clear that Nichiren doesn't simply interpret the phrase by way of a Literal Reading, but rather interprets it on the level of "(B) by way of a Contemplative Reading of the Essential Section for the Latter Day". This means that even if Nichiren states that *"we should make the Shakyamuni Buddha of the Essential Section our object of devotion"*, it cannot be understood literally. We will return to this issue in the next section.

---

[27] Concerning the transmitted Four Phrases under the aspects of the "Fivefold Significance of the Daimoku" see above page 94.

A definition of the One Great Secret Law

In the »On the Five Guides to Propagation (A letter to lay priest Soya)« (1275) Nichiren speaks of the "One Great Secret Law".

> In order to provide a remedy for those who are guilty of the two offenses of committing the five cardinal sins and slandering the Law, [the Buddha] devised and left behind his *One Great Secret Law*. (p. 1032 / II. 547)

After which, the Buddha entrusted the heritage of the Law to the four Bodhisattvas of the Earth.

> And what is this Law that he entrusted to them? It is that which discards *the breadth of the Lotus Sutra* and seizes upon *its outline*, discards its outline and seizes upon *its essential point*, namely, the five characters of Myō-hō-ren-ge-kyō, which represent *the fivefold significance of name, body, doctrine, function, and teaching*. (p. 1032 / II. 549)

Thus, the One Great Secret Law is the "five characters of the Daimoku entrusted to the Bodhisattva Jōgyō" which corresponds to the "Fivefold Significance", an interpretation also found in »On Receiving the Three Great Secret Laws". For the Daimoku is nothing other than the Dharma body which functions as the seed of enlightenment in the Latter Day.

> Now that we have already entered the Latter Day of the Law. The persons who formed a relationship with the Buddha during the time he was in the world have little by little diminished in number, and all those who have the capacity to attain Buddhahood through the two categories of provisional and true sutras have disappeared. Now is the time for Bodhisattva *Fukyō* to appear in the world in this latter age and to sound his poison drum. [...]
> The five characters of the Daimoku should be used to implant *the seed of Buddhahood*. (p. 1027 / II. 543 f.)

Consequently, this "(D) Buddhism of Sowing based on the Essential Section for the Latter Day" represents the core teaching of Nichiren's lifetime and in this way "(A) the Lotus Sutra for the Latter Day" is revealed. The above can be summarized in the following schema, which is based on references to the concept in Nichiren's later writings completed on Mt. Minobu.

One Great Secret Law		"The five characters of the Daimoku" = "The seven characters of chanting Daimoku" which represents the supreme doctrine of Instant Enlightenment of Ichinen Sanzen or the Three Major Principles

Three Great Secret Laws	*Honmon no Honzon*	The Eternal Buddha Shakyamuni
	Honmon no Daimoku	Chanting the Mystic Law of Nam-myō-hō-ren-ge-kyō
	Honmon no Kaidan	The High Sanctuality to be constructed at the moment of attaining Kōsenrufu

2. The multilayered structure of the Three Great Secret Laws

However, it is necessary to be attentive to the fact that Nichiren's understanding of the Three Great Secret Laws, which he arrived at in his last years on Mt. Minobu, represent his particular proclamation, based on a Literal Reading of the Essential Section over and against all other teachings. For Nichiren's understanding was rooted in his constant awareness of his own unique significance in the Latter Day, an awareness which contrasted dramatically with that of the other Great Masters of earlier periods. By way of example:

- In »On the Five Guides to Propagation (A letter to lay priest Soya)« (1275), Nichiren speaks of the *"Honmon no Kaidan"*, as noted above, yet in the context of considering the Kaidan, *the ordination platform,* of the Tendai school on Mt. Hiei.

> The Great Teacher Dengyō accomplished something that neither Nanyüeh nor T'ien-t'ai had done by setting up *an ordination platform for the precepts of perfect and immediate enlightenment* on Mt. Hiei. Thus, throughout the entire land of Japan, every Buddhist priest without exception became a disciple of the Great Teacher Dengyō. (p. 1030 / II. 549)

- Likewise, in the same Gosho, Nichiren speaks of the "Secret Law" which he alone would propagate, although it was known to the other great master of the previous two periods.

> The essential *secret Law*, which Mahākāshyapa, Ānanda, Nāgārjuna, Vasubandhu, T'ien-t'ai, Dengyō, and the other great sages knew about but did not proclaim or propagate, is plainly embodied in the text of the Lotus Sutra. It is also very clear that it is not found in the treatises and commentaries. (p. 1037 / II. 555)

- In »On Receiving the Three Great Secret Laws« Nichiren makes a radical distinction between "Nichiren's Daimoku" and the "Daimoku that other masters have practiced".

CHAPTER 5

> As to the Daimoku there are two meanings dependent on the previous two periods and the Latter Day of the Law. In the first period both the Bodhisattvas Vasubandhu and Nāgārjuna were satisfied with chanting the Daimoku only as a practice for oneself. During the second period Nan-yüeh, T'ien-t'ai and others chanted Nam-myō-hō-ren-ge-kyō as a practice for themselves, but they didn't preach it for others. This daimoku was a theoretical practice.
>
> Now what I, Nichiren, today chant in the Latter Day of the Law is different from that chanted by previous generations, for it is *Nam-myō-hō-ren-ge-kyō as both a practice for oneself and for others*. It is the five characters corresponding to the "Fivefold Significance of Name, Body, Doctrine, Function and Teaching". (p. 1022 / II. 986)

Incidentally, it might appear surprising that all the other great masters had known about the Daimoku of Nam-myō-hō-ren-ge-kyō in the 1,000 years prior to Nichiren. Yet this particular way of understanding the tradition of the Daimoku is part of Nichiren's rhetoric in order to position his own particular teaching within Buddhist history. The same rhetoric is evident when Nichiren states: "*even Amida could attain enlightenment by reciting Nam-myō-hō-ren-ge-kyō*" (see above page 196). From the perspective of the supreme doctrine of Instant Enlightenment Nichiren opens up and integrates all Buddhist teachings into his system. This should be considered to be an "inclusive approach".

- In »The Votary of the Lotus Sutra Will Meet with Persecution« (1274), Nichiren makes reference to other great masters when speaking of the Great Secret Laws.

> Nāgārjuna and Vasubandhu were both scholars who produced a thousand works. However, they expounded only the provisional Mahayana teachings. Though they understood the meaning of the Lotus Sutra in their hearts, they did not declare it in words. An oral transmission exists concerning this. T'ien-t'ai and Dengyō went so far as to expound it, but they left unrevealed *the object of devotion of the Essential Section, the four bodhisattvas, the sanctuary*, and *the five characters of Nam-myō-hō-ren-ge-kyō*[28]. (p. 965 / I. 449)

- In »Letter to Gijōbō« (1273) Nichiren provides a more profound explanation as to the philosophical foundation of the Three Great Secret Laws.

> As to the essence of this Sutra, it is really important to take notice of the teachings of the Mutual Containment of the Ten Worlds, of the hundred

---

[28] Reading the last sentence, some might be left with the impression that Nichiren speaks of the "Four" Great Secret Laws including the "Four Bodhissatvas". However, this is not the case. Later we will discuss their significance.

> worlds and thousand factors, and of the three thousand realms in a single moment of life (Ichinen Sanzen). These teachings are described in the work entitled »Great Concentration and Insight".
> Next, the teaching of the Life Span Chapter is what I, Nichiren, personally depend on. Although T'ien-t'ai and Dengyō also understood it in a general way, they never put it into words or proclaimed it. The same is true of Nāgārjuna and Vasubandhu. The verse section of the Life Span chapter states, "[...] *single-mindedly desiring to see the Buddha, not hesitating even at the cost of their lives"*. Because of this passage, I have revealed the Buddhahood in my own life. The reason is that it is this sutra passage that has enabled me to accomplish *the Three Great Secret Laws based on the Ichinen Sanzen of Action as found in the Life Span Chapter*. But keep this secret, keep it secret. [...]
> *"Single-mindedly desiring to see the Buddha"* may be read as follows: single-mindedly observing the Buddha, concentrating one's mind on seeing the Buddha, and when looking at one's own mind, perceiving that it is the Buddha.
> Having attained the fruit of *Buddhahood endowed with the eternally inherent Three Bodies*, I may surpass even T'ien-t'ai and Dengyō, and excel even Nāgārjuna and Mahākāshyapa. (p. 892 / 389 f.)

In this passage Nichiren also compares himself to the other great masters of the previous two periods. Now, he explains that his *"Honmon"* is not just the Essential Section of the LS, but it is intrinsically related to the Life Span Chapter. Thus:

> The "Three Great Secret Laws of the Essential Section" mean those which are "based on the Ichinen Sanzen of Action as found in the Life Span Chapter.

Nichiren took over the doctrine of Ichinen Sanzen which had been expounded by T'ien-t'ai in his »Great Concentration and Insight« and transformed it by way of a Contemplative Reading of Shakyamuni's Eternal Realization as revealed in the Life Span chapter (B).

The revelation of Shakyamuni's Eternal Realization in the Life Span Chapter is expressly noted in the quotations taken from »On Receiving the Three Great Secret Laws". For example:

> The Object of Devotion that will be constructed is based on the teaching of the Life Span Chapter as the lord of the teachings, Shakyamuni endowed with the original and natural three bodies, who has a profound and deep relationship to this world. (p. 1022 / II. 986)

CHAPTER 5

> *The Honzon, the Kaidan and the Five characters of Daimoku of the Essential Section* which the Buddha practiced *at the very moment of attaining enlightenment* [in the remotest past] (p. 1021 / II. 984)

Strictly speaking, however, there is no mention at all of the Three Great Secret Laws in the Life Span chapter itself.

Only Nichiren himself interpreted Shakyamuni's Eternal Realization in terms of the One Great Secret Law which he then elaborated into the three aspects which are in accord with the Three Disciplines of Precept, Meditation and Wisdom.

In fact, he particularly emphasizes this idea once again in the same Gosho.

> This passage in the Life Span Chapter [...] refers to *the Ichinen Sanzen that the [Buddha] realized when he attained enlightenment in the far distant past.* (p. 1023 / II. 987)

This means, according to Nichiren's understanding:

The One Great Secret Law, the foundation of the Three Great Secret Laws, is the Mystic Law, which Shakyamuni realized "at the moment of his eternal realization," which in itself represents the supreme principle of Instant Enlightenment of Ichinen Sanzen based on the Mutual Containment of the Ten Worlds. It is the "Tathāgata Nam-myō-hō-ren-ge-kyō".

(A) The One Great Secret Law
= the supreme principle of *the Instant Enlightenment of Ichinen Sanzen*

⬇

The Three Great Secret Laws
corresponding to **the Three Disciplines of Precept, Meditation, and Wisdom**

↙ ↓ ↘

Kaidan   *Honzon*   *Daimoku*

(B) **Shakyamuni's** Eternal Realization

(C) **Nichiren's** realization of Instant Enlightenment

(D) **We** chant Daimoku to the Gohonzon in the Latter Day

Identifying the transmission of Shakyamuni's Eternal Realization as the function of the practice of chanting Daimoku before the Gohonzon, Nichiren can speak of the *"Buddha endowed with the original and natural three bodies"*. As this should be understood as the universal Buddhahood inherent within our own lives, Nichiren speaks thus: *"I have revealed Buddhahood in my own life"* or *"that Buddhahood endowed with the eternally inherent three bodies"*, by *"single-mindedly observing my own mind"*. Such expressions refer to Nichiren's personal experience of "Observing the Mind" from a perspective of a Contemplative Reading of the Essential Section for the Latter Day.

Consequently, when we undertake the same practice of mantra meditation by taking Nichiren as our particular exemplar, we can thereby realize Instant Enlightenment in our current time.

Once again, I will summarize the important points from the perspective of "the fourfold interpretative level of the Buddhism of Sowing".

(A) In the case of the Three Great Secret Laws, Nichiren elaborates his theory with reference to the viewpoint of the Essential Section, so he doesn't need to proclaim the superiority of the Lotus Sutra as a whole. However, he still employs a system of comparative evaluation to emphasis both the overall superiority of the LS and the superiority of the Essential Section particularly.

(B) On the face of it, his theory is with respect to the Three Great Secret Laws based on the "Essential Teaching". Yet the theoretical foundation for each of them is to be found in *"the doctrine of the Ichinen Sanzen of Action as expounded in the Life Span chapter"* which *"Shakyamuni practiced at the very moment of attaining enlightenment in the remotest past"*. He *"attained the fruit of Buddhahood endowed with the eternally inherent three bodies"*, which Nichiren also attained. Then, given this particular fact of attainment by Shakyamuni Buddha understood from the perspective of a contemplative reading of the Essential Section, Nichiren reformulates as the supreme principle of the Instant Enlightenment of Ichinen Sanzen. Based on this universal principle of the Mystic Law he thereby envisions the enlightened Dharma world of the primordial Buddha without beginning. This is the foundation upon which the subsequent stages of his theory are built.

(C) Nichiren inherited the Mystic Law in his role as a reincarnation of the Bodhisattva Jōgyō and manifested it in a concrete form by his inscription of a Mandala. By way of such inscription, Nichiren enabled the "enlightened world" as depicted in the form of the Ceremony in the Air to break through into our actual "world of suffering" in the Latter Day.

(D) Consequently, chanting the *Honmon no Daimoku* before the *Honmon no Honzon* enables us to activate the eternal Buddhahood within our own lives. This is the practice of "Observing one's Mind" for the Latter Day, which is nothing other than the practice of Instant Enlightenment. And at this very moment the place of practice manifests its significance as the *Honmon no Kaidan*. The "enlightened world of the other side" thereby is manifested concretely in "the suffering world of this side".

> Eternity breaks through here and now.

For this is implicit in the paramount significance given by Nichiren to the doctrine of Ichinen Sanzen in Actuality.

3. The Multifaceted Significance of *Honmon no Honzon*

We have considered the multiple levels of meaning of the Three Great Secret Laws, yet it should be borne in mind that at each interpretive level, meaning is transformed. However, this does not apply to the Daimoku, as its meaning and significance always remains the same, i.e. as the "five characters of the Mystic Law = seven characters of chanting it", irrespective of the level of interpretation. With respect to the Object of Devotion based on the Essential Section, its meaning can be summarized according to each level of interpretation as follows.

(B) Although speaking of "Shakyamuni, the lord of teachings of the Essential Section", "the Essential Section" actually means the "Life Span chapter" and "Shakyamuni, the lord of teachings" should be reinterpreted as "Shakyamuni, *the lord of teachings endowed with the original and natural three bodies, who upholds has profound relationship with this world*".

> "Shakyamuni Buddha" no longer refers to a particular historical person but rather to a universal concept denoting an enlightened state of life, which manifests as the principle of Ichinen Sanzen.

This can be represented in a concrete and economical form as the Mandala endowed with the Ten Worlds.

(C) Nichiren metaphorically understood himself to be none other than the rebirth of the Bodhisattva Jōgyō entrusted with the mission to propagate the Mystic Law. More profoundly, Nichiren manifested that original Buddhahood universally inherent in each and every life by practicing the Mystic Law. The profound truth of Nichiren's "Instant Enlightenment as an ordinary person" is concretely manifested in the form of the Ten Worlds Mandala which he inscribed.

(D) To enable all people to actually attain Buddhahood in the "world of suffering" in the Latter Day, the practice of the Mystic Law is paramount. By practicing the Mystic Law, we can manifest the supreme principle of the

Instant Enlightenment of Ichinen Sanzen. This enlightened state of life should be considered to be the Unity of the Person and the Law. Consequently, those who chant Daimoku before the Gohonzon can observe the actuality of their own Instant Enlightenment reflected in the Gohonzon.

In the concluding remarks to Chapter One of Part Three, I noted that Nichiren considered his own ultimate teaching to be that of "the Instant Enlightenment of all ordinary people" (D) primarily in the early years before Sado, while he had still to develop his own unique doctrinal standpoint, but also subsequently in his later years after his exile on Sado, at which time he gave it concrete expression in the form of the Mandala Honzon. With respect to the Gohonzon this ultimate doctrine represents the doctrinal standpoint of "the Superiority of the Law to the Person". And interestingly, this very standpoint can be undoubtedly found in two of Nichiren's writings quoted from below.

»On Reciting the Daimoku of the Lotus Sutra« (1260)

This Gosho was written two months before completing »On Establishing the Correct Teaching for the Peace of the Land". Nichiren's discourse focuses on the theoretical foundation for both the Daimoku and the Honzon.

> Question: For persons who place their faith in the Lotus Sutra, what is the proper object of devotion, and what rules are to be followed in acts of worship, and what kind of practice is to be carried out on a daily basis?
>
> Answer: First, with regard to *the object of devotion*, one should [use] the eight volumes of the Lotus Sutra, or one volume, or one chapter, or one may inscribe simply *the daimoku of the Sutra* as the object of devotion, just as it is described in the Dharma Teacher and the Supernatural Powers chapters of the Sutra. And those persons who are able to do so should also *write out the names of the Tathāgata Shakyamuni and the Buddha Tahō, or fashion images of them, and place these on the left and right of the Lotus Sutra*. And if they are further able to do so, they should fashion images or write out the names of the Buddhas of the ten directions and the bodhisattva Fugen and the others.
>
> As for the rules to be followed in worship, one should always *sit upright when in front of the object of devotion*. Once one leaves *the place of practice*, however, one can practice as one wishes at any time and in place where one walks, stands still, sits, or lies down. As a daily practice, one should *chant the Daimoku, Nam-myō-hō-ren-ge-kyō*. [...]
>
> The two characters of *myōhō* of the Daimoku contain within them the heart of the Lotus Sutra, namely, *the doctrine of three thousand realms in a single moment of life* (Ichinen Sanzen) set forth in the Expedient Means chapter, and *the doctrine of the Buddha's attainment of enlightenment in the far distant past* (Kuonjitsujō) set forth in the Life Span Chapter. [...]

> All Buddhas are emanations of the one Buddha, Shakyamuni. Therefore, [...] *they are all brought together within the two characters of myōhō*. For this reason, the benefits to be gained by reciting the five characters of Myō-hō-ren-ge-kyō are great indeed. All the Buddhas, all the daimoku of the various sutras, are opened up and merged in the Lotus Sutra. Taking notice of *this opening up function of the Mystic Law*, one should recite the daimoku of the Lotus Sutra. (p. 12 f. / II. 228 f.)

To summarize:
- In his time, condemnatory of the widespread popular practice of Nenbutsu, Nichiren passionately addressed the question as to what should be regarded as the practice of the Lotus Sutra in the Latter Day.
- The basic form of the practice is to *"chant the Daimoku of Nam-myō-hō-ren-ge-kyō"*. However, this should be understood to mean *"the Mystic Law containing the doctrine of Ichinen Sanzen in the Expedient Means chapter, and the doctrine of the Eternal Realization in the Life Span chapter"*. This necessarily implies that the practice of the Mystic Law is the means by which all ordinary people can realize the Instant Enlightenment of Ichinen Sanzen. Consequently, one should *"recite the Daimoku in awareness that it contains the merits of all Buddhist teachings and practices."*
- The basic practice is to sit and chant before the object of devotion, which represents the Mystic Law. Thus, the propagation of the Daimoku is of paramount significance in meeting the challenge raised by the Nenbutsu and other teachings. However, it is interesting to note that Nichiren had already at this early stage envisioned the image of the Treasure Tower in which *"Shakyamuni and Tahō sit on the left and right of the Lotus Sutra."* Thus, we can conclude from this writing:

Nichiren's fundamental teaching is the chanting of the Mystic Law of Ichinen Sanzen based on Shakyamuni's Eternal Realization.

»*Questions and Answers on the Object of Devotion*« (1278)

There are a number of Nichiren's writings which emphasize that the daimoku of the Lotus Sutra is the source which brings forth all Buddhas; however, here we will focus on the Gosho which is primarily concerned with the matter of the *Honzon* and which proclaims that *not a Buddha (Person) but the Mystic Law (Dharma) should be the object of devotion*.

Nichiren inscribed a part of the Mandala Gohonzon for Jōkenbō and other priests at Seichōji temple. Jōkenbō asked Nichiren what was the reason that the honzon should represent the aspect of the Law, since it was usual in those days for all believers to put their faith in Buddhas. Nichiren firmly advised him at the conclusion of the Gosho to *"set aside all other practices and devote yourself only to this object of devotion, praying wholeheartedly for your next life"*. Nichiren's reasoning with respect to the Honzon focused on its representation of the aspect of the Law.

> Question: In the evil world of the latter age, what should ordinary people take as their object of devotion?
> Answer: They should make *the daimoku of the Lotus Sutra* their object of devotion. [...]
> Answer: There is a reason why these other [ten] schools have a Buddha as their object of devotion, while this school, the Tendai, has a sutra as the object of devotion.
> Question: What then is the reason? Which is superior, a Buddha or a sutra?
> Answer: As the object of devotion one should select that which is superior. And now, in this latter age, I, Nichiren, too, following the example of the Buddha and T'ien-t'ai, take the Lotus Sutra as the object of devotion. *I do so because the Lotus Sutra is the father and mother of Shakyamuni Buddha, the eye of all the Buddhas*. Shakyamuni, Mahāvairochana, and all the other Buddhas of the ten directions were born from the Lotus Sutra. Therefore, as the object of devotion I now take that which is capable of bringing forth such a life force. (p. 365 / II. 787)

Nichiren's argument is relatively simple and can be summarized in brief:
- It considers which Object of Devotion is effective for leading to the attainment of Buddhahood all ordinary people in the evil world of the Latter Day.
- One should not worship Buddhas but rather "the Daimoku of the Lotus Sutra for the Latter Day", that is, the Mystic Law which brings forth all Buddhas.
- Here, Nichiren clearly expresses his standpoint as to *"the superiority of the Law in comparison to that of the Person."*

Nevertheless, in this Gosho we can't find any other theoretical foundation that might powerfully persuade one to embrace his doctrinal stance. Yet, on a closer look, there can be found a firm rebuttal against any doubt as to the necessity of revering the superiority of the Lotus Sutra.

> The Tripitaka Master Pu-k'ung's translation of »The Rules of Ritual Based on the Lotus Sutra« says that *one should regard Shakyamuni and Tahō Buddha as the objects of devotion for the Lotus Sutra*. Why do you go against their views in the matter? (p. 365 / 787)

This passage is found before Nichiren's critical observation that "all the ten Buddhist schools make Buddhas the object of worship". In this context Nichiren further argues.

> Even though one may pay honor to the Buddhas Shakyamuni and Tahō of the Lotus Sutra, this Sutra itself should be honored as the object of devotion if we consider the issue from the perspective of the *Lotus Samadhi*. As for the statement in the Tripitaka Master Pu-k'ung's »Rules of Rituals«, it is based on the text of the Treasure Tower chapter and makes *the lord of teachings of the Lotus Sutra* the object of devotion. But this does not accord with the true intent of the Lotus Sutra. The object of devotion that I have mentioned earlier, *the Daimoku of the Lotus Sutra*, is *the object of devotion for all Buddhas such as Shakyamuni, Tahō, and others of the ten directions*. It represents the true intent of the votary of the Lotus Sutra.
> (p. 365 / II. 788)

»The Rules of Ritual Based on the Lotus Sutra«, which the Indian Tripitaka Master Pu-k'ung (Amoghavajra, 705-774) of the Chinese esoteric school translated into Chinese, is, as the title suggests, concerned with the "Rituals and Rules for manifestation as the *Lotus Sutra King* through Yoga Contemplation". It gives a particular interpretation of the Lotus Sutra and describes the method by which it should be practiced in an esoteric manner. A particular type of mandala is described which is similar to the esoteric Womb Realm Mandala with the threefold layered structure: In its center the two Buddhas in the Treasure Tower should be portrayed on an eight-petalled lotus flower while around it eight Bodhisattvas, four heavenly kings and other deities should be portrayed. In front of this mandala, one practices the three kinds of secret tantra: forming a finger sign (*mudra*), reciting a mantra

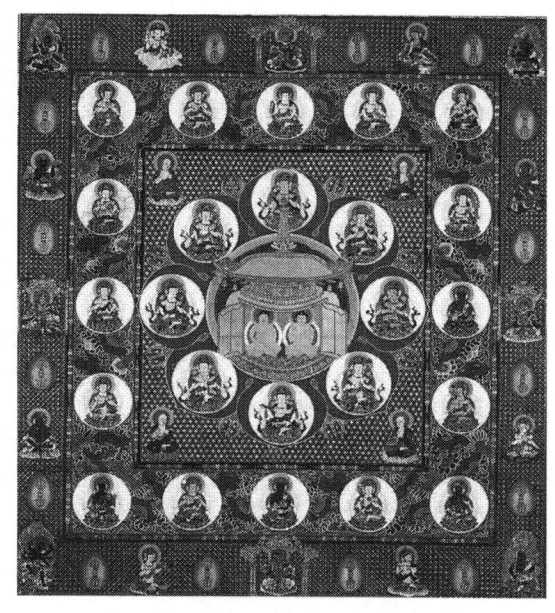

An example of Lotus-Mandala in esoteric manner

(*dharani*) and attaining to the mind state of a Buddha (*yoga*). This is to thereby enter into a profound meditative state of mind (*the Lotus Samadhi*), by which the practitioner attains to the experience of being a Lotus Sutra king. For awakening to this unity with the Dharma body of the truth actually means nothing other than "immediate enlightenment in one's present form."

Incidentally, Nichiren was deeply familiar with the sutras and doctrines of Vajrayana, including the writings of *Kōbō-Daishi Kūkai* (774-835), the founder of the Japanese Shingon school. For example, Nichiren quotes from Kōbō's »The Doctrine of Attaining Buddhahood in One's Present Form« notably in »Attaining Buddhahood in One's Present Form (Reply to Myōichinyo)« (July 1280, p. 1256 / I. 1053). In fact, this writing of Kōbō itself refers to »The Rules of Ritual Based on the Lotus Sutra«, as well as to esoteric sutras such as the *Mahāvairochana Sutra* and the *Vajrasekhara Sutra*. Thus, there is no doubt that Nichiren was deeply and decisively influenced by the Vajrayana doctrine of immediate enlightenment, although he criticized it as inferior to the teachings of the Lotus Sutra.

> Chanting Daimoku before the Mandala-Gohonzon means:
> placing your hands together to symbolize the principle of the mutual containment of the Ten Worlds (*mudra*), reciting the Mystic Law which brings forth all Buddhas (*dharani*) and visualizing the enlightened state of Ichinen Sanzen (*yoga*). This is to enter a meditative state of mind (Lotus samadhi), while experiencing oneness with the Gohonzon represents the *Tathāgata Nam-myō-hō-ren-ge-kyō*.
> At this point, Instant Enlightenment is attained.

Nichiren's main argument for this is grounded upon his particular interpretation of Shakyamuni's Eternal Realization in the Life Span Chapter, i.e. in terms of the immediate enlightenment of Ichinen Sanzen. This is also the case with respect to the above quotation from Pu-k'ung's »Rules of Ritual«. For Nichiren *"considers the matter with reference to the state of lotus samadhi"*. From the perspective of a Contemplative Reading of the Essential Section, the two Buddhas represent Initial Enlightenment as described in the Theoretical Section before Shakyamuni's revelation of his true identity. Consequently, *"the lord of teachings of the Lotus Sutra"* should not be made the object of devotion. For it is *"the votary of the Lotus Sutra,"* who practices to attain the supreme principle of Instant Enlightenment of Ichinen Sanzen in the Latter Day, as *his true intent* is to make *the Daimoku of the Lotus Sutra* the object of devotion.

Nichiren's ultimate standpoint is to consider the Mystic Law itself as the cause which brings forth all Buddhas, as can be clearly seen in his writing »Letter to the Brothers« (1276).

> The Lotus Sutra is the eye of all Buddhas. It is the original teacher of Shakyamuni Buddha himself, the lord of teachings. (p. 1080 / I. 494)

4. The Ambiguity of the *Honmon no Kaidan*

The place for observing the indestructible diamond -like precepts

With respect to the *"Sanctuary of the Essential Section"*, Nichiren considered it to be a radical alternative to the *"ordination platform for the precepts of perfect and immediate enlightenment on Mt. Hiei"* (see above at page 246). Initially, as such an alternative, Nichiren may have conceived of a unique form of ordination for his future disciples. Yet this is unpersuasive, as Nichiren was undoubtedly aware of the decadent and corrupt character of the Latter Day.

> During this period, people neither uphold the precepts nor break them; only those without precepts predominate within the country.
> (»Encouragement to a Sick Person (Letter to Nanjō Hyōe Shichirō)«, p. 1495 / I. 78)

Further, Nichiren was aware of his uniquely significant status, although he always remained humble about it.

> I am a monk without precepts.
> (»Cloth for a Robe and an Unlined Robe«, p. 971 / II. 602)

Consequently, Nichiren regarded the keeping of the precepts as no longer having any meaning: he was especially skeptical of the value of upholding the precepts as the means of attaining to Buddhahood. As a radical alternative, for Nichiren only keeping and practicing faith in the Mystic Law should be considered to have significance. This would be to observe a very special precept.

> Myō-hō-ren-ge-kyō, the heart of the Essential Section of the Lotus Sutra, contains the benefit amassed through the countless practices and meritorious deeds of all Buddhas throughout the three existences. Then, how can these five characters not include the benefits obtained by observing all the precepts?
> Once having embraced this perfectly endowed Mystic Precept, no practitioner can break it, even if he should try. It is therefore called the *"Precept of the Diamond Chalice"*.
> Only by observing this Mystic Precept have the Buddhas of the three existences become Buddhas endowed with the three bodies—the Dharma body, the reward [wisdom] body, and the manifested [physical] body, which are each without beginning or end.

> (»The Teaching, Practice, and Proof«, p. 1282 / 481 f.)

The five characters of the Mystic Law are endowed with an *"indestructible precept just like a diamond"* which, moreover, actually signifies the doctrine of Ichinen Sanzen.

> This priceless gem, the doctrine of Ichinen Sanzen [as revealed by Shakyamuni's eternal realization], was then placed in a diamond-like indestructible wrapping, the five characters of Myō-hō-ren-ge-kyō, which has then been bequeathed to us especially, for the salvation of the troubled and impoverished beings of this latter age.
> (»Reply to Ōta Saemon-no-jō«, p. 1016 / II. 749)

Consequently, as the One Great Secret Law is endowed with the function of the Mystic Precept, which when unfolded corresponds to the Three Disciplines of Precepts, Meditation and Wisdom. Thus, all the Three Great Secret Laws are necessarily endowed with this same function. For the *Honmon no Daimoku* is to chant the Mystic Law to attain the Instant Enlightenment of Ichinen Sanzen, while the *Honmon no Honzon* represents the enlightened state of life of *the primordial Buddha endowed with the three bodies without beginning and end*. So, considered, the chanting of Daimoku is the *cause* by which the Mystic Precepts are kept, while the *effect* is the manifestation of Buddhahood as represented in the form of the Mandala Honzon. Only so is Buddhahood manifested in our own ordinary lives. The place in which this mystic event is enacted, which is characterized by the Simultaneity of Cause and Effect, thereby gains its profound significance as the *Honmon no Kaidan*. This represents a radically new understanding of the concept of *Kaidan*.

The One Great Secret Law
= the Mystic Law *of Ichinen Sanzen*

⬇

The Three Great Secret Laws

Daimoku   *Honzon*

Kaidan

The *Kaidan* can be defined as "*the place for observing the precepts*" in contrast to its original meaning of an *ordination platform*.

The place of practice

In fact, when considered from the perspective of our daily practice, the place where we chant Daimoku before the Gohonzon is in actuality our "place of practice" where the "world of suffering" is transformed into an "enlightened world". Metaphorically, this is symbolized by the Ceremony in the

CHAPTER 5

Air and the emergence of the Treasure Tower. Indeed, the place of practice and the body of an ordinary person chanting Daimoku is nothing other than an actual manifestation of that same Treasure Tower (D). This is exactly how it was conceived by Nichiren himself:

> In the Latter Day of the Law, no Treasure Tower exists other than the persons of the men and women who embrace the Lotus Sutra. It follows, therefore, that whether eminent or humble, high or low in social rank, those who chant *Nam-myō-hō-ren-ge-kyō* are themselves the Treasure Tower, and, likewise, are themselves the Tathāgata Tahō. [...]
>
> You may think you offered gifts to the Treasure Tower of the Tathāgata Tahō, but that is not so. You offered them to yourself. You, yourself, are *a Tathāgata of Original Enlightenment endowed with the three bodies in one body*. You should chant *Nam-myō-hō-ren-ge-kyō* with this conviction. Then the place where you chant Daimoku will become the dwelling place of the Treasure Tower. The sutra reads, *"If there is any place where the Lotus Sutra is preached, then my Treasure Tower will come forth and appear in that spot"*.
>
> Faith like yours is so extremely rare that I will inscribe the Treasure Tower especially for you. [...] This is the reason for my advent in this world.
>
> (»On the Treasure Tower (Letter to Abutsubō)«[29], p. 1304 / 299 f.)

Thus, Nichiren makes it clear that in chanting Daimoku the Treasure Tower itself emerges both from the body of the person and from the place of practice. Consequently, the Instant Enlightenment of Ichinen Sanzen, as represented by Shakyamuni's Eternal Realization, takes place here and now (D). And this understanding of the Instant Enlightenment of Ichinen Sanzen can be applied in an identical way to the life of Nichiren himself (C).

> I inherited *the ultimate secret Law* from Shakyamuni Buddha, the lord of teachings, at Eagle Peak, and I preserve it secretly within my thorax. Thus, my heart under the breast is where all Buddhas enter nirvana; my tongue, where they turn the wheel of the Law; my throat, where they are born into this world; and my mouth, where they attain enlightenment. Be-

---

[29] Saikakudoppo (pseudonym) regarded this Gosho as apochryphal for a long time, but not after he had discovered the source of the passage quoted below which refers to the idea of "My body is a treasure tower". Nichiren seems to have written this passage by way of reference to the poetic verses on immeditate enlightenment found in »The Illuminating Secret Commentary on the Five Cakras and the Nine Syllables". This is a major work of *Kakuban* (1095-1144), a priest of the Shingon school, and the young Nichiren made a copy of this treatise in 1251.

> cause this mountain [Minobu] is where such a wondrous votary of the Lotus Sutra dwells, how can it be any less sacred than the pure land of Eagle Peak? This is what [»The Words and Phrases of the Lotus Sutra« mean when] it is stated, *"Since the Law is mystic, the person is noble; since the person is noble, the land is worthy of respect"*.
>
> (»The Person and the Law (Reply to Nanjō)«, p. 1578 / I. 1097)

Given the quotation above, the idea that the life of an ordinary person who chants Daimoku is most adequately represented by the majestic Treasure Tower, a manifestation of indestructible Buddhahood, as the original and true purpose of the Three Types of Learning is realized.

5. The Three Great Secret Laws as inherited by Jōgyō

The Mystic Law inherent within Jōgyo's own life

There is an additional significant matter with respect to the Three Great Secret Laws, i.e. Nichiren's self-understanding, as expressed as: *"I inherited the ultimate secret Law from Shakyamuni Buddha, the lord of teachings, at Eagle Peak, and I preserve it secretly within my thorax"*. A similar self-understanding is found in „On Receiving the Three Great Secret Laws«.

> At the beginning of the period of more than 2.000 years [after the Buddha's passing], in my capacity as the leader of all the numerous Bodhisattvas [of the Earth], I, *Nichiren, certainly received these Three Great Secret Laws by oral transmission from the lord of teachings [Shakyamuni]. And the propagation which I now undertake do not differ at all from the transmission at Eagle Peak. For it conforms exactly to the three most important issues of the Essential Section.* (p. 1022 / II. 987)

After the Buddha revealed his true identity and spoke about his Eternal Realization, he entrusted his direct disciples from the remotest past, the Bodhisattvas of the Earth, with the mission to propagate the Mystic Law in the Latter Day. Interpreting the "entrustment" in this way, Nichiren identifies himself as the leader of those whom *"received the Three Great Secret Laws by oral transmission"*, specifically as quoted above *"I preserve it secretly in my fleshy thorax"* (C). Indeed, in order to transform the concept of the Mystic Law and to unfold its three characteristics as an actual practice for the Latter Day, Nichiren's self-understanding as "Jōgyō with his inheritance" is especially significant.

In »The Object of Devotion for Observing the Mind« it is emphasized again and again, that the Bodhisattvas of the Earth have received an exclusive entrustment of the Dharma. To quote some particularly relevant passages:

Chapter 5

> As to the five characters of Nam-myō-hō-ren-ge-kyō, the heart of the Essential Section of the Lotus Sutra, Shakyamuni Buddha [...] summoned from beneath the earth the great bodhisattvas as numerous as the dust particles of a thousand worlds and, as he preached the eight chapters, transferred it solely to them.
> (p. 247 / I. 365)

> Essentially, the great bodhisattvas taught by the Buddha in his provisional status and the great bodhisattvas who gathered from the other worlds were not qualified to inherit the Life Span Chapter which reveals the eternal Buddha's inner truth. At the dawn of the Latter Day evil people who slander the correct teaching would be found widely throughout the land, so Shakyamuni Buddha [...] summoned the multitude of great bodhisattvas from beneath the earth. He entrusted them with the five characters of Myō-hō-ren-ge-kyō, the heart of the Life Span Chapter, for the enlightenment of all ordinary beings in the land of Jambudvīpa.
> The bodhisattvas taught by the Buddha in his provisional status were not qualified to accept this transmission as they had not been disciples of Shakyamuni Buddha since the time in which he had first set his mind to attain enlightenment in the remotest past. [...]
> Miao-lo says, "The children propagate the Law of the father, and this benefits the whole world." The Supplement to »The Words and Phrases of the Lotus Sutra« states, "Because the Law manifests eternal realization, it was entrusted equally to all persons of eternal realization."
> (p. 250 / I. 370 f.)

It should be especially noted, that the Mystic Law which led Shakyamuni to immediate enlightenment in the remotest past is nothing other than the eternal Dharma. The Bodhisattvas of the Earth, who have been entrusted with the mission to propagate this Law, also possess a primordial and eternal nature. They have been in fact the original disciples of Shakyamuni Buddha since his Eternal Realization in the remotest past (see id. and p. 253/ 373). This can best be understood, if we interpret this concept in the sense that both Shakyamuni and Jōgyō represent the Mystic Law characterized by the Mutual Containment of the Ten Worlds based on Original Enlightenment without beginning.

Consequently, as the most important matter is the propagation of this eternal Mystic Law for attaining Buddhahood in the Latter Day, Nichiren expressly identified himself as the leader of the Bodhisattvas of the Earth. Let's consider this further below.

Jōgyō will appear in the Latter Day

While on Sado in January 1274, Nichiren wrote »The Votary of the Lotus Sutra Will Meet Persecution« and for the first time spoke of the Three Great Secret Laws. The corresponding passage is quoted again (see above page 247).

> Nāgārjuna and Vasubandhu were both scholars who produced a thousand works. However, they expounded only the provisional Mahayana teachings. Though they understood the meaning of the Lotus Sutra in their hearts, they did not declare it in words. An oral transmission exists concerning this. T'ien-t'ai and Dengyō went so far as to expound it, but they left unrevealed *the object of devotion of the Essential Section,* **the four bodhisattvas**, *the sanctuary,* and *the five characters of Nam-myō-hō-ren-ge-kyō*.
>
> Their reasons were, first, because the Buddha had not transferred these teachings to any of them, and second, because the time and the people's capacity did not satisfy the requirements. Now the time has arrived, and **the four bodhisattvas** *will surely make their advent.* I, Nichiren, was the first who knew this. (p. 965 / I. 449)

Nichiren here gives three reasons as to why the great masters of previous generations did not establish the three Great Secret Laws of the Essential Section:
1) this mission had not been entrusted to them,
2) the time was not ripe, and
3) the people's capacity had not yet so deteriorated as to require a Dharma which would be greater and powerful than that of the provisional Shakyamuni Buddha.

These three reasons are in essential in accord with the Five Guides to Propagation, although the first reason would appear to relate to the concept of a "national master". In fact, this reason suggests that Nichiren's own self-identification is the most important condition needing to be fulfilled not only in order to proclaim a radically new doctrine but also in order to establish a new form for the object of devotion.

Thus, at first sight, »The Opening of the Eyes« would appear to provide doctrinal confirmation that Nichiren should indeed be considered as the "votary of the Lotus Sutra in the Latter Day". Practicing in accord with the Buddha's teaching, Nichiren could expect to provoke the three kinds of enemies to persecute him as proof of his mission in Japan in the Age of the Latter Day. Thus, after having demonstrated with his own body that he had fulfilled the "prophecies" found in the LS, Nichiren considered the entrustment of the One Great Secret Law by Shakyamuni to Jōgyō. This event is depicted in the Supernatural Power chapter and serves Nichiren's own self-identification and legitimation (B). By identifying himself as Jōgyō, the recipient of Shakyamuni's transmission, Nichiren was entrusted with and authorized to unfold the Mystic Law of the Three Great Secret Laws (C).

A further important matter is addressed in the quotation above. The *"Four bodhisattvas"* who are referred to alongside the Three Great Secret Laws are not the Bodhisattvas of the Earth found inscribed on the Mandala-honzon but those who *"will surely make their advent"* in the Latter Day. It is necessary to make a clear difference between these two distinct understandings, as this will become important when we consider the *"Problem with the statues made of one Buddha and four bodhisattvas"* (section 5 of chapter 7). For the leader of the Bodhisattvas of the Earth Jōgyō is in fact Nichiren himself, who speaks expressly about this self-identification:

> I inherited *the ultimate secret Law* from Shakyamuni Buddha, the lord of teachings, at Eagle Peak, and *I preserve it secretly within my thorax*.
> (»The Person and the Law (Reply to Nanjō)«, p. 1578 / 1097)

Nichiren attained to the supreme principle of Instant Enlightenment
as found in Shakyamuni's Eternal Realization (B)
which is the Mystic Law entrusted to Jōgyō (C)
in the form of the Three Great Secret Laws.
Based on this, the practice of "chanting Daimoku before the Mandala-honzon", is for ordinary people in the Latter Day
to attain to Instant Enlightenment in actuality (D).

Selecting the Heart of the Lotus Sutra

Shortly after Nichiren settled on Minobu in May 1274, he completed »Selecting the Heart of the Lotus Sutra«, which was addressed to Toki Jōnin, and spoke once again of the Three Great Secret Laws, particularly with reference to his own self-identification with Bodhisattva Jōgyō. At first sight, this Gosho seems to reflect the new understanding which Nichiren had first begun to develop on Sado, found in »The Opening of the Eyes« (February 1272), »The Object of Devotion for Observing the Mind« (April 1273) and »The Votary of the Lotus Sutra Will Meet Persecution« (January 1274).

The »Selecting the Heart of the Lotus Sutra« considers the question *"for whom the Lotus Sutra was preached?"* and concludes that it is *"for the people of the Latter Day such as Nichiren"*. After a discussion of the sutras and commentaries, Nichiren arrives at the conclusion:

> To bring salvation to those who slander the Lotus Sutra, the only thing which is effective are the five characters of Myōhō-renge-kyō. [...]

> I, Nichiren, have set aside both the Comprehensive and the Abbreviated Version and favor only the Essence of the [LS]. That is, *the five characters of Myō-hō-ren-ge-kyō which were transmitted to Bodhisattva Jōgyō.*
> (p. 336 / II. 488 f.)

This "three step reduction method" had already been used in »The Daimoku of the Lotus Sutra« (1266). However, he signed this letter as a "follower of Dengyō", a learned monk belonging to the Tendai school. Thus, the perspective of a Literal Reading of the LS remains in the foreground.

> To accept, uphold, read, recite, take delight in, and protect all the eight volumes and twenty-eight chapters of the Lotus Sutra is called the *Comprehensive practice*.
> To accept, uphold, and protect the Expedient Means chapter and the Life Span Chapter is called the *Abbreviated practice*.
> And simply to chant one four-phrase verse or the daimoku, and to protect those who do so, is called the *Essential practice*.
> Hence, among these three kinds of practice, comprehensive, condensed, and essential, *the Daimoku is defined as the Essential practice.*
> (p. 942 / I. 143)

In this early work, Nichiren considers his doctrinal stance to be quite simply "the heart of the LS is daimoku" and makes reference also to the abbreviated version of the Expedient Means chapter of the Theoretical Section, as well as to the Life Span Chapter of the Essential Section. Subsequently, in »The Object of Devotion for Observing the Mind«, to make a clear distinction for the purpose of comparison, he defines the abbreviated version as the "the Life Span chapter and two halves before and after it":

> The Essential Section of Shakyamuni's lifetime and that which is for the beginning of the Latter Day are both pure and perfect [in that both lead directly to Buddhahood]. Shakyamuni's, however, is for the harvest, and the latter is for the sowing. The core of his teaching is one chapter and two halves [before and after the Life Span chapter], and the core of mine is the five characters of the daimoku alone.   (p. 249 / I. 369)

At this point, we should pay attention to the implications of this "three step reduction method". It should not be understood only as reductive simplification, but rather as the essence of the LS as interpreted during two distinct temporal periods: the abbreviated version of "one and a half chapters" is only valid for the harvest during Shakyamuni's lifetime, while for the Latter Day only the Essential version of Daimoku should be considered as valid for the Sowing. This distinction itself reflects the comparison between the "LS of the Shakyamuni's lifetime" and "LS of the Latter Day". Nichiren selects the latter as the Daimoku for Sowing and is consistent when he states:

CHAPTER 5

> Now, in the Latter Day of the Law, both the Lotus Sutra and the other sutras are of no use. Only Nam-myō-hō-ren-ge-kyō [has the power of benefit to lead to enlightenment].
> («The Teaching for the Latter Day (Reply to Ueno)«, p. 1545 / I. 902)

Thus, given the above, we arrive at the following equation:

> LS of the Latter Day
> = Daimoku of Sowing
> = the Mystic Law transmitted to Jōgyō
> = the One Great Secret Law

Based on this, the Three Great Secret Laws can be expanded.

> Question: In these two thousand and more years since the passing of the Buddha, what are these "Secret Laws" that were left unrevealed by Nāgārjuna, Vasubandhu, T'ien-t'ai, and Dengyō?
> Answer: They are the Object of Devotion of the Essential Section, the Sanctuary of the Essential Section, and the five characters of the Daimoku of the Essential Section. («Selecting the Heart of the Lotus Sutra« p. 336 / II. 488)

In this way, Nichiren reinterprets the LS with the purpose of "selecting the Mystic Law for the Latter Day". His approach is particularly with respect to a Contemplative Reading of the Essential Section. From this perspective, Nichiren "discovered" the Mystic Law of Sowing which was hidden *"deep beneath the lines"* and was nothing other than Shakyamuni's Eternal Realization, with which he now identified himself as the Bodhisattva Jōgyō, to whom the Mystic Law had been transmitted (C).

> When [...] the nation has been plunged into disorder, there is no doubt that such sages as *Bodhisattva Jōgyō* will emerge, establish *the Three Secret Laws of the Essential Section*, and carry out *the propagation and dissemination [Kōsenrufu] of Myō-hō-ren-ge-kyō* widely throughout the four continents and the region within the four seas! (p. 338 / II. 491)

This passage expresses Nichiren's absolute resolve:

> By establishing the One Great Secret Law transmitted to Jōgyō in the form of the Three Great Secret Laws, Nichiren will establish the foundation for the worldwide propagation of the Mystic Law.

6. The bloodline of the faith which flows to the votaries of the Lotus Sutra

Without a doubt, Nichiren consistently maintained that the "five characters of the Mystic Law -equal- the seven characters of chanting Daimoku" had been transmitted by the eternal Buddha Shakyamuni (B) in the form of an "oral transmission" or "transmission to Jōgyō" (C). Moreover, as already noted (see above page 167), he powerfully proclaims it even at the very beginning of his mission.

> On April 28, 1253, I, Nichiren, for the first time clearly proclaimed the transmission of this large carriage drawn by a white ox which signifies the One Vehicle of the Lotus Sutra.
> (»The Large Carriage Drawn by a White Ox«, p. 1543 / I. 723)

This transmission of the Mystic Law by the Eternal Buddha to "Jōgyō = Nichiren" during the Ceremony in the Air is the doctrinal foundation which legitimizes the chanting of Daimoku.

With respect to the matter of transmission, a series of writings were addressed to Sairenbō, a learned priest, originally of the Tendai school. He must have met Nichiren in Sado while he himself had been exiled to Sado for some unknown reason during an earlier period. As he had great knowledge of Tendai teachings, Sairenbō asked many questions in order to clarify the similarities and differences between Tendai doctrine and the doctrine of Nichiren. Among the many significant writings addressed to Sairenbō, the inherited character of the Mystic Law is particularly elaborated on in »The Heritage of the Ultimate Law of Life« (1272), which replied to a question of Sairenbō while still on Sado.

> The bloodline regarding the ultimate Law of life and death [as transmitted from the Buddha to all living beings] is Myō-hō-ren-ge-kyō. For Shakyamuni and Tahō, the two Buddhas in the Treasure Tower, transferred the five characters of Myō-hō-ren-ge-kyō to Bodhisattva Jōgyō who is carrying it with him as a heritage unbroken since the infinite past.
> (p. 1336 / I. 216)

For Nichiren, the Mystic Law inherited by Jōgyō is the Dharma body itself which is present throughout eternity (C).

> Shakyamuni and Tahō, the two Buddhas, represent also the two phases of life and death. Because of this, there is in no way any difference between the Shakyamuni Buddha of Eternal Realization, the Lotus Sutra which leads all people to Buddhahood, and us ordinary human beings. To chant Myō-hō-ren-ge-kyō with this understanding is to inherit the ultimate Law of life and death. This is a matter of the utmost importance for

> Nichiren's disciples and lay supporters, and this is what it means to embrace the Lotus Sutra. (P. 1337 / I. 216)

This "heritage regarding the Ultimate Law of Life and Death" means to embrace and to practice the same Mystic Law as the Eternal Buddha did. Only then will the supreme principle of Instant Enlightenment based on the Dual Structure of Life and Ichinen Sanzen be activated in our lives. At this moment, the bloodline of the Mystic Law flows.

In chanting Daimoku before the Gohonzon,
we, the ordinary people of the Latter Day (D), will manifest our true identity as the votaries of the LS, the Bodhisattvas of the Earth.
In this way we will be directly connected to
the Eternal Buddha Shakyamuni (B) and to
the reincarnation of Bodhisattva Jōgyō, Nichiren (C).
We thereby all manifest the unity of person and law.
Only thus will the *"heritage of faith"* (p. 1338 / I. 218) flow.

This ultimate perspective can be found inscribed on the Mandala Honzon. However, it should be particularly noted, that the universal "Heritage of the Faith" is radically distinct from any institutional matter relating to the transmission of the teaching or the bloodline of faith in any Nichiren-related sect or organization.

Chapter 6
The Principle of Attaining to Buddhahood

1. The Bodhisattvas of the Earth embody the principle for activating Buddhahood

In continuation, we further develop the concept of "Jōgyō's inheritance of the five characters of Myō-hō-ren-ge-kyō". As already discussed, even though it has been stated that Shakyamuni revealed his true identity by casting off his shadow, he is nevertheless to be considered the Buddha of "Initial Enlightenment" in so far that we remain on the level of literal reading. For he *"originally practiced the bodhisattva way"* characterized by the practice of the six pāramitās and "became a Buddha" at a particular point in the past of countless kalpas. This path to the attainment of enlightenment requires a long process of development from sowing, through ripening, to the harvest, as it is dependent upon a "gradually advancing practice over many kalpas in order to cut off all desires and discard the human body". Thus, although the Life Span chapter would seem to have been intended as a depiction of the "Eternal Buddha Shakyamuni", it is nevertheless still based upon a conventional "view of attaining enlightenment through the process of cause and effect". Nichiren himself understood this Buddha in terms of a "Buddha representing the effect", which he then reinterpreted from a perspective of a Contemplative Reading for the Latter Day.

> The Essential Section of Shakyamuni's lifetime and that for the beginning of the Latter Day are both pure and perfect [in that both lead directly to Buddhahood]. Shakyamuni's, however, is *for the Harvest*, and the latter is *for the Sowing*. (»The Object of Devotion for Observing the Mind«, p. 249 / I. 369)

Further, the Bodhisattvas of the Earth are described as those who are *"all golden in hue, with the thirty-two features of a Buddha and an immeasurable brightness"* (LS, p. 252 f.). These resplendent characteristics, along with the deepest wisdom and limitless virtue, are understood as evidence of unceasing devotion to the Buddha way since the immemorial past. Nichiren particularly highlighted this idea.

> The great bodhisattvas as numerous as the dust particles of a thousand worlds appeared, rising up out of the ground. Even Fugen and Manjushrī, who had been regarded as the leading disciples of Shakyamuni, could not compare to them. [...]
> Then Bodhisattva Maitreya began to consider the matter in his mind. He said to himself: [...] As for these great bodhisattvas who have appeared

> from the earth, *what kind of Buddha is their teacher?* Surely, he must be a Buddha who is incomparably superior to Shakyamuni, Tahō, and the emanation Buddhas from the ten directions! [...] Now from what land did these great bodhisattvas come, *what Buddha did they follow, and what great teaching have they practiced?*"
>
> (»The Opening of the Eyes«, p. 211 f. / I. 252 f.)

Nichiren focused on an especially radical idea, which was the very opposite of the traditional view of attaining Buddhahood. The Bodhisattvas of the Earth are those *"Bodhisattvas emerging from the empty space underneath the Sahā World"*, as described in the LS. This means, they are emerging from an enlightened world, yet they are nevertheless intimately related to this world of suffering. They are related with wisdom and virtue so that, *"when they appear in the midst of the gathering of the other bodhisattvas, they look like so many resplendent gods from the heaven of Indra (Shakra) amidst a troop of apes"* (see id., p. 211 / I. 252). As they are so wonderous, who must be their master? So *"surely he must be a Buddha who is incomparably superior to Shakyamuni, Tahō, and all other Buddhas"*.

Articulating the doubts of all the participants, Bodhisattva Maitreya asks the Buddha what kind of great Law and under what kind of Buddha have they studied and practiced. To dispel these doubts, Shakyamuni speaks and reveals his true identity as a Buddha who had attained enlightenment in the remotest past. This Eternal Buddha is the original source of all Buddhas and direct master to each of the Bodhisattvas of the Earth. Further, their realization is of such profundity, that it could never be attained by any conventional Buddhist practice. So what kind of Great Dharma is this?

Historically, devotees of the LS appear to have conceived of the Mahayana Bodhisattva of the One Buddha Vehicle by reference to the metaphorical image of the bodhisattvas emerging from the enlightened world beneath the earth. This suggests that they differed quite radically from a conventional understanding of a bodhisattva seeking Initial Enlightenment. Rather, their conception is better understood as a "Bodhisattva who is in essence a Buddha". This symbolizes a radically innovative idea with respect to attaining enlightenment, i.e. in terms Instant Enlightenment being understood as the activation of Buddhahood (effect) within the ordinary person of the Nine Worlds (cause).

One again, we will consider the significance of the eternity of the Bodhisattvas of the Earth with reference to »On the Five Guides to Propagation (A letter to lay priest Soya)". This Gosho gives three reasons why the Bodhisattvas of the Earth are especially qualified to propagate the Great Dharma in the Latter Day.

> The great bodhisattvas as numerous as the dust particles of a thousand worlds who emerged from the earth have first of all lived in this Sahā World for an incalculably long period of time; second, they have been disciples of Shakyamuni Buddha since the far distant past, when he first set his mind on and attained enlightenment; and third, these bodhisattvas were the first persons in the Sahā World to receive the seed of Buddhahood from the Buddha. Therefore, in terms of the bonds of karma from the past that tie them to the Sahā World, they surpass the other great bodhisattvas. (p. 1032 / II. 550)

The Bodhisattvas of the Earth are, just like the Eternal Buddha, deeply related to this world of suffering and have received the seed of enlightenment as his first disciples. Because this seed was sowed in the remotest past, they have been practicing the same Dharma and are thereby endowed with the same enlightened state and characteristics as the Buddha himself (B, C).

In this context, Jōgyō's inheritance of the Saddharma (the Right Dharma of the LS) is the Mystic Law which Nichiren selected for the people in the Latter Day. As Nichiren stated in »The Object of Devotion for Observing the Mind«.

> *The Essential Section of Shakyamuni's lifetime* and *that which is for the beginning of the Latter Day* are both pure and perfect [in that both lead directly to Buddhahood]. Shakyamuni's, however, is *for the Harvest*, and the latter is *for the Sowing*. (p. 249 / I. 369)

In the passage, Nichiren makes a clear distinction between *"the Essential Section of Shakyamuni's lifetime"* (B) and *"that for the beginning of the Latter Day"* (C). Thus, he introduced a perspective of comparison between the Buddhism of Sowing and that of the Harvest. In this way, Nichiren selected the seed of enlightenment which represents the Original Cause of the Eternal Buddha Shakyamuni. For this is *the supreme principle of the Instant Enlightenment of Ichinen Sanzen based on the Mutual Containment of the Ten Worlds*.

2. The duality of the primordial Buddha without beginning

Previously, as noted when referring to "the doctrine of original cause and original effect" as outlined in »The Opening of the Eyes«, the Eternal Buddha Shakyamuni should be regarded as the "Buddha presenting the Effect" on a literal level of interpretation. However, from the perspective of a deeper contemplative reading, Shakyamuni became the Buddha of "Original Cause - equals- Original Effect" based on the practice of the Mystic Law (B). As this is the same Mystic Law which is to be practiced, "the *Essential Section of*

Shakyamuni's lifetime and *that for the beginning of the Latter Day are both pure and perfect [in that both lead directly to Buddhahood]"*. However, the practitioners of Shakyamuni's lifetime understood this to mean that the teaching amounted to a harvest of the fruit of their practice (the doctrine of Original Effect) while those in the Latter Day understand the teaching to amount to a sowing of the seed (the doctrine of Original Cause), as they have not yet received the seed.

Further, with respect to "Original Effect" in the "principle of Original Cause -equals- Original Effect", Nichiren conceived of a novel concept, i.e. the "primordial Buddha without beginning", as understood in »On the Superiority of the Lotus Sutra when compared to the Shingon Teachings« (1264).

> Most of the sutras speak of the Buddha as having gained correct enlightenment for the first time, and do not reveal *the primordial Buddha endowed with the three bodies since time without beginning*. If Tathāgata *Dainichi* (Mahāvairochana) had presented an erroneous view of attaining Buddhahood without cause, then he would be but a mere name without any substantial reality. Thus, the Life Span chapter revealed the truth as to this significant matter. For Shakyamuni Buddha is like the single moon in the sky, while all the other Buddhas and bodhisattvas are like the reflection of the moon floating in ten thousand different bodies of water.
>
> (p. 124 / II. 280)

Similarly, the Shakyamuni Buddha within our lives is the *"the primordial Buddha endowed with the three bodies since time without beginning"* as similarly defined later in »The Object of Devotion for Observing the Mind« (p. 249 / I. 365).

The concept of the primordial Buddha has the double meaning of both the Original Effect of Shakyamuni's Eternal Realization and the Buddhahood inherent in our own lives.
In other words, Shakyamuni's Eternal Realization is understood as the original source of realizing enlightenment and provides assurance that all ordinary people are endowed with this potentiality for Buddhahood.

Once again, I would like to emphasize that undoubtedly a concept of Original Enlightenment can be found in Nichiren's thought. Above, with respect to this, we have quoted several terms which Nichiren used in his Gosho, e.g.:

- *"the primordial Buddha endowed with the three bodies since time without beginning"* (»On the Superiority of the Lotus Sutra in comparison to the Shingon Teachings« and »The Object of Devotion for Observing the Mind«)

- "Buddhas endowed with the three bodies—the Dharma body, the reward [wisdom] body, and the manifested body, which are each without beginning or end" (»The Teaching, Practice, and Proof«)
- "the lord of teachings Shakyamuni equipped with the original and natural three bodies" („On the Receiving of the Three Great Secret Laws«)
- "the fruit of Buddhahood equipped with the eternally inherent three bodies" (»Letter to Gijōbō«)
- "the Tathāgata endowed with the original and everlasting three bodies" (»Reply to Myōichinyo«)
- "the everlasting Buddha nature" (»Cloth for a Robe and an Unlined Robe« and »On the Protection of the Nation«)
- "the Mutual Containment of the Ten Worlds of Original Enlightenment" (»On the Ten Dharma Worlds«)

All these phrases are essentially related to Shakyamuni's Eternal Realization in the Life Span chapter. As it can be understood as a prototype of the Immediate Enlightenment of Ichinen Sanzen, philosophically it is consistent to speak of all ordinary people in terms of "original enlightenment" within "the original Ten Worlds without beginning and end" or of their possessing "the everlasting Buddha nature".

- "Common people like ourselves, who have been submerged in the sufferings of birth and death since time without beginning and who never so much as dreamed of reaching the shore of enlightenment, become the Tathāgatas who are originally enlightened and endowed with the three bodies." (»The Teaching, Practice, and Proof«)
- "You, yourself, are a Tathāgata of Original Enlightenment endowed with the three bodies in one body". (»On the Treasure Tower (Letter to Abutsubō)«)
- "A common mortal is an entity of the three bodies, and a true Buddha". (»The True Aspect of All Phenomena«)

The principle of "the Instant Enlightenment of ordinary people" is, for NB, the doctrinal foundation upon which the original Buddhahood in our lives is activated and manifested by chanting the Mystic Law.

Yet this philosophical stance is radically distinct from the "medieval Tendai doctrine of original enlightenment" which sought to legitimate the status of quo by simply regarding all ordinary people just as they are, and the world just as it, as the actual manifestation of original enlightenment. It would, therefore, be precipitate to immediately assume any Gosho should be considered apocryphal simply because it contains such terms as *"original enlightenment"*, *"without intention"*, *"three bodies in on body"* and so on.

Conversely, if you discard or ignore such elements in Nichiren's thought, you will be left only with the "enlightened world" of the Essential Section, i.e. with an understanding based only on the perspective of a literal reading. Consequently, an understanding of the triple aspect of "the Instant Enlightenment of ordinary people" would be seriously defective, as it would be lacking in the essential elements which characterize the original thought of Nichiren (B · C · D).

Further, the practical consequence would be to shift the focus away from upholding the Mystic Law and rather towards the worship of Buddhas, Bodhisattvas or founders of sects, particularly by the recitation of sutras and verses. With this orientation towards the temple, with its priests and rituals, the most important dimension of NB is lost, i.e. that each of us should chant Daimoku before the Mandala Honzon in order to realize his or her own Instant Enlightenment (D). To worship any Buddha who merely represents the effect of Buddhist practice is not the true intention of Nichiren, and it is inconsistent with modern Nichiren Buddhist thought which should be grounded upon a radical Buddhist humanist understanding.

3. Instant Enlightenment is exclusively for ordinary people

The Mystic Law embodies the principle of "original cause -equals- original effect", which is the seed of enlightenment for eternal realization. This is the Dharma body which Nichiren selected as the Dharma body for all ordinary people in the Latter Day, and Nichiren himself, as the leader of the Bodhisattvas of the Earth, received it from the remotest past during the Ceremony in the Air in order to that he might propagate it in the Latter Day. The Bodhisattvas of the Earth should be considered to be all ordinary people within the Nine Worlds who emerge from the enlightened world of Buddhahood. Thus, they can be characterized with an ontological double structure in terms of both the principle of "the Nine Worlds -equals- the Buddha World" and in terms of their embodiment of the principle of Instant Enlightenment which "opens up Buddhahood in the bodies of all ordinary people".

That is to say, they share the same Mystic Law of the Simultaneity of Cause and Effect, which Shakyamuni had practiced as a bodhisattva in the remotest past. The eternal Buddha Shakyamuni and the Bodhisattva Jōgyō are therefore in apposition.

> This is about the *Honzon*, the *Kaidan* and the five characters of the *Daimoku* of the Essential Section which the Buddha practiced at the moment of attaining enlightenment. [...] His abode is the enlightened Land of Eternally Tranquil Light. *The abode of the Lord of Teachings is the everlasting entity of the three bodies without intention. And the same is true of his*

> *disciples.* On this occasion [of speaking of his eternal realization], the Buddha summoned the four bodhisattvas such as Jōgyō all the way from the depths of the Earth of Eternally Tranquil Light and transmitted [these secret laws] to them.
> (»On the Receiving of the Three Great Secret Laws«), p. 1021 / II. 984)

The Mystic Law which embodies the principle of "original cause -equals- original effect" is that which the Bodhisattva Jōgyō inherited and bears deep within his life, it is none other than the Dharma body by which *"all ordinary people attain the Buddha way"*. This idea is synonymous with the phrase found in chapter 2 of the LS: *"If there are those who hear the Law, then not one of them shall fail to attain Buddhahood"*. Nichiren quotes this phrase frequently and particularly refers to the attainment of Buddhahood by all ordinary people, e.g. as explained in his writing »Winter Always Turns to Spring (Letter to Lay Nun Myōichi)« (1275).

> Those who believe in the Lotus Sutra are as if in winter, but winter always turns to spring. Never, from ancient times on, has anyone seen or heard of winter turning back to autumn. Nor have we ever heard that a believer in the Lotus Sutra turned into an ordinary person. The sutra states, *"If there are those who hear the Law, then not one of them shall fail to attain Buddhahood"*. (p. 1253 / II. 536)

To chant Nam-myō-hō-ren-ge-kyō is the direct way to the realization of Instant Enlightenment and each ordinary person can be transformed into a "Bodhisattva Buddha" who exists in actuality by activation of the principle of cause and effect. In this way, Nichiren radically reinterprets the meaning of *"becoming a Buddha"*.

> When the Amida Buddha was *still an ordinary mortal*, it was through practicing the five characters of Myō-hō-ren-ge-kyō that he was able to attain Buddhahood. It is nowhere stated that he gained perfect enlightenment by reciting Namu-Amida-butsu. Myō-hō-ren-ge-kyō is that which opens up, and Namu-Amida-butsu is that which is opened up.
> (»The Superiority of the Daimoku over Amida's Name«, p. 115 / II. 1003)

> The Buddhas of the three existences of past, present, and future, when they were *still ordinary mortals*, all offered their lives to the Lotus Sutra and thus were able to become Buddhas. (»On Namu«, p. 1299 / II.1073)

For Nichiren, to become a Buddha always means to practice the Mystic Law as an ordinary person. There is no process of gradual development or step by step attainment. Consequently, no self-depreciation is implied when Nicheiren states:

> I, Nichiren, am an ordinary mortal at the nominal stage of identity.
> (»On the Buddha's Prophecy«, p. 507 / I. 400)

Thus, with respect to this:

> there is no Buddha other than each ordinary person
> who lives in this world of suffering and chants Daimoku.

4. The inter-relationship between Daimoku and chanting Daimoku

As for the "Daimoku" itself, we can distinguish between the "five characters of the Mystic Law" and the "seven characters of chanting the Mystic Law". In fact, Nichiren frequently uses both phrases interchangeably so that any difference in meaning between each of the phrases is often not apparent. This might suggest that Nichiren himself, although aware of the distinction which can be made between the meaning of each of the two phrases, nevertheless wished to stress their inseparability and interdependence. In other words, "the Dharma body that we practice" (five characters) is equal to "the practice of the Dharma body" (seven characters). For this Dharma body is the Mystic Law that represents the principle of Instant Enlightenment based on "Original Cause -equals- Original Effect". To practice the Mystic Law (cause) is to realize or to activate Buddhahood (effect). Nichiren saw the prototype of this process of the simultaneity of cause and effect in the event of Shakyamuni's Eternal Realization (B).

> The Original Enlightenment or Buddha nature inherent in one's life will be
> activated and manifested (effect) by practicing the Mystic Law (cause).
> This is thereby nothing but the manifestation of the Mystic Law of
> the Simultaneity of Cause and Effect itself.

Thus, in practicing we can observe on the one hand an identity of original cause and original effect, or the ordinary person and Buddha, while on the other hand we can observe a unity of person and law. These aspects need to be kept in mind, if we are to understand the multiple significance of the Daimoku itself, which is found inscribed not only at the very center of the Mandala Honzon but also represents its whole richness of meaning.

We have considered above the three-layered structure with reference to: the eternal Buddha (*the deepest layer B*), Nichiren (*the intermediate layer C*), and to ourselves (*the surface layer D*) (see above page 241).

As the practice of chanting Daimoku by all people in order to realize Buddhahood has a universal significance, it is necessary to emphasize not a particular Buddha representing original effect, but rather the Law for Sowing representing original cause. Nichiren considered that this could be explained by the three-phase process of Sowing, Ripening and Harvest. For the Mystic Law is the source of all Buddhas. As many fruit grow from one seed, so many Buddhas arise from one Mystic Law. In both cases, there is an identity between source and fruit.

> Even one seed, when planted, multiplies. [...] Though there is only one unlined robe, when it is presented in offering to the Lotus Sutra, it is offered to all 69,384 characters of the sutra, each of which is a Buddha. These Buddhas have [...] the revelation of [eternal realization] and the immeasurable life span as their lives, *the everlasting Buddha nature* as their throats, and the wonderful practice of the Single Vehicle as their eyes.
> (»Cloth for a Robe and an Unlined Robe« p. 970 / II. 602)

As the Buddha represents the fruit grown from the seed of Buddha nature, there is an ever-abiding significance to the three-phase process as it is by that very process that "everlasting Buddha nature" is unfolds. This aspect is addressed in the Gosho below:

> To illustrate, it is like seeds that sprout, grow into plants, and produce rice. Though the form of the rice changes, its essence remains the same. Shakyamuni Buddha and the written words of the Lotus Sutra are two different things, but their heart is one. Therefore, when you cast your eyes upon the words of the Lotus Sutra, you should consider that you are beholding the living body of the Tathāgata Shakyamuni.
> (»The Pure and Far-Reaching Voice (Reply to Shijō Kingo)«, p. 1122 / I. 333)

Furthermore, since the Mystic Law both represents and brings forth and unfolds Buddha nature, as Nichiren regarded it as all encompassing. It is "the seed of Ichinen Sanzen" from which all Buddhas grow. This aspect had already been expounded in such writings as »The Opening of the Eyes« and »Letter to Akimoto« (see the section above "The superiority of the Sowing in comparison to the Harvest", p. **Fehler! Textmarke nicht definiert.** f.).

By contrast, if a Buddha represents only the effect, then such a Buddha may serve as a particular model for attaining enlightenment, yet such a Buddha can never be a universal model for the practice of all ordinary people. For only a Buddha of Eternal Realization representing the source for all Buddhas can be a universal model for all ordinary people. Thus, it is imperative to understand the universal Mystic Law and the practice of chanting Daimoku as a Buddhism of Sowing. For this concerns the very form of practice by which self-realization can be actualized, it is not merely about the worship of a Buddha who is another person. Consequently, the most urgent task is for us to practice the Mystic Law of Sowing by ourselves in order to activate and unfold the Instant Enlightenment inherent within our own ordinary lives (D).

> Now in the Latter Day of the Law, only the teaching remains; there is neither practice nor proof. There is no longer a single person who has formed a relationship with Shakyamuni Buddha. Those who possessed the capacity to gain enlightenment through either the provisional or true Mahayana sutras have long since disappeared. *In this impure and evil age, Nam-myō-hō-ren-ge-kyō of the Life Span chapter, the heart of the Essential Section, should be planted as the seeds of Buddhahood for the first time in the hearts of all those who commit the five cardinal sins and slander the correct teaching.* [...]
> I, Nichiren, am an ordinary man at the nominal stage of identity. [...] I sow the seeds of Buddhahood with only the five characters [of Myō-hō-ren-ge-kyō].   (»The Teaching, Capacity, Time, and Country«, p. 1276 / I. 473)

> *Now, in the Latter Day of the Law, both the Lotus Sutra and the other sutras are of no use.* Only Nam-myō-hō-ren-ge-kyō [has the power of benefit to lead to enlightenment. ...] To mix other practices with this Nam-myō-hō-ren-ge-kyō is a grave error. A lantern is useless when the sun rises.
> (»The Teaching for the Latter Day (Reply to Ueno)«, p. 1545 / I. 903)

Both passages quoted above emphasize that the Buddhism of Sowing is the practice for the people in the Latter Day. When Nichiren says that even the Lotus Sutra is of no use, he reasons from the perspective of the Dharma body of Sowing selected as uniquely suited to the Latter Day. For only the chanting of the Mystic Law is identical to the "*Nam-myō-hō-ren-ge-kyō of the Life Span chapter*" (D).

The multiple meanings of the Daimoku can now be summarized as follows.

The "LS of the Latter Day" signifies:

(A) the "*five characters of Daimoku, Myō-hō-ren-ge-kyō*",
(B) but on a deeper level
- the "*Five Characters of Nam-myō-hō-ren-ge-kyō, the heart of the Essential Section of the Lotus Sutra*"   (»The Object of Devotion for Observing the Mind« and »Selecting the Essence of the Lotus Sutra«)
  or more precisely
- the "*five characters of the Daimoku of the Essential Section which the Buddha practiced at the moment of attaining enlightenment*"
  („On Receiving the Three Great Secret Laws«)

(C) The Daimoku can also be understood in terms of
- the "*five characters of the Daimoku entrusted to the Bodhisattva Jōgyō*"
  (»On the Five Principles of Propagation«, »Selecting the Essence of the Lotus Sutra«, and »The Heritage of the Ultimate Law of Life«).

(D) Finally, the Daimoku must have a unique meaning for all ordinary people in the Latter Day which can be expressed as the "Ichinen Sanzen in Actuality".

- *"The doctrine of Ichinen Sanzen is hidden in the depths of the Life Span chapter of the Essential Section"*; *"The doctrine of Ichinen Sanzen begins with the concept of the Mutual Containment of the Ten Worlds"*; *"Ichinen Sanzen represents the seed of enlightenment of all Buddhas"*

  (»The Opening of the Eyes«).

- *"This jewel of Ichinen Sanzen was wrapped in the five characters of the Mystic Law, which is indestructible like a diamond, and it has been left for all of us, the poor people of the Latter Day"*

  (»Reply to Ōta Saemon-no-jō«).

- *"The Three Great Secret Laws based on the Ichinen Sanzen just as found in the depths of the Life Span chapter"*   (»Letter to Gijōbō«)

"The seven characters of Daimoku, Nam-myō-hō-ren-ge-kyō" signify "the practice of chanting the five characters of the Mystic Law".

(B) Nichiren found this practice from a deep reading and understanding of Shakyamuni's Eternal Realization as narrated in the Life Span chapter. For Nichiren, this is nothing other than a manifestation of the enlightened world of Ichinen Sanzen based on the Mutual Containment of the beginningless Ten Worlds.

(C) In upholding the Mystic Law transmitted to him as Bodhisattva Jōgyō, Nichiren practiced only that Law which manifested the Instant Enlightenment of Ichinen Sanzen inherent within his own life.

(D) Finally, if we chant Daimoku, we can attain to a realization of the same enlightened life as Nichiren, although necessarily there will be individual differences, related to depth of understanding and commitment to practice, as well as differences related to personal and family karma.

Each one of us, the ordinary people of the Latter Day,
manifest the very same Immediate Enlightenment of Ichinen Sanzen
as that of both the Eternal Buddha and Nichiren himself.
Each one of us manifests the principle of
the "ordinary person as Buddha".
B = C = D.

Chapter 7
A systematic interpretation of the Gohonzon

1. Ambiguities in any theory of the Honzon with respect to the Person and the Law

Nichiren began to propagate his innovative teaching on the LS and to promote the practice of "Daimoku -equals- Chanting daimoku", which became standardized it in the form of the "Three Great Secret Laws of the Essential Section". Although his teaching was necessarily subject to change over the course of his eventful life, we have emphasized that the essential heart of his teaching nevertheless remained unchanged from the beginning of his public mission. The doctrinal foundation of his teaching is to be found in *the supreme principle of the Instant Enlightenment of Ichinen Sanzen based on the Mutual Containment of the Ten Worlds*. As for the *Honmon no Honzon*, Nichiren elaborated on its structure and particular characteristics in a systematic manner in »The Object of Devotion for Observing the Mind«. Nevertheless, it is important to note that Nichiren would seem to have conceived of the *"Three Great Secret Laws of the Essential Section"* at the beginning of his public mission, as can be seen in his early writing »On Reciting the Daimoku of the Lotus Sutra« (see above the quotation, page 265).

Next, we will consider some articles relevant to this matter published in »Lotus Buddhist Studies (*Hokke bukkyō kenkyū*) No. 21 & 22« (2015).

Kazuhiro Miura seeks to elucidate "the essence of the Honzon" and he distinguishes between *"the Person-centred Honzon"* and *"the Law-centered Honzon"*, a distinction he considers to be determined by how a particular Honzon has been inscribed (22: 69). Thoroughly exploring Nichiren's writings, he arrives at the concusion that *"as far as the theory of the Honzon before Sado is concerned, there is only reference to the concept of the 'lord of teachings'. There is no theory with respect to the Honzon"* (22: 74). Given this context, *"the doctrinal position of the superiority of the Law when compared to the Person represents an extraordinary innovation,"* in that the LS itself or the Daimoku has been made into the Honzon, i.e. the Law itself becomes the focus of devotion, as Nichiren expressly states in »On Reciting the Daimoku of the Lotus Sutra« (22: 73). Against this background, Miura considers each form of the Honzon in each period before and after Sado. In conclusion, he states:

> Because even in »The Object of Devotion for Observing the Mind« there are expressions affirming both a Person-centered and a Law-centered Honzon, any judgement in favor of one or the other (or both) might be

permitted as appropriate. This uncertainty has caused difficulty for any theory of the Honzon in our time. (22: 78 and 83).

Similarly, when referring to the relationship between the Bodhisattvas of the Earth and the Daimoku at the center of the Mandala Honzon, Kōdō Shikata, a Nichiren-Shōshū-related scholar, raises a doubt that *"wholly consistent conceptions are to be found in Nichiren's writings"* (21: 268).

Taking the above observations seriously, I consider that three problematic issues remain:
- ✓ Is it not so that doctrinal confusion on the theory of the Honzon has led to a proliferation in the variety of forms which have been established as objects of worships (as can be seen in many Nichirenshū-affiliated temples)?
- ✓ Is it not so that any method which classifies a Honzon only as Person-centered or as Law-centered is simply not able to provide a coherent theory of the Honzon?
- ✓ Is it the inconsistency found in Nichiren's writings or our own intellectual limitation which leads us to find many ambiguous or contradictory conceptions in the Gosho?

Nevertheless, as I see it, Nichiren himself has in fact left us a heritage of clear and coherent doctrine: so, I will attempt to outline his theory of the Honzon in a systematic manner. I am proposing a hermeneutical method by way of classification of the distinct levels of interpretation found in Nichiren's discourse. For example, using this method of multiple reading, what Miura implies by the "Person-centered Honzon" can be best understood at the level of Literal Reading, i.e. from the perspective of the superiority of the LS over against all other sutras as well as from the perspective of the superiority of the Essential Section over against the Theoretical Section (A & B). By contrast, the "Honzon based on the Daimoku" is understood by Nichiren from the perspective of a Deeper Contemplative Reading (C & D). However, in reality, neither the Person-centered nor the Law-centered Honzon can exist alone. For Nichiren, the Daimoku means the practice of we ourselves chanting daimoku, whereby both aspects are ceaselessly present in the unity of Person and Law.

Incidentally, Miura misses the implication of the inclusion of the "four Bodhisattvas of the Earth" on the object of worship, as understood in »On Reciting the Daimoku of the Lotus Sutra« (see 21: 73). Taking into consideration that this Gosho war written in 1260 before Sado, it seems to me only natural that these four leaders of the Bodhisattvas of the Earth should gain a special significance not only because of their entrustment with the Law during the Ceremony in the Air, but also because Nichiren himself had given them a special significance, given the Three Great Secret Laws. This is an interpretation on the level of a contemplative reading of the Essential Section, which Nichiren understood to be crucially important in the period after Sado.

Consequently, only after Sado did Nichiren inscribe all the Ten Worlds on the Mandala Honzon, so that the enlightened world of Ichinen Sanzen could be made manifest in a concrete form on the Gohonzon. At the same time, by emphatically emphasizing the perspective of a Contemplative Reading of the Essential Section, Nichiren consolidated several aspects of his teaching expounded prior to Sado into his final teaching, the practice of which is to "chant the daimoku before the Ten Worlds Mandala Honzon."

2. Three different types of Gohonzon

In order to explicate Nichiren's doctrinal development, the changes he progressively made to the form of the Gohonzon will be briefly summarized here:[30]

1) The so-called "toothpick Honzon" (No. 001) was inscribed on October 9, 1271, in Echi shortly after the persecution at Tatsunokuchi. Nichiren used a small piece of twig torn a tree branch to write only the Daimoku of Nam-myō-hō-ren-ge-kyō and the two Sanskrit syllables symbolizing *Fudō* and *Aizen* to the right and left.

2) The so-called "Gohonzon transmitting the quintessence" (No. 028) inscribed in December 1274 consists of the Daimoku only, other than some phrases from the LS. Nichiren appears to have inscribed this, the simplest form of the Mandala for this period, in order to bestow it

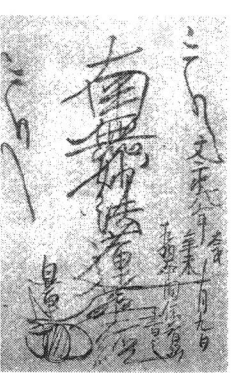

No. 001

No. 028

---

[30] For the various forms of the Gohonzon, I cite the 123 mandalas listed in Japanese: http://juhoukai.la.coocan.jp/mandara/mandaraitiran.html. Though some internet sites seem to have been deleted, there is still reference to 125 of Nichiren's Mandalas:
https://www.youtube.com/watch?v=CB3fTV74yco&feature=youtu.be.

Given the composition and structure of the Honzon both in the form of Mandalas and Statues, Toshitaka Takahashi classifies them in seven types such as 1) the Law-centered Honzon with Daimoku only, 2) the Shakyamuni Buddha alone or with four Bodhisattvas, 3) the two Buddhas in the Treasure Tower with four Bodhisattvas, … and 7) the ten worlds mandala in the sense of the Object of Devotion for Observing One's Mind. However, I personally consider that only the Ten Worlds Mandala as Gohonzon expresses Nichiren's ultimate intention.

upon his followers some time after he wrote »On Reciting the Daimoku of the Lotus Sutra«, i.e. between 1260 and 1272.

The Mandala (No. 002 till 007), dated 16. June 1272, includes the two Buddhas inscribed as Namu-Shakyamuni-Butsu and Namu-Tahō-Nyorai on each side of the Daimoku.

3) In case of the Mandala (No. 012), which was presumably given to Abutsubō in 1274, and the Mandala (No. 017) with is inscribed with Nichirō's signature, the four Bodhisattvas have been added. This results in the form of the Treasure Tower with Two Buddhas and Four Bodhisattvas, yet the central focus point in the Buddha diptych are always the seven characters of the Daimoku.

4) The so-called "Gohonzon of Ichinen Sanzen" (No. 008) includes on each side of the two Buddhas other bodhisattvas, as well as Demon Mother and her Children. A phrase from Miao-lo concerning Ichinen Sanzen (see above page 196) is also inscribed on each side.

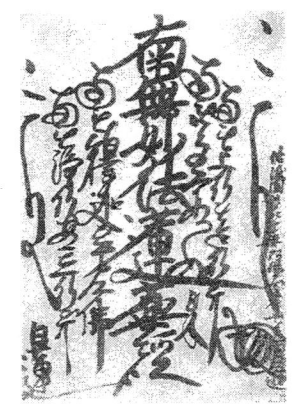

No. 012

5) In the Mandala known as the "Honzon for the realization of Buddhahood by women" (No. 009), which was presumably given to Sennichi-ama, and which is also designated the "First manifestation of the Honzon on Sado" (authenticity established), dated July 8, 1273, representations of all Ten Worlds are included.

6) In later Mandala Honzons such as the so-called "Deathbed Gohonzon" (No. 081), dated March 1280, and the so-called "Gohonzon for transmitting the Dharma" (No. 101), dated November 1280, in addition to the Ten Worlds the four Heavenly Kings are included. Thereby, Nichiren's Mandala Honzon attains to its final form.

Consequently, the Mandalas which Nichiren inscribed have a variety of characteristics reflecting a progressive elaboration over the course of his public mission. We can classify them into three basic types, which represent the three steps Nichiren employed in order to express the essence of the LS.

No. 101

1) The "essential version of the Gohonzon" which represents earliest and simplest form, inscribed with the Daimoku only or sometimes with additional Sanskrit letters to the right and left.
2) The "abbreviated version of the Gohonzon" which is inscribed with the Daimoku and the two Buddhas. With the addition of the four Bodhisattvas, this type is designated as that with "One Tower with two Buddhas and four Bodhisattvas".
3) The "comprehensive version of the Gohonzon" inscribed with representations of the Ten Worlds and the Four Heavenly Kings, dating from the period after Sado.

Not only for historical reasons but also from a doctrinal perspective, it is important to consider the differences between these three types of the Gohonzon, which at the same time highlight significant characteristics which apply to each Mandala Gohonzon when considered as a focus for devotion. Consequently, we can once again employ three hermeneutical levels, i.e. B, C, and D, in order to analyze the multilayered structure of the Gohonzon. Level B refers to the "enlightened world" envisioned in the Essential Section of the LS itself and the Gohonzon can be understood as reflecting each of these three layers of meaning.

3. The significance of the "essential version of the Gohonzon"

Chanting Daimoku is the primary practice for our times

The essential version of the Mandala honzon represents the simplest form and is inscribed with the Daimoku along with only the Sanskrit seed-syllables for the Vajrayana deities, Fudō and Aizen, to the right and left. As noted above, Nichiren's writing »On Reciting the Daimoku of the Lotus Sutra« describes this early form of the Gohonzon, and we find reference to the significance of the Daimoku as follows:

> The two characters of myōhō of the Daimoku contain within themselves the heart of the Lotus Sutra, namely, the doctrine of Ichinen Sanzen set forth in the "Expedient Means" chapter, and the doctrine of the Buddha's attainment of enlightenment in the far distant past set forth in the "Life Span" chapter. [...]
>
> All Buddhas are emanations of the one Buddha, Shakyamuni. Therefore, [...] they are all brought together within the two characters of the Mystic Law. For this reason, the benefits to be gained by reciting the five characters of Myō-hō-ren-ge-kyō are great indeed. All the Buddhas, all the daimoku of the various sutras, are opened up and merged in the Lotus Sutra.

> Taking notice of *this opening up function of the Mystic Law*, one should recite the daimoku of the Lotus Sutra. (p. 13 / II. 228)

Even at this early stage in his mission, Nichiren was already proclaiming the daimoku of the Lotus Sutra as that practice appropriate for the Latter Day (A), which he understood as the Mystic Law based on the Ichinen Sanzen of Shakyamuni's Eternal Realization (B). This formulation with respect to the Daimoku indicates the supreme doctrine of the Instant Enlightenment of Ichinen Sanzen. Chanting Daimoku is the primary practice and this understanding remained consistent throughout Nichiren's mission.

> As for the rules to be followed in worship, one should always *sit upright when in front of the object of devotion*. Once one leaves *the place of practice*, however, one can continue to practice as one wishes every time and everywhere if one walks, stands still, sits, or lies down. As a daily practice, one should *chant the Daimoku, Nam-myō-hō-ren-ge-kyō*. (ibid.)

With respect to the Honzon, Nichiren had a tolerant attitude as long as the Lotus Sutra or its core teaching contained in the Daimoku is at the center as the object of devotion. He seemed to be relatively open to other forms.

> One should [use] the eight volumes of the Lotus Sutra, or one volume, or one chapter, or one may inscribe simply *the daimoku of the Sutra*, for use as the object of devotion, as is indicated in the "Teacher of the Law" and the "Supernatural Powers" chapters of the Sutra. And those persons who are able to do so should also *write out the names of the Tathāgata Shakyamuni and the Buddha Tahō, or fashion images of them, and place these on the left and right of the Lotus Sutra*. And if they are able to do so, they should also fashion images or write out the names of the Buddhas of the ten directions and the bodhisattva *Fugen* (Universal Worthy) and the others. (ibid.)

These ambiguous remarks with respect to the shape and structure of the Honzon might lead to some misapprehensions about the Gohonzon. However, it is most important to remember that for Nichiren the chanting of Daimoku always meant not only the chanting of Nam-myō-hō-ren-ge-kyō before the Honzon but also meant the chanting of Daimoku at all times and places. For the essence or core concept behind the Honzon is the Daimoku of the Lotus Sutra, the source of enlightenment for all Buddhas.

Here we will consider in more detail the essence or core concept behind the Honzon, when viewed from some different perspectives.

How to deal with the statue of Shakyamuni Buddha

The core concept behind the Honzon is *"the Lotus Sutra or its Daimoku"* (»On Reciting the Daimoku of the Lotus Sutra«), *"the Lotus Sutra or the daimoku of the Lotus Sutra"* and *"the lord of teachings of the Lotus Sutra"* (»Questions and Answers on the Object of Devotion«) as well as the *" Shakyamuni the lord of teachings of the Essential Section"* (»On Repaying Debts of Gratitude«). In each case, the "Lotus Sutra" is identified as being superior to the pre-Lotus Sutra teachings, while the *"lord of teachings Shakyamuni of the Essential Section"* indicates the superiority of that Buddha to the Buddha of the Theoretical Section.

When Nichiren moved from Seichōji to Kamakura in 1254, he settled down in a hermitage in Matsubagayatsu. Shortly after he submitted his remonstrance on the religious policy of the Shogunate, »On Establishing the Correct Teaching for the Peace of the Land«, his hermitage was attacked by a group of soldiers and Nenbutsu followers on August 27, 1260. In referring to this event, Nichiren speaks of his devotion to a statue of Shakyamuni Buddha.

> And on another occasion the little retreat where I was living, where I had enshrined a statue of Shakyamuni Buddha as the object of worship, and where I stored the texts of the various sutras, was attacked and destroyed, and the statue of the Buddha and sutra texts were not only trampled upon but thrown into the mud and filth.
> (»Rulers of the Land of the Gods«, p. 1525 / II. 623)

In February 1279, although the Mandala Honzon had first been inscribed for some time, Nichiren praised Nichigennyo who had ordered to build "a wooden statue of Shakyamuni Buddha.

> I have inscribed the Gohonzon for your protection. I have previously received two thousand coins, and now receive another thousand from my lay supporter, Lady Nichigen-nyo, *who fashioned the wooden statue, three inches in height, of Shakyamuni Buddha, the lord of teachings in the threefold world.*
> (»Concerning the Statue of Shakyamuni Buddha Fashioned by Nichigen-nyo«, p. 1187 / II. 811)

Nichiren's followers seem to have embraced the idea that they should worship Shakyamuni Buddha as revealed in the Life Span chapter, while Nichiren emphasized that this Buddha is the original source for all Buddhas in his letter. In the same letter, Nichiren stresses this aspect further.

> Shakyamuni Buddha is like the moon in the sky, and the various other Buddhas, bodhisattvas, and beings are like the reflections floating on ten thousand different bodies of water. Thus, a person who fashions a single image of Shakyamuni Buddha is in effect making images of all the Buddhas of the worlds in the ten directions.
> (ibid., p. 1188 / II. 812)

As these examples demonstrate, Nichiren seems to have readily accepted even the statues of Shakyamuni Buddha as one variant of the Honzon as long as it represented the eternal Buddha Shakyamuni of the Life Span chapter. This doctrinal stance can best be understood in terms of the superiority of the Essential Section when compared to the pre-Lotus Sutra teachings and the Theoretical Section.

Shakyamuni as the Buddha of Ichinen Sanzen

Nevertheless, it does not follow that such a form of worship offered to the eternal Buddha Shakyamuni represents the true intention of Nichiren. Even while indulgent of a wide variety of forms of worship and shifts in perspective, the core of the Mandala Honzon always remains the Daimoku at its center, the prominent seven characters of Nam-myō-hō-ren-ge-kyō. Nichiren never inscribed *Nam-hokekyō* (devotion to the Lotus Sutra), *Nam-myōhō* (devotion to the Mystic Law), or *Nam-Shakamuni-Butsu* (devotion to the Buddha Shakyamuni) nor *Nam-kuonjitujō-Shakuson* (devotion to the eternal Buddha Shakyamuni). By contrast, the seven characters of Nam-myō-hō-ren-ge-kyō has an ambiguous fullness, which embraces utterly the notion of the Lotus Sutra, the two characters of Myōhō and the five characters of Myō-hō-ren-ge-kyō, as well as the eternal Buddha Shakyamuni.

Interestingly, Nichiren similarly praised Toki Jōnin's construction of a Buddha statue in his writing "Concerning the Statue of Shakyamuni Buddha Made by Toki« (1270) before his Sado exile. However, we need to pay attention to Nichiren's reasoning at the beginning of his letter.

> With regard to the statue of Shakyamuni Buddha you have made, in fact you have made and revealed *the Buddha of Ichinen Sanzen found within one's heart*, which since time without beginning had never been revealed!
> (p. 950 / II. 354)

Nichiren considered that the Buddha statue represented the *"Ichinen Sanzen found within one's heart"* if the Buddha of the Life Span chapter is understood from the perspective of a Contemplative Reading of the Essential Section (B). This particular point of view becomes more obvious, as noted above, when the Ten Worlds Mandala Honzon is interpreted with such phrases as

- *"the true doctrine of Ichinen Sanzen based on the principle of the Mutual Containment of the beginningless Ten Worlds"* (»The Opening of the Eyes«),
- *"the Shakyamuni Buddha of the Essential Section, the lord of teachings, endowed with the original and natural three bodies"* (»On Repaying Debts of Gratitude«, »The Opening of the Eyes«).

> The eternal Buddha Shakyamuni can be respected due to the superiority of Essential Teaching to all other teachings. However, he should not be made to the object of worship for our current times.

Daimoku as the power of transformation

From the perspective of a *Contemplative Reading of the Essential Section for the Latter Day*, the seven characters of Nam-myō-hō-ren-ge-kyō are, as already stressed above, understood in terms of the supreme principle of the Instant Enlightenment of Ichinen Sanzen in Actuality. By chanting Daimoku Instant Enlightenment will be activated in the body of an ordinary person. This fundamental position remained unchanged over the course of Nichiren's life after the proclamation of daimoku.

By also inscribing the two Vajrayana deities of Fudō and Aizen at each side of the Daimoku at the center of the Honzon, Nichiren radically transformed the literal meaning of the Daimoku as simply the "title of the Lotus Sutra". For it powerfully enhanced the significance of the Daimoku for practice. It thereby underlines the belief that it is only by chanting Daimoku that Buddhahood can be activated in the Nine Worlds of all ordinary people. The fact of Instant Enlightenment activated by chanting Daimoku amounts to a radical principle of spiritual transformation, which both deities represent:

Na m(u) myō hō ren ge kyō

Aizen — *Fudō*

> *Fudō* represents the transformation of the physical pains of birth, aging, illness and death into blissful liberation, while *Aizen* represents the transformation of the suffering of the "three mental poisons", ignorance, desire and aversion, pride and envy, into enlightenment.

Both in body and in mind we can overcome every kind of difficulty and attain to a happy and fulfilled life by chanting daimoku, that is to say, by activating our life force and wisdom, as well as by purifying all delusion and negative karmic tendencies. For this is the core belief behind the practice of Nichiren Buddhism.

Incidentally, the principle of transforming the three poisons into a purgative medicine is a doctrine which derives from Nāgārjuna, the key intellectual source behind the Mahayana philosophy of emptiness. Primarily because of his understanding of Nagarjuna, Nichiren considered the Mystic Law of the

Lotus Sutra to be best defined in terms of the "doctrine of immediate enlightenment of all ordinary people", as can be seen in his writing »On Attaining Buddhahood in One's Present Form (Reply to the wife of Ōta)« (1275).

> Regarding the character myō in the five characters Myoho-renge-kyo, [...] only Bodhisattva Nāgārjuna got to the very heart of this character by interpreting it in his »Treatise on the Great Perfection of Wisdom« as "[The Lotus Sutra which is] like a great physician who can change poison into medicine".
>
> The *"poison"* in the above passage indicates the first two of the four noble truths, the "truth that all existence is suffering" and the "truth that suffering is caused by selfish craving as well as by karmic cause and effect which binds living beings to the sufferings of birth and death". These are truly the poisons to outdo all poisons. But the ultimate function of "myō" (mystic) is to change this poison by way of transforming the "sufferings of birth and death into nirvana" and "earthly desires into enlightenment". The good medicine deserves its reputation when it can change poison into medicine. (p. 1006 / II. 585)

4. The Law-centered Honzon attended by the eternal Buddha

As for the "abbreviated version of the Gohonzon", there are other than the particular Mandalas dating from the Sado period, two forms which consist of statues of the "One Buddha and Four Bodhisattvas" or the "One Tower with the Two buddhas and the Four Bodhisattvas." These are still popular in the Nichirenshū temples. Yet I want to consider whether these forms can meet the intention of Nichiren himself.

The One Buddha and the Four Bodhisattvas

Kōki Shibusawa, priest of Nichiren Shū and researcher, comments on this Honzon style:

> The Honzon style of the One Buddha and the Four Bodhisattvas was held to be the standard form in the so-called "Ōsaki Study" which had been carried out predominantly among the scholars of Risshō University, as this style served to make clear that the One Buddha is the eternal Buddha Shakyamuni. (21: 207)

In support for this particular interpretation of the Honzon, reference is made to the phrase below, found in »The Object of Devotion for Observing the Mind«, which has been much esteemed by advocates of the Buddha-centered Honzon.

CHAPTER 7

> 此時地涌千界出現本門釈尊為脇士一閻浮提第一本尊可立此国。
> （『観心本尊抄』、昭定 720 頁、御書 254 頁）

Nichiren wrote many of his writings in Sino-Japanese characters, as in the above quotation, and thereby left room for varied kinds of interpretations depending on where commas are placed in order to make meaningful phrases. For example, in the above phrase there is no comma between the units of meaning and it is difficult to clearly discern who is the attendant to whom.

The English translation of WND states as follows.

> At this time the countless Bodhisattvas of the Earth will appear and establish in this country the foremost object of devotion in the entire world, which *depicts Shakyamuni Buddha of the Essential Section attending [the eternal Buddha]*.
> (p. 254 / I. 376)

This translation reflects a particular interpretation, but the key question is the last sentence which refers to the relationship between the Bodhisattvas of the Earth (Jōgyō) and the eternal Buddha. Who attends whom? The English translation appears to assume the traditional interpretation of NS, according to which the "eternal Buddha" indicates Nichiren himself. In which case, should Nichiren, the eternal original Buddha, appear as the rebirth of **Jōgyō in the Latter Day, attended by** Shakyamuni Buddha of the Essential Section? And should this Buddha be represented on the Mandala Honzon? Yet such a reading doesn't make much, given its ambivalent meaning. For Shakyamuni Buddha of the Essential Section does not appear in the Latter Day and Nichiren himself cannot be the eternal original Buddha.

To return to the traditional understanding as found in the Ōsaki Study, Miura, himself a Nichirenshū-affiliated scholar, considers the relationship discussed above in the same way. Thus, *"Shakyamuni Buddha appears attended by the Bodhisattvas of the Earth"* (22: 75). Further, he understands it as that relationship which is represented on the Honzon based on the "theory of the teaching lord", i.e. the Buddha.

And, in fact, there is no doubt that during the Ceremony in the Air, the Bodhisattvas of the Earth are portrayed as attendants to the eternal Buddha Shakyamuni, flanking the prominent characters of the Daimoku itself.

> This true object of devotion looks like this: The Treasure Tower dwells in the air above the Sahā world [...]; Myō-hō-ren-ge-kyō appears in the center of the tower with the Buddhas Shakyamuni and Tahō seated to the right and left, and, flanking them, the four bodhisattvas, followers of Shakyamuni, led by Jōgyō.
> (ibid., p. 247 / I. 365)

Jōgyō appears at the dawn of the Latter Day

However, we have been considering a description from the LS whose meaning transcends a literal reading and which should more correctly be understood by way of a contemplative reading of the Essential Section (B). For on such a reading, it foretells the fact that Nichiren will appear as a rebirth of Jōgyō in order to inscribe the Gohonzon (C). Prior to the above quotation, Nichiren speaks of the matter of *"the seed of Buddhahood, Ichinen Sanzen"* and of *"Shakyamuni in our heart"*, as well as of *"the transmission of the Mystic Law of the Essential Section to the Bodhisattvas of the Earth"* (p. 253 / I. 373). It is this which they will emerge to propagate.

> In the Middle Day of the Law, [great teachers like] Nan-yüeh and T'ien-t'ai [...] expounded [the doctrine of Ichinen Sanzen] in principle, but they did not establish the actual practice of the five characters of Nam-myō-hō-ren-ge-kyō and the object of devotion of the Essential Section. [...]
>
> Now, at the beginning of the Latter Day of the Law, [...] At this time the Bodhisattvas of the Earth appear in the world *for the first time* solely to bring the medicine of the five characters of Myō-hō-ren-ge-kyō to the ignorant people of the Latter Day. (ibid., p. 253 / I. 373)

Jōgyō is entrusted with the mission to initiate the "practice of chanting daimoku before the Gohonzon" in order that all ordinary will attain to the Instant Enlightenment of Ichinen Sanzen. In order to particularly emphasize this, Nichiren radically distinguished between *"the Essential Section of Shakyamuni's lifetime and that revealed at the beginning of the Latter Day"*.

> Shakyamuni's, however, is the Buddhism of the harvest, and this is the Buddhism of sowing. (ibid., p. 249 / I. 363)

The Mystic Law entrusted to Jōgyō is for sowing the seed of enlightenment, that is, for the Instant Enlightenment of Ichinen Sanzen for all ordinary people of the Latter Day (B, C, and D). Consequently, there is no need to worship the eternal Buddha Shakyamuni who represents the Buddhism of the harvest. Nor will this Buddha appear in the Latter Day. So, it is nonsensical to expect Jōgyō to accompany the eternal Buddha.

In the Buddhism of Sowing only the practice of chanting daimoku is required for the people of the Latter Day to realize the supreme principle of the Instant Enlightenment of Ichinen Sanzen.
For it is for this purpose alone
that Jōgyō has appeared to inscribe the Mandala-Gohonzon
in order to bring to complete the ultimate practice of chanting daimoku based on the Three Great Secret Laws.

Nichiren employs the narrative pattern of Jōgyō's appearance in the Latter Day as quoted above.

> Now, at the beginning of the Latter Day of the Law, [...] At this time the Bodhisattvas of the Earth appear in the world for the first time solely to bring the medicine of the five characters of Myō-hō-ren-ge-kyō to the ignorant people of the Latter Day. (ibid., p. 253 / I. 373)

Further, a similar understanding is expressed in the same Gosho.

> The bodhisattvas emerging from the earth [...] are certain to *appear at the beginning of the Latter Day*. [...] "This good medicine" is the heart of the "Life Span" chapter, or Nam-myō-hō-ren-ge-kyō, which is endowed with [the *fivefold significance* of] name, body, doctrine, function, and teaching. (ibid., p. 251 / I. 372)

Likewise, in the »Letter to Shimoyama« (1277).

> The great bodhisattvas emerging from the earth will *appear at the beginning of the Latter Day of the Law* to teach all the living beings of the entire world to chant the five characters of Nam-myō-hō-ren-ge-kyō, which are the heart of the "Life Span" chapter of the Essential Section. (p. 346 / II.688)

As these examples demonstrate, Nichiren consistently employed a narrative pattern which held that at the dawn of the Latter Day the Bodhisattva of the Earth Jōgyō will appear to proclaim the "Mystic Law = chanting daimoku" to all ordinary people.

With respect to this, amongst the Mandala Honzons inscribed by Nichiren there is one Mandala of particular interest, the so-called "*Mannenkugo no Daihonzon*" (No. 016), dated December 1274. This is unique in that as it also includes a laudatory inscription which expresses Nichiren's own self-identification with Jōgyō, along with the usual characteristics found on other Mandalas.

> More than 2,220 years have passed after the passing of the World-Honored One. Despite this, this Daihonzon does not yet exist among the three countries of India, China and Japan. Either it was unknown or although known it has never been propagated. Our merciful father kept it secret with his wisdom and left it for the Latter Day. *In the age after the [fifth of the] five hundred years, Bodhisattva Jōgyō has appeared in the world to propagate this for the first time.*
> Inscribed in December 1274 on [Mt. Minobu]

Who is Attending whom?

In this context, we need to consider what is meant by *"attending upon someone"*. In fact, the answer can be found in the phrase which Miura himself quotes from »The Object of Devotion for Observing the Mind«.

> During the two millennia of the Former and Middle Days of the Law, statues were made to represent *the Shakyamuni Buddha* of Hinayana, thereby *making* Manjushrī and Universal Worthy *his attendants*. *The Shakyamuni Buddha* of the provisional Mahayana, the Nirvana Sutra, and the Theoretical Section of the Lotus Sutra *made* Mahākāshyapa and Ānanda *his attendants*. Even though statues and paintings were made of Shakyamuni Buddha during the two millennia, no image or statue was made of *the Buddha of the "Life Span" chapter*. Only in the Latter Day of the Law will the representation of that Buddha appear. (p. 247 / I. 367)

Given this way of thinking, a rather simpleminded interpretation of the text would be as follows: "the Honzon makes Shakyamuni Buddha of the Essential Section *its attendant*". For clarity, I will punctuate the sentences thus:

> 此時地涌千界出現、本門釈尊為脇士一閻浮提第一本尊、可立此国

It then reads:

> At this time the countless Bodhisattvas of the Earth will appear and establish in this country the foremost object of devotion in the entire world, *which makes Shakyamuni Buddha of the Essential Section its attendant*.
> (p. 254 / I. 376)

This should be understood as:

> When the Bodhisattva Jōgyō appears in the Latter Day, he will not make the eternal Buddha Shakyamuni the object of worship (B),
> but he will establish the object of devotion
> centered upon the Mystic Law transmitted by himself (C).
> Only in this way can Nichiren establish the Buddha way for all ordinary people to realize the Instant Enlightenment of Ichinen Sanzen (D).
> In this respect Shakyamuni Buddha of the Essential Section represents a prototype for the "Tathāgata of Nam-myō-hō-ren-ge-kyō",
> based on the "principle of original cause -equals- original effect" and in "unity with the Mystic Law".
> The eternal Buddha serves as the foundation to the practice of the Mystic Law and thereby represents the primordial foundation of
> the Ten Worlds Mandala Honzon itself.

Given this understanding, the Daimoku in the center of the Mandala Honzon represents the person of the eternal Buddha Shakyamuni himself chanting the Mystic Law, while the whole Mandala reveals the "enlightened world" (B). Since this Mystic Law is transmitted through the Mandala (C), we, all ordinary people in the "world of suffering" of the Latter Day, can practice the Mystic Law and attain to a realization of our own enlightened state of life (D).

Consequently, it is not the case as Miura states that *"Shakyamuni Buddha appears attended by the Bodhisattvas of the Earth"* (22: 75). For in the Latter Day the eternal Buddha does not appear in actuality, only Jōgyō does. Nor can this Buddha attend upon Jōgyō in the Latter Day, as Nichikan of NS claimed. For in this context, the Eternal Buddha is of significance only in relation to the object of devotion which Jōgyō will establish.

5. Concerns about the use of statues of "the one Buddha and the four bodhisattvas"

One more important aspect is the relationship of the one Buddha and the four Bodhisattvas. Miura refers to the passage below, especially the phrase that *"Only in the Latter Day of the Law will a representation of that Buddha appear"* (»The Object of Devotion for Observing the Mind«, p. 247 / I.367).

> During the two thousand years of the Former and Middle Days of the Law, [...] bodhisattvas and teachers constructed images of and built temples and pagodas to the Buddhas of other worlds or to the Shakyamuni Buddha of Hinayana, of provisional Mahayana of the pre-Lotus Sutra teachings, or of the Theoretical Section of the sutra. No one in India, China, or Japan, however, neither rulers nor subjects, revered *the object of devotion of the "Life Span" chapter of the Essential Section and the four great bodhisattvas*. (ibid.)

Miura reads the last sentence as *"indicating the form of the One Buddha and the Four Bodhisattvas"* (22: 76). However, before this phrase, Nichiren speaks of the entrustment of the Mystic Law to Jōgyō, the characteristics of the Honzon to be established and its appearance in the Latter Day. Subsequently, Nichiren goes on to speak about the propagation of the Mystic Law as entrusted to Jōgyō for the people in the Latter Day. Yet it is clear that the "four Bodhisattvas" referred to together with the Honzon do not signify those inscribed on the Honzon itself. Rather, they refer only to the Bodhisattva Jōgyō who will appear to establish the Honzon in the Latter Day. For this is exactly the same context in which the "four Bodhisattvas" are given a particular significance in connection with the Three Great Secret Laws.

In »The Votary of the Lotus Sutra Will Meet Persecution«, dated January 1274, Nichiren outlined for the first time the nature of the Three Great Secret Laws.

> [Though Nāgārjuna and Vasubandhu] understood the meaning of the Lotus Sutra in their hearts, they did not declare it in words. [...] T'ien-t'ai and Dengyō went so far as to expound it, but they left unrevealed *the object of devotion of the Essential Section*, **the four bodhisattvas**, *the sanctuary*, and *the five characters of Nam-myō-hō-ren-ge-kyō*.
>
> Their reasons were, first, because the Buddha had not transferred these teachings to any of them, and second, because the time and the people's capacity did not satisfy the requirements. Now the time has arrived, and **the four bodhisattvas** will surely make their advent. I, Nichiren, was the first who knew this. (p. 965 / I. 449)

Thus T'ien-t'ai and Dengyō had left the mission of establishing the Three Great Secret Laws only to the person who was authorized to undertake it. Nichiren understood himself to be the person so authorized to establish the Mystic Law, entrusted to Jōgyō, in the form of the Three Great Secret Laws.

Miura considers the Honzon with the "one Buddha and four Bodhisattvas" as an example of a honzon belonging to the "category related to the lord of teachings" (22: 76). Yet this type of Buddha-centered Honzon can never manifest the supreme principle of the Instant Enlightenment of Ichinen Sanzen based on the principle of the Mutual Containment of the Ten Worlds, either on the level of Shakyamuni's Eternal Realization (B), or in the sense of Jōgyō's secret enlightenment (C), or on the level of our practice of chanting daimoku (D).

Hanano comments that *"there are in Nichiren's writings many statements about Shakyamuni Buddha of the Essential Section as the object of devotion, but no statement about statues of the one Buddha and four Bodhisattvas as the Honzon"* (14: 29).

Nor do I believe that Nichiren ever considered that the worship of the eternal Buddha could of itself lead to the attainment of Instant Enlightenment. Isn't that the case?

6. Is the Eternal Buddha identical to Shakyamuni Buddha in the Treasure Tower?

In the last two sections, with respect to Jōgyō's mission in the Latter Day as described in »The Object of Devotion for Observing the Mind«, we criticized the appropriateness of a Honzon comprised of "one Buddha and four Bodhisattvas", as understood by Shibusawa and Miura. We will now revisit this issue from a rather different perspective.

Shikata does not accept the Standard Showa reading which has transcribed the relevant sentence as *"the Bodhisattvas of the Earth appear and become attendants to Shakyamuni Buddha of the Essential Section"* (21: 264). As an alternative, he reads the sentence in the same way as the traditional sectarian scholars of NS Taisekiji, so that the sentence is read as *"Shakyamuni is the attendant of the Daimoku itself found at the center of the Mandala Honzon"* (ibid.: 265). His reason for this is that the Eternal Buddha is identified with Shakyamuni Buddha sitting within the Treasure Tower.

Curiously, on the level of a literal reading, the Eternal Buddha himself does not participate in the Ceremony in the Air nor is he inscribed on the Mandala Honzon. Shakyamuni simply relates the story about his Eternal Realization thereby revealing his true identity. The Daimoku at the center may signify Shakyamuni Buddha, but then there are only the "seven characters of Nam-myō-hō-ren-ge-kyō", not the "five characters of Myō-hō-ren-ge-kyō" nor "Nam-the eternal Shakyamuni Buddha". For there is only one Shakyamuni inscribed on the Gohonzon, as the ordinary form of the Mandala endowed with the Ten Worlds demonstrates, just as is described in »The Object of Devotion for Observing the Mind«.

> Myō-hō-ren-ge-kyō appears at the center of the tower with the Buddhas Shakyamuni and Tahō seated to the right and left. (p. 247 / I. 365)

So, is Shakyamuni within the Tower identical to the Eternal Buddha?
Nichiren makes a clear distinction between the two Buddhas.

> Both the teachings before the Lotus Sutra and the Theoretical Section of the Lotus Sutra itself tell us that Shakyamuni Buddha, *the lord of teachings*, attained enlightenment for the first time in this world. [...]
> Now, the Essential Section of the Lotus Sutra says that Shakyamuni Buddha, *the lord of teachings*, attained Buddhahood uncountable major world system dust particle kalpas ago, and that the cause that made this possible was the practice he had carried out at that time. (p. 243 / I. 357)

Shakyamuni is at the same time both the Buddha of Initial Enlightenment and the Buddha of Eternal Realization. As innumerable wondrous Bodhisattvas emerged from the depths of the earth, the participants at the Ceremony of the Earth suspected that the vast wisdom and compassion of their master was undoubtedly other than the Shakyamuni of Initial Enlightenment.

> As for these great bodhisattvas who have appeared from the earth, *what kind of Buddha is their teacher? Surely, he must be a Buddha who is incomparably superior to Shakyamuni*, Tahō, and the emanation Buddhas from the ten directions! (»The Opening of the Eyes«, p. 211 / I. 253)

Shakyamuni Buddha of Initial Enlightenment is just one manifestation of the eternal Buddha.

However, both of them are designated the lord of teachings, as the passage above the a.m. quotation has established. Thus, Shakyamuni within the Tower is also known as the lord of teachings.

> Shakyamuni Buddha, the lord of teachings, and Tahō Buddha sit side by side in the Treasure Tower like the sun and moon, and the Buddhas who are emanations of Shakyamuni come from the ten directions and are ranged beneath the trees like so many stars. (ibid., p. 225 / I. 272)

Nichiren speaks of Shakyamuni as if he is both the historical Buddha sitting in the Treasure Tower and the original Buddha representing the source of his many emanations. Are they identical?

Again, Shakyamuni is the lord of teachings from India and sits in the Treasure Tower.

> In India, when Shakyamuni Buddha, the lord of teachings, was preaching the Lotus Sutra as described in the "Treasure Tower" chapter, he summoned all the various Buddhas and had them take their seats upon the ground. Only the Tathāgata Dainichi (Mahāvairochana) is seated within the Treasure Tower, on the lower seat to the south, while Shakyamuni Buddha was seated on the upper seat to the north. [...] Shakyamuni Buddha, *the lord of teachings*, sits in the seat above Tahō Buddha who had made a disciple of the Tathāgata Dainichi (Mahāvairochana) in each Realm. This Shakyamuni Buddha is known as a *practitioner of the Lotus Sutra*. (»On Repaying Debts of Gratitude«, p. 310 / I. 712)

In this passage, Shakyamuni Buddha is portrayed as the greatest Buddha surpassing all other Buddhas, including Tahō Buddha who is attended by his disciple the Tathāgata Dainichi in the Tower. The superiority of Shakyamuni is based on his eminence as a *"practitioner of the Lotus Sutra"* (A). This dimension opens up a new perspective from which to understand Nichiren's unique understanding of Shakyamuni as both Buddha of initial enlightenment and Buddha of Eternal Realization yet as *identical* with respect to their practicing the Mystic Law of the Instant Enlightenment of Ichinen Sanzen (A=B). This represents Nichiren's ultimate perspective of a deeper contemplative reading for the Latter Day. Thus:

> Not only each Shakyamuni Buddha (A, B), but also Jōgyō, Nichiren (C), and we ourselves (D) all share the same true identity
> as the votary of the Lotus Sutra based on the Instant Enlightenment
> of Ichinen Sanzen by chanting daimoku
> (A=B=C=D).

Now, as "Shakyamuni" within the Treasure Tower retains his dual identity as the Buddha of Initial Enlightenment and the Buddha of eternal realization, "the lord of teachings" is seated within the Tower as "Shakyamuni" as an attendant to the daimoku at the center, as Shikata suggests. Yet in this case, the seven characters of the Daimoku at the center, the Mystic Law representing Eternal Realization, would appear to be separated from the Buddha practicing the Law. Consequently, the question remains at to whether the Daimoku at the center represents the Law alone or the unity of the Person and the Law. Given the dual identity of Shakyamuni, we should regard Shakyamuni within the Tower as manifesting his actual identity at the moment of his eternal realization. As a result, we can accept that Shakyamuni Buddha within the Tower manifests his *dual identity* as both the Buddha of Initial Enlightenment and the Buddha of the eternal realization. We can discover this subtle distinction in the passage quoted below:

> I, Nichiren, was the first to spread the Mystic Law entrusted to Bodhisattva Jōgyō for propagation in the Latter Day of the Law. Though he alone was so empowered, I was also the first, to construct [the object of devotion] by inscribing *Shakyamuni Buddha* who represents the *primordial Buddha* as revealed in the "Life Span" chapter of the Essential Section, Tahō Buddha who appeared when the "Treasure Tower" chapter of the Theoretical Section was preached, and the Bodhisattvas of the Earth who arrived with the "Emerging from the Earth" chapter.
> (»The True Aspect of All Phenomena«, p. 1359 / I. 384)

And in fact, Nichiren did inscribe the Mandala-Gohonzon by depicting the Ceremony in the Air, with its participants including both the two Buddhas and the four Bodhisattvas. However, at the moment when Shakyamuni spoke of his Eternal Realization in the remotest past, he thereby revealed his true identity as "the primordial Buddha." In this respect, the central Daimoku manifests the Eternal Realization of this primordial Buddha (B).

With respect to this primordial layer, each of the two Buddhas can be further distinguished, each being identified with one of the two universal aspects of Instant Enlightenment, as realized by the primordial Buddha Shakyamuni.

> A commentary states that "the profound principle of the true aspect is the originally inherent Myō-hō-ren-ge-kyō". [... This can be explained also in terms of] the two aspects of reality and wisdom. Tahō stands for reality, *Shakyamuni for wisdom*.
> (»Earthly Desires Are Enlightenment (Reply to Shijō Kingo)« of 1272, p. 1117 / I. 318)

This way of understanding Shakyamuni Buddha within the Tower definitely transcends his identity as the historical Buddha of Initial Enlightenment. Indeed, it suggests that in some sense he should be considered the eternal Buddha symbolizing "wisdom". At this level of a deeper contemplative reading, the central Daimoku would be regarded as the Mystic Law for Instant Enlightenment in the Latter Day (D).

> On the primordial layer of interpretation of the Mandala,
> the Daimoku at the center represents eternal realization.
> In this context Shakyamuni within the Tower
> can be considered to be the eternal Buddha (B)
> who also represents the "wisdom" which realizes enlightenment (D).
> The relationship between Shakyamuni within the Tower and
> the Daimoku representing Eternal Realization (B) can also be understood
> to apply to the relationship between Nichiren himself (signature) and
> the Daimoku representing the realization of Instant Enlightenment (C).

However, although the above might be understood by a variety of interpretations, and although Shakyamuni Buddha within the Treasure Tower does speak of his own eternal realization, nevertheless Shakyamuni should not be considered to be the eternal Buddha himself. Rather, the Daimoku at the center represents Instant Enlightenment understood as "Shakyamuni's eternal realization."

As we are now considering the characteristics of the Mandala Honzon, we should take a closer look at the following passage from »The Object of Devotion for Observing the Mind«.

> As to the five characters of Nam-myō-hō-ren-ge-kyō, the heart of the Essential Section of the Lotus Sutra, Shakyamuni Buddha [...] summoned from beneath the earth the great bodhisattvas as numerous as the dust particles of a thousand worlds and, as he preached the eight chapters, transferred it solely to them. *This true object of devotion looks as follows:*
> The Treasure Tower dwells in the air above the sahā world governed by *the original Buddha*; Myō-hō-ren-ge-kyō appears in the center of the tower with the Buddhas *Shakyamuni* and *Tahō* seated to the right and left, together with *the four bodhisattvas, followers of the world-honored Shakyamuni, led by Jōgyō*[31]. (ibid., p. 247 / I. 366)

---

[31] WDN's translation states: "Myō-hō-ren-ge-kyō appears at the center of the tower with the Buddhas Shakyamuni and Tahō seated to the right and left, and, *flanking them, the four bodhisattvas, followers of Shakyamuni,* led by Jōgyō." This interpretation doesn't take account of the distinction between "Shakyamuni Buddha" in the Tower and the "world-honored Shakyamuni" (*Shakuson*),

With respect to this passage, I would like to clarify some aspects. First, Nichiren says that "Shakyamuni Buddha" transferred the "five characters of Nam-myō-hō-ren-ge-kyō" to the Bodhisattvas of the Earth. Strictly speaking, the Mystic Law doesn't belong to him, but to the eternal Buddha Shakyamuni. So, if Shakyamuni Buddha is able to transfer it, he can do so only in his dual identity as the eternal Buddha or, alternatively, on behalf of the Eternal Buddha, although necessarily this similarly highlights *the dual identity of Shakyamuni within the Tower*.

Further, *"this* true object of devotion[32]*"* refers to the Mystic Law with which Jōgyō has been entrusted to propagate. On a superficial literal reading the transmission of the Law has taken place, although on the level of a deeper contemplative reading Jōgyō has been carrying the Law originally deep within himself from the eternal past. Thus, *"this true object of devotion"* refers to the Honzon which Nichiren in his capacity as Jōgyō would inscribe.

One further important matter needs to be addressed. The Treasure Tower which dwells in the air above the sahā world is the domain of *"the original Buddha"*, surely indicating the eternal Buddha. The Buddha *Shakyamuni* sits to the left of the Daimoku at the center of the tower. *"The four bodhisattvas"* sit to the right and to the left, yet not as followers of *Shakyamuni*, but as the original eternal disciples of *"the world-honored Shakyamuni"*, himself the eternal Buddha. They are sitting at the same level as the Buddhas Shakyamuni and Tahō on the Mandala Honzon. Thus, Nichiren makes a clear distinction between Shakyamuni who speaks of Eternal Realization and the Eternal Buddha Shakyamuni.

Given this context, we will revisit the passage which makes reference to the Three Great Secret Laws found in the writing »On Repaying Debts of Gratitude«.

> Japan and the other countries throughout the entire world should all *make Shakyamuni Buddha of the Essential Section their object of devotion.* In that case, the *Shakyamuni* and Tahō who sit together in the Treasure Tower, all the other Buddhas, and the four bodhisattvas headed by Jōgyō, will act as attendants to *this Buddha.* (p. 328 / l. 735)

The *"Shakyamuni Buddha of the Essential Section"* is understood here as the object of devotion in that not only the four bodhisattvas but also the two Buddhas within the Tower serve as his attendants (B).

---

whose followers are the four Bodhisattvas of the Earth. They don't flank the two Buddhas, Shakyamuni and Tahō, but the Eternal Buddha or the Daimoku.

[32] WDN's translation uses the term *"the* true object of devotion" as though Nichren himself spoke of it only in general terms. It misses the essential point as who will inscribe and which Law will be inscribed in the form of the Honzon.

The reason for this we find in the writing »On the Three Great Secret Laws« in which Nichiren speaks of Shakyamuni'.

> The Honzon, the Kaidan and the five characters of the Daimoku of the Essential Section *which the Buddha practiced at the moment of attaining enlightenment.* (p.1021/ -)

> The doctrine of Ichinen Sanzen *which* the great world-honored *Shakyamuni practiced at the moment of attaining enlightenment in the remotest past.* (p. 1023 / -)

This means that the One or the Three Great Secret Laws have been established on the foundation of the supreme doctrine of the Instant Enlightenment of Ichinen Sanzen which the eternal Buddha practiced at the moment of his eternal realization. The Mandala Honzon therefore manifests the enlightened Dharma World of Ichinen Sanzen and this can be only actually made visible in the form of the Mandala endowed with all Ten Worlds.

It is most plausible to understand
the whole Mandala Honzon as the manifestation of that enlightened state attained by *the eternal Buddha Shakyamuni (B).*

Consequently, although Shakyamuni Buddha speaks of his Eternal Realization in the Life Span chapter in terms of the Eternal Buddha representing the Mystic Principle of the Original Effect, in fact he is not the same Buddha as the Eternal Buddha (B).

In so far as the structure of the Mandala Honzon is concerned, the Eternal Buddha cannot be identical to Shakyamuni Buddha within the Tower. Consequently, the sentence in question does not mean, as Shikata states, that "*Shakyamuni becomes the attendant of the Daimoku at the center of the Mandala Honzon*" (22: 265).

7. The relationship between the Daimoku and the Eternal Buddha

In a symposium Hanano referred to "*Shakyamuni Buddha of the Essential Section*" (»On Repaying Debts of Gratitude«) and posed the question as to how "the relationship between this Buddha and the Law of Nam-myō-hō-ren-ge-kyō" should be understood (21: 197). I myself would agree with the opinion of most of the participants, i.e. to "regard the Great Mandala of Ichinen Sanzen as the object of devotion in the Unity of Person and Law" (ibid.: 203). However, I would also stress the dimension of "Action", i.e. that *Shakyamuni's*

Eternal Realization is actualized by chanting daimoku. The enlightened state of life represents the world of Ichinen Sanzen, in that all the Ten Worlds are mutually contained in beginningless Buddhahood. Consequently, the practice of chanting daimoku manifests the Original Cause, while the Original Effect is Instant Enlightenment in terms of "the ordinary person -equals- Buddha". From the perspective of a contemplative reading of the Essential Section, it would be correct to consider "the Great Mandala as the 'One Buddha' manifest as the 'Tathāgata Nam-myō-hō-ren-ge-kyō'" (ibid.: 198), but this aspect also suggests the prototype for attaining to enlightenment (B).

Further, from the perspective of a contemplative reading of the Essential Section for the Latter Day, this same principle should be applied equally to all ordinary people chanting daimoku (D). In this sense, all who chant daimoku should be known as "Tathāgata Nam-myō-hō-ren-ge-kyō", be they the eternal Buddha Shakyamuni, the Bodhisattvas of the Earth, and all the participants at the Ceremony in the Air, as well as all ordinary people in the Latter Day, who like Nichiren chant daimoku before the Mandala Honzon.

This means, as noted frequently above, *"the Shakyamuni Buddha of the Essential Section is to be made the object of devotion"* is the Eternal Buddha of the Life Span chapter to be distinguished from all other Buddhas expounded in the pre-Lotus Sutra teachings, as well as the Theoretical Section of the LS. However, transcending this level of interpretation, the Eternal Buddha of the Ceremony in the Air should be understood to have gained a more universal significance by the inscription of the Mandala Honzon for the Latter Day (B). Consequently, *"the Shakyamuni Buddha of the Essential Section"* manifests as the central Daimoku representing the principle of Instant Enlightenment and the enlightened life of the wisdom body, which immediately with the whole Mandala Honzon represents the enlightened Dharma World, Ichinen Sanzen based on the Mutual Containment of the Ten Worlds.

Further, importantly, Shakyamuni's revelation of his true identity opens up a radically new perspective on the Ceremony in the Air which is itself revealed as the "everlasting pure land of beginningless Ichinen Sanzen". Doesn't this enlightened world signify the "body" or the essence of the Eternal Buddha Shakyamuni?

In interpreting the complex signification of all aspects of the Mandala Honzon, the central Daimoku signifies the Mystic Law representing the source of all the Buddhas, including the Eternal Buddha himself, no, more exactly the chanting of the Mystic Law. From the perspective of a contemplative reading of the Essential Section, the seven characters of Nam-myō-hō-ren-ge-kyō at the center of the Mandala Honzon indicates Shakyamuni's chanting of the Daimoku (B). However, from the perspective of its significance for the Latter Day, Shakyamuni's Eternal Realization is to be re-interpreted in terms of a universal principle for the attainment of enlightenment, so that it will be activated here and now and the beginningless primordial Buddha will be made manifest from within us (C, D).

To summarize the last two sections:

➢ On a superficial literal reading, Shakyamuni Buddha within the Treasure Tower is the Buddha who reveals his true identity, which is the manifestation of his dual identity as both Shakyamuni Buddha and the Eternal Buddha. Consequently, he is also known as "the Shakyamuni Buddha of the Essential Section". Thus, Shakyamunis Buddha has the dual identity as the Buddha of Initial Enlightenment and as the Buddha of Original Enlightenment. Nevertheless, both Buddhas represent the aspect of effect.

➢ The inscription of Shakyamuni Buddha on the Mandala Honzon from the perspective of a contemplative reading of the Essential Section, indicates his sitting within the Treasure Tower and his speaking of his eternal realization. Nevertheless, he is not the Eternal Buddha himself. For it is the central Daimoku which signifies the attainment of his eternal realization, representing Instant Enlightenment and eternal Buddhahood (B). The whole Mandala Honzon represents Ichinen Sanzen based on Instant Enlightenment. And it is these aspects which are distinguished from Shakyamuni Buddha within the Tower.

➢ We will discuss this aspect in detail later, but Nichiren himself understood the two Buddhas within the Tower to represent the two aspects of wisdom and reality. Their fusion is an expression of exactly that state of life which is made manifest when the Instant Enlightenment of Ichinen Sanzen takes is activated by chanting the Mystic Law. For this "fusion of wisdom and reality" (*Kyōchi-myōgō*) is an expression of the enlightened state of life of the Eternal Buddha. It takes concrete form as the unity of Person and Law at the primordial level of the Mandala Honzon. Consequently, Shakyamuni Buddha within the Tower cannot signify the Eternal Buddha himself.

➢ Thus, the sentence in question refers to the eternal Buddha, and this Buddha is manifested as the Mandala Honzon understood in terms of the unity of Person and Law (B). However, when Jōgyō appears and transmits the Mystic Law in the form of the Mandala Honzon for all ordinary people in the Latter Day, he brings the universal Law for the Sowing to the foreground (C). Consequently, the eternal Buddha representing this unique aspect of original effect is pushed into the background as a support for the universal wonderful Law. For Jōgyō who appears in the Latter Day can never be an attendant to the eternal Buddha in the actual world.

➢ "Shakyamuni Buddha of the Essential Section" represents Instant Enlightenment based on the principle of Original Cause and Original Effect understood in terms of the Unity of person and law, as manifested by his Eternal Realization (B). So far, he is identical with the Tathāgata Nam-myō-hō-ren-ge-kyō. Thus, each of those who chant the Mystic Law in the Latter Day should equally be regarded as a votary of the Lotus Sutra as each will manifest identical qualities as those of the Tathāgata Nam-myō-hō-ren-ge-kyō, activating the Instant Enlightenment of Ichinen Sanzen based on the Mutual Containment of the Ten Worlds (C, D). This enlightened state of life is reflected in the Ten Worlds Mandala Honzon (D).

8. An Appropriate Limit to any worship of the sect's founder

As considered above, Shikata employs a traditional NS sectarian approach when interpreting the sentence in question above, perhaps in order to give some form of doctrinal foundation to the theory of Nichiren as the eternal original Buddha: *"the leader of the Bodhisattvas of the Earth, Jōgyō, makes the Shakyamuni Buddha of the Essential Section his attendant"* (21: 267). However, this thesis is based on an assumption that Nichiren was "the Tathāgata of the Wisdom Body at the Original Beginning in the Remotest Past" who thereby should be considered to be more fundamental than Shakyamuni Buddha of Eternal Realization and, further, that this original Buddha would subsequently appear as Nichiren, a rebirth of Jōgyō in the Latter Day. This represents a mythological understanding of *the descent of a deity to earth*. Further, it is not appropriate that a Bodhisattva should make the eternal Buddha his attendant. This particular mode of understanding by extension culminates in the worship of the founder of the sect, yet here it is especially incoherent, given the absurdity of the claim that Nichiren himself is the only true Buddha for the Latter Day of the Law.

Without a doubt, Nichiren sought to transmit to us the practice of the Mystic Law for our Instant Enlightenment and did not demand that we worship either himself, Shakyamuni Buddha or the Eternal Buddha, as the object of devotion. Nichiren identified himself with Jōgyō and transmitted the Mystic Law, with which he was entrusted, in the form of the Three Great Secret Laws. Nichiren did powerful assert a claim as to his own unique role and the paramount importance of his mission in the Latter Day (C). Thus:

> Nichiren, the votary of the Lotus Sutra is more precious than Shakyamuni Buddha, the lord of teachings.   (»Letter to Shimoyama«, p. 363 / II. 710)

But, the above assertion by no means legitimates the theory that Nichiren is the only true Buddha based on a particular understanding of the doctrine of Eternal Original Buddha.

As to the statue form *one Buddha with four bodhisattvas*, this surely represents a viewpoint of Shakyamuni Buddha of Eternal Realization from the perspective of a literal reading. In this case, a particular form of faith in, and worship of, the Eternal Buddha is embraced. Shikata refers to this form and an alternate form, consisting of *two Buddhas with the four bodhisattvas* (21: 269 f.).

Additionally, Shibusawa noted the existence of a form of *one tower with two Buddhas and four bodhisattvas* and remarks that in all three cases frequently *"the Great Mandala has been installed behind these statues while the statue of the founder Nichiren is set in front of them"* (21: 207). In each case, a form of faith which incorporates worship of the founder seems evident.

The Honzon style consisting of one tower, two Buddhas, and four Bodhisattvas with a Mandala behind them and a statue of Nichiren in front of them

At this point, I will give a brief outline of the different doctrinal orientations found within the Nichiren school. I have attended many times the Gongyo service at Nichirenshū temples and I have gained the impression that Gongyo has a highly-ritualized orientation, comprising a litany of recitations from different chapters of the Lotus Sutra. Hanano calls this style of practice *"the expansive practice of Odaimoku"* (ibid.: 205) because *"Nichiren Shū considers the Daimoku (the One Great Secret Law) as its essential practice and therefore accepts a variety of objects of worship"* (ibid.: 211). By contrast, he denotes the style of practice of NS and SG as *"the restrictive practice of the Honzon"*. Yet, curiously enough, I never observed in a Nichiren Shū Gongyo service the ardent daimoku recitation as normally found in NS and SG, although Nichiren Shū does have additional Shōdaikai meetings of lay believers under the guidance of priests.

Under my system of classification of the distinctive hermeneutical levels, I would categorize the faith and practice style of Nichiren Shū as "that centered around a literal reading of the Lotus Sutra". With regards to the practice style of NS, although the Dai-gohonzon is conceived of in terms of the Oneness of Buddha and Dharma, the form of faith is based on the theory that Nichiren is the Eternal Original Buddha. Thus, this style of practice can be regarded as a type centered around the eternal Buddha, and on the doctrinal level as "that type centered around a deeper contemplative reading of the Essential Section". Yet in contrast to this "faith in the Buddha and the

Founder centered around the Personal aspect of the Honzon", I would consider a more authentic and profound faith and practice to be that of "a type centered around a deeper contemplative reading of the Essential Section for the Latter Day". Such a faith requires the exclusive chanting of daimoku as the essential practice for us ordinary people to realize Instant Enlightenment, along with faith in the Gohonzon which is centered around the Mystic Law of the Instant Enlightenment of Ichinen Sanzen based on the Mutual Containment of the Ten Worlds (D).

9. Toward a theory of Nichiren as true Buddha in the sense of "ordinary person as Buddha"

The significant unity between the central Daimoku and Nichiren's Signature

Further, underlying the understanding that *"the leader of the Bodhisattvas of the Earth, Jōgyō, makes Shakyamuni Buddha of the Essential Section his assistant"*, Shikata speculates that the theory on Nichiren as original Buddha may have become prominent as it is based on a form of Mandala Honzon characteristic of the period after 1280, in which *"the Daimoku and the signature of Nichiren form a unity"* (21: 267). With respect to this, Miura notes an interesting fact that *"after the writing of »Questions and Answers on the Object of Devotion« (1278) the aspect of the Person became barely manifest on the Honzon"* (22: 84). Referring to this writing, he introduces an idea of the late Kōdō Yamashita who claimed to see *"a change in Nichiren's thinking, which is related to the change in his signature"* (ibid.) This refers to Nichiren's signature which moved from left to center directly beneath the Daimoku at the center of the Mandala Honzon. Can this change explain the genesis of the theory on Nichiren as Original Buddha reflected in the doctrine of the "Oneness of Buddha and Dharma"?

First, I would emphasize that Nichiren did push his ultimate doctrinal position to the fore in his later years on Mt. Minobu as he had inscribed the Ten Worlds Mandala Gohonzon for the realization of Instant Enlightenment. In the passage quoted above, taken from »The Teaching for the Latter Day (Reply to Ueno)«, written in the same year as »Questions and Answers on the Object of Devotion«, Nichiren made a very bold statement:

> Now, in the Latter Day of the Law, both the Lotus Sutra and the other sutras are of no use. Only Nam-myō-hō-ren-ge-kyō [has the power to benefit and to lead to enlightenment]" (p. 1545 / II. 903).

As a further example let's have a look at the Mandala-honzon (No. 92) inscribed for Jaku-nichibō, a disciple of Nikkō, on May 8, 1280. Nichiren's signature is clearly at the center directly under the central Daimoku. This gives a vivid impression of the oneness of Daimoku (law) and Nichiren (person). However, I would like to offer a correction to the theory on Nichiren as original Buddha by a critique based on Nichiren's own ultimate doctrinal position grounded in his view on such ideas as *the superiority of the Sowing over against the Harvest, a contemplative reading of the Essential Section for the Latter Day, and the Instant Enlightenment of all ordinary people.*

Above, I have already summarized the three-layered structure of the Mandala Honzon: in Section "6The four-layered dimensional structure of the Gohonzon"; in Chapter "4. From the perspective of a Contemplative Reading of the for the Latter Day" (see above page 240 f.). I would like to summarize once again:

➢ For all ordinary people in the Latter Day of the Law, who no longer have a direct relationship to the eternal Buddha Shakyamuni (B), Nichiren establishes the Mystic Law as transmitted to Jōgyō in the form of the Three Great Secret Laws (C). In this capacity, Nichiren should be considered to be the master of the Mystic Principle of the Original Cause who brought this Mystic Law to the fore. This is in order that we ourselves are able to realize the Instant Enlightenment of Ichinen Sanzen by chanting daimoku (D).

➢ Further, as the Mystic Law represents the supreme principle of enlightenment based on the Mutual Containment of the Ten Worlds, we can ourselves manifest the same enlightened state of life in our current circumstances, i.e. as "ordinary people as the true Buddha", just like the founder Nichiren (B = C = D).

➢ To put it in a different way, Nichiren discovered the supreme principle of the Instant Enlightenment of Ichinen Sanzen based on the Mutual Containment of the beginningless Ten Worlds in the realization of eternal enlightenment by Shakyamuni (B) and inscribed it in the form of the Ten Worlds Mandala Honzon for observing one's own mind. This Mandala manifests the same enlightened state of life as Nichiren himself in his capacity as Jōgyō. Thus, Nichiren is the primary exemplar both of practice and effect, based on the Ichinen Sanzen of Actuality in the Latter Day (C).

As emphasized above, in section "5. The Three Great Secret Laws as inherited by Jōgyō" (see above page 260 f.), Nichiren's unique self-understanding can be seen in two of his writings from his later years on Mt. Minobu:

> I inherited the ultimate secret Law from Shakyamuni Buddha, the lord of teachings, at Eagle Peak, and I preserve it secretly in my fleshy thorax.
> («The Person and the Law (Reply to Nanjō)», p. 1578 / I. 1097)

> At the beginning of the period of more than 2.000 years [after Buddha's passing] in my capacity as the leader of all the numerous Bodhisattvas [of the Earth] I, Nichiren, certainly received these Three Great Secret Laws by oral transmission from the lord of teachings [Shakyamuni].
> («TheThree Great Secret Laws», p. 1022 / II. 987)

Thus, Nichiren regularized Jōgyō's inheritance of the Secret Law in the form of chanting daimoku before the Ten Worlds Mandala Honzon.

➢ Further the final form of "Nam-myō-hō-ren-ge-kyō Nichiren" at the center of the Mandala Honzon signifies the fact that Instant Enlightenment has actually been activated in the person of Nichiren as he chants Daimoku. The unity of person and law is thereby made manifest and Nichiren himself manifests as the true Buddha. Of course, strictly speaking, this Buddhahood should only be understood after the model of an "ordinary person as Buddha", who alone can exist in actuality. Without a doubt, Nichiren is the founder of Nichiren Buddhism and the lord of the teachings in the Latter Day, who demonstrated the power of chanting daimoku by overcoming all difficulties and *transforming the sufferings of birth and death into nirvana and earthly desires into enlightenment, as well as the world of suffering into the enlightened world* (C).

Next, it is necessary to develop a more complete understanding on the practice of the Mystic Law for all ordinary people in the Latter Day. With respect to this, the form and character of the Gohonzon and the significance of the Daimoku at its center, will be interpreted initially on the "surface" (D). These issues will be discussed later in the next chapter.

Making a single individual a prototype for all without distinction

Here, I will emphasize that aspect which Nichiren himself consistently maintained as essential, i.e. the "practice of chanting daimoku before the Mandala-Honzon". This can be conceived as a form of universal "meditation practice" for the realization of enlightenment by all ordinary people. Briefly, in support, I would make reference to the Gosho »The Unanimous Declaration by the Buddhas« (1279), as representative of a particular form of practice which is known as "the perfect and immediate meditation (*endon shikan*) for the Latter Day" in traditional Tendai Buddhism.

➢ In this Gosho, Nichiren repeatedly affirms a world view of the unity of all phenomena with their essence by stating that the "Buddhahood" of our own lives, of the whole of nature and of all Buddhas is identical. This essential entity is known as the "Tathāgata of Original Enlightenment". However, this term can be rather confusing as it gives the impression of a personal entity creating and sustaining the entire universe. Yet all traditional Buddhist terms, such as the Tathāgata, Buddhahood or Dharma nature are related to this essential entity which is universal and permanently existing without beginning and without end and transcendent of any kind of distinctions and discriminations. For ease of understanding, it is better to translate such terms into a more contemporary form, such as "cosmic life" which Ikeda inherited from Toda. The term "five elements or agents" which is employed in the quotation below refers exactly to the universal components of all phenomena and it makes it relatively easy for us to perceive our body in the fullness of its cosmic existence, a manifestation of that very cosmic life.

> The five elements are earth, water, fire, wind, and space. [...] They are thus equivalent to the five characters Myō-hō-ren-ge-kyō. These five characters are what make up the entity of the individual human being, and hence that entity exists eternally in its original state, it is the *Tathāgata of Original Enlightenment*. [...] Ordinary people who follow *the teaching of perfect and immediate meditation* understand this truth from the beginning of their Buddhist practice, and therefore they are able to *realize Instant Enlightenment*, to enjoy that state of being which is indestructible like a diamond. (p. 567 / II 849 f.)

➢ The statement that "My body is a Tathāgata of Original Enlightenment" indicates an identity and fusion with cosmic life and thus underlines the insight that "I am a part of the universe." It refers to the level of observing Buddhahood (cosmic consciousness) which is inherent in our own lives. Our Instant Enlightenment is attained when we realize that our life is a manifestation of cosmic life and when we become aware that we are connected to the whole of nature and the universe. This insight into our own lives is of universal and egalitarian validity, as the attainment of enlightenment is open to all without distinction.

> The Lotus Sutra speaks of [the appearance, the nature and the entity of the *Tathāgata of Original Enlightenment* ...]. The Ten Factors pervade the Ten Worlds. These Ten Worlds are born from the mind of the individual and constitute the eighty-four thousand teachings. *Here a single individual*

> *has been used as an example, but the same thing applies equally to all living beings.* (p. 564 / II 844)

➢ In the same way as "*taking an individual person as an example*," and although the Shakyamuni of Eternal Realization might surely serve as the prototype for Instant Enlightenment, we should also take Nichiren's faith and behavior as exemplary for our own life of faith and behavior. However, since Buddhahood is universally without distinction and intrinsic to each of our own lives, any thought of restricting faith to the worship of Nichiren himself (or any Buddha or Bodhisattva) necessarily conflicts with Nichiren's own true intention.

➢ When our heart or Ichinen is in unity with cosmic life, the realization that this cosmic entity is inherent to our own lives means that there is no longer any need for a "gradual progress in meditation practice," as it is better understood as Tendai's ultimate teaching of "perfect and immediate meditation".

> The sentient beings and the environment of the Ten Worlds are the Buddha of the Dharma body, one who possesses the virtue of the three bodies in a single entity. Once one has understood this, one will fully realize that all phenomena are the Buddhist Law. This state is called the *nominal stage of identity*. From this one proceeds onward directly to the attainment of Buddhahood. Thus, in the teaching of perfect and immediate enlightenment there are no successive stages of practice. (p. 566 / II. 847 f.)

The meaning of this term "the nominal stage of identity" has been explained previously at footnote 8 (see above page 49) of Part 1, Chapter 4. Each of us who embrace the Mystic Law and chant daimoku enters into this stage as it is there that the realization of Instant Enlightenment is assured.

➢ The realization of Instant Enlightenment has two significant meanings of "immediately at this moment" and "in the present form just as you are". This implies that there is never any requirement to renounce and destroy the spiritual darkness of ignorance and all carnal desires which that are normally regarded as the root of suffering in life. No, on the contrary, spiritual darkness is not separate from Dharma nature, the essential nature of phenomena, just as carnal desires themselves do not exist separate from enlightenment. Consequently, to cut off all these apparently negative aspects of life would be to deny any possibility of spiritual development, of openness to the Dharma nature and of the attainment of enlightenment.

> The Tathāgata of Original Enlightenment becomes one's own body and mind. [...]. While one fails to understand this, one is in a state of ignorance. [...]. When one wakes to and understands this mind, this is called awakening to the essential nature of phenomena. Thus, *ignorance and awakening*

> *are simply different names for this single mind. [...] there is only the one mind. Therefore one should not cut off or do away with ignorance.*
> (p. 564 / II 844)

➤ The teaching of transforming an ordinary person into a Buddha by immeasurably long-term austerities designed to eliminate all the carnal desires is known as a provisional teaching for "the instruction of others". By contrast, the Lotus Sutra alone represents a teaching for "practicing as one's self" or for "observing one's own mind" for it directly reveals that enlightenment which was attained by the Buddha himself as a result of his own practice.

> One should know that immediate enlightenment is not to be found anywhere outside one's own body. Though the mirror of one's own mind and that of Buddha's mind are the same mirror, we cannot see our own true nature because we are looking at the back of the mirror. For this reason, we are said to be deluded by the spiritual darkness of ignorance. On the contrary, the Tathāgata looks at the front of the mirror and observes the principle underlying his own nature. [...]
> The doctrines for instructing others are like looking at the back of a mirror, while the practice of observing one's own mind for the realization of enlightenment is like looking at the front of a mirror.   (p. 570 / II. 852)

Chanting Daimoku is like a practice of looking at a mirror from the front, which reflects our own enlightened state of life. To worship the eternal Buddha Shakyamuni or Nichiren, regarded as the true Buddha, cannot therefore be the object of practice.

➤ From the perspective of a literal reading, Nichiren divides all the teachings of Shakyamuni into provisional teachings for the instruction of others and into the true teaching of practice for one's self. However, they are opened up from his ultimate perspective by a "Contemplative Reading of the Essential Section for the Latter Day", in which they are integrated into the exclusive *"practice of chanting daimoku for one's self and others"*. The proclamation and propagation of this exclusive practice was Nichiren's true intention and his unshakable determination.

> It represents the original intention for which the Buddhas of the three existences made their appearance in the world, the direct way for attaining Buddhahood by all living beings.   (p. 572 / II 856)

Some examples of substituting another's name for Nichiren's signature

Consequently, there is no doubt that Nichiren, for those of us who follow his teachings, is the great master in our contemporary age. Nichiren

Daishōnin deserves our ultimate respect as the primary exemplar of an ordinary person as true Buddha. Yet, although it might sound most inappropriate, shouldn't we perhaps substitute own name for Nichiren's signature on the Mandala Honzon, in order to thereby observe more easily our own enlightened state of life? I mean by this not only that we can observe our own enlightened state of life reflected in the mirror of the Mandala, but also that we take Nichiren as our primary exemplar, whom we seek to follow as Bodhisattvas of the Earth.

With respect to this, there is an interesting fact: Nichirō, Nisshō and Nichijō (Toki Jōnin) inscribed their own Mandalas after Nichiren's death and pointedly inscribed their own name in place of Nichiren's signature directly under the central Daimoku (see Mandara 2017). Further, Nichiren was designated as *"Nam-Nichiren-Shōnin"* or *"Nam-Hossu-Daishi"*, placed beside *Dengyō-Daishi* on the Honzon. This form of amendation seems to have reflected their particular understanding that each of us who chant daimoku manifests Instant Enlightenment in the unity of person and law.

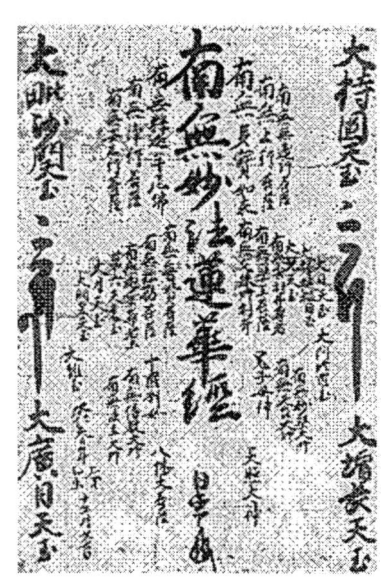

Nichijō's Honzon of 1295

However, I personally feel uneasy with this type of amendation, as if I would thereby place myself in a central position and only consider Nichiren Daishōnin as one of the great masters within the LS traditional lineage. This is not only as it gives me an uneasy feeling, but also as the alignment of "Nam-myō-hō-ren-ge-kyō Nichiren" also has the particular significance that Nichiren himself embodied the Mystic Law in his capacity as Bodhisattva Jōgyō. If we ignore this aspect, we would disrespect his great achievement in his capacity as "the votary of the Lotus Sutra of the Latter Day". Further, we might thereby lose our true orientation for the practice of our faith. Thus, we can never really put our own heart or our own self in place of our true object of devotion, nor indeed as focus in any meditative practice for observing the enlightened mind. Consequently, I feel much more affinity with the traditional lineage of Nikkō, who adopted Nichiren's own original style of Mandala inscription, and always subsequently inscribed his own Mandalas down the center with "Nam-myō-hō-ren-ge-kyō Nichiren".

In conclusion, chanting Daimoku to the Mandala Gohonzon is the meditative practice to realize Instant Enlightenment. In this, we observe in the Gohonzon of Ichinen Sanzen the aspect which appears as the "Unity of Person and law". At this moment, we observe ourselves connected directly to all cosmic life, as well as to the Eternal Buddha Shakyamuni, Bodhisattva Jōgyō, and Nichiren Daishōnin himself. Thus, it is only natural that Nichiren concluded his Gosho with the full title »The Unanimous Declaration by the Buddhas of the Three Existences regarding the Classification of the Teachings and Which Are to Be Abandoned and Which Are To Be Upheld« with the sentence below:

> You should carry out the practice of Myō-hō-ren-ge-kyō single-mindedly in harmony with all the Buddhas of the three existences, and, without any obstruction, attain enlightenment. (p. 575 / II. 861)

Chapter 8
The Ten-Worlds-Mandala of Ichinen Sanzen

1. The Fusion of Wisdom and Actuality

We will now take a further step in our consideration of the particular Mandala characterized by "One Tower, Two Buddhas and Four Bodhisattvas". For this form of Mandala can be viewed as representative of the core elements found on the Ten-Worlds-Mandala.

The fusion of wisdom and actuality represents Instant Enlightenment

In the Gosho »On Repaying Debts of Gratitude«, "Shakyamuni Buddha, the lord of the Essential Section" was declared to be the Object of Devotion as one of the Three Great Secret Laws.

> So, it is that Shakyamuni and Tahō sit together in the Treasure Tower, while all the other Buddhas, and the four bodhisattvas headed by Jōgyō, will act as assistants to the [eternal] Buddha. (p. 328 / l. 735)

With respect to the relationship between the Buddha Shakyamuni, the lord of teachings and Buddha Shakyamuni within the Treasure Tower, its implications have been discussed previously in chapter 4, Section 6. There I arrived at the conclusion that, on the level of a literal reading, the seven characters of the central Daimoku signify the Eternal Buddha Shakyamuni, while both of the two Buddhas and the four Bodhisattvas are arranged as his attendants. Thus, the form of the Mandala represents the Ceremony in the Air, in that Eternal Realization is made manifest and the eternal law transmitted.

As the two Buddhas and the four Bodhisattvas are significantly prominent on the "complete version of the Gohonzon," I would now like to consider them from the "perspective of a contemplative reading of the Essential Section for the Latter Day". On level of a literal reading, the Treasure Tower appeared in the place of Shakyamuni's preaching of the Lotus Sutra in order to affirm its truth. By contrast, at the level of a contemplative reading, the image of the two Buddhas sitting side by side within the Treasure Tower signifies the principle of the "Fusion of Actuality and Wisdom" (D). The particular aspects of this will now be illustrated.

First, as previously noted with respect to "Shakyamuni's dual identity" (see above page 297), a matter considered by Nichiren in »Earthly Desires Are Enlightenment (Reply to Shijō Kingo)«, dated 1273, the two Buddhas are defined in terms of wisdom and actuality.

> A commentary states that "the profound principle of the true aspect is the originally inherent Myō-hō-ren-ge-kyō". [As to this *true aspect of all phenomena* ...] all phenomena correspond to Tahō, and the true aspect corresponds to Shakyamuni.
>
> These can be also understood in terms of the two elements of *reality and wisdom*. Tahō stands for reality, Shakyamuni for wisdom. Though the reality and the wisdom are two different elements, they are not two, and thus, they present *secret enlightenment*.
>
> These are teachings of prime importance. They are also what is called "earthly desires are equal to enlightenment," and "the sufferings of birth and death are equal to nirvana". (p. 1116 f. / I. 317)

Each of the principles such as *the true aspect of all phenomena* and *the Fusion of Actuality and Wisdom* manifest the analytical aspect of the Instant Enlightenment of Ichinen Sanzen. This perspective is even more clearly expounded in »The Essentials of Attaining Enlightenment (Reply to Soya)«, dated 1276, which begins by quoting a phrase from the Expedient Means chapter of the LS: "*The wisdom of the Buddhas is infinitely profound and immeasurable.*"

> Aren't the sutra and the commentary stating that the way to attain Buddhahood lies within the two elements of reality and wisdom? In that case, *reality means the essential entity of all phenomena, and wisdom means the body illuminating and manifesting this true nature*. Thus, when the riverbed of reality is *infinitely* broad and deep, the water of wisdom will flow ceaselessly. *When this reality and wisdom are fused, one attains Buddhahood immediately*.
>
> The sutras expounded prior to the Lotus Sutra cannot lead to Buddhahood because they are provisional and expedient teachings that *separate reality and wisdom*. The Lotus Sutra, however, unites the two as a single entity. [...] *By realizing this Buddha wisdom, one attains Buddhahood*. [...]
>
> What then are these two elements of reality and wisdom? They are simply the five characters of Nam-myō-hō-ren-ge-kyō. Shakyamuni Buddha called forth the Bodhisattvas of the Earth and entrusted to them these five characters that constitute the essence of the sutra. The Lotus Sutra states that Bodhisattva Jōgyō and the others will appear in the first five

hundred years of the Latter Day of the Law to propagate *the five characters, the embodiment of the two elements of reality and wisdom*. The sutra makes this perfectly clear. (p. 1055 / I. 746)

The passage above makes it clear that to chant the Mystic Law for realization of Instant Enlightenment means to become fused with the essential entity of all phenomena throughout the universe and to thereby manifest the enlightened state in each of our own lives. The fusion with limitless cosmic life (Buddhahood) enables the life of all ordinary people (Nine Worlds) to shine forth brilliantly. It means, to quote a contemporary phrase, that "I am equal to the cosmos" and that we are connected to everything in the nature and throughout the whole universe. This aspect actually makes manifest the significance of the central Daimoku, as well as that of the two Buddhas on the Mandala from a perspective of a contemplative reading for the Latter Day (D). It is also particularly related to the Dharma body and the form of practice for our contemporary age.

> The Mystic Law transmitted to Jōgyō is the Law which Shakyamuni practiced in order to become the eternal Buddha immediately.
> By embracing this Law, "*we will naturally be endowed with the same benefits as he*" (»The Object of Devotion for Observing the Mind«).
> Thus, we are able to attain Instant Enlightenment
> in a simple and natural way.

The fusion of wisdom and actuality represents the essence of the eternal Buddha

Consequently, deep behind the attribution of wisdom and actuality to each of the two Buddhas, Shakyamuni's Eternal Realization itself is characterized as the Fusion of Actuality and Wisdom (B). This dimension is particularly stressed, for example, in »Establishing the Correct Method of Contemplation«, dated 1274.

> How wonderful the Law can be described in terms of *the three truths* or *the threefold contemplation* or *the three thousand realms*, which can be found as the culmination of the doctrines which T'ien-t'ai was able to elaborate in his thought. Yet This Mystic Law is the master of all Buddhas. [...] it represents *the state of life of the eternal Buddha who attained the highest stage of perfect enlightenment, the ultimate fruit of Buddhahood*. [...] The Lotus Sutra says: "That which can only be understood and shared between Buddhas" [...]. *The Mystic Law, the Law that the Buddha in his original state attained as a result of the fusion of reality and wisdom*, is something which any Buddha in his provisional status and the other Buddhas

could never encompass in their thought. Much less, then, could bodhisattvas or ordinary mortals! (p. 530 / II. 515)

> The "Mystic Law which the Buddha in his original state attained as a result of the Fusion of Actuality and Wisdom" is the Dharma body "which can only be understood and shared between Buddhas" and represents "the state of life of the eternal Buddha who attained the highest stage of perfect enlightenment, the ultimate fruit of Buddhahood.

Further, with respect to "Instant Enlightenment representing the unity of actuality and wisdom," Nichiren took a harshly critical attitude against T'ien-t'ai's method of contemplation by pointing out the limitations in a mere *"doctrine which T'ien-t'ai elaborated in his thought"* and which, therefore, could never attain to the highest state of eternal realization.

The present work contends that the T'ien-t'ai's method of meditation does not discard either the Theoretical or the Essential Section of the LS, although it is based on a contemplative reading which transcends a literal reading. At the same time, it should be understood that the Mystic Law is superior to T'ien-t'ai's method of *threefold contemplation in a single mind* and represents *"a doctrine of the greatest significance, concerning a realm which can only be shared between one Buddha and another"* (ibid.).

To clarify this difference: T'ien-t'ai and Dengyō realized within their own minds the Wonderful Law which is expressed in the two characters of *myōhō*. It symbolizes the practice of observing the Law in one's own mind. In contrast to this contemplative method, Nichiren propagated a method of practice of the Mystic Law which had been transmitted by the eternal Buddha to Jōgyō. The fundamental difference lies in the nature of the Dharma body itself which is to be practiced. T'ien-t'ai's contemplation is for observing the Mystic Law in one's own mind, which is formulated in terms of the doctrine of Ichinen Sanzen, based on the Ten Factors of the Theoretical Section. Thus, the Ten Worlds are theoretically equal, but the Nine Worlds are understood to be basically distinct from Buddhahood. This theory of Ichinen Sanzen was transformed by Nichiren into the doctrine of "Ichinen Sanzen in Actuality", based on the Essential Section, which represents the Mystic Law of "Original Cause -equals- Original Effect", based on the Mutual Containment of the beginningless Ten Worlds.

> The heart of the teachings received by the Great Teacher T'ien-t'ai and handed on by him is this doctrine of *the wonderful Law expressed in a single word*. *The threefold contemplation in a single mind* is in the end simply nothing other than a method of practice designed to enable one to realize this wonderful Law. The threefold contemplation represents the cause,

> and the wonderful Law represents the effect. But the effect is already present in the cause, and the cause is already present in the effect. One is thus contemplating *the Mystic Law in which both cause and effect are present simultaneously*, and that is why this method can achieve the results which it does.
> (p. 531, II. 517)

In the case of T'ien-t'ai's method of contemplation, the cause of practice and the effect of attaining Buddhahood are distinct from each other. Thus, inevitably the goal is achieved by making progress only step by step, and ultimately in vain. By contrast, in the case of practicing the Mystic Law which embodies the principle of *the simultaneity of cause and effect* or defined as "the ordinary person is fundamentally equal to those who are enlightened", chanting the Mystic Law is likewise equal to Instant Enlightenment. This is a distinctive type of practice which does nothing other than actualize Buddhahood or Original Enlightenment. Consequently, the effect of attaining enlightenment which the *threefold contemplation in a single mind* aims to attain is already achieved in the chanting of daimoku representing the practice of the cause.

In actuality, T'ien-t'ai's method of contemplation will lead you to observe the world of Ichinen Sanzen in your own mind step by step. By way of contrast to this gradual process of meditation, we will actually experience the cosmic life of infinite extent and depth by chanting Daimoku before the Mandala-Gohonzon.
I would call this Nichiren Buddhist practice of mantra meditation the "*perfect and immediate contemplation for the Latter Day*", (*mappō no endonshikan*).

2. The theoretical and practical consequences for the theory of the ordinary person as true Buddha

In the previous section, the principle of the Fusion of Actuality and Wisdom has been defined as an expression of that immediate enlightenment which can be realized by practicing the Mystic Law. Further, it indicates a decisive and dramatic change in understanding NB. The Ceremony in the Air, and the world of the Eternal Realization as depicted in the LS (B), will emerge immediately in the world of the Latter Day (D). All the principles and characteristics related to the "world of enlightenment" as described in the sutras will be realized as actual events, through the concrete practice of chanting the Mystic Law in the "world of suffering". This is nothing other than the theoretical and practical consequence of the theory of the ordinary people as true Buddha.

Keeping the Treasure Tower in one's own heart

If the two Buddhas Shakyamuni and Tahō symbolize the two aspects of wisdom and actuality, the Treasure Tower itself also assumes a new significance. The fact that Instant Enlightenment takes place here and now can also be taken to mean that those who chant daimoku before the Gohonzon keep the Treasure Tower within their own hearts. This idea is most vividly expressed in »On the Treasure Tower (Letter to Abutsubō)«, dated March 1272, from the perspective of a contemplative reading. It is philosophically coherent.

> The closed tower symbolizes the Theoretical Section, and the open tower, the Essential Section. This reveals *the two elements of actuality and wisdom*. This is extremely complex, however, so I will not go into further detail now. In essence, the appearance of the Treasure Tower indicates that only on hearing the Lotus Sutra will the three groups of voice-hearers *perceive the Treasure Tower within their own lives*.
>
> *Now Nichiren's disciples and lay supporters are also doing this*. In the Latter Day of the Law, no Treasure Tower exists other than in the persons of the men and women who embrace the Lotus Sutra. It follows, therefore, that *whether eminent or humble, high or low, those who chant Nam-myō-hō-ren-ge-kyō are themselves the Treasure Tower, and, likewise, are themselves the Tathāgata Tahō*. No Treasure Tower exists other than Myō-hō-ren-ge-kyō. The daimoku of the Lotus Sutra is the Treasure Tower, and the Treasure Tower is Nam-myō-hō-ren-ge-kyō. (p. 1304 / I. 299)

The above is certainly a metaphorical mode of discourse peculiar to Nichiren, yet *"perceiving the solemn and precious Treasure Tower bedecked with brilliant jewels within one's own heart"* represents a perspective grounded on a contemplative philosophy.

> You may think you offered gifts to the Treasure Tower of the Tathāgata Tahō, but that is not so. You offered them to yourself. You, yourself, are *a Tathāgata of Original Enlightenment endowed with the three bodies in one body*. You should chant *Nam-myō-hō-ren-ge-kyō* with this conviction. Then the place where you chant daimoku will become the dwelling place of the Treasure Tower. The sutra reads, *"If there is any place where the Lotus Sutra is preached, then my Treasure Tower will come forth and appear in that spot"*.
> (»On the Treasure Tower (Letter to Abutsubō)«, p. 1304 / I. 299 f.)

The idea that the Treasure Tower of the Lotus Sutra will appear before the person who chants Daimoku represents a metaphorical understanding that Instant Enlightenment is actualized. However, this actualization is already anticipated and reflected in the form of the Mandala Honzon.

The two Buddhas represent the function of the Mystic Law

In a similar manner, »The true aspect of all phenomena (Reply to Shijō Kingo)« (1273) describes the significance of the two Buddhas sitting side by side from a perspective of a contemplative reading. In the "enlightened world" (D), their relationship will be reversed. The significance of the two Buddhas will be correspondingly altered. Our world here and now gains the significance of actuality, while the world of the Sutra recedes to become "its shadow (trace)". Apart from the issue of the authenticity of this Gosho, this relationship amounts to "the perspective of a contemplative reading for the Latter Day," which is the ultimate destination at which Nichiren's teaching arrives. It is philosophically coherent and consistent with other Nichiren sources, so I will rely on this Gosho without any qualms.

»The True Aspect of All Phenomena« begins with a question as to its definition, which by reference to the Expedient Means chapter, has a straightforward and clear answer.

> The true aspect of all phenomena signifies that each entity of all phenomena is present in the entity of Myō-hō-ren-ge-kyō. (p. 1359 / I. 383)

This particular statement clearly highlights, as noted above, Nichiren's *holistic world view and is a form of absolute monism, as the Mystic Law encompasses the whole universe*. From this perspective, each of the two Buddhas manifests a particular symbolic character, rather than each being understood metaphorically or in a literal sense.

> Thus, the entire realm of phenomena [from hell to Buddhahood] is not different than the five characters of Myō-hō-ren-ge-kyō. Even the two Buddhas, Shakyamuni and Tahō, performing their functions based on the benefit of the five characters of the Mystic Law, appeared and seated together within the Treasure Tower, nodding in mutual agreement. No one but Nichiren has ever revealed teachings like these before. (ibid.)

In this passage, Nichiren does not, as he normally does, provide an interpretation of certain phrases with reference to the Sutras or Commentaries nor is his understanding based on the perspective of a contemplative rather than a literal reading. Quite the contrary, for he takes *a particular holistic world view, based on an absolute monism of the Mystic Law which encompasses the whole universe,* as his starting-point a particular holistic mystical philosophy, from whence he seeks to re-evaluate the significance of the two Buddhas. Ultimately, he now understands the two Buddhas as symbolic manifestations of the function of the Mystic Law.

The last sentence of the above quotation indicates that Nichiren was fully aware of the astounding originality of this approach to the interpretation of the Lotus Sutra. Furthermore, this extraordinary originality is also evident in his inscription of the Mystic Law as transmitted to Jōgyō in the form of a Mandala-Honzon.

Nichiren then proceeds to further explicate the symbolism of the two Buddhas within the Treasure Tower.

> No one else other than Jōgyō, [... and other leaders] among the Bodhisattvas of the Earth can appear [... in the Latter Day] and spread the five characters of Myō-hō-ren-ge-kyō, the Dharma body [the essence of all phenomena], but also give concrete form to the ceremony of the two Buddhas seated side by side in the Treasure Tower. This is because of *the doctrine of Ichinen Sanzen of Action based on the Life Span chapter of the Essential Section.*
>
> *Therefore, the two Buddhas called Shakyamuni and Tahō serve to represent the functions [of the Mystic Law] while Myō-hō-ren-ge-kyō is the true Buddha.* This is what is described in the sutra as "the Tathāgata's secret and his transcendental powers". The "Tathāgata's secret" refers to the entity of the Buddha's three bodies, the true Buddha. "His transcendental powers" refers to the functions of the three bodies, provisional Buddhas. *A common mortal is an entity of the three bodies, and a true Buddha.* A Buddha is a function of the three bodies, and a provisional Buddha.
>
> In that case, though it is thought that Shakyamuni Buddha possesses the three virtues of sovereign, teacher, and parent for the sake of all of us living beings, that is not so. On the contrary, *it is common mortals who endow him with the three virtues.* (ibid.)

To emphasize once more, the Mystic Law represents the universal essence of all phenomena throughout the whole world and throughout the universe, embodying the principle of Ichinen Sanzen based on the Mutual Containment of the Ten Worlds. When we embrace and chant the Mystic Law, it manifests in our life in the form of a Unity between Person and Law so as to actualize Instant Enlightenment. The realization of the principle "the ordinary person – equals- Buddha" is itself a manifestation of the "true Buddha in actuality". From this perspective, the Buddhas described in the Sutra are symbolic representations of the concept of "Buddha", which reflects our own dignity and our own greatness.

The practitioner of the daimoku will manifest as the true Buddha who exists in actuality

It is from the perspective of a contemplative reading that the theory on the ordinary person as true Buddha can be best understood (D). I will summarize the main points.

1) Jōgyō, the supreme leader of the Bodhisattvas of the Earth, propagates the Mystic Law in the Latter Day, as one of the participants in the Ceremony with the two Buddhas sitting within the Treasure Tower.
2) The fundamental principle of both the Daimoku and the Mandala is the *"doctrine of Ichinen Sanzen in Actuality based on the Life Span chapter of the Essential Section,"* i.e. the actualization of the *principle of Instant Enlightenment of Ichinen Sanzen based on the Mutual Containment of the Ten Worlds*.
3) Practicing this Mystic Law leads directly to the Buddha way and represents the seed of all Buddhas which allows the *"original and true Buddha of Myō-hō-ren-ge-kyō"* to be made manifest.
4) That which is realized by Instant Enlightenment is the *Tathāgata Nammyō-hō-ren-ge-kyō*. By contrast to this "true Buddha of actualization", the two Buddhas depicted in the Sutra will signify "the Buddha manifesting the noble functions of the true Buddha."
5) In other words, the Fusion of Actuality and Wisdom is the principle which defines the enlightened world or the state of Ichinen Sanzen.
6) When we practice chanting the Daimoku in Actuality, in the "world of suffering," Instant Enlightenment will manifest that Buddhahood within us, that within all ordinary people of the Nine Worlds. We will thereby demonstrate that we are the true Buddha in Actuality, manifesting the characteristics of the "ordinary person -equals- Buddha" endowed with the three bodies. That is to say: our own lives will be replete with the wonderful qualities of the Tathāgata of Original Enlightenment, such as life force, wisdom, compassion, etc...
7) At this point, the traditional view of the Buddha is radically reversed. In contrast to the idea that a true Buddhas exists in the world of suffering, all the Buddhas of the "enlightened world" inscribed on the Mandala Honzon, such as the two Buddhas within the Treasure Tower and the Buddhas of the three existences and the ten heavenly directions, are significant merely as "functions and shadows of the true Buddha" (D).
8) The world of the Mandala-Honzon which on the surface represents the world of enlightenment as described in the Sutra, now reflects the world of Instant Enlightenment which will be manifested by the practice of chanting daimoku in our actual world of suffering. For the state of life representing our own Instant Enlightenment in "truth and actuality" is anticipated in the world of the mandala world by its function of "transcendent reflection". The literal world of Eternal Realization is to be realized here and now in a concrete form, as "Ichinen Sanzen in Actuality".
9) Consequently, all ordinary people encountering this mandala world are to be regarded as the actual true Buddha manifesting the principle of "the ordinary person as true Buddha".

This radical philosophical innovation turns on its head any conventional understanding of NB, e.g. that primarily found in traditional Nichirenshū temples. Some traditional Nichiren Buddhists may feel perplexed and resent any radically innovative approach to NB doctrine which goes beyond a literal reading of the LS. For this requires a radical change of perspective away from a ritual-centered form of worship of the Buddha and attendant Bodhisattvas towards the "enlightened world" itself, which demands a more pro-active and dynamic form of practice whereby practice is for one's own Instant Enlightenment within this "world of suffering". What is more, in case of Nichiren Shoshu theory and practice, Instant Enlightenment based on the principle of the ordinary person as true Buddha is restricted wholly to Nichiren himself as the true and original Buddha, which amounts to nothing other than a most egregious form of "founder worship".

For, in so far as Nichiren's doctrinal concept for the realization of Buddhahood is concerned, it depends on no Buddha nor Buddhist to as redeemer. As only the chanting of daimoku assures Instant Enlightenment, it is universally applicable to all ordinary people without distinction. Nichiren was himself wholly aware of the radical innovativeness of his own teaching when he stated: *"No one but Nichiren has ever revealed teachings like these"*. It is only this radically innovative and contemporarily relevant Nichiren teaching which alone can be accepted by SGI, or more generally by contemporary lay Buddhists orientated towards an ethic of radical individual responsibility, including a radical aspiration to self-realization[33].

3. The Ten World Mandala as the Realization of Ichinen Sanzen in Actuality

As for the Mandala endowed with all Ten Worlds, we will consider it by reference to both the essential and the abbreviated form of the Honzon. The whole mandala represents the Ceremony in the Air on the level of a literal reading. However, from the perspective of a contemplative reading, it consistently represents the Mystic Law transmitted to Jōgyō, which manifests the three supreme principles of Shakyamuni's Eternal Realization. Consequently:

> In order for the Mandala to manifest the supreme principle of
> the Instant Enlightenment of Ichinen Sanzen
> based on the Mutual Containment of the Ten Worlds,
> all the Ten Worlds must be inscribed on it.

---

[33] With respect to the cultural context of the embracing of Buddhism in Germany see Matsudo 2015.

Given that, I would now like to look once more at the significance of the principle of the dual life structure in its relation to the Mandala-Honzon. Shikata states:

> The innumerable bodhisattvas of the Earth represent the Nine Worlds. Thus, when the Bodhisattvas face the two Buddhas Shakyamuni and Tahō, this indicates the principle of "Nine Worlds -equal- Buddhahood" and "Buddhahood – equals – the Nine Worlds". And both the Nine Worlds and Buddhahood are attendants to the Daimoku at the center. As the Daimoku is central to the principle of the Mutual Containment of the Ten Worlds, this makes the Mandala the foremost Honzon throughout the whole entire world. (21: 266).

However, the fact that the Bodhisattvas and the two Buddhas face each other does not in itself explain how they symbolize the principle of the Mutual Containment of the Ten Worlds. Nor is it clear how the Daimoku itself is central to this principle simply because both the Nine worlds and Buddhahood are its attendants. For this principle indicates the fact that each world is endowed with each of the other Nine Worlds. Given this fact, each world is necessarily endowed with the potentiality to manifest one hundred worlds within itself, ultimately manifesting up to three thousand aspects. Because all the representatives of the Ten Worlds inscribed on the Mandala-Gohonzon are themselves practicing the Mystic Law, each of them is manifesting the character of the Instant Enlightenment of Ichinen Sanzen based on the Mutual Containment of the Ten Worlds. This same structural principle can be applied to the whole Mandala.

In an iconographic manner, each of the representatives of all the Ten Worlds as well as the whole mandala itself are together manifesting the vast world of interdependent being which is Ichinen Sanzen.

This world of suffering itself is the enlightened world of eternal realization

As we have noted above, at the level of "(B) a literal reading of the Essential Section for the Latter Day," the Daimoku at the center manifests "Eternal Realization", i.e., the "chanting of Daimoku by the eternal Buddha Shakyamuni", while the whole mandala itself manifests the "enlightened world of Ichinen Sanzen in Actuality". This is just as quoted above in »The Opening of the Eyes". To quote once again:

> When we come to the Essential Section of the Lotus Sutra, [...] those matters as expounded in the Essential Section are revealed. This is precisely *the doctrine of original cause and original effect*. In this case, the

> Nine Worlds are all present in *beginningless Buddhahood* and Buddhahood is inherent in *the beginningless Nine Worlds*. This *true* principle of the Mutual Containment of the Ten Worlds constitutes the true hundred worlds and thousand factors and thus *the true doctrine of Ichinen Sanzen*, the true three thousand realms in a single moment of life.
> (p. 197 / I. 235)

Eternal Realization can be also defined as "*the lord of teachings Shakyamuni endowed with the original and natural three bodies who has formed a deep and intimate relationship to this world*" (»On Receiving the Three Great Secret Laws«, p. 1022 / II. 986). The Tathāgata himself actually signifies the enlightened world of Ichinen Sanzen, i.e. our world in actuality. But as our actual world of suffering is also revealed as the true pure land, a radical reversal of perspective on our actual world takes place.

> When this everlasting past was revealed, it became apparent that all the other Buddhas were emanations of Shakyamuni. [...]
> In the earlier sutras and the Theoretical Section of the Lotus Sutra, all the regions of the ten directions were called pure lands while this present world was declared as an impure land. But now, [in the Life Span chapter], *this relationship has been reversed, revealing that this world is the true pure land* so that the so-called pure lands of the ten directions should be regarded as merely unreal projections of those in impure lands.
> (»The Opening of the Eyes«, p. 214 / I. 256)

Our world of suffering is transformed in significance as itself the land of enlightenment. This is nothing other than the "world of contemplation in the Latter Day". This particularly transformative perspective on the world is notably highlighted in »The Object of Devotion for Observing the Mind«.

> The latter half of the ["Emerging from the Earth"] chapter, the "Life Span" chapter, and the first half of the following "Distinctions in Benefits" chapter are revelation. [...]
> The Buddha who revealed in these [*one chapter and two halves*] is not the Shakyamuni of Initial Enlightenment. His teaching is also distinguished from [the Theoretical Section] *as great as the difference between heaven and earth*. Because the eternal character of the Ten Worlds has been revealed, the character of the realm of the land and its natural environment is also made manifest. Thus, as to the doctrine of Ichinen Sanzen, there is *only a fine distinction [between the Theoretical and the Essential Section] as thin as a bamboo membrane*.
> All the three teachings like the Theoretical Section and the first four flavors of teachings as well as the Immeasurable Meanings Sutra and the Nir-

> vana Sutra, which were preached "according to the capacities of the people" and represent teachings which are therefore easy to believe and easy to understand. In contrast, the Essential Section, which transcends the three categories, is difficult to believe and difficult to understand, for it directly reveals the" Buddha's own enlightenment." (p. 249 / I. 368)

We can interpret this passage in the following way. The teaching master of the Theoretical Section is the Buddha of Initial Enlightenment, while the Life Span chapter with two halves is speaking of the Tathāgata of Original Enlightenment. Consequently, between the *"teaching of the Buddha's own enlightenment"* and the *"teachings preached according to the capacities of a variety of people"* there is *an enormous* as vast as that *between heaven and earth*. With respect to the doctrine of Ichinen Sanzen of the Essential Section, as the beginningless Mutual Containment of the Ten Worlds has been revealed, the land and its natural environment is also revealed as possessing a dual structure of "the world of suffering -equals- the world of enlightenment". Consequently, the Instant Enlightenment of Eternal Realization is regarded as the "Ichinen Sanzen of Original Enlightenment" (B). Nichiren transmits this Mystic Law into the Latter Day as the Dharma body of practice (D). Here, the Mystic Law is the same, the only difference being in terms of "time": either "the Essential Section of Shakyamuni's lifetime" or "the contemplation of the Essential Section in the Latter Day". It is this difference which is as fine as a *"bamboo membrane."*

> The Essential Section of Shakyamuni's lifetime and that revealed at the beginning of the Latter Day are **both pure and perfect** [in that both lead directly to Buddhahood]. Shakyamuni's, however, is the Buddhism of the harvest, and **this is the Buddhism of sowing**. The core of his teaching is one chapter and two halves, and **the core of mine is the five characters of the Daimoku alone**. (p. 249 / I. 370)

The "doctrine of Ichinen Sanzen in Actuality of the Essential Section" is based on the concept of "Ichinen Sanzen of Original Enlightenment." Moreover, this is the Mystic Law which also represents the principle of "original cause -equals- original effect", Nichiren highlighted the idea of "the sowing of the seed" as the Dharma body of practice in the Latter Day.
This is to enable all ordinary people to realize Instant Enlightenment in the world of suffering.

Ichinen Sanzen in Actuality for the Latter Day

Nichiren's own distinctive interpretation of "Ichinen Sanzen in Actuality for the Latter Day" is particularly evident in its radical contrast with T'ien-t'ai's doctrine of Ichinen Sanzen. Even though both teachings are defined theoretically as the principle of the Mutual Containment of the Ten Worlds, there is a radical distinction in practical orientation between "aiming at Initial Enlightenment" and "beginning from Original Enlightenment".

> Putting the Theoretical Section to the fore while leaving the Essential Section in the background, [Nan-yüeh and T'ien-t'ai] fully revealed the meaning of Ichinen Sanzen in terms of the hundred worlds and thousand factors. Though they expounded the Mutual Containment of them *in principle*, they did not practice the *five characters of Nam-myō-hō-ren-ge-kyō in actuality*, nor did they established the Object of Devotion based on the Essential Section. (p. 253 / I. 375)

Thus, to practice T'ien-t'ai's method of meditation is only to contemplate an ideal state of enlightenment as understood in terms of the "theoretical doctrine of Ichinen Sanzen." By contrast, in practicing Nichiren's "Ichinen Sanzen in Actuality," each ordinary person can realize Instant Enlightenment in this world of suffering.

Before the Mandala-Honzon which reflects the Instant Enlightenment of Eternal Realization, each practices *the five characters of Nam-myō-hō-ren-ge-kyō in actuality*, which represents its original cause. Only so is the Instant Enlightenment of Eternal Realization actualized here and now.

Eternal Realization manifests in one's own heart

Thus, as the Gohonzon represents "the world of enlightenment," Instant Enlightenment based on Ichinen Sanzen in Actuality can only occur in "this world of suffering" as an event in actuality (D). Chanting the Mystic Law will actualize the supreme principle of Instant Enlightenment by "transferring to us *Shakyamuni's practices and the virtues*" and "*we will naturally be granted the same benefits as he*" (p. 246 / I. 365). After this passage, Nichiren describes all the Ten Worlds in the Mandala-Honzon in terms of "*our own states of life*" (B). This radical change of perspective is essential, in order to truly apprehend the nature of the Instant Enlightenment of Ichinen Sanzen based on the Mutual Containment of the Ten Worlds as reflected on the Gohonzon (D).

> Shakyamuni Buddha, who has attained perfect enlightenment, is our own flesh and blood. The benefits and merits resulting from his practices are our bones and marrow. [...]
> The Shakyamuni Buddha within our lives is *the primordial Buddha endowed with the three bodies since time without beginning*, revealed more than innumerable major world system dust particle kalpas ago. [...]

> The bodhisattvas Jōgyō [and the others] represent the world of the bodhisattva within ourselves. The Great Master Miao-lo says: *"You should understand that one's life and its environment at a single moment encompass the three thousand realms. Therefore, when one attains the Buddha way, one puts oneself in accord with this fundamental principle, and one's body and mind at a single moment pervade the entire realm of phenomena".*
> (p. 246 f. / I. 365 f.)

When practicing Mystic Law in the Latter Day, the world of Ichinen Sanzen signifies our own mind and body, as well as to the natural environment in which we dwell. These aspects are all included in the principle for realizing Buddhahood and this Buddhahood will be realized in actuality. Moreover, when Nichiren says that *"the Shakyamuni Buddha within our lives is the primordial Buddha endowed with the three bodies since time without beginning,"* he considers the eternal Buddha as a symbol manifesting our own dual life structure, i.e. the "ordinary person -equals- Buddha". On the level of a literal reading of the LS, Shakyamuni's "attaining enlightenment in the remotest past" refers to that Buddha as the subject of a time-bound ordinary narrative, yet on a deeper reading what should actually be understood from this narrative is that Shakyamuni is has rather only a symbolic function as "the primordial Buddha without beginning" (B) and who thereby reveals the "eternal character" of existence beyond the everyday experience of time and space. In this way, the world of Eternal Realization, which represents the principle of "original cause -equals- original effect", in actuality reveals the world of Ichinen Sanzen without beginning. Consequently, when we will ourselves realize Instant Enlightenment in actuality simply by embracing and practicing the Mystic Law of the simultaneity of cause and effect. For the mythic Ceremony in the Air, which symbolizes eternity (B), will itself thereby be actualized here and now (D).

While chanting daimoku before the Gohonzon, we manifest this enlightened world of Ichinen Sanzen and at the same time we can observe our own Instant Enlightenment. This is exactly why the Mandala is known as "the object of devotion for observing the mind."

Nichiren's Gosho of that title, considers this very matter from the outset:

> The observation of the mind means to observe one's own mind and to find the Ten Worlds within it. This is what is called observing the mind. For example, though we can see the six sense organs of other people, we cannot see our own. *Only when we look into a clear mirror do we see, for the first time, that we are endowed with all six sense organs.* [...]
> Only in the clear mirror of the Lotus Sutra and of the Great Teacher T'ien-t'ai's Great Concentration and Insight can one see one's own Ten

Worlds, hundred worlds and thousand factors, and three thousand realms in a single moment of life.

Question: What part of the Lotus Sutra do you refer to, and what section of T'ien-t'ai's commentaries?

Answer: The Expedient Means chapter in volume one of the Lotus Sutra states, "The Buddhas wish to open the door of Buddha wisdom to all living beings". This refers to the world of Buddhahood inherent in the Nine Worlds. The Life Span chapter states: "Thus, since I attained Buddhahood, an extremely long period of time has passed. My life span is an immeasurable number of asamkhya kalpas, and during that time I have constantly abided here without ever entering extinction. Good men, originally I practiced the bodhisattva way, and the life span that I acquired then has yet to come to an end but will last twice the number of years that have already passed." Here the sutra refers to the Nine Worlds inherent in Buddhahood. [...]

The sutra says, "Sometimes I speak of myself, sometimes of others" and so on. Thus, the world of Buddhahood contains the Ten Worlds.

(p. 240 / I. 356)

As to the principle of the Mutual Containment of the Ten Worlds, the Mandala-Honzon manifests the enlightened character of all Ten Worlds. It means the principle of "Nine or Ten Worlds endowed with Buddhahood," the perfect manifestation of Buddhahood throughout the whole world. As a reflection of this world of Ichinen Sanzen, we also actualize that "Buddhahood inherent within our own life of Nine Worlds."

In actualizing *Buddhahood inherent in the Nine Worlds* by chanting Daimoku, *the Nine worlds inherent in Buddhahood* will be manifested. This means, for example, that the state of hell can be transformed into that of Buddhahood.

4. The Mystic Law is itself the original master of the eternal Buddha

In the world of suffering, no individual Buddha can lead all people on to the Buddha way if any one of them should be incapable of attaining enlightenment.

The temporary forms that the Buddha manifests in response to the capacity of the people are not the true Buddha. Rather than the Buddha with thirty-two features and eighty characteristics, it is *the characters of the Lotus Sutra* that are the true Buddhas. Thus, during the Buddha's lifetime there were people who believed in the Buddha, but never became Buddhas themselves. After the Buddha's passing, of those who believe in the Lotus Sutra *"not one will fail to attain Buddhahood"*. These are the golden words of the Tathāgata.

(»Cloth for a Robe and an Unlined Robe«, p. 970 / II. 602)

Those Buddhas, who appeared in the world to provide teachings for others in accord with their capacities, are all provisional Buddhas. Only that teaching which the Buddha himself practiced can lead all people to the Buddha way without fail. That teaching itself should be the "true Buddha" emphasizes that function of the Mystic Law which is to bring forth all Buddhas.

> The Buddhas throughout the three existences attain enlightenment because *they take this sutra as their teacher*. The Buddhas of the ten directions guide living beings with the teaching of the One Vehicle as their eyes.
>
> (»Letter to the Brothers«, p. 1079 / I. 493)

For while the Great Master of all Buddhas is the Eternal Buddha Shakyamuni, his Original Master is none other than the Mystic Law itself.

> *The Lotus Sutra is the eye of all the Buddhas. It is the original teacher of Shakyamuni Buddha himself, the lord of teachings.* (ibid., p. 1080, / I. 494)

The Mystic Law has the two aspects of "Original Cause" representing practice by each ordinary person and "Original Effect" representing the Buddha which is the fruit of that practice. Now all ordinary people should practice the Mystic Law of Instant Enlightenment in the world of suffering of the Latter Day. Consequently, it is necessary to discard the eternal Buddha (original effect) and to set up the practice of chanting Daimoku, representing his original master (D). Let's remind ourselves of the following answer found in »Questions and Answers on the Object of Devotion«.

> Question: In the evil world of the latter age, what should ordinary people take as their object of devotion?
>
> Answer: They should make *the daimoku of the Lotus Sutra* their object of devotion. [...]
>
> *Because the Lotus Sutra is the father and mother of Shakyamuni Buddha, the eye of all the Buddhas.* Shakyamuni, Mahāvairochana, and all the other Buddhas of the ten directions were born from the Lotus Sutra. Therefore, as the object of devotion I now take that which is capable of bringing forth such a life force. [...]
>
> *The Buddhas are beings who have been born, and the Lotus Sutra is that which has given birth to them. The Buddhas are the body and the Lotus Sutra is the soul.*
>
> (p. 365 / II. 787 f.)

Thus, we get the equation:

> The "object of devotion for observing the mind" is for the sake of
> all ordinary people in the Latter Day
> = the Daimoku of the Lotus Sutra
> = *the father and mother of Shakyamuni Buddha,
> the eye of all the Buddhas*
> = the "Lotus Sutra which gives birth to all Buddhas"

In this letter which was addressed to Gijōbō of Seichōji, Nichiren proclaims the superiority of the LS over all other sutras and teachings. Yet from the perspective of a contemplative reading for the Latter Day, the LS which is capable of giving birth to all Buddhas should be considered to be not simply the LS or its title but rather the Daimoku understood in a particular sense as the "Mystic Law of giving birth to all Buddhas". For this Mystic Law is nothing other than the chanting of Daimoku for realization of the three supreme principles of the Instant Enlightenment of Ichinen Sanzen based on the Mutual Containment of the Ten Worlds. So, although Nichiren speaks of both the LS and daimoku, Nichiren himself only chants the seven characters of *Nam-myō-hō-ren-ge-kyō* which he inscribed at the center of the Mandala-Honzon. Given this context, when Nichiren speaks generally of the LS in terms of the LS which transcends all the eight teachings, he understands it as "the LS for the Latter Day."

Although the above has previously been addressed in Chapter 5, Section 4 "The Ambiguity of the Honmon no Honzon," let's now summarize the main points considered:

1) The seven characters at the center of the Mandala signify the "Lotus Sutra", that is, "the Mystic Law = chanting of Daimoku" itself. Thus, we need to complement the itemized list.

> The "object of devotion for observing the mind" for the sake of
> all ordinary people in the Latter Day
> = the "Lotus Sutra which gives birth to all Buddhas"
> = *the Lotus Sutra for the Latter Day*
> = the Mystic Law -equals- the chanting of Daimoku
> = *Nam-myō-hō-ren-ge-kyō* in actuality or the chanting of the Mystic Law
> representing the principle of "original cause- equals- original effect"
> = the realization of the Instant Enlightenment of Ichinen Sanzen
> based on the Mutual Containment of the Ten Worlds.

This interpretation actually refers to the most general level of "A. *the Lotus Sutra for the Latter Day*". If we regard this level as the foundation of a multilayered structure upon which the Daimoku at the center of Mandala-Honzon gains its primary significance, it is essential to have regard to the fourfold structure for interpreting the Daimoku's significance, which is dependent on different "persons", as below:

The four-layered structure for interpreting the significance of the central Daimoku

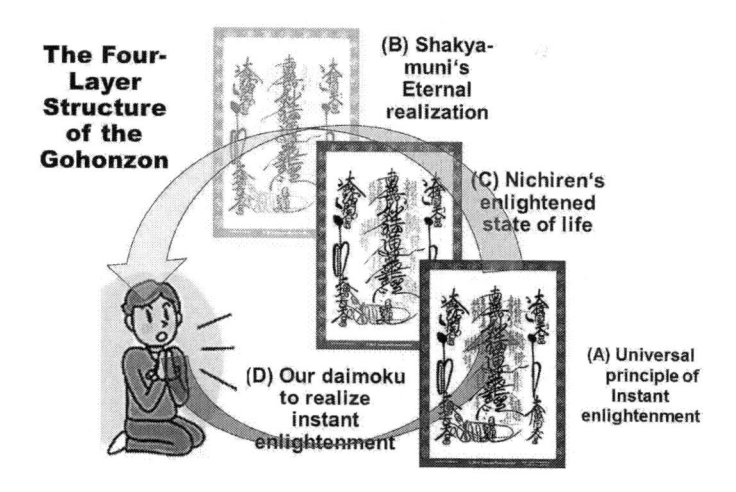

The Four-Layer Structure of the Gohonzon

(B) Shakyamuni's Eternal realization

(C) Nichiren's enlightened state of life

(A) Universal principle of Instant enlightenment

(D) Our daimoku to realize instant enlightenment

A. The Realization of the Instant Enlightenment of Ichinen Sanzen by chanting Daimoku = Tathāgata Nam-myō-hō-ren-ge-kyō as the Unity of Person and Law
B. The Realization of the Instant Enlightenment of Ichinen Sanzen by the eternal Buddha Shakyamuni
C. "The Mystic Law = the Chanting of daimoku" transmitted to Jōgyō deep within the heart of Nichiren
D. Realization of the Instant Enlightenment of Ichinen Sanzen by all ordinary people in the Latter Day

---

2) Consequently, although the seven characters of the central Daimoku on the Honzon signify the Eternal Realization at the level of a literal reading, from the perspective of a contemplative reading it also signifies the realization of Instant Enlightenment by the *Tathāgata Nam-myō-hō-ren-ge-kyō in the Unity of Person and Law* in actuality. What is more, at the same time, the whole Mandala-Honzon manifests the enlightened world of Ichinen Sanzen.

3) Further, if we regard the participants in the Ceremony in the Air as the representatives of all Ten Worlds, this aspect signifies the universal significance which each of them manifests by their devotion to the Mystic Law by chanting Daimoku. Thus, the central Daimoku of the Honzon is universally applicable to all those who chant Daimoku and signifies that each of

them is manifesting the character of Instant Enlightenment in the same way.

4) In other words, the three supreme principles related to Instant Enlightenment at the moment of Eternal Realization represents *holographically* the world of Ichinen Sanzen pervading both each of the Ten Worlds and pervading the whole Mandala. For it is the enlightened world of Ichinen Sanzen, made manifest in the Tathāgata of Original Enlightenment.

5) As each member of the Ten Worlds manifest the Instant Enlightenment of "The Nine worlds -equal- Buddhahood" based on Eternal Realization, the whole Mandala-Honzon manifests the principle of "Buddhahood -equals- the Nine Worlds."

Up to this point, we have been considering the "other world of enlightenment" where the world of the mandala is understood from the perspective of a contemplative reading for the Latter Day.

These aspects are clearly illustrated by Nichiren in »The Real Aspect of the Gohonzon (Reply to Nichinyo)«, dated August 1277. With respect to the significance of the Gohonzon, the following passage is especially important:

> This mandala is in no way my invention. [...]
> Without exception, all these Buddhas, bodhisattvas, great sages, and, in general, all the various beings [...] dwell in this Gohonzon. *Illuminated by the light of the five characters of the Mystic Law, they display the dignified attributes that they inherently possess. This is the object of devotion.*
> This is what is meant when the sutra says "the true aspect of all phenomena". Miao-lo stated: "The true aspect invariably manifests in all phenomena, and all phenomena invariably manifest in the ten factors. The ten factors invariably manifest in the Ten Worlds, and the Ten Worlds invariably manifest in life and its environment." It is also stated that the profound principle of the true aspect is the originally inherent Myō-hō-ren-ge-kyō. The Great Teacher Dengyō said, "[*Ichinen Sanzen is itself the wisdom body of limitless joy*]; this is the Buddha of extraordinary honorable appearances." Therefore, this Gohonzon shall be called the great mandala never before known; it did not appear until more than 2,220 years after the Buddha's passing. (1243 f. / I. 831 f.)

The statement here, "*Illuminated by the light of the five characters of the Mystic Law, they display the dignified attributes that they inherently possess,*" means that all the beings of the Ten Worlds manifest Buddhahood in terms of "*Ichinen Sanzen as the wisdom body of limitless joy*". Thus, because the Mandala assures us of the possibility that we all can manifest this dignified appearance through the practice of chanting Daimoku, it is the "great mandala never before known", isn't it?

So, with respect to as the chanting of the "five characters of the Mystic Law" manifests *"Ichinen Sanzen as the wisdom body of limitless joy,"* we may observe this principle and its threefold significance in the Gohonzon itself.

The threefold significance of the Gohonzon representing the principle of the "enlightenment of Ichinen Sanzen"

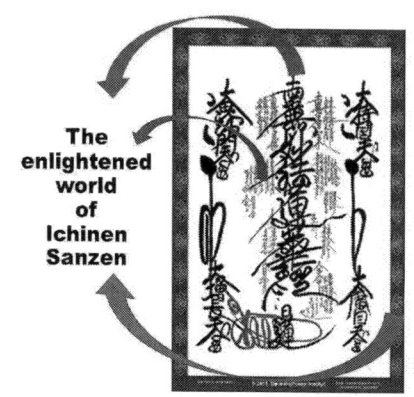

The enlightened world of Ichinen Sanzen

(1) The central Daimoku represents it

(2) Each of ten worlds represents it

(3) The entire Mandala represents it

1) The central Daimoku signifies the realization of the Instant Enlightenment of Ichinen Sanzen by chanting daimoku
  = Tathāgata Nam-myō-hō-ren-ge-kyō in the unity of person and law
2) Each of the Ten Worlds manifests the same realization.
3) The whole Mandala itself manifests the same realization.

5. Fusion with the Mandala-Honzon

If we chant the Mystic Law before the Mandala-Honzon, the "enlightened world" depicted there become manifest as an actuality within our "world of suffering" (D). To achieve this end, the Mystic Law which has the universal character of enabling all people without distinction to realize Buddhahood through its practice, and which is represented by the central Daimoku, should be most prominent. In this way, the relationship between the practitioner and the Mandala for observing the mind can be easily grasped as the "Fusion of Actuality and Wisdom". Generally, the following four aspects should be taken into consideration.
1) You will participate in the Ceremony in the Air as one of representatives of the Ten Worlds, as depicted on the Gohonzon. One might also express this aspect as viewing it as entry into the "enlightened world" of the Tathāgata of Original Enlightenment. Thus, this can be understood, as Kanno noted, as "entering the Mandala world by chanting Daimoku before

the Mandala-Honzon which depicts the Ceremony in the Air" (21: 191). Indeed, this particular aspect is powerfully expressed by Nichiren in »The Real Aspect of the Gohonzon (Reply to Nichinyo)«.

> This Gohonzon also is to be found simply in the two characters for *Shinjin* (believing heart). This is what the sutra means when it states that one can "gain entrance through faith alone" [LS, chap. 3]. Since Nichiren's disciples and lay supporters believe solely in the Lotus Sutra, "honestly discarding expedient means and not accepting even a single verse of the other sutras" [ibid.], they can enter the Treasure Tower of the Gohonzon.
> (p. 1244 / I. 832)

2) At the same time, this eternal ceremony is actualized here and now within the sacred time and space. In the life of one who chants Daimoku in the "world of suffering", the "enlightened world" of beginningless Ichinen Sanzen will be made manifest. Likewise, in the same Gosho:

> Never seek this Gohonzon outside yourself. *The Gohonzon exists only within the mortal flesh of us ordinary people who embrace the Lotus Sutra and chant Nam-myō-hō-ren-ge-kyō.* The body is the palace of the ninth consciousness, the unchanging reality which reigns over all of life's functions.
> (ibid.)

3) Further, in chanting Daimoku, you enter the Treasure Tower and it appears in your own life. These complimentary aspects illustrate precisely the Fusion of Actuality and Wisdom. This fact is best defined as "my body = the Treasure Tower", e.g. as found in »On the Treasure Tower" (Letter to Abutsubō)«.

> In the Latter Day of the Law, no Treasure Tower exists other than in the persons of the men and women who embrace the Lotus Sutra. It follows, therefore, that *whether eminent or humble, high or low, those who chant Nam-myō-hō-ren-ge-kyō are themselves the Treasure Tower, and, likewise, are themselves the Tathāgata Tahō.* [...]
> *You, yourself, are a Tathāgata of Original Enlightenment endowed with the three bodies in one.* You should chant Nam-myō-hō-ren-ge-kyō with this conviction. Then the place where you chant Daimoku will become the dwelling place of the Treasure Tower.
> (p. 1304 / I. 299 f.)

4) Additionally, the fusion of the person who chants with the Mandala-Gohonzon manifests that realization of Instant Enlightenment which is reflected on it. For the Mandala functions just as a mirror which reflects that person's enlightened life.

Chapter 8

With respect to this metaphor of a mirror, already in his early writing »On Attaining Buddhahood in This Lifetime« (1255), Nichiren gave guidance as to how to "polish the mirror of your heart". Thus:

> When deluded, one is called an ordinary being, but when enlightened, one is called a Buddha. This is similar to a tarnished mirror that will shine like a jewel when polished. *A mind now clouded by the illusions of the innate darkness of life is like a tarnished mirror, but when polished, it is sure to become like a clear mirror, reflecting the truth of Dharma nature.* Arouse deep faith, and diligently polish your mirror day and night. How should you polish it? Only by chanting Nam-myō-hō-ren-ge-kyō.
> (p. 384 / I. 4)

Indeed, the metaphor of a mirror concretely suggests also "the mirror for observing one's mind". Further, there is a vast difference as to whether one looks into the mirror from the front or from the back.

> *The practice of observing one's mind for realizing enlightenment is comparable to the looking at the front of a mirror.*
> (»The Unanimous Declaration by All the Buddhas«, p. 570 / II. 852)

Similarly, this is a main theme found in »On Attaining Buddhahood in This Lifetime«:

> The observation of the mind means to observe one's own mind and to find the Ten Worlds within it. [...] *It is like this only when we look into a clear mirror do we see, for the first time, that we are endowed with all six sense organs.* (p. 240 / I. 356)

Distinct from ordinary mirrors, the "object of devotion for observing the mind" permanently reflects the enlightened state of life. For this is a clear mirror for observing the Buddhahood in our own heart, which means, to activate it within our lives.

So, if we remind ourselves of the idea that "one is oneself the Treasure Tower":

> Now, the entire body of the Honorable Abutsu is composed of the five elements of earth, water, fire, wind, and space. These five elements are also the five characters of the daimoku. Abutsubō is therefore the Treasure Tower itself, and the Treasure Tower is Abutsubō himself. [...] *You may think you offered gifts to the Treasure Tower of the Tathāgata Tahō, but that is not so. You offered them to yourself.* You, yourself, are a Tathāgata of Original Enlightenment endowed with the three bodies in one.
> (»On the Treasure Tower (Letter to Abutsubō)«, p. 1304 / I. 299)

Given this aspect, that we are inherently the revered Tathāgata, we might have the following insight as to our adoption of a reverential attitude towards the Gohonzon, which enable us to appreciate our practice more deeply.

> When the bodhisattva Fukyō [Never Disparaging] makes his bow of obeisance to the four kinds of [priests and lay] believers, the Buddha nature inherent in the four kinds of believers of overbearing arrogance bows in obeisance to the bodhisattva Fukyō. It is like the situation *when one faces a mirror and makes a bow of obeisance: the image in the mirror likewise makes a bow of obeisance to oneself.* (p. 769 / OTT 165)

With respect to the above, I have refrained from quoting from »The Record of the Orally Transmitted Teachings« (OTT) in order to avoid any misunderstanding which might be the case if I sought to base my theory on a Gosho whose authenticity is generally considered to be problematic. Nevertheless, OTT can be considered as a writing which reflects Nichiren's own thought and it is consistent only if we read it from the perspective of a contemplative reading for the Latter Day. Especially as, it seems to me, this writing is philosophically consistent with Nichiren's teaching as found in his authenticated writings if it is considered under the aspect of a "theory on the ordinary person as true Buddha" viewed from a "perspective of a contemplative reading for the Latter Day."

6. Buddhahood omnipresent throughout the whole cosmos

Nichiren Buddhism presupposes an everlasting and omnipresent "Buddha nature" which can also be expressed as *"the primordial Buddha without beginning"* and *"the Tathāgata of Original Enlightenment"*. This Buddhahood is not just inherent in our own heart and life, but it pervades all nature and the whole universe itself as the "essence of all phenomena". This concept is best expressed by terms such as the "true aspect of all phenomena", "Ichinen Sanzen based on the Mutual Containment of the Ten Worlds", as well as by the idea that "everything is contained within the two characters of the Mystic Law."

> All things and events in nature and the universe, as well as in all Buddhas and within our own heart, are contained within the Mystic Law.
> The whole universe is the Dharma World of Buddha Nature or the Cosmic Life.

All phenomena in the universe represent the manifestation of the cosmic life which is their essence. Let's take a closer look at the particular view which

Chapter 8

Nichiren held with respect to the Mystic Law, conceived as the Buddhahood of all phenomena:

> *Myō-hō-ren-ge-kyō is the Buddha nature of all living beings.* The Buddha nature is the Dharma nature, and the Dharma nature is enlightenment. The Buddha nature possessed by Shakyamuni, Tahō, and the Buddhas of the ten directions, [...] by all living beings from the realm where there is neither thought nor no thought above the clouds down to the flames in the lowest depths of hell—*the Buddha nature that all these beings possess is called by the name Myō-hō-ren-ge-kyō*. Therefore, if you recite this Daimoku once, then the Buddha nature of all living beings will be summoned and gather around you. At that time the three bodies of the Dharma nature within you—the Dharma body, the reward body, and the manifested body—will be drawn forth and become manifest. This is called *attaining Buddhahood*. To illustrate, when a caged bird sings, the many birds flying in the sky all gather around it at once; seeing this, the bird in the cage strives to get out.
> (»Conversation between a Sage and an Enlightened Man«, p. 498, / I. 131)

Since the Buddhahood of all things in the universe is the Mystic Law, it is only natural that when one chants the Mystic Law, which actualizes one's Buddhahood, the Buddhahood of all things resonates with and responds to one's chanting.

> As for the meaning of *Myō-hō-ren-ge-kyō*: The Buddha nature inherent in us, ordinary people; the Buddha nature of Brahmā, Shakra, and the other deities; [...] and the Mystic Law that is the enlightenment of the Buddhas of the three existences, are *one and identical*. This principle is called *Myō-hō-ren-ge-kyō*. Therefore, when once we chant Myō-hō-ren-ge-kyō, with just that single sound we summon forth and manifest the Buddha nature of all Buddhas; all existences; all bodhisattvas; [...] and all other living beings. This blessing is immeasurable and boundless.
>
> *When we revere Myō-hō-ren-ge-kyō inherent in our own life as the object of devotion, the Buddha nature within us is summoned forth and manifested by our chanting of Nam-myō-hō-ren-ge-kyō. This is what is meant by "Buddha".*
>
> To illustrate, when a caged bird sings, birds who are flying in the sky are thereby summoned and gather around, and when the birds flying in the sky gather around, the bird in the cage strives to get out. When with our mouths we chant the Mystic Law, our Buddha nature, being summoned, will invariably emerge. *The Buddha nature of Brahmā and Shakra, being called, will protect us*, and the Buddha nature of the Buddhas and bodhisattvas, being summoned, will rejoice. [...]

> All Buddhas of the three existences, too, attain Buddhahood by virtue of the five characters of Myō-hō-ren-ge-kyō. They refer to *the Mystic Law* that represents the "reason why the Buddhas of the three existences appear in the world" and, at the same time, *"that enables all living beings to attain the Buddha way"*. You should take notice of these matters thoroughly and, on the path of attaining Buddhahood, chant Nam-myō-hō-ren-ge-kyō without arrogance or attachment to biased views.
>
> («How Those Initially Aspiring to the Way Can Attain Buddhahood through the Lotus Sutra», p. 557 / I. 887 f.)

The analogy of the caged and uncaged singing birds is beautifully simple yet profound. Ontologically, it can be schematized as follows:

The "Buddha nature representing the essence of all phenomena,"
has two aspects:
All phenomena are inherently endowed with Buddha nature
which can be defined as "immanent Buddhahood"
(The Nine worlds -equal- Buddhahood).
Further, that Buddha nature which contains all phenomena throughout the universe is correspondingly known as "transcendent Buddhahood"
(Buddhahood -equals- The Nine worlds).
Thus, this is a universal perspective on the Dharma world
which represents an absolute monism with respect to Buddha nature.
All phenomena are manifestations of "Buddha nature or the cosmic life"
and all exist within its "field."
Therefore, when you call forth the Mystic Law, that Buddha nature inherent within your own life, by reciting Nam-myō-hō-ren-ge-kyō,
not only the Buddha nature within your own life,
but also the Buddha nature of all beings throughout the universe will be invoked. Each resonates with the other as they are in correspondence.
All the Buddhist heavenly deities will then protect you as well.
Thus, the Instant Enlightenment within the life of all ordinary people
actualized by chanting Daimoku is grounded upon access to
the Buddha nature within your own life
which is identical with that of the whole cosmos.

---

7. The four-fold level of interpretation of the Buddhism of Sowing and the four-layered structure of the Gohonzon

As considered above, we have defined the four-fold level of interpretation of the Buddhism of Sowing from the perspective of "a contemplative reading of the Essential Section for the Latter Day". This had been necessary in order

CHAPTER 8

to arrive at a conclusion that Nichiren's ultimate doctrinal stance is the "theory of the Instant Enlightenment of all ordinary people" in the Latter Day. This theory is the foundation for the practice of Nichiren Buddhism in the 21st Century. So, to conclude, the levels of interpretation and the significance of the Gohonzon and Daimoku with respect to them can be schematized in tabular form as below:

	The four-fold level of interpretation of the *Buddhism of Sowing* and the four-layered structure of the Gohonzon in the *theory of the Instant Enlightenment of all ordinary people* which is to be established from the perspective of a *contemplative reading of the Essential Section for the Latter Day*.				
Interpretation level	Significance of chanting Daimoku	Practitioner chanting Daimoku	Significance of the central Daimoku in the Gohonzon	Form of the Gohonzon = Realization of Instant Enlightenment	
A) LS of the Latter Day	Daimoku of the LS	All Buddhas and all people in the world	One Great Secret Law	The Mystic Law = Chanting daimoku	
B) Essential Section of the Latter Day	Practicing the principle of the Instant Enlightenment of Ichinen Sanzen based on the dual structure of life	Primordial Layer: The eternal Buddha Shakyamuni	The eternal Buddha chanting daimoku	The eternal Realization = A prototype of Instant Enlightenment of ordinary person	
C) Contemplative Reading of the Essential Section For the Latter Day		Intermediate layer: Nichiren as Jōgyō	Nichiren practicing the Mystic Law transmitted to Jōgyō	Nichiren's enlightened state of life as the true Buddha of the Latter Day	
D) The Attainment of Buddhahood by all ordinary people in the Latter Day		Surface: Ourselves, all ordinary people of the present day	Ourselves chanting the Mystic Law of Sowing	A clear mirror reflecting our enlightened state of life	

Concluding Remarks

> Now, no matter what, strive in faith and consistently remain as a votary of the Lotus Sutra and my disciple for the rest of your life. If you are of the same mind as Nichiren, you must be a Bodhisattva of the Earth. And if you are a Bodhisattva of the Earth, there is not the slightest doubt that you have been a disciple of the eternal Buddha Shakyamuni.
> (»The True Aspect of All phenomena«, p. 1360 / I. 384)

All those who chant Daimoku are without exception a disciple of Nichiren Daishōnin and therefore a Bodhisattva of the Earth, regardless of any distinctions with respect to doctrinal understanding, ritual forms and traditional lineage or organizational affiliation. Chanting Daimoku minimally represents the common practice of all Nichiren Buddhists. Consequently, as I hold the belief that all Nichiren Buddhists should work together in unity for widespread propagation (Kōsenrufu), I would designate this a "universalist stance on the chanting of Daimoku."

> All disciples and lay supporters of Nichiren should chant Nam-myō-hō-ren-ge-kyō with the spirit of many in body but one in mind, transcending the mind which makes distinctions among themselves to become as inseparable as fish and the water in which they swim. This spiritual bond is the basis for the universal transmission of the ultimate Law of life and death. Herein lies the true goal of Nichiren's propagation. When you are so united, even the great desire for Kosenrufu can be fulfilled. But if any of Nichiren's disciples disrupt the unity of many in body but one in mind, they would be like warriors who destroy their own castle from within.
> (»The Heritage of the Ultimate Law of Life«, p. 1337 / I. 217)

We should never betray this most sincere wish of Nichiren. For it was an expression of Nichiren's own great encompassing compassion.

> If Nichiren's compassion is truly great and encompassing, Nam-myō-hō-ren-ge-kyō will spread for ten thousand years and more, for all eternity, for it has the beneficial power to open the blind eyes of every living being in the country of Japan, and it blocks off the road that leads to the hell of incessant suffering.
> (»On Repaying Debts of Gratitude «, p. 329 / I. 736)

Above, I have cited some passages from Gosho, emphasizing the inherent dignity of all human beings and of each of their lives. Yet, as well as Nichiren's deep concern for each individual's humanity, there is an underlying sharp edge to Nichiren's criticism of any kind of alienating religious practice, characteristically expressed by statements such as:

> Though Shakyamuni Buddha is supposed to possess the three virtues of sovereign, teacher, and parent for the sake of all living beings, [...]. On the contrary, *it is common mortals who endow him with the three virtues.*
> (»The true aspect of all phenomena (Reply to Shijō Kingo)«, (p. 1359 / I. 383)

Nichiren advanced this radically innovative idea some six hundred years before the German philosopher Ludwig Feuerbach (1804-1872) developed a similar critique of traditional Christian belief. Each were concerned with the self-alienating behavior of human beings who thereby suffered as a consequence of projecting their own perceived positive characteristics upon an idealized Creator God; and the more this transcendent God was perceived to be omnipotent, omnipresent, and omniscient, the more they perceived themselves to be miserable, weak and poor in the spirit. God was therefore nothing other than the idealized projected essence of human beings themselves. Consequently, all should make themselves fully aware of, and free from, such false projections. Only by a full-awareness of the higher and benevolent side of their nature as being inherent within themselves, can dignity, love and true freedom return. All should strive for human liberation from their own self-alienation. For the same reason, Nichiren Buddhism can never be a religion of worship focused on any transcendent Buddhas or Bodhisattvas, including any founder of a sect. I wish to inherit and pass on Nichiren Buddhism as a practical philosophy for human liberation and self-realization which overcomes any kind of self-alienation and enjoins radical self-responsibility.

In the foreword to this book, I pointed out that there had been a spiritual streaming toward the SG Renaissance movement, which exemplified new humanism of the 1990's, as the quotation taken from »Human Revolution« (Volume 11) highlights. Once again, I would like to affirm the sublime and magnificent goals of this movement.

> The Buddhism of Nichiren Daishōnin is not a religion of authority, power, nor a religion for religion. Also, it is not a religion for one ethnic group or one nation alone. It is exactly a religion for all human beings, for all humankind, for human rights. A fundamental solution for both racial discrimination and ethnic conflict can be found in the humanism based on this Buddhism of the Daishōnin. In this respect, Kosenrufu must be nothing other than the struggle for human rights in order to attain dignity, freedom and equality for all human beings. And this is a social mission which Soka Gakkai should take. (From »Human Revolution«, Vol. 11, "Trial")

Nichiren Buddhism can only be for the attainment of dignity, freedom, equality and happiness for all human beings. This is the non-negotiable starting point and at the same time the answer to the question of "What is Nichiren Buddhism for? What is this faith and practice for?"

Reference

The references used in this book are predominantly Japanese documents that will be listed up with additional Romanized name of authors.

Related to the Soka Gakkai 創価学会関係

【「創価学会会則　教義条項」の改正について全国県長会議から原田稔会長】、2014年11月8日 聖教新聞掲載
In English: "Nichiren Buddhism Is for All People", Dec. 12, 2014, *World Tribune*, p. 9.,
https://www.worldtribune.org/2016/07/nichiren-buddhism-people/

【「会則の教義条項改正に関する解説」（上）（下）創価学会教学部】、2015年1月29・30日 聖教新聞掲載

SOKAnet
「教学用語検索 Study term search」　　http://www.k-dic.sokanet.jp/
「勤行について About the Gongyo」
http://www.sokanet.jp/ shinkaiin/gongyo.html

SGI-SEIGI、『法華経の智慧』から学ぶ「永遠の法」と「永遠の仏」単体版
http://www.sgi-seigi.com/

Miyata, Kōichi, 宮田幸一、「学問的研究と教団の教義―創価学会の場合 日本宗教学会第74回学術大会　発表 2015/9/5」
http://hw001.spaaqs.ne.jp/miya33x/shukyogakkai.html
「SGI 各国の HP の教義紹介の差異について」(12-10-2013)
http://hw001.spaaqs.ne.jp/miya33x/sgihp.html

Suda, Haruo, 須田晴夫、「宮田論文への疑問　―　日蓮本仏論についての一考察 2016/9/14」
http://file.www4.hp-ez.com/haruosuda/file_20160922-132507.pdf

Ikeda, Daisaku, and Derbolav, Josepf, 池田大作、J.デルボラフ［対談］、『二十一世紀への人間と哲学: 新しい人間像を求めて』(1989年、河出書房)
Search for a new humanity: a dialogue between Josef Derbolav and Daisaku Ikeda, edited and translated by Richard L. Gage, New York, Weatherhill, 1992

Related to Nichiren Study 日蓮研究関係

Dai-Nichiren『大日蓮』「邪教創価学会の目指すもの・松戸行雄の邪説を破す」1994年12月号~1996年3月号

http://tidouji.la.coocan.jp/dainitirenn/matu/matumokuji.htm

Hanano, Jūdō, 花野充道、「日蓮の本尊論と『日女御前御返事』」、『法華仏教研究　第14号』、2012年

- ≪シンポジウム≫「日蓮教団の教義と信仰の現状」、『法華仏教研究　第21号』、2015年
- 『不動・愛染感見記』の真偽をめぐる諸問題に関する一考察」、『法華仏教研究　第23号』、2016年

Ishizuki, Toshiyuki, 石附敏幸、「日蓮と鎌倉幕府」、『法華仏教研究　第21号』、2015年

Kanno, Hiroshi, 菅野博史、≪シンポジウム≫「法華経の平等思想と優劣思想」、『法華仏教研究　第21号』、2015年

Kawasaki, Hiroshi, 川崎弘志、「日蓮聖人の生涯と遺文の考察（四）」、『法華仏教研究　第21号』、2015年

- 「種種御振舞御書に関する一考察」、『法華仏教研究　第21号』、2015年

Mamiya, Keijin, 間宮啓壬、「日蓮に見る女人救済〈統括版〉」、『法華仏教研究　第22号』、2016年

Mandara, Ken, »The mandala in Nichiren Buddhism. Special Feature: The 'Honmon Kaidan Dai-gohonzon' of Nichiren Shōshū Taisekiji«, Nichiren Mandala Workshop Study, 2015.
https://nichirenmandala.weebly.com/uploads/4/4/4/0/44406171/ specialissue_plankmandala.pdf

- "How Nichiren's disciples were influenced by the Gohonzon they received and the moji-mandala versus the tridimensional honzon". Essay by Ken Mandara, The Nichiren Mandala Study Workshop
https://nichirenmandala.weebly.com/uploads/4/4/4/0/44406171/jnbs_xii2017.pdf

Miura, Kazuhiro, 三浦和浩、「日蓮聖人の本尊論とその展開」、『法華仏教研究　第22号』、2016年

Miyata, Koichi, 宮田幸一、「『守護国家論』について」(2000)、「日有の教学思想の諸問題」(2009)、「『本尊問答抄』について」(2013)「日興の教学思想の諸問題」(2014)、「優陀那日輝『本尊略弁』の構成と諸問題」(2017)等すべて HP で閲覧可。http://hw001.spaaqs.ne.jp/miya33x/index.html

Nishiyma, Shigeru, 西山茂、「内棲宗教の自立化と宗教様式の革新 ─ 戦後第二期の創価学会の場合─」、『沼義昭博士古稀記念論文集　宗教と社会生活の諸相』、隆文館、1998年

Ozaki, Makoto, 尾崎誠、「ヘーゲルと法華思想」、『法華仏教研究　第23号』、2016年

Saikaku Doppo, 犀角独歩 『阿仏房御書』
　　http://blog.livedoor.jp/saikakudoppo/archives/51938719.html
Shibusawa, Kōki, 渋澤光紀、≪シンポジウム≫「日蓮教団の教義と信仰の現状」、『法華仏教研究　第21号』、2015年
Shikata, Kōdō, 四方弘道、「『観心本尊抄』の「本門釈尊脇士」について」、『法華仏教研究　第２１号』、2015年
Suda, Haruo, 須田晴夫、『新版　日蓮の思想と生涯』、鳥影社、2016年
Sueki, Fumihiko, 末木文美士、末木『日蓮入門　― 現世を撃つ思想』、ちくま新書、2000年
- 「世俗化と日蓮仏法 ― 松戸行雄の『凡夫本仏論』をめぐって」、『シリーズ日蓮　第五巻　現代世界と日蓮』、春秋社、2015年
Suguro, Shinjō, 勝呂信靜、「御遺文の真偽問題－その問題点への私見－」、『日蓮宗 現代宗教研究所所報　第32号』、1998年
　　http://www.genshu.gr.jp/DPJ/syoho/syoho32/s32_086.htm
Takahashi, Toshitaka, 高橋俊隆、「本尊・始顕本尊」
　　http://www.myoukakuji.com/html/telling/benkyonoto/index162.htm
Tamura, Kanji, 田村完爾、「日蓮聖人の本迹論とその展開」、『法華仏教研究　第21号』、2015年
The Collection of Nichiren Shonin's Mandalas 日蓮聖人大漫荼羅一覧
　　http://juhoukai.la.coocan.jp/mandara/mandaraitiran.html
　　https://www.youtube.com/watch?v=CB3fTV74yco&feature=youtu.be.
Nichiren Shonin Gohonzon Shu —O'Mandalas by St. Nichiren [1222-1282]
　　http://nichirenscoffeehouse.net/GohonzonShu/001.html
　　(*This site seems to be deleted*.)
Nichiren Shoshu, The Liturgy of Nichiren Shoshu, Head Temple Taiseki-ji edition:
　　https://de.scribd.com/doc/34254294/The-Liturgy-of-Nichiren-Shoshu

Related to Yukio Matsudo 松戸行雄関係

松戸行雄、『人間主義の「日蓮本仏論」を求めて ― 創価ルネサンス運動の基礎付けのために』、みくに書房、1992年。
- 『日蓮思想の革新 ― 凡夫本仏論をめぐって』、論創社、1994年
- 『平成の教義論争 ― 日蓮正宗の「反論」を嗤う』、みくに書房、1995年
- 「日蓮仏法の現代的再構成のために」、『法華仏教研究　第 21 号』、2015年
- 「ドイツ人仏教徒の自己理解について」、『法華仏教研究　第２２号』、2016年

Matsudo, Yukio
- "Protestant Character of Modern Buddhist Movements". In Buddhist Christian Studies, Vol.20, Honolulu: University of Hawaii Press. 2000. Pp. 59-69.
- Nichiren, der Ausübende des Lotos-Sutra, 2009 (Norderstedt 2004)
- Hairetischer Protest – Reformatorische Bewegungen im Buddhismus und Christentum, Norderstedt 2009.
- *Faszination Buddhismus – Beweggründe für die Hinwendung der Deutschen zum Buddhismus*, Norderstedt, 2015
- *Neue Entwicklungen innerhalb der Soka Gakkai*, Materialdienst 2/2017 (EZW)

Yukio Matsudo & Susanne Matsudo-Kiliani

Transform your energy – Change your life! Nichiren Buddhismus 3.0, 2016.

Change your Brainwaves – Change your Karma! Nichiren Buddhismus 3.1, 2017.

Glossary
- English Translation of Japanese Buddhist terms

All the Buddhas of the three existences and the ten directions 三世十方の諸仏 *Sanze-jippō no shobutsu*

All sentient beings are endowed with Buddhahood (Buddha nature) 一切衆生悉有仏性 *Issaishujō shitsuubusshō*

All sentient beings will carry out the Buddha way 一切衆生皆成仏道 *Issaishujō kaijōbutsudō*

Attaining to Buddhahood or Realizing enlightenment 成仏 *Jōbutsu*

Attaining to enlightenment in the remotest past 久遠実成 *Kuon jitsujō*

Bodhisattvas of the Earth 地涌の菩薩 *Jiyū no bosatsu*

Buddhahood -equals- or is the same as the Nine Worlds 仏界即九界 *Bukkai-soku-kyūkai*

Buddha 仏 *Hotoke*

Buddhism of Sowing 下種仏法 *Geshubuppō*

Ceremony in the Air 虚空会 *Kokūe*

Changing poison into medicine 変毒為薬 *Hendokuiyaku*

Comprehensive, abbreviated and essential version of the LS or Gohonzon 広略要の法華経または御本尊 *Kō-ryaku-yō no hokekyō* or *Gohonzon*

Dai-Gohonzon of the High Sanctuary of the Essential Teaching 本門戒壇の大御本尊 *Honmon kaidan no dai-gohonzon*

Doctrine of Nichiren as the Eternal Orginal Buddha 日蓮久遠本仏論 *Nichiren kuon-honbutsu ron*

Doctrine of Nichiren as the Original Buddha 日蓮本仏論 *Nichiren honbutsuron*

Dual life structure = *Mutual Containment of the Ten World*

Dual Life Structure = *Principle of the Mutual Containment of the Ten Worlds*

Enlightenment 正覚 *Shōkaku* or 悟り *Satori*

Essential Teaching or Essential Section 本門 *Honmon*

Eternal Buddha Shakyamuni 久遠仏釈尊 *Kuonbutsu shakuson*

Eternal Realization = *Attaining to enlightenment in the remotest past*

Five Guides to Propagation - Teaching, Capacity, Time, Country and the sequence of proclaimed teachings or the Lord of Teachings 教機時国教法流布または教主の五綱五義判 *Kyō-ki-ji-koku-kyōhōrufunosengo* or *kyōshu no gokō* or *gogihan*

Five periods and eight teachings 五時八教 *Goji hakkyō*

Five periods of Kegon, Agon, Hōdō, Hannya and Hokke-Nehan 華厳阿含方等般若法華涅槃の五時 *Goji*

Fivefold Comparison 五重相対 *Gojū sōtai:* 1) Buddhism is superior to non-Buddhist teachings 内外相対 *Naige sōtai,* 2) Mahayana Buddhism is superior to Hinayana Buddhism 大小相対 *Daishō sōtai,* 3) True Mahayana is superior to provisional Mahayana 権実相対 *Gonjitsu sōtai,* 4) The Essential Section of the LS is superior to its Theoretical Section 本迹相対 *Honjaku sōtai,* and 5) The Buddhism of the Sowing is superior to the Buddhism of the Harvest 種脱相対 *Shudatsu sōtai*

Fivefold Significance of Name, Body, Doctrine, Function and Teaching 名体宗用教の五重 *Myō-tai-shū-yū-kyō no gojūgen*

Four teachings of doctrine 化儀の四教 *Kegi no shikyō*

Four teachings of method 化法の四教 *Kehō gi no shikyō*

Fourfold level of interpretation of the Buddhist teaching for the Latter Day 末法の四重解釈レベル *Mappō no shijū kaishaku reberu:* 1) the LS for the Latter Day 末法の法華経 *Mappō no hokekyō,* 2) The Essential Section for the Latter Day 末法の本門 *Mappō no Honmon,* 3) The Buddhism of Sowing for the Latter Day 末法の下種仏法 *Mappō no geshu buppō,* 4) The Chanting of Daimoku for the Latter Day 末法の題目即唱題行 *Mappō no daimoku-soku-shōdaigyō*

Fourfold Rise and Fall - The contemplative teaching is superior to all other teachings considered in the sequence of pre-Lotus teachings, the Theoretical Teaching and the Essentail Teaching of the LS 爾前迹門本門観心の四重興廃 *Nizen-shakumon-honmon-kanjin no shijū kōhai*

Fusion of Actuality and Wisdom 境智冥合 *Kyōchi myōgō*

Hermeneutical judgement system for selecting the superior teachings 教相判釈 *Kyōsō hanjaku*

Honzon in terms of either the Person- or the Law 人本尊または法本尊 *Ninhonzon* or *hōhonzon*

Ichinen Sanzen in Actuality 事の一念三千 *Ji no Ichinen Sanzen*

Initial Enlightenment -equals- or is the same as Original Enlightenment 始覚即本覚 *Shikaku-soku-hongaku*

Initial Enllightenment 始覚 *Shikaku*

Instant Enlightenment or Immediate Enlightenment in one's present fom 即身成仏 *Sokushin-jōbutsu*

Latter Day = Latter Day of the Law = our current times or contemporary age

Mutual Containment of the Ten Worlds 十界互具 *Jikkai gogu*

Mystic Law entrusted to Jōgyō 上行所伝の妙法 *Jōgyō no Myōhō*

Mystical Principle of Original Cause 本因妙 *Hon'inmyō*

Mystical Principle of Original Effect 本果妙 *Hongamyō*

Nine Worlds -equals- or is the same as Buddhahood 九界即仏界 *Kyūkai-soku-bukkai*
One Buddha and Four Bodhisattvas 一仏四菩薩 *Ichibutsu shibosatsu*
One Buddha Vehicle 一仏乗 *Ichibutsujō*
One Great Secret Law 一大秘法 *Ichidai hihō*
One Tower with two Buddhas and four Bodhisattvas 一塔二仏四菩薩 *Ittō nibutsu shibosatsu*
Oneness of Buddha and Dharma 人法一箇 *Ninpō ikka*
Ordinary body as Buddha body 凡身即仏身 *Bonpu-soku-busshin*
Original Enlightenment 本覚 *Hongaku*
Original or True Buddha 本仏実仏 *Honbutsu, Jitsubutsu*
Originally inherent enlightenment 本有本覚 *Honnu hongaku*
Originally inherent without intention 本有無作 *Honnumusa*
Perfect and immediate contemplation for the Latter Day 末法の円頓止観 *Mappō no endonshikan*
Perspective of a Contemplative Reading of the Essential Section for the Latter Day 末法の本門観心の視座 *Mappō no Honmon kanjin no shiza*
Practice of chanting Daimoku 唱題行 *Shōdaigyō*
Primordial Buddha without beginning 無始の古仏 *Mushi no kobutsu*
Provisional Buddha 権仏 *Gonbutsu*
Realizing or Attaining to Enlightenment 正覚 *Shōkaku*
Revealing the true identity by casting aside its shadow 発迹顕本 *Hosshaku kenpon*
Shakyamuni who attained to enlightenment in the remotest past 久遠実成の釈尊 *Kuon-jitsujō no shakuson*
Simultaneity of cause and effect 因果倶時 *Ingaguji*
Six pāramitās 六波羅蜜 *roku-haramitsu*
Six progressive stages of identical enlightenment 六即 *roku-soku*: 1) *theoretical stage of identity* 理即 *ri-soku*, 2) *nominal stage of identity* 名字即 *myōji-soku*, 3) *active stage of identity* 観行即 *myōji-soku*, 4) *resemblance stage of identity* 相似即 *sōji-soku*, 5) *participating stage of identity* 分真即 *bunshin-soku*, and 6) *ultimate stage of identity* 究竟即 *mkukkyō-soku*
Tathāgata endowed with the three bodies of original enlightenment 本覚無作三身如来 *Hongaku musa sanjin nyorai*
Tathāgata of the wisdom body (Samboghakaya) at the original beginning in the relmotest past 久遠元初自受用報身如来 *Kuonganjo jijuyū hōshin nyorai*
Ten Factors of the Life 十如是 *Jūnyoze*
Ten-Worlds-Mandala 十界漫荼羅 *Jikkai mandala*
The threefold contemplation in a single mind 一心三観 *Isshin sangan*

Theoretical Teaching or Theoretical Section 迹門 *Shakumon*

Thesis on the Ordinary Person as True Buddha 凡夫本仏論 *Bonpu honbutsu ron*

Three bodies in one body 三身即一身 *Sanjin-soku-isshin*

Three Bodies of Dharma, Wisdom and Manifestation 法報応の三身 *Hop-pō-ō no sanjin*

Three bodies of original enlightenment without intention 本覚無作三身 *Hongaku musa sanjin*

Three Bodies without Intention 無作三身 *Musa sanjin*

Three disciplines of precepts, meditation, and wisdom 戒定慧の三学 *Kai-jō-e no ksangaku*

Three domains of the present 今此三界 *Konshi sangai*

Three Existences of the past, the present and the future 過去現在未来の三世 *Kako-genzai-mirai no Sanze*

Three fundamental principles of the Instant Enlightenment of Ichine Sanzen based on the Mutual Coontainment of the Ten Worlds 十界互具一念三千即身成仏の三大根本原理 *Jikkaigogu, Ichinen Sanzen, Sokushinjōbutsu no sandai konpon enre*

Three Great Secret Laws 三大秘法 *Sandai hihō:* 1) Object of Devotion of the Essential Section 本門の本尊 *Honmon no honzon,* 2) Daimoku of the Essential Section 本門の題目 *Honmon no daimoku,* 3) High Sanctuary or Place of Practice of the Essential Section 本門の戒壇 *Honmon no kaidan*

Three kinds of proof: documentary, theoretical and empirical 文証理証現証の三証 *Monshō-rishō-genshō no sanshō*

Three kinds of Realm 三界 *Sangai*

Three periods of cultivation from the Sowing through Maturing to the Harvest 種熟脱の三義 *Shu-juku-datsu no sangi*

Three periods: the Former, Middle, and Latter Day of the Law 正法像法末法の三時 *Shōhō-Zōhō-Mappō no sanji*

Three Standards of Comparison 三種の教相 *Sanshu no kyōsō*

Three thousand realms in a single moment of life 一念三千 *Ichinen Sanzen*

Three Vehicles of arhat, pratyekkabuddha and bodhisattva 声聞縁覚菩薩の三乗 *Shōmon-engaku-bosatu no sanjō*

Three virtues of Dharma body, Transcendent Wisdom and Liberation 法身般若解脱の三徳 *Hosshin-hannya-gedatsu no santoku*

Three virtues of sovereign, teacher and parent 主師親の三徳 *Shu-shi-shin no santoku*

Three Ways of Desire, Karma and Suffering 煩悩業苦の三道 *Bonnō-gō-ku no sandō*

Threefold truth of Non-substantiality, Provisional Existence, and the Middle Way 空仮中の三諦 *Kū-ke-chū no santai*

Transformation of the physical pains of birth, aging, illness and death into blissful liberation 生死即涅槃 *Shōji-soku-nehan*

Transformation of the suffering of earthly desires into enlightenment 煩悩即菩提 *Bonnō-soku-bodai*

Two Vehicles of arhat & pratyekkabuddha 声聞縁覚の二乗 *Shōmon-engaku no nijō*

Unity of person and law 人法一如 *Ninpō ichinyo*

World of suffering or the Sahā world 娑婆世界 *Shabasekai*

About the author

Yukio Matsudo, PhD

PhD in Philosophy and post-doc qualification for professorship (Habilitation) in the subjects of Japanese Buddhism and Comparative Religions, Heidelberg University.

After receiving his post-doc qualification, he was active as a lecturer at Heidelberg University on the subjects of Japanese Buddhism and Comparative Religions from 2001-2014.

Dr. Matsudo has been practicing Nichiren Buddhism intensively since 1976 and was a top leader of SGI Germany at a federal level until 2001. He has supported hundreds of people in their practice. This way he could also gain many concrete and important experiences.

SGI-President Ikeda asked him personally to found and run as Director of Research *the European Centre of the Institute of Oriental Philosophy* (IOP) in Taplow Court, UK. In this period from 1990-2000, based on the modern, humanistic and open-minded approach of Daisaku Ikeda, he developed an innovative understanding of Nichiren Buddhist teachings and published a number of books and articles in Japanese, German and English.

Today, Dr. Matsudo is engaged in building a bridge between Buddhism, Western philosophy and new scientific disciplines. As an expert in Nichiren Buddhist Studies he is also active in a research group in Japan, in which prominent scholars are represented from all main denominations of Nichiren schools including Soka Gakkai (IOP).

Made in United States
Orlando, FL
23 July 2022